Human Rights, Ownership, and the Individual

Is it defensible to use the concept of a right? Can we justify rights' central place in modern moral and legal thinking, or does the concept unjustifiably side-line those who do not qualify as right-holders? Rowan Cruft develops a new account of rights. Moving beyond the traditional 'interest theory' and 'will theory', he defends a distinctive 'addressive' approach that brings together duty-bearer and right-holder in the first person. This view has important implications for the idea of 'natural' moral rights—that is, rights that exist independently of anyone's recognizing that they do. Cruft argues that only moral duties grounded in the good of a particular party (person, animal, group) are naturally owed to that party as their rights. He argues that human rights in law and morality should be founded on such recognition-independent rights. In relation to property, however, matters are complicated because much property is justifiable only by collective goods beyond the rightholder's own good. For such property, Cruft argues that a new non-rights property system, that resembles markets but is not conceived in terms of rights, would be possible. The result of this study is a partial vindication of the rights concept that is more supportive of human rights than many of their critics (from left or right) might expect, and is surprisingly doubtful about property as an individual right.

Rowan Cruft is Professor of Philosophy at the University of Stirling. He is the co-editor of *Crime, Punishment, and Responsibility* (OUP, 2011) and of *Philosophical Foundations of Human Rights* (OUP, 2015).

Praise for *Human Rights, Ownership, and the Individual*

'A valuable and original contribution to the recent philosophical literature on rights and human rights...ambitious and wide-ranging...We have only been able to engage with a few of the many topics of great interest and importance on which he has advanced the state of the art...His book is required reading for anyone doing serious work on rights and human rights.'

Allen Buchanan and Gopal Sreenivasan, *Ethics*

'Cruft manages to do what few philosophers are able to do: offer a genuine competitor to extant theories of rights in general, and human rights in particular. The book is replete with arresting insights and does not shy away—on the contrary—from reaching controversial conclusions on (in particular) the grounds and scope of property rights. Cruft's ability to conduct forensic dissections of the literature without losing sight of his overarching aims is extraordinary. With this book, he cements his status as a leading legal, moral, and political philosopher.'

Cécile Fabre, University of Oxford

'A rich and carefully structured book, written with clarity and integrity...The author's appetite for argument is formidable, his intelligence is obvious, and the analysis offered is always thought-provoking and often subtle. While I find myself disagreeing with some of the author's conclusions, the central ideas which drive the argument of the book represent an important advance in the literature.'

N. E. Simmonds, *American Journal of Jurisprudence*

Human Rights, Ownership, and the Individual

Rowan Cruft

OXFORD
UNIVERSITY PRESS

OXFORD
UNIVERSITY PRESS

Great Clarendon Street, Oxford, OX2 6DP,
United Kingdom

Oxford University Press is a department of the University of Oxford.
It furthers the University's objective of excellence in research, scholarship,
and education by publishing worldwide. Oxford is a registered trade mark of
Oxford University Press in the UK and in certain other countries

First published 2019
First published in paperback 2021

Published in the United States of America by Oxford University Press
198 Madison Avenue, New York, NY 10016, United States of America

British Library Cataloguing in Publication Data
Data available

Library of Congress Cataloging in Publication Data
Data available

ISBN 978–0–19–879336–6 (Hbk.)
ISBN 978–0–19–285533–6 (Pbk.)

Preface

Is it defensible to frame moral and legal questions in terms of 'rights'? When is it a good idea to think like this, and when is such thinking misleading by distracting us from our actions' effects on parties who do not qualify as 'right-holders'? In what follows, I offer a defence of the use of 'rights' in contemporary human rights practice and discourse (see Part II), and qualified criticism of its use in relation to property (Part III). Beforehand (in Part I), I develop a new 'Addressive' account of what we mean by rights that draws on insights from the traditional Interest, Will and related theories of rights (e.g. Kind-Desire, Demand, Hybrid theories). The result is a partial vindication of our use of the rights concept.

I have enjoyed writing this book. It would not have been possible without research leave in 2016–17, provided by the British Academy's Mid-Career Fellowship scheme along with institutional leave from the University of Stirling. Earlier thinking on these topics was assisted by a project on the nature of rights that I pursued with Leif Wenar, funded by the Arts and Humanities Research Council from 2010 to 2012. Two workshops have examined successive drafts of the book manuscript: at Stirling in 2017 funded by the Mind Association, the Scots Philosophical Association, and the Society for Applied Philosophy; and at King's College London in 2018 funded by the YTL Centre for Politics, Philosophy & Law. I am very grateful to Joseph Bowen and Massimo Renzo, who organized these events, and to my generous and incisive commentators for their energy and insightfulness: Tom Dougherty, Katrin Flikschuh, Nick Sage, Zofia Stemplowska, Victor Tadros, John Tasioulas, Laura Valentini, and Leif Wenar. I also received generous and helpful comments from two anonymous reviewers for Oxford University Press, and patient guidance from Peter Momtchiloff. Thanks also to April Peake and Rajeswari Sathiyamoorthy for their excellent work on the production process.

I have been lucky to be able to discuss my work in a range of events with a large number of interlocutors including Arif Ahmed, Martin Ajei, Jimmy Altham, Elizabeth Ashford, Daniel Attas, Caesare Atiure, Andrea Baumeister, Chris Bennett, Ricardo Bermúdez-Otero, Samantha Besson, Matthias Brinkmann, Kimberley Brownlee, Allen Buchanan, Susanne Burri, Tom Campbell, Hannah Carnegy, Benjamin Chen, Francis Cheneval, Richard Child, Emilios Christodoulidis, Ioana Cismas, Ben Colburn, Helen Coverdale, Stephen Darwall, Christina Dineen, Alexander Douglas, Luis Duarte d'Almeida, Marcus Düwell, Pavlos Eleftheriadis, Stephen Engstrom, Adam Etinson, Cécile Fabre, Sarah Fine, Michael Garnett, Pablo Gilabert, Margaret Gilbert, Marie Göbel, Carol Gould, Amanda Greene, Andrew Halpin, Alon Harel, Antony Hatzistavrou, Katherine Hawley, Tim Hayward, Jane Heal, Jan-Christoph Heilinger, Alison Hills, Zhengyue Huang, Graham Hubbs, Nien-he Hsieh, Suzie Killmister, Kosuke Kiyama, Christoph Kletzer, Richmond Kwesi, Gerald Lang, Holly Lawford-Smith, Hugh Lazenby, Annabelle Lever, S. Matthew Liao, Hallvard Lillehammer, David Lyons, Mark McBride, Helen McCabe, Christopher McCrudden, Euan MacDonald, Tom McKenna, Mike Martin, Matt Matravers, Saladin Meckled-Garcia, Claudio Michelon, David Miller, Monica Mookherjee, Véronique Munoz-Dardé, Stephen

Munzer, Anh Quan Nguyen, Jim Nickel, Fay Niker, Cara Nine, Torhild Elin Nordtveit, Kieran Oberman, Maggie O'Brien, Onora O'Neill, Tom Parr, Avia Pasternak, Walter Pedriali, James Penner, Chris Pierson, Tom Pink, Theron Pummer, Amit Pundik, Jahel Queralt Lange, Joseph Raz, Mark Reiff, Massimo Renzo, Henry Richardson, Stephen Riley, Emma Ritch, Carol Rose, Markus Rothhaar, Ben Sachs, Irit Samet, Andrea Sangiovanni, Janis Schaab, Peter Schaber, Hubert Schnueriger, Liam Shields, Robbie Shilliam, Andrew Simester, Nigel Simmonds, Tom Sinclair, John Skorupski, Gopal Sreenivasan, Hillel Steiner, Markus Stepanians, Michael Thompson, Jens Timmerman, Jesse Tomalty, Bas van der Vossen, Siegfried van Duffel, Jo Wolff, Kerri Woods, Bill Wringe, and Lorenzo Zucca. I have also benefited enormously from the questions, criticism, and insight of my undergraduate philosophy students in Stirling, and my postgraduate students within the St Andrews–Stirling joint programme.

Special thanks to Jim Nickel and Trish White for allowing me to co-host one of the British Academy workshops in Miami Law School. And further special thanks to my past and present Stirling philosophy colleagues for their careful attention to my work in progress: Amanda Cawston, Fiona Doherty, Philip Ebert, Kent Hurtig, Colin Johnston, Adam Linson, Alisa Mandrigin, Giacomo Melis, Giovanni Merlo, Alan Millar, Peter Milne, Fay Niker, Sonia Roca-Royes, Peter Sullivan, Jesse Tomalty, Lauren Ware, Mike Wheeler, and Crispin Wright.

Extra thanks for long conversations to my colleagues Adrian Haddock and Simon Hope, and to Joe Bowen, Matt Clark, Brian Ho, Ambrose Lee, Simon Căbulea May, and David Owens. Many thanks of course to Matthew Kramer for sustained criticism and support early in the project, and to Laura Valentini and Ariel Zylberman for unstinting support and repeated, constructive criticism throughout. And for lengthy constructive and critical discussions over many years, to Leif Wenar.

Antony Duff and Sandra Marshall have read and commented on the manuscript; they have also supported me, and done a vast amount for philosophy in Stirling, since I started my career in 2002. I admire and learn a great deal from them. Their example has inspired my own hopes for intellectual rigour and depth, and for leading a full, rich academic life.

I am very grateful to all those mentioned, and to Gemma Robinson, May and Tom, plus all the wider Crufts and Robinsons. Everyone has shaped my thinking, but, of course, all errors are my own.

Stirling, December 2018.

Contents

Part II. Human Rights for the Right-Holder's Sake

Acknowledgements

Some parts of Chapter 2 use material already published as 'The Circularity of the Interest and Will Theories of Rights', in M. McBride (ed.), *New Essays on the Nature of Rights* (Hart 2017), and are reprinted here with permission.

1

Introduction

1.1 The Aim: Vindicating Rights

In this book, I defend the concept of a right as something humans need in order to understand our relations to one another and to non-human animals. Yet in one interesting sense we do not need the concept. Or, at least, we do not need the concept of a *violable* right, or what Hohfeld calls a 'claim-right': a right constituted by a duty owed to the right-holder, whose violation wrongs the right-holder.[1] Human society could survive, in roughly recognizable form, without thinking in terms of this concept. We will see in Part III of this volume that even capitalism could cope without the concept.

The reason for this is that whether a duty is owed to someone, correlating with their right, need make no 'extensional' difference to what ought to happen, where this means no difference to the overt behaviour people ought to perform. This might seem a surprising claim, and I expand on it throughout Part I of this book.[2] The idea is captured in the thought that if I am under a duty not to kill you, then I remain duty-bound not to kill you whether this duty is owed to you as your right, to your parents as their right, to God, or to nobody. In Chapters 2–4, I develop an addressive conception of rights which entails that *any* pattern of behaviour required or permitted by people's rights—including secondary patterns such as demands anticipating or triggered by violations—could be equally required or permitted by duties owed to nobody and uncorrelated with rights.[3] A duty's being someone's right affects how we should *think* of our actions in relation to the duty (e.g. as 'wronging you', or 'demanding in my own name as right-holder'), but makes no necessary difference to what should be done, extensionally conceived. This dispensability of the concept is, I suggest, reflected in historians' debates about whether rights—as duties owed to someone—are a modern invention. According to some, the Ancient Greeks and Romans lacked our rights notion; it is a medieval or perhaps a specifically Christian creation or discovery.[4]

---

[1] Hohfeld 1964. [2] See especially Section 3.5, and also Section 13.3.

[3] I argue that all the actions frequently associated with rights—such as demanding, waiving, resenting, receiving apology or compensation, forgiving—can in appropriate circumstances be performed by third parties on behalf of a right-holder, and can also in appropriate circumstances be performed in relation to duties owed to nobody, correlating with no right. For someone who comes from very different premises to roughly the same conclusion, see Gilbert 2018, ch. 12, section 8.1 (on moral theory's main conclusions surviving whether or not there are moral *rights*).

[4] See Brett 1997, Tierney 1997, Siedentop 2014; for the view that the Ancients had the concept, see Miller 1995; Garnsey 2007, ch. 7; Donahue 2010.

I will not enter the historical debates, but if the idea of a violable right really is a contingent, recent creation, and one whose use is dispensable as a generator of action, then this should prompt us to seek justification for its use. Maybe its role is purely ideological, giving a positive flavour (as 'my rights') to duties that would, if purged of their association with rights, be revealed as mechanisms for hiding injustice or for feeding selfishness. For example, consider feminist concerns about rights to privacy within the domestic sphere, or Marxist concerns about rights of property. The relevant privacy rights are constituted centrally by duties of non-interference within the domestic realm, while property rights are constituted centrally by duties not to trespass on or use an item. Focusing on these duties *as rights* gives priority to the individual right-holder in our thinking: the party who, as right-holder, will be wronged if the duty is violated. One plausible feminist and Marxist complaint is that such a focus diverts attention away from the many parties who are profoundly affected by the duties in question yet are not right-holders: these might include members of the domestic household who are not themselves householders, or those who are left homeless or starving by the duties not to trespass that constitute others' property. Focusing on the duties in question *as rights* seems to direct attention towards the beneficiaries of the required behaviour (the domestic householder and the owner), thereby helping to hide injustices within the domestic sphere or injustices generated by exclusionary property distributions.[5] A related concern is the Confucian view that focusing on a right-holder as 'the' party who is wronged when a duty is violated overlooks the effects of such duty-violation on the wider group in which the party is situated.[6] A surprisingly similar concern about rights emerges from conservative thought: here, the complaint is often that rights think-ing generates a 'claimant culture' which forgets the costs of compliance with correlative duties: by drawing our attention to the party who will qualify as wronged if a duty is violated, the rights concept leads us to focus on the duty's benefits to that party, at the expense of due consideration of the costs of those who must fulfil the duty.[7] Taken together, the theme unifying the concerns outlined is that the rights concept, by highlighting a particular party as 'the wrongable party' in relation to a given duty, is excessively narrowing, focusing our attention on the fate of the right-holder at the expense of the fates of the many others entwined with any given duty.

This book defends our use of the rights concept against this and other charges. I will argue that we can justify thinking in terms of rights, and hence thinking of our peers as wrongable beings, because this offers a distinctively illuminating way of understanding our moral relations to others, including relations that are 'natural' in the sense that they obtain independently of our recognizing them. We can also justify

---

[5] For feminist concerns about rights that include but go beyond that in the main text, see the useful summary in Reilly 2009, p. 3; for Marxist concerns, see, e.g. Marx 2000.

[6] See Ihara 2004.

[7] This concern is frequently encountered in those who worry about the 'proliferation' of rights talk; for an early expression, see Cranston 1973. Note the similarity to the left-wing concern about the effects of property rights on the propertyless: in both cases, the concern is that focusing on certain duties *as rights* ignores the costs of these duties for the duty-bearers.

thinking in terms of rights as a way of understanding how the legal and social duties we create reflect and augment these natural relations. In a sense to be explained in Chapter 4, a party has a right if a duty-bearer is formally required, by the nature of her duty, to conceive that party second-personally as potentially addressable as 'you, on whom I act', and if the right-holding party (if appropriately capable) is formally required to conceive herself first-personally as 'I, on whom you act'. Identifying a right involves identifying an addressive recognitional relationship between duty-bearer and right-holder that would be missed if their relation was taken simply as that between duty-bearer and a rights-independent third party. The rights relationship makes no extensional difference to how the parties should behave compared to a relationship structured by duties owed to nobody; but it is of vital significance to how they should think of their relationship. Without it, our conception of our duties would alienate us from one another in thought.[8]

This view of rights as 'addressive duties' has important implications for the idea of natural rights, that is, duties that as a matter of nature—independent of intentional social creation or recognition—take the form of rights. I argue in Part II (and anticipate in Chapter 5) that duties with an addressive rights-type structure only obtain *naturally* when an individual or collective addressable party's good manages largely on its own to place someone under a duty, independently of any social conventions, and independently of whether this would serve the good of others beyond the party in question. Conventionally and legally created rights, by contrast, need not be grounded by the right-holder's good, though they can be.[9] This contrast between *rights grounded in a broadly 'individualistic' manner by what they do for the right-holder* and *rights grounded by how they serve other people or values beyond the right-holder* is absolutely crucial to the book. The former category includes all natural rights, and I argue in Part II that it is partially definitive of anything correctly called a 'human right', including both legal and natural human rights: legal human rights are rights that give legal expression to natural human rights, and I argue that the latter must be morally grounded primarily by what they do for the right-holder.[10]

Part III turns to rights justified by what they do for beings or values beyond the right-holder's good—rights that are not justifiable for the right-holder's own sake. Parts I–II tell us that such rights cannot be natural rights, but we often have strong reasons to create them through law and convention, and to respect them when they are created. But I argue that sometimes the rights-type structure of such creations is misleading. For example, I argue that conceiving property as a right does, in many circumstances, play something close to the problematic ideological role identified earlier: it misleads us into overlooking the fact that most trespassory duties are

---

[8] And of course how we think might well have knock-on effects on how we behave. See Section 5.1.

[9] My view is therefore that the account of *rights in general* developed by Raz is, on close inspection, true of *natural rights* but fails to encompass many socially or legally created rights (including morally justified legal rights whose justification is independent of the right-holder's interests). See Raz 1986, ch. 7. See also Rainbolt 2006 for a view similar to Raz's.

[10] This contradicts Buchanan 2013, and is in some ways similar to the 'Mirroring View' he rejects. See this volume, Chapter 9.

morally grounded primarily by how they serve the common good, rather than by the good of the individual right-holder. Unlike property, most legal-conventional rights grounded by how they serve beings other than the right-holder protect the right-holder in her performance of duties defined by an other-directed role—such as parents' rights to care for their children or civil servants' rights to extract taxes. Because the role of 'owner' carries no defining other-directed duty of office that can remind people that the rights definitive of the role ultimately serve people other than the right-holder, conceiving property as a right is misleading. It can make it seem too like one of the fundamental human rights of Part II. I explore the implications of this fact, and its relation to how all our morally justified rights—including merely legal rights grounded in what they do for values other than the right-holder's good—define the sphere of moral respect for the right-holder. I will propose a significant change in how we should think about some of 'our' property but one which, at least in its direct initial effects, makes minimal extensional difference to our behaviour: we should not think of property as our 'rights' but merely as others' duties that we control. I explain this idea of 'controllership' more fully in Chapter 13. This change would not directly affect our overt behaviour, but it would improve our thinking and thereby indirectly improve our political actions, leading to enhanced public debate and policy decisions.

We end up with a partial vindication of the language of rights. It is essential to understanding some of our natural relationships, including those captured by and extended through law and convention with the idea of human rights. But it is also on occasion misleading, including sometimes in one of its canonical uses, namely, property.[11] This path—from conceptual-analytic rights theory to a defence of human rights and a (qualified) rejection of the rights concept in relation to property—has not been trodden before, though it is close in certain respects to that of the philosophical radicals, perhaps especially Proudhon. But dominant historical figures from the seventeenth to the nineteenth centuries such as Locke, Hume, Kant, Fichte, or Hegel tend to defend property alongside other fundamental rights: often as the primary right. More recent insightful work defending human rights rarely engages either with analytic theories of the nature of rights or with property, though there are exceptions.[12] I believe a full assessment of our use of the concept of a right requires engaging *both* with the contemporary flowering of the idea of 'human rights' in theory and practice *and* with the historically central and (arguably) even today practically more influential idea of property as a right. Keeping this combined focus will, I suggest, result in a partial vindication of the rights concept that is more supportive of human rights than many of their critics (from left or right) might expect, and is surprisingly doubtful about property as an individual right.

[11] One might say that I defend a version of the 'high liberalism' (in which property and related economic rights have a lower status than more basic rights) that Tomasi (2012) criticizes; more precisely, I show in Chapter 13 that classical liberalism surprisingly undermines property's status as an individual right.
[12] See, e.g. Waldron 1988; Thomson 1990; Nickel 2000 and Nickel 2007, ch. 8.

1.2 In Defence of Rights as Duties Owed to the Right-Holder

I discuss Hohfeld's famous taxonomy of forms of right in Chapter 6. But there are two points that might strike readers or opponents of Hohfeld, which I should address now.

First, some might have noticed that even if rights of the type on which I focus—rights constituted by duties owed to a right-holder (that is, Hohfeldian claim-rights)—make no extensional difference to how people should behave, other types of rights within Hohfeld's taxonomy clearly do. Hohfeldian *power-rights*, for example, are constituted by an ability to create new duties for someone, and Hohfeldian *immunity-rights* are constituted by another's inability to create such duties for one.[13] Such abilities and inabilities can obviously make a difference to what should be done. For instance, in exercising our power to elect a member of parliament, we collectively make a difference to the duties borne by the elected person, to how we ought to behave towards her, and, potentially, to the law of the land governing how we ought to behave in many spheres. Because they seem indispensable to any system of rules, rights of this type cannot plausibly be a modern invention, even if a settled word to refer to them only emerged recently. As Wenar puts it, 'even the most rudimentary human communities must have rules specifying that some are entitled to tell others what they must do. Such rules ascribe rights.'[14]

Yet my central interest in this book is Hohfeldian claim-rights: rights constituted by duties owed to the right-holder, duties whose violation wrongs the right-holder. They are dispensable and (arguably) historically contingent in the manner outlined earlier. Why focus on these extensionally dispensable forms of right, rather than those which seemingly make 'more of a difference'? Despite their extensional dispensability, Hohfeldian claim-rights are, I suggest, central to our willingness to ascribe a rights-type character to any other Hohfeldian position, such as the powers and immunities outlined above. Someone with Hohfeldian power to create new duties, and immune from others' attempt to create such duties for them, would nonetheless in my view probably not be best described as a 'right-holder' if no duties were owed to them. They would appear more like a regulatory authority, overseeing a system of duties as a 'third party' even in their possession of power. That is, their powers and immunities would not be called 'rights'. I do not make this as the dogmatic claim that such a body's powers and immunities *must* fail to be classifiable as rights; my sense is simply that it might often be unclear whether such a body's powers and immunities were to be called rights or not.[15] This is one reason to follow

---

[13] Hohfeld 1964, pp. 50–64 and this volume, Section 6.2. Those who know Hohfeld must excuse my simplification in the main text; of course as Hohfeld defines them *powers* include abilities to create new powers and immunities as well as duties, and abilities to remove duties and thereby create privileges; and Hohfeldian *immunities* can similarly include immunities from the creation of new powers, etc. I overlook this for simplicity in the main text.

[14] Wenar 2015, section 3.

[15] It would be similarly unclear whether the Hohfeldian-privilege-bearing inhabitants of Hobbes's state of nature should be conceived as holding rights *if we prescind from the fact that they can turn their privileges into Hohfeldian claims through the social contract*. Would we really call this privilege a '*right* of nature' if we

Hohfeld in taking claim-rights—constituted by duties correlating with and owed to the right-holder—as the core of rights: they confer rights status on all the other Hohfeldian forms. Note further that claim-rights are the only form of right which it is logically possible to violate; I return to the significance of this in Chapter 6.

A second likely complaint, this time levelled by anti-Hohfeldians, is that by assuming Hohfeld's framework, and in particular by focusing on claim-rights constituted by duties owed to the right-holder, I overlook the possibility of rights having an independent existence, distinct from any duties which the rights serve to ground. This complaint normally takes the form that rights are *grounds* of duties and should not be logically yoked to what they serve to ground.[16] In response, we should note first that this move does not seem attractive in relation to legal or conventional rights and duties. It seems rather implausible to say that my conventional duty (under university rules) to hand my essay in on a certain date is grounded in my tutor's distinct right to this, or that my legal duty to allow someone who has purchased a parking space to use that space is grounded in their distinct right to the space. The relevant rights genuinely exist in the cases in question (tutors have rights to essays being handed in, drivers to parking spaces they have purchased), but they are no more than the 'flip-side' of the duties, and in each case the relevant right–duty pair is grounded by a distinct set of values that underpin the system as a whole: in the first case, these are the values of education, of students' and tutors' interests, and of the wider public in an educated citizenry; in the second case, they are the values of efficiency in traffic management. In such cases, the rights do not 'come first', grounding the duties.[17]

The anti-Hohfeldian proponent of my second complaint might concede that, with regard to *legal or conventional* rights, there is truth in the Hohfeldian thesis that a party's (claim-)right to X is in some sense constituted by another party's duty to do or secure X. But they might insist that matters are different when it comes to natural

were unable to escape the state of nature in which no duties are owed to us—that is, if were stuck forever as beings who could not be wronged? (Hobbes 1958 [1651], ch. 13; compare 'Nowheresville' in Feinberg 1970).

[16] See, e.g. Raz 1986, pp. 170–1, 183–6; Waldron 1984, pp. 10–11. Note that Kramer has pointed out that a right can ground a duty even if the two are logically correlative (just as my desire for a downward slope in my garden can justify the creation of a (logically equivalent) upward slope viewed from the other end (see Kramer 1998), p. 39)). Note also that the complaint in the main text is sometimes accompanied by the claim that a given right, such as the right to health care, should be taken to ground a range of duties which change over time as context and needs change; those who press this point claim that the Hohfeldian view that a right is constituted by a duty owed to the right-holder cannot accommodate the way that rights serve to ground changing sets of duties (Raz 1986, p. 171). Against the latter contention, Kramer has decisively pointed out that the 'dynamic' feature whereby a right can ground a range of duties changing over time can be captured equally in terms of Hohfeldian claim-rights: as involving an abstractly specified right–duty pair grounding a range of more specific right–duty pairs which change over time (Kramer 1998, p. 43). For example, my abstract right to health care correlating with my state's duty to provide it grounded, in 1980, a very specific right to drug X correlating with a very specific duty to provide drug X, while now in 2018 it grounds a different specific right to treatment Y with its correlative specific duty.

[17] Compare Anscombe 1981a, at p. 101: she considers 'You can't sit there, it's N's place', writing that if we separate out 'you can't sit there' and 'it's N's, and 'if we ask what the thought [either "it's N's..." or "you can't sit there"] is, and for what it is a reason, we'll find that we can't explain them separately...Of course, *once these linguistic practices* exist, we can detach the two parts from one another and "it's N's" can appear as an independent reason, e.g. a reason why one will not do something.' This is, I think, Hohfeld's correlativity point restated.

rights: here the right really can exist independently of whatever duties it grounds. Yet this, I suggest, leaves it unclear what distinguishes a right from either a value or a good. If rights are—as in the suggestion under consideration—simply the grounds of duties and *can exist independently of duties*, then rights seem to play a role most naturally ascribed to the idea of value or good; it is not clear what distinguishes them as *rights*. I pursue this argument further throughout the book, partly via Part I's defence of my new Addressive Theory of what rights are, and more extensively via Part II's demonstration of the importance of the Hohfeldian model even in conceiving *natural* rather than created rights. At the end of Section 8.2, I show why we might think that when the interests or other goods of particular people on their own ground duties for others to act, there is some attraction to identifying the right with the relevant interest or good. But even if this is correct, and hence natural rights can in some sense be identified with the valuable aspects of the right-holder which ground them, this does not impugn Hohfeld's correlativity axiom; it does not entail that a right can exist independently of a correlative duty. For the relevant grounding interest, freedom or other valuable aspect of the right-holder will, if we have a natural right in this case, itself constitute a reason constitutive of a duty for someone. There are no natural rights without natural duties. In Chapter 9, I explain how this Hohfeldian view is compatible with fairly demanding natural socio-economic rights—for example, rights to housing and subsistence supplies—despite the concerns some raise that any correlative duties must be either unjustifiably demanding or indeterminate in their content and allocation. We will find a major place for socio-economic rights correlating with important duties borne by the state, by individuals, and by humanity as a whole.

1.3 Terminology: Recognition-Independent, Uncreated, Natural, Moral, and Morally Justified Rights

I eschew the term 'moral rights' in this book, because I find it ambiguous: it could mean any right whose existence or bindingness is morally justified; or it could mean any right that exists simply in virtue of its moral justification, independently of whether it has been created or recognized by social convention. In the first sense, the phrase 'moral rights' encompasses all morally justified legal and conventional rights as well as any pre-legal 'natural' rights. So conceived, the concept captures all those rights whose violation constitutes moral disrespect for the right-holder, for we will see (Section 5.3) that morally justified conventional rights of mine, such as my rights as a teacher or owner of a field, play as significant a role in delineating the sphere of moral respect around me as those rights that I hold independently of law or convention. Yet the second sense, which reserves the phrase 'moral rights' for something equivalent to 'natural rights', is more common in the literature; I fear that this can obscure the way morally justified *legal* and *conventional* rights shape what it is to show moral respect to the right-holder, and can also obscure the commonalities between this second conception of moral rights and the older idea of natural rights.

Rather than 'moral rights' in the second sense above, I use the phrase 'natural rights'. I do not intend this to imply rights conferred by some metaphysically loaded, theological conception of a law of nature.[18] Nor do I intend it to refer to the rights we would hold in an asocial 'state of nature'.[19] I doubt that a truly *asocial* condition is possible for humans, and in my usage many of our 'natural rights' include rights generated by features of our social context—such as natural rights to vote, or natural rights against discrimination in employment decisions. Instead of theological or asocial conceptions, 'natural right' in my usage refers to any right whose existence is recognition-independent: that is, any right that exists whether or not anyone ever thinks that it does. Such a right cannot have been created by law, convention, or promising, for such rights only exist if someone at some point (perhaps only implicitly) thinks that they do. (Note that it could still have been *created*, but not in a law-making or promising way: by tripping you up and injuring your leg, I create for you a right that I telephone for an ambulance. This right qualifies as a 'natural right' in my sense, in that it exists in the circumstances whether or not anybody recognizes that it exists.) So conceived, natural rights are in a certain sense pre-legal or pre-conventional. The term 'natural' seems appropriate for such rights, in that their existence depends not on acts of law-making or promising aimed at creating them, but on what might contrastingly be seen as natural features of the context.

In what follows, I refer frequently to 'morally justified rights', where these can include both morally justified legal or conventional rights, and pre-legal or pre-conventional rights that have a 'purely moral' existence. I also refer frequently to 'natural rights', and endeavour to make clear my conception of such rights as recognition-independent.[20]

---

[18] Compare Finnis 1980.   [19] Compare Hobbes and Locke.

[20] Note my nonstandard exclusion of promissory rights from the natural rights. Because promising is, in effect, a two-person form of law-making or convention-creation, promissory rights are non-natural for me. See Section 12.3 for further discussion in relation to the right to transfer property by consent.

PART I

Rights as Addressive Duties

2

Rights' Elusive Relation to Interests

2.1 Introduction to Part I: Identifying When and To Whom a Duty Assigns Rights

My topic in Part I is the nature of Hohfeldian claim-rights: that is, the question what it is to be owed a duty, and what it is for that to be one's right. We will see that the interestingly mixed insights of the traditional 'Interest' and 'Will' theories of claim-rights, when combined with more recent theories including the new Addressive account I develop in Chapter 4, carry important implications for what can be a natural right: implications whose import makes central the distinction, animating Parts II and III, between rights justifiable for the right-holder's sake and those not so justifiable.

Now, Hohfeldian claim-rights and their flip-side, directed duties, have a distinct form: they are 'bipolar'[1] in that they connect one party, a duty-bearer (who might have a duty to do something positive or to refrain from doing something), with a second party, a right-holder to whom the duty is owed. I will follow standard usage in calling duties owed to a party 'directed duties'. A bearer of any form of duty—e.g. in morals, law, etiquette, aesthetics, and whether directed or not—does wrong of the relevant type if they violate it. What is distinctive of a *directed* duty of whatever type is that violating it *wrongs a particular party or set of parties*: the party or parties to whom the duty is owed. This party or these parties are the *victim* or *victims* of the violation. Wronging someone *ceteris paribus* triggers further directed duties to make amends to the victim through apology and recompense.[2]

Bipolar or directed duties thus contrast with their monadic, undirected fellows. While violation of an undirected duty might trigger undirected duties of rectification, the violation is wrong but does not wrong anyone in particular: there is no victim who has been violated. Thus, for example, if environmental legislation to protect rare birds does not give us legal duties owed to the birds but simply undirected duties to treat them in certain ways then the birds are, in Thompson's memorable words, 'raw materials for wrongdoing' rather than wrongable beings under the law.[3] It should, I think, be an open question whether there are any genuinely undirected duties. Standard examples include duties of beneficence and duties to behave respectfully in

---

[1] See Weinrib 1995, Thompson 2004, and Darwall 2012.

[2] These contentions—in particular, that a duty's directedness marks it as one whose violation *wrongs* the party to whom it is directed—have been contested recently by Cornell 2015. I rebut Cornell's approach in Section 6.1—see especially note 1.

[3] Thompson 2004, p. 372.

relation to inanimate objects: for example, a duty to contribute some of one's income to charity, or a duty not to destroy an uninhabited planet, or not to damage the Grand Canyon.

My Introduction (Chapter 1) contends that whether a duty correlates with a right makes no extensional difference to how people should behave compared to its being undirected—even though it makes a difference to how people should think. But, strictly speaking, it is a duty's *directedness* which makes no extensional difference to people's behaviour, and there is a distinction to draw between this and a duty's being a *right*. Directed duties are partially constitutive of any violable or infringeable rights.[4] But there might also be duties that we are willing to see as directed but that we hesitate to call 'rights'. A good example is duties of gratitude. These are directed duties owed by a beneficiary to their benefactor. Failure to express gratitude wrongs the person to whom it is owed. But nonetheless we might feel uneasy to regard the benefactor as holding a *right* to their beneficiary's thanks.[5] I will suggest—in Section 6.1—that our hesitancy in calling this a right, along with some hesitancy in refraining from doing so, reflects the fact that it is unclear whether the directed duty in such cases possesses all of the cluster of features associated with rights proper. In particular, in the gratitude case it is unclear whether and to what extent there exists a power of enforcement on behalf of the benefactor—although the duty of gratitude clearly qualifies as 'addressed to' the benefactor in my sense (see Sections 4.1–5.4). My contention will be that the more powers of action (demand, waiver, enforcement) a person holds on their own behalf in relation to a duty owed to or directed at them, or the more such powers someone else holds on their behalf, the more apposite it is to call it that person's 'right'. In the gratitude case, the duty possesses some but not all of the relevant features. This means that there is often an extensional difference (constituted by differing powers to demand or enforce) between a directed duty that is a right and a directed duty with the same content that fails fully to qualify as a right.[6]

In the ensuing Chapters 2–3, I examine attempts to explain what has to be added to an undirected duty to turn it into a directed duty owed to someone—that is, what determines to whom, if anyone, a given duty is owed. I assess each attempt initially in reductive spirit, as trying to analyse the bipolarity of directed duties and rights in a

[4] I follow Judith Thomson in using 'violation' to refer to the unjustified, inexcusable non-fulfilment of a duty, while 'infringement' refers to non-fulfilment that is justified or excused according to the rules of the normative system (Thomson 1990, p. 122).

[5] Thanks to John Skorupski for drawing this to my attention. Different cases involving the same divergence between directed duties and rights are found in Cornell 2015 and Wenar 2013 at p. 214, n. 24; see this volume, Section 6.1 for discussion.

[6] Note that this extensional difference is not inevitable. A duty could be owed to someone, and be accompanied by extensive powers of demand and enforcement, yet these powers not be exercisable on behalf of the relevant party to whom the duty is owed. The relevant powers might, like similar powers existing in relation to an undirected duty, simply be exercisable by anyone as a member of the moral community without thereby being exercised for the sake of the party to whom the duty is owed. A duty accompanied by powers like this would be extensionally identical to a similar directed duty accompanied by similar powers exercisable on behalf of the person to whom the duty is owed; the latter duty would qualify as a right and the former would not, even though both are accompanied by extensive powers allowing and enjoining extensionally equivalent actions. I discuss this further in Chapter 3.

way that does not itself appeal to any bipolar notion. I take the attempts in this way because this is how their authors intend them.[7] On this 'reductive analysis' reading, each approach is taken to appeal to the idea of a monadic duty to which some further non-bipolar concept is added in order to deliver a bipolar duty. We will see that on inspection, the approaches in the literature—Interest Theory, Will Theory, Demand Theory, Hybrid Theory, Kind-Desire Theory—have some limitations as reductive accounts. If construed in a form faithful to ordinary usage, they have to be understood in ways that are informative but circular—or so I will argue. Purged of circularity, they cannot deliver a full analysis reflecting actual usage. My alternative Addressive Theory, developed in Chapter 4, is not a reductive analysis of directedness in terms that are external to the rights/direction conceptual framework, but I will argue that its circularity is not problematic or vicious. Part of the work of Chapter 4 is to show the appeal of such a non-reductive approach. I argue that no reductive approach will be able to accommodate the fact that we can create rights wherever we want, through law and convention, independently of any relation to directedness-independent interests, desires, or powers of the right-holder. Chapter 5 integrates Chapter 4's non-reductive Addressive account with the important insights that can be found in the Interest, Will, Kind-Desire, and related theories. The result is an account of what we mean by *a duty's being owed to someone* that, although non-reductive, nonetheless reveals its distinctive role in our thinking, thereby enabling us more fully to understand the concept, and thereby to see the reasons for and against using it.

2.2 Raz's Justificatory Interest Theory: Sufficient but Unnecessary for Right-Holding

It is attractive to think that what distinguishes *duties owed to me as my right* from other duties to which I am related is that my rights—or duties owed to me—are good for me: they serve my well-being. Discussing Villey on Roman law, Tierney writes:

Villey maintains that, although there existed at Rome practical situations that we should discuss in terms of rights, the concept of an individual right was lacking in classical jurisprudence.[...] For instance, in discussing urban servitudes, Gaius wrote of a *ius altius tollendi*. At first glance it seems clear enough that Gaius was writing about a right in the modern sense, a "right of building higher". But Gaius went on to mention a "*ius ... non extollendi*". We cannot possibly translate this as "a right of not building higher". So Gaius's concept of a *ius* is just not congruent with our concept of a right. [/] It is the same with Ulpian's famous definition of the function of justice – to render to each his right (*suum ius cuique tribuere*). Here again we seem at first sight to be dealing with the modern idea of inherent individual rights. But Villey points out that *ius* here has a different meaning. It refers to the just share [...] In this sense the word *ius* could imply a disadvantage to an individual. Villey observes that the *ius* of parricide was to

---

[7] This is, I think, evident in Raz's canonical statement of his Interest Theory (1986, p. 166): the concepts of 'well-being', 'sufficient reason', and 'duty' are all meant to be taken in a directedness-independent way; I think it is also implicit in Steiner 1994, p. 62, and in Wenar 2013's formalizations (pp. 208–9 and 218–19).

be sewn up in a sack of vipers and thrown into the Tiber. Again the meaning of *ius* is not congruent with our idea of a right.[8]

A natural response to these claims is to maintain that the modern concept of a right refers to a requirement of justice, or a duty, that *serves someone's well-being*. The parricide's *ius* is not her right because it is not good for her.[9]

In the remainder of this chapter, I explore the attractions and pitfalls of this approach, which has become known as the 'Interest Theory of Rights'; I also go on to explore Wenar's recent proposal to shift rights theory from interests to desires. I will argue that no version of an Interest or Desire Theory succeeds in giving combined non-circular necessary and sufficient conditions for a duty's being owed to someone (and hence, when the extra conditions alluded to in Sections 2.1 and 6.1 are fulfilled, for that duty's being someone's right). But Raz's justificatory version of the Interest Theory gives an important non-circular sufficient condition for a duty's being owed to someone, and Kramer's and Wenar's distinct theories give necessary conditions for a duty's being owed to someone, but conditions that at least in certain rare cases have to be taken circularly: rights necessarily serve certain interests—or in Wenar's case, kind-based desires—but in some odd cases that is only because they *create* or *constitute* the relevant interests or desires.[10] These complex results pose three questions for rights theory to answer about the relationship between directed duties, interests, and desires, and I outline these at the end of the chapter. My aim throughout will be—like that of other theorists of rights—to find a unifying account that can explain the shared feature of natural rights or directed duties, morally justified legally or conventionally created rights or directed duties, and any morally unjustified legal-conventional rights or directed duties: the feature that explains why all of these are *directed* duties and hence rights.

Raz's well-known theory holds that a right exists when an interest grounds a duty. Raz puts it this way:

'X has a right' if and only if X can have rights, and, other things being equal, an aspect of X's well-being (his interest) is a sufficient reason for holding some other person(s) to be under a duty.[11]

In light of the point in Section 2.1, I will focus on this as a theory of a *duty's direction*: of what it is for a duty to be owed to someone.

---

[8] Tierney 1997, p. 16. Thanks to Leif Wenar for drawing my attention to this passage.

[9] And if there is a sense in which it *is* good for her, then perhaps it can be her right. For more on Hegel's purported right to be punished, see Section 4.6.

[10] Note also that on my account of interests, Kramer's Interest Theory fails to accommodate morally unjustified rights—though rival conceptions of interests might deliver different results. See Section 2.3 below.

[11] Raz 1986, p. 166. Those who follow Raz include Waldron 1993, Fabre 2000 and 2006, and Tasioulas 2015; Rainbolt 2006 is also close. I would add that Raz's influence can also be seen in structurally similar theories which place some value other than *interests* at the heart of rights, but which still regard rights as grounded by the importance of the right-holder's possession of or relation to the value in question. See, for example, Griffin 2008, in which *agency* plays broadly the same role in relation to human rights that Raz ascribes to well-being for all rights; or see Nussbaum 2006, in which capability plays this role; see also the Razian role for interests in Beitz 2009 at p. 109. In the discussion below I ignore Raz's 'X can have rights' clause.

In interpreting the quotation above, it is best to reframe 'sufficient reason for holding...'. Raz is not saying that someone is owed a duty whenever there is sufficient practical reason to *hold* (e.g. to assert) that someone else has a duty.[12] Nor is Raz's 'sufficient reason' epistemic. A person's interest could constitute epistemic reasons for inferring the existence of a duty without that person being owed the duty.[13] It is better to read Raz as saying that X is owed a duty if and only if X's interest is a sufficient *reason for the existence* of that duty, where 'reason' is not here essentially about the directing of reasoning, but rather indicates a *ground*.[14] In this sense a sufficient reason for the existence of a duty is something sufficient to make it the case that the duty exists, that is, that someone is duty-bound. With this clarification in place, Raz can be read as offering a reductive analysis of a duty's direction: an otherwise undirected duty is owed to some party if and only if that party's interest is sufficient to ground the duty.

'Interest' here means an 'aspect of well-being', which might but need not be something the relevant person 'takes an interest' in. Further, Raz makes clear that a duty can be owed to someone without serving that person's interests *on balance*, and the 'sufficient to ground' clause in Raz's theory accommodates this.[15] For example, my interest in not being tortured can ground your duty not to torture me even if on balance I would do better if you tortured me or if you were under no duty not to torture me—perhaps because I am in some desperate situation where you can only save my loved ones by torturing me. Nonetheless, my interest in not being tortured could be sufficient to ground your duty here.[16]

There are two ways to understand what might make an interest sufficient to ground a duty. One results in an attractive but extremely radical theory of directed duties. The second makes the theory collapse.

The first interpretation sees a given interest as sufficient to ground a duty only if that interest has some independent importance on its own—that is, only if that interest's importance is not wholly derived from how serving that interest will serve further values such as the interests of others. On this interpretation, your duty not to torture me is owed to me because my interest in not being tortured (which plays a sufficient role in grounding this duty)[17] is of some independent importance: even if

---

[12] Suppose the only way to avert a disaster for someone is to tell everyone else that you have a duty (perhaps you can only save someone from the mob's wrath by distracting it by claiming, loudly, to be under a duty). It follows neither that the relevant duty exists nor—if it does—that it is owed to the person who you save.

[13] Suppose Mary is the only person who knows where the fire escape is. In a fire, I have a strong interest in doing what Mary says. This interest of mine might constitute a sufficient epistemic reason for observers to infer that both I and my colleagues have a duty to obey Mary in a fire. But I do not hold a right here (suppose my colleagues' obeying Mary will not help me escape). I doubt Mary has a right to be listened to either.

[14] For discussion of the nature of grounds, and the distinction between moral grounds for duties and legal or conventional grounds for duties which lack moral grounding, see Sections 5.1–5.2, plus Chapter 7.

[15] Raz 1986, p. 180.   [16] Whether the duty is then justifiably infringeable is a further question.

[17] A further difficult interpretative issue concerns what it is for an interest to be *sufficient* to ground a duty: must the interest ground the duty on its own, no matter the burdens the duty imposes? Or must the interest simply play *a major role* in grounding the duty, or a major role in the *positive case in favour* of the duty (as opposed to the considerations counting against the duty's existence)? This question in its most

lots of people will gain from my not being tortured, the importance of my interest in not being tortured is independent of this.

This first interpretation has theoretical attractions. It makes a duty's direction neatly mark out parties whose interests are of independent importance sufficient to ground it. This is the kind of distinctive role within normative topology for which it would be plausible to have a special linguistic marker like 'owed to' or 'a right'.

However, the first interpretation is extremely radical. It rules out the possibility of duties—even merely legal or conventional duties—owed to parties whose interests lack independent importance. But we commonly take duties to be owed to business corporations and other entities (clubs, universities) whose interests derive all their importance from their role in serving the interests of others (such as their members or other human beings).

The first interpretation also rules out the possibility of duties owed to someone whose interests, although independently important, do not play a significant role in grounding them. There seem to be many examples of duties that are owed to people even though the independent importance of the interests of the people to whom they are owed plays no part in their grounding. Raz himself mentions parents' rights to child benefit payments within the British benefits system.[18] These are justified by the interests of the child, plus perhaps the wider importance of morally permissible public policies that have been legitimately adopted. The parents' own interests need play no independently important role in this justification. Yet if the appropriate system is set up, parents are right-holders, owed duties to be paid benefits by the state. The prime minister's right to declare war is similar. Ordinary citizens owe (limited) duties to the prime minister to allow her to declare war: not to impede or obstruct her in the declaration. These duties are *owed to* the prime minister, and the prime minister is disrespected when they are violated. But these duties are grounded in the interests of the citizenry as a whole and in considerations about the smooth running of states. They are not grounded in the prime minister's own personal interests. Also consider trivial property rights like my right over this computer. This—I will argue in Part III—is grounded in how a property system serves the common good (construed as potentially divergent from the individual's good). Your duty not to use the computer is owed to me even if I gain nothing from the computer, and even if I am the sort of self-sufficient person who gains nothing from having a property system in operation overall. I still have a justified right over the computer, so long as I acquired it according to the common-good-grounded rules. But it does not seem that my interest need have played any role whatsoever in grounding it.[19]

---

general form—namely, the differing roles the individual right-holder's good can play in grounding different rights—is taken up in detail in Chapter 8.

[18] Raz 1994, p. 50.

[19] For conceptions of the common good as not having to include everyone's good, see the 'utilitarian' approach sketched in Section 13.2. Also see my Cruft 2006 for an argument against individualistic approaches to property, including Lockean self-ownership-based approaches. Compare also Nozick's 'historical' theories of justice, which make justified property rights depend only on how they were acquired and subsequently transferred, independently of the transferee's interests (Nozick 1974, ch. 7, and see this volume, Section 12.3). Raz gives more examples in his Raz 1994, including a pregnant woman's right not to be executed (the duty is owed to the woman but grounded in the interests of the foetus) (p. 50), and a town

Later in this book, I will return to the examples above.[20] I will find reason to support some of the radical conclusions implied by this first interpretation of Raz's theory. For example, I will find some reason to conclude that I am not 'really' the holder of property rights over 'my' computer: these are, rather, in a sense really held by the community whose interests ground the system. This radical conclusion involves no change in the *existence* or *contents* of the duties standardly taken to bind us (you still have a duty not to take 'my' computer, and I still have control over that duty as the person who can sell, give away, or bequeath the computer for whatever reason I see fit), but only in our conception of *to whom they are owed* (if you were to take it, you would wrong the community and not me, despite my powers of control over this community-directed duty).[21] But it should be clear that this would still be an extraordinarily radical conclusion, requiring a major rethink of our normative world. For that reason among others, I resist following this conclusion through in every case. On grounds explained in Chapter 14, I allow that business corporations can genuinely hold rights even though their interests lack intrinsic moral importance and hence cannot be the true ground of duties.[22] I also allow that the government's duty to make child benefit payments is genuinely owed to me, even though my child's well-being is what grounds this duty, and that citizens' duties to allow the prime minister to declare war are genuinely owed to her, even though the interests of the citizenry as a whole ground these duties. But maintaining that these are genuine rights requires abandoning the first interpretation of Raz's theory.

Raz favours a second interpretation of his theory of rights, which he thinks can accommodate these counterexamples. He claims that an interest can be sufficient to ground a duty in his sense even when the importance of that interest depends entirely on how serving or respecting that first interest serves the further interests of other parties. Thus he suggests that a journalist's right not to have her notes taken from her is grounded by the journalist's interests—but he adds that the journalist's interests ground the relevant duties precisely because serving these interests serves the common good; the journalist's interests have no independent duty-grounding importance.[23] Similarly, in discussing the rights of officials and corporations, Raz

---

planner's right to devise a preservation scheme (the duty to respect the planner's office is owed to the planner but grounded in the interests of the city's inhabitants) (p. 53).

[20] See especially Chapters 13–14. Note that what is special about these examples is that they involve duties owed to *a party whose own interests fail to ground them*; it is not simply that such duties could be grounded by what they do for parties others than those to whom they are owed (many fundamental human rights, such as the right to freedom of expression, *could* be grounded by what they do for parties beyond the right-holder), but that the duties in question *are not successfully groundable* simply or primarily by what they do for the party to whom they are owed (see Chapter 8 on this; by contrast the right to freedom of expression, I argue later, is groundable simply by the right-holder's interests independently of what it does for others, even though its serving others *could also* work to ground it).

[21] Note that even the contents and existence of duties of compensation or rectification need not change on this approach: you could still have to pay me compensation when you take the computer. But our conception of this payment would change: your making the payment to me would be a matter of *duty owed to the community*: for the community's sake, you have to make the payment to me. I return to this in Chapter 3 and again, in relation to property, in Section 13.3.

[22] But see the end of Section 14.3 for some limits to the idea of businesses' rights.

[23] Raz 1986, p. 179.

writes 'rights protect the interests of right holders. But these interests need not be intrinsically valuable. The reason for protecting them may be that by doing so one does protect the interests of others.'[24]

This second interpretation of the kind of importance an interest can have in grounding a duty within Raz's theory might seem to accommodate the counterexamples, but on inspection it leads to the theory's collapse. This second interpretation allows that a particular interest can attain duty-grounding status by inheriting all its duty-grounding importance from other interests or other factors—e.g. interests which will be served by the duty via the serving of the particular interest. But then can't any interest whatsoever that is served by a duty for which there are independent grounds inherit the duty-grounding importance of those independent grounds? It would be very problematic if this were so. For example, we would find ourselves saying that my employer's duty to pay my salary is a duty which is owed not only *to me* but also *to my local shopkeepers*. Because I spend my salary in their shops, they have an interest at stake in my being paid, and on this second interpretation it is unclear how we could stop that interest inheriting the duty-grounding importance of my own interest in my salary: the shopkeepers' interest is served by the way the duty serves my own interest.[25] But surely my employer's legal duty to pay my salary is not itself owed to local shopkeepers as well as to me.

One might try to block this move by adding that only interests which are furthered *necessarily* by the fulfilment of a duty can be seen as their 'grounds'. (My employer's paying my salary is necessarily in my interests in some respect if not on balance; its relation to my local shopkeepers' interests is much more contingent.) There is merit in this but—even apart from difficulties considered in the next section—it involves giving up on the idea of a duty's direction as genuinely determined by the interests that *ground* it.[26] Even interests *necessarily* served by a duty are not aptly described as its 'ground' if their importance is wholly derived from other interests.

For example, notice how artificial it is to describe parents' interests as one ground for the existence of the duty to pay child benefit payments, once we accept that such parental interests only possess duty-grounding importance because serving these interests will serve children.[27] Similarly, note how artificial it is to describe the prime minister's interest in declaring war as the ground for our duty to allow her to do so. It is much more natural to 'look through' the artificial interests here (i.e. those with only derivative importance) and refer to the underlying interests of primary importance— the children's interests or the people's interests—as the ground of the relevant duty. Similarly again, note the artificiality in referring to Microsoft's interests as the ground of our duties to Microsoft—rather than referring to how a system of corporations with rights can serve the common good. My point is not that there is a problem with the very idea of interests borne by corporations, by state officials on behalf of the people, or by parents on behalf of children. But referring to the immediate artificial or

---

[24] Raz 1984, p. 20.   [25] The example, in a different context, derives from Kramer's 2010, pp. 31–9.

[26] It also converts Raz's theory into Kramer's; see discussion in Section 2.3.

[27] This is not to deny the deny importance of parents' own interests in their children's well-being; but we could surely justify the right whether or not they had such interests.

other-directed interests as the *ground* of duties when these interests only gain any duty-grounding importance through their relation to other underlying interests seems misleading. It can seem apt to say—in a helpfully clarifying tone—that children's interests are *really* the ground for the child benefit system, that the people's interests are *really* the ground for the prime minister's right to be unimpeded in declaring war, or that efficiency or other common goods are the *real* ground for corporations' rights. If there are any duties that are groundable independently of any interests (one might think, along Kantian lines, of duties required by consistency in willing), then again it can seem apt to say that even if some individuals' interests are necessarily served by such duties, their *real* ground is the interest-independent consideration.[28]

The appropriate conclusion is that if a duty's direction is to be characterized as marking the interests which ground it (as Raz suggests), then this must be understood in line with the first interpretation, with its deeply radical consequences. The second interpretation of Raz's theory (and his favoured one) cannot make proper sense of an interest as a ground.[29] But the first interpretation is too radical to succeed as a necessary condition for right-holding or for duties to be owed to someone. Microsoft, parents, and the prime minister are genuinely owed legal duties in the examples in the preceding paragraph. Raz's theory on its first interpretation fails to accommodate these cases.

But in my view, Raz's theory still gives a *sufficient* condition for a duty's being owed to someone. If some party's interest or well-being (a party who might be an individual person, an animal, a group) is sufficiently important largely on its own to place some other party under a duty, then it seems to me that as Raz tells us, this duty must be owed to the relevant party. It might seem to follow that, for example, the state's duty within the British welfare system to make child benefit payments *must* be owed to children, even if it is also owed to their parents. But this does not follow, because the child's interest is not the only significant factor needed to make it the case that there is a duty to make child benefit payments. The legal duty's justification depends also (and centrally) on democratic approval of the system adopted, and the duty's existence depends on its being legally created. We can take this example as hinting at the fact, to be defended in Chapters 5 and 7–8, that what Raz has given us is actually an account of *natural* rights or *natural* directed duties: of duties owed to someone whether or not their existence or direction is recognized, and independently of their creation in law or convention. When someone's interest on its

---

[28] Fitting such a possibility with the Razian position would require allowing interests to inherit duty-grounding status not only from other *interests*, but also from interest-independent considerations. For more on the idea that Raz's account of what it is for an interest to *ground* a duty collapses into the idea of an interest's being *served* by a duty if 'grounding' is taken too broadly, see Cruft 2017.

[29] On its second interpretation, Raz's theory ends up as a theory which says that a duty is owed to any being or body whose interests are *necessarily served* by its fulfilment. This is actually Kramer's theory of rights, the pertinent difference being the presentational point that Kramer explicitly abandons Raz's claim that duties can only be owed to beings whose interests *ground* them, while Raz maintains this notion of grounding by interpreting it too broadly to mean anything distinctive. For more on Kramer's theory, see Section 2.3.

own makes it the case that another is duty-bound, then that duty is owed to the bearer of the interest.

We will see in Chapter 7 that all naturally directed duties fit Raz's account—so it turns out that natural rights, unlike created legal-conventional rights, cannot be grounded primarily by values other than the right-holder's good. Some legal and conventional rights and directed duties also come close to fitting Raz's analysis: those rare legal rights justifiable directly by the good of an individual—see Section 9.2. But even they are not *made to exist* simply by the right-holder's good; they are merely *justified* simply by this; their existence still depends on their creation, not simply on the interests of the party to whom they are owed. Further, we will see that the vast majority of legal and conventional rights are not justifiable simply by how they serve the particular party to whom they are owed, but can be justified only by how they serve others too.

2.3 From Kramer's Non-Justificatory Interest Theory to Wenar's Kind-Desire Theory

One way to accommodate the cases with which Raz struggles—those in which a duty is owed to someone whose interests are not its ground—is to see directedness simply as marking parties whose interests are necessarily at stake in relation to a duty, rather than those whose interests ground it. This is another kind of distinctive role within normative topology for which it would be plausible to have a special linguistic marker like 'owed to' or 'a right'—and it is the approach favoured by Kramer, following Bentham.[30]

An apparent problem for Kramer (and indeed for Raz) is that some duties—even morally justified ones—seem to do *nothing whatsoever* for the well-being of those to whom they are owed, not even contributing to it in some small respect. An example is that of ugly, valueless plastic garden gnomes inherited from a relative I never knew nor cared for. Your duties not to use these gnomes are, perhaps, owed to me although it is hard to see any sense in which they contribute to my well-being.[31] Given the doubts about property rights to be developed in Part III, I should mention another example, and duties of office seem to furnish many cases: even if I loathe my job as manager, do not need the salary, and would be better off in every respect if my employees anarchically rebelled, nonetheless those employees owe me (limited) duties of obedience, duties correlating with my managerial rights. To accommodate these cases, Kramer specifies that a given duty to PHI is owed to any human, animal, or group who is necessarily placed, by the duty-bearer's PHI-ing, in a state or situation that it is *typically* beneficial for a human, animal, or group in the relevant

---

[30] Kramer 1998 and 2010.

[31] See my Cruft 2004 at pp. 372–3. Another example is a trivial promissory duty which I accept (as promisee) absent-mindedly, without any interest served by what is promised. It is not totally clear to me that such promises really are binding, but if they were they would provide a similar counterexample. See Raz 2012 and my Cruft 2013 at p. 213.

context to be in.[32] Note that unlike Raz, Kramer does not make the right-holder's interests the *ground* or *justification* of their right.[33]

I say more about Kramer's theory after introducing an alternative. Wenar offers an original new theory that supplies a different approach to the problem. Like the Interest Theories, Wenar makes a duty's direction turn on who is served by that duty's fulfilment, but 'served' here refers to the satisfaction of *desires* rather than of well-being-defined *interests*. Further, for Wenar the relevant desires are those one holds in virtue of the kinds (including roles) specified by the normative system within which the relevant duties fall. He first formulates his theory in terms of role-based desires, and then develops this into a kind-desire version (in which roles are one type of kind), formalized thus:

Consider a system of norms S that refers to entities under descriptions that are kinds, D and R. If and only if, in circumstances C, a norm of S supports statements of the form:

1. Some D (qua D) has a duty to *phi* some R (qua R); where '*phi*' is a verb phrase specifying an action, such as 'pay benefits to', 'refrain from touching', 'shoot', and so on;
2. Rs (qua Rs) want such duties to be fulfilled; and
3. Enforcement of this duty is appropriate, *ceteris paribus*;
   then: the R has a claim-right [is owed a duty] in S that the D fulfil this duty in circumstances C.[34]

In what follows, I set aside Wenar's third clause (the enforceability clause), because Wenar sees his first two clauses as sufficient for determining a duty's direction; the third clause distinguishes those directed duties which we can call 'rights' from those duties that are still directed but are not rights.[35] I return to this clause when I develop a similar thesis in Section 6.1.

In focusing on role- or kind-based desires, Wenar follows Raz's suggestion that 'rights are vested in right-holders because they possess certain general characteristics'.[36] Where Kramer takes this idea as defining rights or directed duties by what is *typically* in the *interests* of a human, animal, or group, Wenar defines them by the

---

[32] I here follow Kramer's exposition in his 2010, p. 32. In Kramer 1998, the idea that rights must *necessarily* serve their holders is outlined via 'Bentham's test' (where Kramer puts it as the thesis that when detriment to someone is sufficient to establish a duty's breach then the duty is owed to them; pp. 81–3); the explication of 'serving' and 'detriment' in terms of what is *typically* beneficial comes at pp. 93–7. I discuss the indexing to humans, animals, and groups later (Sections 3.2 and 4.5); obviously, this should be read as saying that for a duty to be owed to a given *human*, its fulfilment necessarily has to place that human in a state or situation that would be typically beneficial for a *human*; for it to be owed to a given *animal*, we should read it indexed to 'animal' and so on. Note also that Kramer's own exposition gives necessary but insufficient conditions for a duty's direction because he states his theory in a way that does not assume that any duty exists (Kramer 2010, p. 32). It is, I contend, fair to read his account as giving a sufficient condition of the type outlined: a condition whose fulfilment is sufficient to establish a duty's direction. Recent work on Kramer's 'Bentham's Test' includes Frydrych 2017, McBride 2017, Kurki 2018.
[33] We should note also that Kramer's account refers to the benefits of the full action enjoined by the duty. Even if part of an action (or an action under a partial description) would necessarily be beneficial for the typical human, a duty enjoining this action will not be owed to the person it affects unless the full action (under the description used in specifying the duty) places the person in a position that would be beneficial for the typical human.
[34] Wenar 2013, p. 219; for the role version see p. 209.   [35] Ibid., p. 214, section X and note 24.
[36] Raz 1986, p. 180, referenced by Wenar 2013 at pp. 205–6.

desires that we ascribe to *role*-bearers or to members of natural *kinds*. Wenar shows how these moves enable his theory to accommodate directed duties with which Interest Theories struggle, such as a right of a kamikaze pilot to her allocation of fuel—something that it is hard to see as in her interests (even in Kramer's 'typical' sense) but which, given her role, she desires.[37]

Wenar notes that the desires we ascribe to role-bearers or to members of natural kinds can be distinct both from any given person's desires or well-being and from the desires or well-being that groups of actual persons have as a matter of statistical frequency. Wenar makes clear how free-floating his notion of role- and kind-based desires is: 'When travelling through King's Cross station in London you may hear a recorded announcement saying that members of the station's staff will be happy to help passengers. Even if every individual who works at King's Cross is entirely misanthropic, we still say that all staff members, qua staff members, are happy to help passengers.'[38] So on Wenar's understanding, a party's role- or kind-based desires are determined by her role or kind in a way that makes them independent of both the well-being of that party, and of the desires or pro-attitudes 'in that party's head', those specific to her psychology. By making a duty's direction determined by role-/kind-based desires, rather than actual or typical interests, Wenar avoids cases that are problematic for both Raz and Kramer.

Kramer's theory struggles with morally unjustified social or legal rights, while Wenar's does not. For example, I would dispute the claim that the 'rights' of an organized crime boss serve their typical holder's genuine interests, despite material appearances to the contrary. They perhaps serve interests definitive of the boss's role within the criminal organization, but not her true interests. Wenar can accommodate this, as his analysis merely aims to locate claim-rights within whatever normative system is under analysis, whether it be good or bad. Within the normative system of the mafia, the crime boss qua boss within the (informal) rules of the criminal organization, will want the satisfaction of the relevant duties (e.g. duties held by her subordinates).[39]

In my view, both Kramer's and Wenar's theories of directed duties are very attractive. It is hard to think of *morally justified* rights or directed duties that qualify as counterexamples to either Kramer's or Wenar's theory. I had an initial worry that this was because it was natural to take both theories, implicitly, in a circular way when thinking about cases: my thought was that it is natural to ascribe typical interests or role-/kind-based desires only because one already thinks a duty is owed to someone. For instance, take the conventional duty borne by private soldiers to

---

[37] Wenar 2013, p. 205. Could Kramer reply that the typical kamikaze pilot's well-being is served by her allocation of fuel—and indeed by her successful completion of a mission that kills her—because her well-being requires her to be able to do her job? Perhaps, if the job is itself morally justified. But what if kamikaze missions are not justified? Can they still serve the well-being even of an unwilling pilot? I doubt it, but even the unwilling pilot has a right to the fuel within the system of military, role-based norms.

[38] Wenar 2013, p. 215.

[39] Compare Wenar on the unjustified legal right to arrange one's child's marriage, and on unjustified property (Wenar 2013, p. 205). Note that Raz also fails to accommodate unjustified rights, because the duties in question are by hypothesis ungrounded.

salute military officers.[40] Is this duty—to salute officers—owed to officers, or to the monarch, or to nobody? My worry was that—to put it in Wenar's terms—we most naturally ascribe to military officers a *role-based desire* to be saluted by private soldiers only if we make the prior assumption that the duty to salute is owed to officers. Or, to put this in Kramer's terms, we most naturally ascribe to typical humans who are military officers an *interest served* by being saluted by private soldiers only if we make the prior assumption that the duty to salute is owed to officers.

On further inspection, I think this particular concern is unjustified in all but odd cases. Both Kramer and Wenar take pains to explain how interests (for Kramer) or kind-based desires (for Wenar) can be identified in non-circular ways that are independent of the relevant party's being owed the duty in question.[41] In Section 2.5, I explain how they could address my initial circularity concerns about the military officer case above. We will see that this leaves a few odd cases as outstanding problems for the theories as non-circular necessary conditions on being owed a duty. But the real trouble will be for the theories as *sufficient* rather than as *necessary* conditions: it is reflection on this that can drive us to circular versions of the theories. Because, as legal positivism tells us, we can make duties owed to whomever we want through law-making, we should not be compelled to see a duty as owed to a party only when her or his independent interests or desires are served by that duty. Before getting to this point, it will be useful to say more on when being owed a duty creates a circular, directedness-dependent interest in or desire for its own fulfilment (Section 2.4); after that, I return to my concern about the theories as a necessary condition on duties' direction (returning to the military officer case), and we will see how limited the reach of this concern is (Section 2.5); then I move on to the point about positivism and the theories as sufficient conditions (also in Section 2.5).

2.4 Desires and Interests Created by Rights

There are two ways in which someone's interest or their kind-based desire can be conjured into existence by their being owed a duty. First, all morally justified directed duties necessarily generate a distinctively *status-based* interest in—and, I would add, a *status-based* kind-desire for—their own fulfilment, borne by the party to whom they are owed. Consider the full range of morally justified duties owed to a person, including morally justified but legally or conventionally created duties owed to that

---

[40] See my earlier discussion in Cruft 2013, pp. 210–2.

[41] See, for example, Wenar's account of how to identify duty-derived role-based desires: 'Those within a system of norms understand its positions, and so understand what those who occupy its positions have a duty to do. Above we saw some duty-derived attributions of desires based on the principle that a role-bearer wants to do her job, to fulfil her responsibilities. A journalist wants to break the story, a parent wants to do what's best for her child—so a journalist wants his notes to be private, and a parent wants to receive child support. In such analyses, the R's desire for the D's duty fulfilment flows from a more basic desire: that she be able successfully to carry out her own duties' (2013, p. 215). Compare Wenar's later discussions allowing non-circular role-normative identification of further role-based desires, and stipulative and kind-normative identification of kind-based desires (2013, p. 216 and pp. 221–2); compare also Kramer's non-circular identification of interests in his discussion of highly unusual interests (Kramer 2001, pp. 87–9); throughout his 2001 and 1998 essays, Kramer identifies interests in a non-circular way.

person, such as my duty to do what the person says because she is my manager, or my duty to hand my work in to her on time because she is also my tutor. As noted in Section 1.3, these duties—including both the conventional directed duties just mentioned and what we might see as the natural directed duties correlating with natural rights (e.g. my duty not to assault her)—delineate the sphere of moral respect for the person in question. If I assault them, or indeed if I simply fail to do what they requested as my manager, or fail to hand my essay in on time to them, I show disrespect to them. These morally justified directed duties constitute ways of wronging someone which mark what it is to show disrespect to them.

Now (to take the Interest Theory first) it seems to me that everyone has an interest in being respected and being shown respect; that is, each person's well-being is necessarily diminished in a certain way if they are not respected. The interest here can plausibly be described as a status interest.[42] These facts about respect and status mean that any morally justified right is one whose fulfilment necessarily serves the right-holder's interests in a certain way: namely, in this status way. But this interest is parasitic on, rather than determinative of, a duty's direction.[43] Is there a parallel status interest in the fulfilment of morally unjustified rights? It is tempting to think this, for example, to ascribe to the organized crime boss a status interest in the 'respect' shown by those who pay her protection money. But I would favour a more moralized conception of respect, and hence of the attendant status interest. In my view, the crime boss's well-being is not really enhanced by the 'respect' shown in such payments, and this is because they do not show true respect. I would even deny that the payments themselves enhance her well-being.[44]

Nonetheless (to turn to the Kind-Desire Theory) even in *unjustified* cases a duty owed to someone seems to me to create a distinctive kind-based desire—in Wenar's sense—for its own fulfilment: a desire constituted by one's occupying the role or status of 'party to whom a duty is owed'. That is, in my view, a member of the latter kind (a bearer of an 'owed to' role) must, *qua owed a duty*, want its fulfilment. They want the respect owed to themselves as a party to whom a duty is owed—even if this is just the pseudo-'respect' owed to the crime boss. This desire for respect-as-fulfilment-of-duty just seems to me to go along with falling under the kind 'party to whom a duty is owed': this particular kind-based desire is an inevitable concomitant of any directed duty (whether morally justified or not), and it is conceptually generated by the duty's direction. We could call this kind-based desire a 'status desire' for the duty's fulfilment. It is parasitic on, rather than determinative of, a duty's direction.[45] Now, I recognize that some might not share my confident sense that there is such a status kind-desire generated by every directed duty. But if there *is* such a status kind-desire, then *it* cannot be what we appeal to if we want to use

---

[42] For theorists who stress this status interest, but look primarily at the status constituted by *natural* rather than *legally created* duties owed to the person, see Kamm 1996 and Nagel 2002, ch. 3.

[43] Ripstein makes a somewhat similar point in referring to the 'rights theory of interests' (Ripstein 2013, p. 180). Note that I do not suggest that *all* interests are conjured into existence by being owed a duty; only this special status interest is. See this volume, Section 5.3 for full discussion of this status interest.

[44] See note 39 and accompanying text.

[45] Such a status desire is, in my view, borne by *any party to whom a duty is owed*, including corporations, animals, dead people. For more on parties other than living adult humans, see Section 4.5.

Kind-Desire Theory to generate a non-circular explanation of when a duty is owed to someone. It is important to add that Wenar does not himself appeal to such a circular status desire in his explanations.[46]

There is a second way in which many rights or directed duties—morally justified and unjustified—contingently create further desires for and interests in their own fulfilment. Such desires and interests are *not* a necessary feature of the rights in question, in the way that the status desire is in my view necessary to all rights, and the status interest is necessary to morally justified rights. The second way in which rights create desires and interests is, rather, contingent on particular circumstances, and involves directed duties, and respect for them, *causing* the development of desires or interests in their own fulfilment. Examples of what I have in mind include the way that once a legal right becomes the social norm, people develop expectations based on 'their rights' that generate genuine interests and desires.

We should be careful in identifying the circular desires and interests here. An undirected duty to PHI might, contingently and over time by causal mechanisms, create desires (perhaps including kind-based desires) and interests which are served necessarily by PHI-ing—but such desires and interests are created by an *undirected duty* rather than by a *right*. An Interest Theory or Desire Theory might have to say that in such a situation what was previously an undirected duty has now, by creating desires or interests in its own fulfilment, become a right.[47] But this is not circularity for the theories. The circular case involves those interests or desires of mine which are created, again contingently and over time via causal mechanisms, by the existence of a *duty owed to me* (or a *right of mine*). For example, it is quite plausible that because I am a property owner or a manager, I might contingently come to gain interests generated specifically by the fact that duties not to use particular items or to do as I say *are owed to me*. Perhaps I come, through various psychological mechanisms, to gain great pleasure (and hence develop an interest) in people's thinking of me as 'propertied' or 'owed obedience', and this requires that my property and managerial rights be respected.[48] Similarly, perhaps due to psychological pressures generated by my ownership or managerial rights I come to embody the kinds 'proud homeowner' or 'obsessive manager', with their attendant kind-based desires for respect and obedience. (Few normative systems involve such kinds, of course, but they make occasional appearances in our psychology, and in sitcoms: we know the 'script' for the roles 'proud homeowner' and 'obsessive manager', and sometimes we try to live by or find ourselves living by these scripts, or we see others doing so.) Referring to

---

[46] See note 41 above. And see the final paragraph of Section 2.5 for the worry that in developing his theory to accommodate legal positivism, Wenar might sometimes be compelled to appeal to such status desires, despite his own avoidance of them. A similar claim can be made about Kramer.

[47] By denying that any duties are undirected, Kramer would deny this possibility (see his 1998). Similarly, I do not think this possibility would arise for Wenar's theory because the relevant kind-based desires in his theory are internal to the normative system that generates the duties, rather than creatable downstream from the system (2013). But alternative Interest and Desire Theories might allow for the possibility outlined in the main text.

[48] Note that this is distinct from the status interests my property rights and managerial rights create, for these status interests are served by respect for my rights independently of whether I take pleasure in such respect.

such *rights-created* interests or kind-based desires in order to explain why the duty not to use certain property or to do as I ask is owed to me would be circular.

2.5   Avoiding Circularity for Kramer and Wenar

Non-circular versions of Kramer's or Wenar's theories must exclude both rights-created *status* interests or desires and rights-created *contingent* interests or desires from those 'typical interests' (Kramer) or 'kind-based desires' (Wenar) which identify the people to whom a duty is owed.[49] And, as noted at the end of Section 2.3, both theorists do indeed offer non-circular accounts which avoid appealing to problematically circular interests and desires.[50] For instance, in relation to the saluting case Wenar can claim that unless saluting *helps military officers in some role-based way graspable independently of whether the duty to salute is owed to them*, then the duty will not be owed to them. Wenar can plausibly claim that within a military order that involves a duty to salute officers, being saluted helps the officers smoothly fulfil their function as military leaders—by recognizing hierarchy, maintaining discipline, and so on—whether or not the saluting is owed to them; he can then claim that it is only because saluting serves an officer's non-circular role-based *desire to do their job* that the relevant duty is indeed owed to the officer. Similarly again, Kramer can claim that it is only because others' duties to refrain from using particular land or chattels *benefits someone independently of whether these duties are owed to her* that the duties really are owed to her. That is, Kramer can claim that others keeping off something that a particular person has no duty to keep off is beneficial for that person whether or not the others' trespassory duties are owed to her—and that this non-circular interest makes the relevant duties owed to her.[51]

In both the latter cases, the interests or kind-based desires in question seem to be causally or constitutively downstream of the duties in some sense (for it is not clear

---

[49] To put this in terms of Kramer's 'Bentham's Test' (cf. Kramer 1998, pp. 80–3 and 2010), detriments which consist solely of either *rights-created status detriments* or *detrimental impacts on interests contingently created downstream from rights* must be excluded from the range of detriments which, through their sufficiency for a breach, identify those to whom a duty is owed. Note that Kramer also needs to exclude interests in learning what it is like to be wronged. Even a horrific morally justified legal duty of oppression (see this volume, Section 4.6) 'benefits' its victims by teaching them what oppression is like from the victim's perspective, and I think we should assume that all knowledge is in at least some respects beneficial to the learner. To avoid making legal duties to wrong others owed to them, this interest—in learning what it is like to be wronged—must be excluded.

[50] See the methods for identifying interests and desires referenced in note 41. Note that Wenar's discussion makes clear that we are not allowed, in working out to whom a duty is owed, to cast around for just *any* kind-based desire that someone happens to hold, which the duty serves: the relevant kind-based desires have to be those referred to by the system of norms that includes the duty (Wenar 2013, pp. 218–19). 'Proud homeowner' is not a role or kind referred to by the property system, and hence this odd role's circular, system-created kind-based desires are excluded by Wenar from determining to whom the relevant duties (not to enter a home, etc.) are owed.

[51] Similarly, both Kramer and Wenar could claim that promissory duties whose fulfilment would not serve some directedness-independent interest or directedness-independent kind-desire of the promisee are not owed to the promisee (and, perhaps, are not binding: see Raz 2012). I would question this claim, on the broadly positivist grounds in the main text below: can't we create directed duties where we want through consent (under appropriate conditions), largely independently of the non-circular interests or desires of the promisee?

that officers have a kind-based desire to do their job independently of the system of duties that constitutes them as officers, nor that owners have an interest in a particular area of land wholly independent of the system of trespassory duties—in the way that, say, we all have interests in not being tortured independently of any duties forbidding torture); but these desires and interests are not—so the retort goes—downstream of *the duties' being owed to someone as their right*. Therefore, even purged of circular interests and desires, Kramer's and Wenar's theories are able to accommodate the cases in question.

But there are some odd cases where I find it hard to see how the theories could avoid appealing to the circular interests or desires of Section 2.4. For example, it seems to me that the duty to salute military officers could be owed to officers even if the only interests or kind-desires it served were created by its being owed. Imagine a perverse military system in which officers were to be saluted only at times which impeded rather than enhanced their functioning—e.g. perhaps they were to be saluted only in the heat of battle. Even in this scenario, in which the duty to salute serves no desire or interest other than any created by its being owed, I am tempted to think that the system could still make the duty owed to officers. Its being owed would I think *create* interests and desires satisfying Kramer's and Wenar's theories, but only interests and desires that were circular in one or both of the manners outlined in Section 2.4: most plausibly, *status* interests and desires, those that are generated necessarily by being a party to whom a duty is owed. Further, such a perverse saluting system might in odd scenarios be morally justified—for example, if it were necessary to satisfy the whim of a wealthy backer without whose support disaster would strike some separate vulnerable group. Here we seem to have a morally justified duty owed to officers that does not serve any non-circular interest or non-circular kind-desire of theirs.

One reason to find the example above persuasive is a form of legal positivism: specifically, the view that we should be able through law, convention, or promising, to create rights in a manner untethered by the right-holder's good in any independent sense; that the right-holder's independent interests or desires, including kind- or role-based desires, should constitute no conceptual limit to the rights we can create, even those which might potentially be morally justified. Those unpersuaded by the example of the previous paragraph might be less positivist, taking rights to be more 'tethered' and less 'free-floating': conceptually unable to exist wholly independently of the right-holder's good or desires in some rights-independent sense. I find the example in question persuasive, but I also think such cases must be rare, and this requires explanation—which I return to in Section 5.4.

But whatever one thinks of the debate above (that is, whatever one's view of Kramer's approach or Wenar's approach as non-circular necessary conditions),[52] we should note that the positivism point implies that both Kramer's and Wenar's approaches would fail as non-circular sufficient conditions. To take Kramer first: suppose, as in the retort at the opening of this section, that military officers have an interest in private soldiers fulfilling their duty to salute them, independently of

---

[52] As noted in the previous paragraph, I return to this in Section 5.4.

whether this duty is conceived as owed to officers. The trouble is that even if officers do have this interest, which being saluted serves necessarily, we should be willing to see the duty as owed not to them but rather the monarch if, for example, the military code makes this explicit ('private soldiers owe it to the monarch (and not to anyone else) to salute in the presence of officers'). Such a conception of the duty seems possible no matter the interests of officers. Similarly, being a *named beneficiary* to a contract or promise means that fulfilment of the relevant contractual or promissory duty necessarily benefits one; but again I think it should be an open question whether the duty in such a case is owed to one.[53] Similarly again, Kramer's theory seems to *compel* us to see duties not to impede the prime minister's exercise of her power to declare war as owed to the prime minister, and duties to pay child benefits as owed to parents—for these parties are necessarily placed, by the duties' fulfilment, in a position that is typically beneficial in the relevant way. But it seems to me that we should not be *compelled* to accept this: the duties might or might not be owed to the parties in question, and this depends simply on whether the systems creating the duties make the duties owed to the relevant parties. They could do this, but they need not: a welfare system requiring child benefit payments to be made to parents could (as in the current British system) but need not confer on parents correlative rights.

At one point, Wenar focuses attention on roles defined by duties, and the role-based desires these create: desires to be able to do one's duty, such as parents' desire to be able to fulfil their duty to look after their children.[54] It is doubtful, I think, that the presence of a *duty-derived* role-based desire *must necessarily* make any additional supportive duties (legal-conventional or natural) borne by others to help the duty-bearer fulfil her own duties into supportive duties *owed to that duty-bearer*. Wenar assumes this in arguing that because parents have a duty-derived role-based desire to look after their children, other people's or institutions' duties to help parents (including the state's duty to pay child benefits) will be *owed to* parents.[55] I am not convinced that the presence of a *duty-derived* role-based desire should compel us to conclude this: while the British child benefit system takes the duty to make child benefit payments to parents to be a duty that is owed to parents (as their right), alternative systems could just as plausibly take such duties-to-make-child-benefit-payments-to-parents to be *owed to children* or to something else (perhaps *the community at large*). I think the polity can decide how it wants to conceive of such duties—without being bound to take them as owed to parents, despite the fact that the duties require payments to be made to the parents, and parents have a role-based desire to care for their children. The polity can recognize the existence of this role-based desire, and set up a child benefit system that serves it, without thereby being conceptually compelled to make the duties-to-make-child-benefit-payments duties *owed to parents*. Wenar's theory, like Kramer's, denies this—at least in its more reductive, non-circular form (see next paragraph for something less reductive). In this form, both theories make it necessary that any legal duty to make child benefit

[53] See Kramer 2017, section 10.1, for agreement with the text following the semi-colon; see also Sreenivasan 2017, section 5, for a full exposition of how Kramer's account struggles with third-party beneficiaries to contracts.
[54] Wenar 2013, pp. 215–16.   [55] Ibid.

payments must be owed to parents, no matter how the administration creating the duty conceives it. And that is my principal problem with the theories.[56]

One approach to this problem might be to draw on Wenar's contention that systems can *stipulate* what kind-based desires a party has.[57] (Could Kramer make a similar move? Stipulating the existence of interests—aspects of well-being—is arguably harder to do than stipulating the existence of kind-based desires.) Wenar could note that the law is allowed to stipulate whatever it is that parents desire qua parents-in-the-legal-system. Then in the problem case outlined—a system of duties to make child benefit payments to parents, in which the duties are owed only to children—the law can stipulate that parents, as defined by the legal system, lack a desire for the payments: only children are legally stipulated to have such a desire. And of course the law could make some alternative stipulation, and whatever is stipulated will determine to whom the relevant duties are owed. This move might work, but I worry that it takes us towards circularity. This is because it seems to me that if the law can stipulate the existence of kind-based desires, then it can do this in various direction-independent ways that then have to be excluded from the determination of directedness. For instance, I would suggest that the creation of any legal duty stipulates a kind-desire that the duty-bearer (qua duty-bearer) do what the duty requires. And perhaps law can also stipulate kind-desires 'as such', e.g. by simply stating 'It is stipulated that Xs qua Xs desire Y.' Neither of the latter kind of stipulated desires can be admitted by Wenar's theory as determinative of a duty's direction, if the theory is to avoid the problem in question. Instead, to respect our ability to create directedness wherever we want through law or convention, Wenar needs to draw a distinction among different legally stipulated kind-based desires: a distinction between those which can and those which cannot determine to whom the state's legal duties to make child benefit payments are directed or owed. In the case under consideration, this distinction must *exclude* my legally stipulated kind-based *desire to fulfil my own legal duties as a parent* (a desire that is stipulated, I think, by the creation of legal parental duties for me, and that will as it happens be served by my receiving the child benefit payments), while the distinction must *include* my children's legally stipulated kind-based desire to receive child benefit payments. What justifies us in drawing this distinction? What type of stipulated kind-based desires are allowed on the 'included' side? My suspicion is that the ultimate answer is that we must include only those legally stipulated status desires that reflect the legal duty's

---

[56] Note that Wenar's theory does not deny that the relevant duties could also be owed to children or the community at large (for these bodies might have the relevant kind-based desires); what it denies is that they could be *unowed* to parents, given the kind-based desires parents bear for their children's well-being. I think a polity could decide that the duties are not owed to parents; Wenar rules this out. For somewhat similar examples, see May 2017, perhaps especially the umpire example on p. 94: May argues that an umpire 'wants the bowler to inform her if he intends to start bowling around the wicket', and that this is one of Wenar's system-relative kind-desires, but he does not think we should be compelled to conclude that the umpire is owed this duty. I have found that intuitions about this case vary. See also this volume, Chapter 14 for further discussion; there I defend use of the term 'right' to refer to duties protecting duty-derived roles, but unlike Wenar I do not think all such duties *must be* owed to (and rights of) the role-bearer; we can legitimately choose to make them owed if we wish to. Note further that I am not denying that parents' interests could ground natural duties to assist parents that might be owed to parents.

[57] Wenar 2013, p. 221.

direction—circular desires of the type outlined in the first half of Section 2.4, desires one bears *in one's role as owed the duty in question*. Now, I think any theory has to be circular or at least non-reductive in something like this way if it is to respect the leeway we have to use legal and conventional creation in order to make a duty directed to whomever we want. My own Addressive approach will be non-reductive (see Section 4.3 and the end of Section 4.4 for further discussion of ways to be non-reductive without being viciously circular). But this is to move beyond Kramer's and Wenar's reductive ambitions.

2.6 Prospects for the Desire and Interest Theories

We have seen that both Interest Theory approaches (Raz's and Kramer's), and Wenar's Kind-Desire Theory, struggle with rights protecting the right-holder's duties of office or role, such as the rights which protect politicians, officers, or parents in discharging their role-defined duties. Raz's approach cannot accommodate such rights because the duties of office which they protect are often grounded or justified by common good considerations or other values distinct from the right-holder's own good. Rights protecting these duties inherit these grounds, and are thus not grounded by the right-holder's own interests. Kramer's and Wenar's different approaches, by contrast, in a sense accommodate such rights *too well*, at least if the theories are taken non-circularly: so taken, they force us to see as directed (rights-correlative) any duty that helps someone perform their role, for such a duty will necessarily serve the role-bearer's interest in performing their role, and will necessarily serve her role- or kind-based desire to perform her role.

While Raz thereby fails to give conditions *necessary* for a duty's being owed to someone (for duties can be owed to someone without their interests grounding them), Kramer and Wenar fail to give non-circular conditions *sufficient* for a duty's being owed to someone (for duties need not always be owed to those who are benefited necessarily by their fulfilment, or whose non-circular kind-based desires are served by their fulfilment). And more tentatively I have also argued that Kramer and Wenar fail to give non-circular *necessary* conditions too (for duties can in odd cases be owed to someone while bearing no relation to their non-circular or direction-independent interests or kind-based desires). This complex result, I have argued, still leaves Raz's approach accurate as a non-circular sufficient condition for right-holding, and Kramer's and Wenar's approaches accurate and informative as circular analyses, and near-accurate as non-circular necessary conditions. But we will need a further theory of directed duties—developed in Chapter 4, after discussing the Will and Demand Theories in Chapter 3—to explain why directedness is related to interests and desires in this complicated way. I think we can helpfully distinguish three questions posed by the discussion so far:

1. Why does a duty's being owed to someone necessarily set up a circular status interest or status desire, held by the person to whom it is owed, in its own fulfilment?
2. Why do cases which challenge Kramer's and Wenar's approaches as non-circular necessary conditions on a duty's being owed to someone seem unusual

or rare—like my perverse military saluting rule outlined earlier? In particular, why must *most* morally justified directed duties be such that fulfilling them necessarily satisfies Kramer-style typical interests of the party to whom they are owed, interests that are graspable independently of the fact that the party in question is owed the duty? And why must *most* directed duties be such that fulfilling them satisfies Wenar-style kind-based desires of the party to whom they are owed, desires that again are graspable independently of the fact that the party in question is owed the duty?

3. Why is Raz's approach accurate as a sufficient condition for duties being owed to someone? That is, why must any duty morally grounded by a party's interests be owed to that party?

I develop answers to all three questions in Chapter 5 after introducing my own alternative account of directedness as addressiveness in Chapter 4. In answering the first question, I will suggest that, in a sense, the status interest or desire created by being owed a duty is the flip-side of what one might call a 'Socratic' interest in doing one's duty.[58] But one might wonder whether the second and third questions really need an answer. One might try to rest content with the claim that a duty's direction is a matter of the complex Razian sufficient condition in conjunction with circular versions of Kramer's or Wenar's conditions—or perhaps with Kramer's or Wenar's non-circular conditions as near-accurate necessary conditions. That is, one might try to retain a 'Desire-Interest Theory' of rights composed of a Razian sufficient condition and one or both of Kramer's and Wenar's conditions, taken either in circular interpretations or as non-circular but defeasible or 'for the most part' necessary conditions. Such an approach leaves some important questions unanswered, in particular: whether a duty which necessarily serves some party's direction-independent interests or direction-independent kind-desires, *without* being grounded on their interests, is thereby owed to that party. All we can say of such a case is that it fulfils either a circular or a defeasible 'for the most part' necessary condition (Kramer's or Wenar's) on the duty's being owed to the person, but does not satisfy Raz's sufficient condition. This leaves it open that it might satisfy some other sufficient condition—or it might not. And the idea of a defeasible or 'for the most part' necessary condition is unhelpful. This unhelpfulness need not impugn the approach. Some concepts might lack any further determinacy, and there is no reason to assume that a duty's directedness is not like this. But we will see in the next two chapters that there is more to say, and that the additional condition gleaned from Chapter 3 and the further analysis of directedness developed in Chapter 4 enable us to regard my second and third questions above as genuine questions. Directedness is more than a duty's relation to someone's interests or desires, and we can draw on what more it is in order to explain why directedness has the relation to interests and desires underpinning the three questions above. To put it very briefly at this stage, directedness involves duties which place formal conditions of first- and second-personal apprehension on certain parties, and it will turn out that our interests and desires are complexly bound up with our being formally required to engage in such first-/second-personal thinking.

---

[58] See, e.g. Socrates' famous claim that 'nothing can harm a good man' (Plato 1969 [*The Apology*], 41d).

3

Rights' Elusive Relation to Powers

3.1 Forms of the Will and Demand Theories

Interest Theories of rights are standardly contrasted with Will Theories, which make a duty owed to whoever's will has control over it or over its enforcement.[1] We can also identify a related Demand Theory which makes a duty owed to whoever can demand its fulfilment.[2] My aim in the current chapter is to bring out the truth in the Will and Demand Theories. These theories fail as free-standing accounts of what it is to owe someone a duty. Focusing on one reason why they fail—because they cannot distinguish controlling or demanding a duty *on one's own behalf as the party to whom it is owed* from doing so on behalf of *another* or on behalf of *nobody*—will lead us to the new Addressive Theory of rights developed in Chapter 4.

Interest Theories that explain a duty's direction by reference to its recipients' interests or well-being focus, in formal terms, on a *passive* aspect of those to whom they are owed: right-holders are conceived passively as recipients of well-being.[3] By contrast, the rival Will Theory and Demand Theory approaches focus on the formally *active* aspect of those to whom duties are owed—as *claimants, demanders, complainants, enforcers, waivers, forgivers, punishers, resenters*. Different theorists pick out different characteristic activities. Consider the following list:

A duty is owed to and only to whoever has power[4] to

- waive it (Hart, Steiner)
- demand or claim its fulfilment (Feinberg, Darwall, Gilbert, Skorupski)
- enforce it (Hart, Mill, Skorupski)
- waive the duty of compensation triggered by its violation (Hart)
- demand or claim compensation for its violation (Hart, Darwall, Feinberg)
- enforce compensation for its violation (Hart, Mill)
- complain following its violation (Hart, Mill)
- demand or claim justification for its violation (Forst)
- punish its violation (Mill, Locke)
- forgive its violation (Darwall, Owens)

---

[1] For the standard Interest vs. Will bifurcation, see, e.g. Jones 1994, ch. 2, or Kramer, Simmonds and Steiner 1998.

[2] See Feinberg 1970 and Skorupski 2010, section 12.6.

[3] The passivity here is only formal; I do not deny that well-being essentially includes action.

[4] Some of the powers on this list are Hohfeldian powers (e.g. waiver); others are not but simply involve the possession of force or the permissibility of its exercise (e.g. enforcement). The power to demand fulfilment is rather obscure, and is discussed in more detail in Section 3.6.

- resent or blame its violation (Strawson, Darwall, Mill, Owens)
- receive apology for its violation
- reproach its violation
- some combination of the above.[5]

In response to the Interest Theory's failure as an account of a duty's direction, we might try one of the Will or Demand Theory options outlined above. But I will argue in this chapter that they all fail as analyses of a duty's direction. The truth we can take from the Will and Demand Theories is that every duty is, *ceteris paribus*, permissibly demandable by someone. The trouble is that this does not distinguish directed from undirected duties: *all* duties are *ceteris paribus* permissibly demandable, and this is part of what distinguishes them—as *duties*—from other sorts of reasons. Now, duties *owed to someone* are demandable distinctively on that person's behalf as the person to whom the duty is owed. But the theories have no successful non-circular account of what it is to issue a demand (or in other ways control a duty) on behalf of someone to whom the duty is owed (whether as that person oneself, or as a fiduciary issuing a demand or exercising control on behalf of someone else). The theories are, I will argue, unable to distinguish demands issued or control exercised *on behalf of someone to whom the duty is owed*, from demands issued or control exercised on behalf of the moral community in general—the kind of demanding or controlling that applies to undirected duties. To draw this distinction, we need an additional theory of what it is to owe someone a duty. That will come in Chapter 4, and we will see that a wholly reductive account is unavailable. Beforehand, in the current chapter, I assess the Will and Demand Theories' potential. That will pave the way for Chapter 4 and the eventual uniting, in Chapter 5, of the approach with the insights of the Interest Theory.

One might observe that some actions on the list above—e.g. perhaps forgiveness, receipt of apology, waiver—can seemingly be performed only by the person to whom the relevant duty is owed, and that a theory based on these actions therefore promises to avoid the problem sketched.[6] I criticize this proposal in Section 3.5.

3.2 The Standard Objection: Incapable Beings

First, a familiar objection to any item on Section 3.1's list: it rules out the possibility of duties owed to beings incapable of the relevant activity. This threatens the whole Will or Demand Theory approach. Surely we should see some duties as owed to beings incapable of any activity—such as comatose people—or incapable of any adult

---

[5] The works referred to in this list are: Hart 1955; Locke 1960 [1689], section 7 (on the natural power to punish); Strawson 1962; Feinberg 1970; Mill 1987 [1863], ch. 5; Steiner 1994 and 1998; Darwall 2006 and especially 2012; Skorupski 2010, section 12.6; Forst 2012; Owens 2012; and Gilbert 2018. Of course not all these authors take themselves to be offering an analysis of a right or of a duty's direction (e.g. not Forst, Locke, Owens, or Strawson), but their work can be developed as such an account.

[6] This response mirrors a distinction between 'personal' reactive attitudes (which one can only hold in relation to a duty owed to one) and 'impersonal' such attitudes (which one can hold in relation to duties owed to others or to nobody, as much as to oneself). See Strawson 1962, section 5; Darwall 2012, p. 336; Schaab 2017, section 4.5.

human activity—such as animals or babies.[7] So surely we cannot see the possession of any of the powers listed earlier as necessary for the relevant being to be owed a duty.

One response to this objection observes that in some cases we can construe the relevant power counterfactually. For example, we can ask whether a baby would have the power to waive a given duty if it were grown up. But this only makes sense for parties—like babies who could grow into adults—whose possession of the power in question is possible. It makes no sense to ask whether a cow or rabbit would have the power to waive a given duty if it were...what? If it had any of the powers on Section 3.1's list, it would not be a cow or rabbit.[8]

A second response to the objection observes that a person can demand fulfilment, waive duties, blame or enforce them *on behalf of* someone else, including on behalf of an animal, baby or incapable being—and in such cases this other being is the person owed the duty. This response prompts two concerns. First, the response needs to offer some explanation of what is going on when animals, babies, or other incapable beings (or indeed other capable humans) are such that duties can be waived, demanded, or enforced, etc. *on their behalf*. Whatever condition is introduced as explaining this (i.e. explaining what it is to be such that a duty is demanded, etc. *on one's behalf*) will itself constitute a separate, power-independent account of directedness. Secondly and relatedly, in order to distinguish a person exercising some power on behalf of someone else (and hence not themselves owed the duty) from a person exercising that power on their own behalf (and hence owed the duty), again some appeal needs to be made to some alternative conception of directedness which can underpin this *on one's own behalf/on someone else's behalf* distinction.[9]

3.3 A Less Familiar Objection: Exercising Powers on One's Own Behalf

The *on one's own behalf/on someone else's behalf* distinction highlights a problem that is less familiar in the literature.[10] Not only is possession of any one of the powers listed too exclusive as a *necessary* condition for being owed a duty, it is also too inclusive as a *sufficient* condition: it entails that duties are owed to beings who should rather be seen as third-party advocates on behalf of the 'real' recipient of the duty. When a passer-by demands that a farmer fulfil her duty of care to her cows (perhaps

---

[7] See, e.g. MacCormick 1982, ch. 8; Kramer 1998, pp. 69–70 (where he focuses on Hart's change of heart on this issue). Past and future people can also seem problematic for Will and Demand theories, and there might be specific problems for specific items on my list of powers: e.g. are corporations capable of resentment or forgiveness?

[8] Compare also debates about the status of *humans* who constitutionally could not have been conscious—or constitutionally could not have possessed other important moral properties (see e.g. McMahan 2016). Many thanks to Joseph Bowen for discussion, and see his 2020.

[9] Compare Darwall's similar distinction between individual standing to demand one's own right's fulfilment and representative standing to demand on behalf of the moral community (Darwall 2012; see also Darwall 2006, p. 29). Compare also the discussion of what Bowen calls 'Will Theory 3' in Bowen 2020. Sreenivasan's Complex Hybrid Theory (discussed in Section 3.4) can be seen as a response to the concern I press in the main text: that the Will Theory lacks resources to distinguish those claiming or waiving duties as right-holders from those doing so on behalf of someone else (Sreenivasan 2005, 2010).

[10] For a hint of it, see Raz 1984, p. 5.

they are being abused), the duty is not owed to the passer-by even though she holds this power to demand its fulfilment.[11]

Similarly, the approach seems to make third-party regulators into parties owed duties. For example, suppose that two businesses have contracted to merge in order to become a dominant force within the UK market. The Competition and Markets Authority (CMA) has the power to waive the contractual duties of these businesses if their merger would damage the market. Hart's and Steiner's Will Theory tells us that the relevant contractual duties—duties to undertake the necessary actions in order to merge the businesses—are therefore owed to the CMA, as well as to the parties to the contract.[12]

In both cases, the theory's deliverances are surely a mistake. The mistake emerges from failing to distinguish *powers exercised on one's own behalf as party-owed-the-duty* from powers exercised on behalf of others. When the passer-by issues a demand to the farmer on behalf of the cows, the duty is owed to the cows. When the CMA waives the relevant contractual duties, these are duties owed by the businesses to each other, and the waiver is exercised by the CMA on behalf of the British people. Only if one has power to waive, demand, enforce, etc. some duty on *one's own behalf as party-owed-the-duty* should this power be taken as a sign that one is owed the duty.

Furthermore, note that this notion of 'on one's own behalf' is technical in a circular way. There are several natural senses in which the passer-by or the CMA in the examples above does indeed act on their own behalf. The passer-by has considered the situation herself, has decided how to act, is not just taking orders, and is not purporting to be representative of someone else's views on the matter. Much the same might be true of the CMA (with the addition that it acts ultimately on behalf of the British people). These senses of exercising power 'on one's own behalf' cannot distinguish such bodies from those to whom the relevant duties are owed. It seems that the only sense that allows us to do this is the sense in which a power is exercised 'on one's own behalf' when and only when it is exercised in relation to a duty *owed to one*. It is in this circular sense that duties are owed to beings who exercise power over them 'on their own behalf'.

3.4 Sreenivasan and Powers Held on One's Own Behalf

Sreenivasan's Complex Hybrid Theory offers a non-circular account of 'on one's own behalf'. Sreenivasan couples the Will Theory's focus on powers with Raz's focus on

---

[11] Margaret Gilbert has suggested, in discussion, that demanding issued on behalf of cows (or similar cases involving demands made by third parties) is not genuine demanding, for genuine demanding is made by a right-holder on her own behalf. But, first, it is unclear to me why we should deny that such actions are genuine demandings, given the account of demanding to be developed in Section 3.6. Secondly, if these are *not* genuine demandings, then on Gilbert's proposal that is only because they are not made by the right-holder on her own behalf, in which case a genuine demand is distinguished only circularly from a third party's quasi-demand (as in the cow case): circularly because it depends on some separate conception of what it is to demand *as a right-holder*. (This second retort is developed further in Section 3.5; compare also May 2015, p. 527.)

[12] See, e.g. Steiner 1994, ch. 3.

grounds. He argues that a duty is owed to whoever has a level of power over it which is grounded by her interests. Thus he allows that a baby might be owed a duty (say, the duty not to harm the baby) if that baby's null control over it (as an incapable being) is grounded by the baby's interests. Similarly, an adult human might be owed a duty (say, the duty not to harm the adult) if that adult's fuller control over it is grounded by the adult's interests.[13] In my terms, Sreenivasan can be read as saying that power over a duty is held or exercised 'on-X's-behalf-as-owed-the-duty' if and only if X's interests are the ground for the degree of power held; if the power is instead grounded on something other than X's interests, then the power is not 'on X's behalf'.

With its invocation of *grounds*, Sreenivasan's theory inherits the problems of Raz's. For example, we have various duties to respect authoritative commands issued by our managers, politicians, and corporations for whom we work. These duties are owed to the managers, politicians, and corporations. But the powers of control over these duties borne by our managers, politicians, and corporations are not grounded in the interests of these managers, politicians, and corporations. Instead, they are grounded in a diversity of further interests and values: e.g. the common good values of efficiency and non-domination served by having an economic system that involves corporations with managers who hold rights protecting their duties of office, and the common good values of democratic control served by having a system of politicians with rights protecting their duties of office.[14] Sreenivasan's approach would seem to make the relevant duties owed to (and thereby make the relevant rights be held by) the wider public whose interests ground the level of control managers, politicians, and corporations hold over the duties in question. Perhaps we should be willing to accept this conception of these duties: perhaps in some sense duties to respect authoritative directives from managers, politicians, or corporations are indeed owed to the public at large. But Sreenivasan's approach goes further by erroneously denying that the relevant duties can also be acceptably conceived as owed to (and as rights held by) the specific managers, politicians, and corporations in question. Denying this is, in my view, a very radical departure from standard thinking, a departure which claims that managers, politicians, and corporations have no right to our respecting their directives, not even a legal or conventional right: for Sreenivasan, the relevant duties can only be the wider public's rights, and this impugns his theory.[15]

3.5 Powers Exercisable Only by Those to Whom a Duty is Owed

An alternative to Sreenivasan's way of distinguishing between powers over a duty *exercisable on one's own behalf as the person to whom the duty is owed*, and powers

---

[13] See especially Sreenivasan's useful illustrative discussion of the artist's right to the integrity of her works, in Sreenivasan 2005, pp. 273–4.

[14] For defence of these claims about the values grounding economic and political roles, see Chapters 13–14.

[15] These criticisms of Sreenivasan's account as a necessary condition for a duty's being owed to someone are matched by Kramer's and Steiner's powerful criticisms of it as a sufficient condition (Kramer and Steiner 2007).

over a duty *exercisable on behalf of another or nobody*, is as follows: we focus on those rather specific powers which can *only* be exercised by someone to whom a duty is owed. While many people beyond the person to whom the duty is owed might be both capable and morally permitted to demand and enforce its fulfilment, and to punish its violation, I suggested at the end of Section 3.1 that only the person to whom the duty is owed seems able to forgive its violation, and we might similarly claim that only this person is able to resent its violation, and to waive it.[16] If we restrict ourselves to powers of this type, we avoid having to distinguish power exercised on behalf of a person to whom a duty is owed from the same power exercised by a third party on behalf of another.

One flaw in this strategy, of course, is that it can only deliver a sufficient condition for a duty's being owed to someone. For as Section 3.2 showed us, the strategy cannot accommodate duties owed to babies, animals, or other beings incapable of the powers in question—and I take it that duties can be owed to these beings.[17] An interesting further flaw is that there seem to be impersonal parallels, performable by third parties, for all the activities that one might think can only be performed by the person to whom a duty is owed. For example, even if one defines 'waiver' as something performable only by a party to whom a duty is owed, there is an extensionally equivalent power often possessable by third parties—such as the CMA's regulatory power over merging businesses' contractual duties. In Section 3.3, I happily called this third-party power 'waiver', but perhaps we should reserve a separate term for it such as 'annulment'. But whatever terms describe these powers, the key point is that a power extensionally equivalent to the *waiver power possessed by parties to whom a duty is owed* can be borne by third parties to whom the duty is not owed. Thus when faced with a power to cancel or annul a duty, we cannot know whether it is a 'waiver' power (borne by the person to whom the duty is owed) or a power of 'annulment' (borne by a third party) without some independent grasp on to whom the duty is owed.

Similarly, even if we specify that resentment at a duty's violation can only be felt by violated parties to whom the duty was owed, there is a viable parallel notion of 'impersonal resentment' or 'resentment on another's behalf' that can be felt by third parties. When I observe employees exploited and then sacked by a local employer, I feel resentment on the employees' behalf even though their employer's duties were not owed to me. Perhaps this is better described as 'third-party outrage', but it is parallel to personal resentment.[18] Again, then, if we define resentment at a duty's

---

[16] Compare Gilbert's similar claim about demanding (see note 11). In making the point considered in Section 3.5, a theorist might draw on Darwall's distinction between (i) powers possessed by someone as an 'individual' authority (i.e. someone owed the duty), powers involving 'personal' reactive attitudes and (ii) powers possessed by someone as a 'representative' authority (i.e. as a member of the moral community, rather than as someone owed the duty), involving 'impersonal' reactive attitudes (2012, pp. 32–4; compare Schaab 2017).

[17] For more discussion of this premise, see Section 4.5.

[18] We should here distinguish (a) outrage at violation of a duty that is not owed to me but whose violation harms me (as felt by, e.g. Kramer's local shopkeepers when Kramer's employer fails to pay his salary (see this volume, Section 2.2)) from (b) outrage at violation of a duty that is neither owed to me nor whose violation harms me. David Owens argues that Hume 1975 [1777], pp. 310–11, can be read as holding that anyone in position (a) can feel outrage conceptualizable as resentment (see Owens

violation as something only those to whom the duty is owed can feel, we cannot use the fact that someone is capable of feeling something like resentment in order to determine that the duty is owed to them. In order to determine this, we already need to know, circularly, whether it is the kind of 'true' or 'personal' resentment felt at violation of a duty *owed to one*, or whether it is instead its impersonal parallel ('third party outrage'). And to know this, we seem to need some separate account of what it is for a duty to be owed to someone.

The same point applies to receipt of apology. Even if we define 'apology' as something that must, as a matter of conceptual necessity, be issued to the person to whom the violated duty was owed, we will still face the question, when encountering someone saying sorry, whether they are offering a genuine 'apology' with its defining directedness, or are rather saying sorry 'to the world at large' in a way that need not pick out or be aimed at the violated victim.

Owens claims that forgiveness is the odd one out here: he says it is not conceptually possible for me to forgive a violation, or do anything close to or parallel to forgiving it, if I am not the violated party.[19] But there is some plausibility to the idea that a party can delegate their powers of forgiveness to others: you might give me power to forgive, on your behalf, violations of your rights over some artwork you have created and put into my care, for example. Or consider a priest's power to forgive sin on god's behalf.[20] If forgiveness is primarily the annulment of a wrong-doer's rectificatory duties, then it seems to me that some legal or conventional systems of duties could include *undirected* duties that a central authority has power to annul in this way; this would be an undirected or impersonal power to 'forgive'.[21] These points mean that we cannot appeal to forgiveness to rescue the strategy explored in this section. Its being conceptually possible for a party to forgive violation of a duty does not guarantee that the duty is owed to that party: to know whether it is, we need to know whether the power of forgiveness is being exercised by the party on her own behalf, or on behalf of another or nobody. And to know that, we need already to know to whom the duty is owed.

The failure of this approach underpins the point I made in Chapter 1, that whether a duty is owed to someone makes no extensional difference to what ought to happen. This is because any extensionally described power associated with a given duty, whether exercisable pre- or post-violation, could be equally a power exercisable by someone *as the party to whom the duty is owed*, a power exercisable by someone *on behalf of some other party to whom the duty is owed*, or a power exercisable impersonally by someone as a third party. So any configuration of powers associated with a given duty could obtain equally if that duty were owed to one party, if it were owed to somebody else, or if it were undirected. For example, in response to my argument a critic might retort that when a duty is owed to someone, its violation

---

forthcoming, note 30 and main text). But it will not be resentment of a violation (or infringement) of a duty *owed to one*—unlike the conception of resentment sketched in the main text and favoured by, say, Darwall or Strawson.

[19] Owens 2012, pp. 51–8.   [20] Thanks to an anonymous reviewer for OUP for this useful example.
[21] Kramer (1998) would reject this by rejecting the possibility of undirected duties; he would say that the seemingly 'undirected' duties in my example are actually owed to the law-maker.

triggers remedial duties of apology and compensation, and the latter extensionally distinguish the case of the duty's being owed to someone from what would have obtained if the duty were undirected. But our discussion shows that a duty's violation could trigger remedial duties of apology and compensation, including duties to say 'I am sorry' in front of someone, and to pay that person money, without the latter duties thereby being owed to the relevant party hearing the apology and receiving the money. That party might instead have been tasked, as a third party, with hearing and receiving compensation on behalf of the moral community at large—rather as the CMA and other regulatory bodies are tasked in certain cases. Of course there is a difference between apologising to a party for having violated a duty owed to them, and issuing an apology to be heard by some party who does not take the role of 'violated victim'. My point is simply that this is not an extensional difference. In terms of overt behaviour, the actions can be the same. And my point in Chapter 1 was that a duty's being owed to a particular party, as opposed to its being owed to another or to nobody, therefore need not make a difference to the overt behaviour required of the duty-bearer.[22]

3.6 Prospects for the Will and Demand Theories

Given the problems in Sections 3.2–3.5, I cannot see any hope for a non-circular version of the Will or Demand Theory as a biconditional analysis of a duty's direction. But can the Will or Demand Theory supply a *circular* biconditional? Such a theory would say that duties are owed to whoever either (i) holds powers to exercise certain types of control over these duties on their own behalf (as the party to whom the duty is owed), or (ii) for whom others hold such powers on behalf of the beings to whom these duties are owed.[23]

Which powers should be given centre stage in such a circular theory? Not the power of waiver, I suggest, for the simple reason that some duties (e.g. moral duties not to enslave, criminal law duties not to kill) seem owed to people without being waiveable by anyone. Even adult humans who would be capable of waiver if they possessed the power do not, I contend, possess the power to waive some duties owed to them, including the moral duty of non-enslavement and the criminal law duty not to kill them.[24] Similarly, the power permissibly to enforce seems inappropriate for our purpose here because some duties (e.g. of gratitude) seem owed to people without being permissibly enforceable.[25] The power to forgive is also not what we need. It is unclear that the power to forgive a directed duty's violation can be held by a third party without its having been delegated to that party by the party to whom it was

---

[22] So Darwall's distinction between representative and individual authority (as picked up also by Schaab 2017) marks no extensional difference: in terms of overt behaviour, *waiver, resentment, apology, and demand-issued-on-one's-own-behalf* need not differ from *third-party annulment, outrage, apology-to-the-world-at-large, and demand-issued-on-behalf-of-the-moral-community.*

[23] Note that I claim no priority for exercising power on one's own behalf. I thus deny Thompson's claim that 'apprehension of the duty' is a typical achievement for those owed it (Thompson 2004, p. 368). Those who have to have the relevant powers exercised on their behalf by others because they are non-human animals might well be the typical beings owed duties. See this volume, Section 4.5.

[24] See, e.g. MacCormick 1977.   [25] See Sections 1.2 and 6.1.

owed. So giving this power centre stage would incorrectly nullify clause (ii)'s ability to encompass duties owed to animals, babies, and other beings incapable of such delegation.

In my view, *the power to demand or claim* seems central to all directed duties. If a duty is owed to me, *ceteris paribus* I can (i.e. am permitted and able to, according to the rules of the normative system in question) either demand its fulfilment on my own behalf or others can do so on my behalf.[26] This Feinbergian thesis has much to recommend it. Feinberg famously writes:

> [It] is claiming [=demanding] that gives rights [and directed duties] their special moral significance. Having rights enables us [. . .] to look others in the eye, and to feel in some fundamental way the equal of anyone.[27]

I endorse this view, with the qualification that *either* demanding *on one's own behalf* or having someone else demand *on one's behalf* is sufficient to capture (at least part of) the significant status brought by being owed a duty.[28]

Note that the thesis above has to include a *ceteris paribus* clause. I am not permitted to demand fulfilment of a duty owed to me if so doing would cause the heavens to fall, or indeed if it would have some more trivial but significant demerit. Furthermore, note that there is no pretension to reductive analysis of directedness in the presentation above: *demanding a duty's fulfilment on my own behalf* just is *demanding fulfilment of a duty that is owed to me*, and I am not here suggesting that the 'on my own behalf' notion can be grasped separately from our grasp of directedness. The circularity of the analysis is made further evident by the fact that even in a world in which all duties were undirected (such as Feinberg's 'Nowheres-ville'), citizens could hold the standing to demand fulfilment of duties: they would simply be unable to issue such demands either *on their own behalf as parties to whom the duties were owed* or *on behalf of someone else to whom the duties were owed*.[29] It is the latter types of demanding that are the (circular) truth in the Will and Demand theories.

There is something interesting to glean from this circularity. Demandability is not special to directed duties, but it *is*, I suggest, distinctive of *duties* as opposed to other kinds of reasons. I develop this further in Chapter 7 but the broad idea is that duties are one kind of reason: a reason that is categorical (binding on its bearer whatever

---

[26] Note that even babies or animals are owed duties whose fulfilment suitably placed others can demand on their behalf; for this to be the case, the babies or animals do not have to have engaged in prior delegation of this power to demand—unlike with the power to forgive.

[27] Feinberg 1970, p. 151.

[28] For a similar conception, see Darwall 2006, pp. 18–20. Note that the thesis to which this footnote is attached is compatible with Darwall's claim that *undirected* duties can also be demanded by anyone exercising 'representative authority' *on behalf of the moral community* (Darwall 2012). I neither endorse nor reject this latter claim linking undirected duties to the moral community (though I do think all duties are *ceteris paribus* demandable); I stick to the narrower claim that *directed* duties must, *ceteris paribus*, be demandable *on behalf of those to whom they are owed*. Note also that many apparently 'undemandable' directed duties—e.g. duties of gratitude, or duties to express love within one's loving relationship—are permissibly demandable by third parties on behalf of the person to whom they are owed, even if they are not permissibly or coherently demandable by that person on her own behalf.

[29] For a hint at this point, see May 2012, pp. 120–1.

their particular wishes), of significant (perhaps exclusionary) weight, failure to act on which *ceteris paribus* triggers duties of apology and rectification, and which is *ceteris paribus* demandable from the duty-bearer. Furthermore, I suggest that it is *because* the kind of reason which is a duty applies to its bearer categorically (irrespective of her wishes), and *because* its violation would trigger further duties for her, that it is *ceteris paribus* something that suitably placed others have standing to demand of her. There is much more to say about this which I explore in Section 7.2 (on the link between a reason's categoricality and its demandability) and Chapter 10 (on different parties' differential standing to demand that duties be fulfilled), as well as later in the current section (on the link between demanding and the triggering of rectificatory duties and permission to resent). For present purposes, my claim is simply that someone's having defeasible standing to demand respect for a reason is a mark of that reason's constituting a duty for its bearer.

If duties are demandable, it should be no surprise that directed duties are demandable on behalf of those to whom they are owed—either by the party to whom they are owed or by some other. But what is it to make a demand, whether on one's own behalf or on another's? To demand that someone do something need not create any new reasons for that person to do it: when, as the party owed a duty, I demand that you feed me or refrain from assaulting me, I ask you to do what you already have a duty to do. Some might claim that when I demand that you feed me or refrain from assaulting me, I add a new reason alongside your prior duty-constituted reason to feed or refrain from assaulting me. But this new reason cannot add to your overall balance of reasons: it is not that, when wondering who to feed or not to assault (among those to whom you owe such duties), you should give priority first to those who have demanded this. The purported 'new reason' created by my demand therefore seems normatively inert. On this basis, I reject the view that demanding PHI involves exercising a Hohfeldian power to create a new reason to PHI.

But nor is demanding's role purely epistemic: there is a difference between my reminding you of your duty to feed or refrain from assaulting me and my demanding that you do so. What is this extra that characterizes demanding, if it is not the exercise of a Hohfeldian power? In recent work, Skorupski and May develop complementary accounts which make demanding more than simply asserting the existence of a duty, but deny that it involves creating a new reason for the party subject to the demand. Suppose A has a duty (which might be directed or undirected) to do PHI. Skorupski argues that when someone B demands PHI of A, B is requesting that A do PHI, and furthermore, B is permitted to use force to enforce her request if A does not comply.[30] Similarly, May argues that B's demanding PHI of A communicates to A that were she to violate her duty (by not doing PHI), then B (or perhaps someone else) would be released from some standing duty not to harm A.[31] In other words, for both theorists demanding communicates to the demandee that she will become liable to something undesirable (enforcement, for Skorupski; harm, for May) if she violates her duty. For example, May writes 'Doris has the standing to demand of Boris that he desist in his attack because she becomes free to

---

[30] Skorupski 2010, pp. 310–11.   [31] May ms.

shoot him if he does not.'[32] On both accounts, a demand is rather like a threat, but with a normative ('I am *permitted* to harm you or use force on you if you do this') rather than a committing-intentional ('I *will* harm you or use force on you if you do this') aspect.

I am broadly sympathetic to this account, with two caveats. First, we must interpret the harm to which the demandee is liable in a broad manner. If I telephone someone to demand that she come to pick me up as promised, it is not clear that I thereby communicate that unless she comes to pick me up, I or others will be released from certain standing duties protecting my addressee *from harm or enforcement taken in the sense of events that could have a significant negative impact on her well-being.*[33] Her failure to pick me up as promised might do no more than trigger quite trivial remedial duties, and permit no more than mild resentment on my part. Nonetheless, it seems to me that liability to some such 'negative' consequences is an essential part of what is communicated by any demand of the type we are considering. (And this should be no surprise, given that the demands in question demand fulfilment of duties, and duties' violation always *ceteris paribus* has some such 'negative' consequences for the violator.)

The second caveat is that simply communicating the existence of liabilities of this kind is not in itself sufficient for demanding. We can imagine drawing someone's attention to the fact that their failure to fulfil a duty would trigger liability to Skorupski-style enforcement or May-style harm without such attention-drawing constituting a demand. I think it is quite hard to imagine a case where someone says 'I am permitted to use force on you if you do not do this' without this statement constituting a demand. But such cases are possible—for example in educating children about the nature of rules, or in legal textbooks issued by an authority. What this shows is that there is something extra that distinguishes demanding PHI of someone from informing them of the Skorupski-/May-type liabilities that will be triggered by their not PHI-ing (and, recall, we have seen that this 'extra' is not the exercise of a Hohfeldian power to create a new duty to PHI).

In my view, we get close to understanding what this 'extra' is when we observe that demanding has a distinctive illocutionary force: in the jargon, it has 'world-to-word direction of fit', like commanding.[34] But unlike commanding, demanding is not an act that creates a new duty. Instead, demanding is a speech act with 'world-to-word fit' that articulates some pre-existing duty. When I demand something of someone, I *call on them* to do what they have a duty to do, rather than simply *informing* them of this or of the consequences of their not doing it. Now, I recognize that what exactly this notion of 'illocutionary force' means in this context is unclear. But I contend that May-/Skorupski-type liabilities to permitted resentment, and to the triggering of remedial duties, are *necessary* if a demand is to possess the threat-like illocutionary flavour that constitutes it as a demand. It is just that such liabilities are not sufficient: something distinctly 'world-to-word' in the force of the speech act must also be present.

---

[32] Ibid.   [33] This discussion and the example were generated by comments from Laura Valentini.
[34] See, e.g. Green 2015, section 3.1. I am grateful to Laura Valentini for suggesting this speech-act-type approach to the distinctiveness of demanding.

I cannot pretend to have offered a full account of demanding, but this partial account will be useful in what comes. The account applies both to demanding on one's own behalf and on another's behalf. When one demands fulfilment of a duty on one's own behalf and one's demand goes unmet, any remedial duties owed by the addressee will be owed to one (and any May-/Skorupski-style negative consequences that one is then permitted to inflict will also be made on one's own behalf). By contrast, demands made on behalf of another trigger remedial duties owed to the other (and any May/Skorupski inflictions or enforcements etc. made on the other's behalf). In neither case are the remedial duties created by the demand; they would apply equally to violated duties whose fulfilment nobody demanded. But their presence—as costs triggered if the demand goes unheeded—is necessary to confer the appropriate illocutionary force on the action in question, making it a demand.

In this chapter, I defended the view that at the heart of the Will and Demand theories is the insight that if one is owed a duty, then someone (perhaps oneself, or perhaps another) can, other things being equal, demand its fulfilment on one's behalf. But we saw that this is little help for someone who does not yet know to whom a duty is owed: to identify a person who can demand its fulfilment need not be to identify the person to whom the duty is owed. To identify this person, we need to know whether the demander can demand the duty's fulfilment *on her own behalf as the person owed the duty*, or *on behalf of some other to whom the duty is owed*. To draw this distinction, the Will and Demand theories cannot help us. We need a further account of what it is to be owed a duty—and Chapter 2 tells us that extant versions of the Interest Theory fail as biconditional accounts that could help. I turn to an alternative in the next chapter.

4

Rights' Relation to the First and Second Person

4.1 Overview of the Addressive Theory

Chapter 3 told us that a duty that is owed to someone is, other things being equal, demandable on that person's behalf. But how do we distinguish on whose behalf a demand to fulfil a duty can be made? We saw that neither Will nor Demand theories can answer this without circularity. The Interest and Desire theories of Chapter 2 tell us that a person to whom a duty is owed—and hence on whose behalf a demand can be made—is a person whose interests ground the duty (Raz), or who is placed by fulfilment of the duty in a position that necessarily serves her role- or kind-based desires (Wenar), or that would necessarily be in the interests of a typical person so placed (Kramer). But I argued that many morally justified legal or conventional duties can be owed to people whose interests do not ground them (Section 2.2), and that sometimes such a duty can necessarily serve (direction-independent) role-/kind-desires or place someone in a typically beneficial situation without being owed to that person (Section 2.5).

In the current chapter, I develop a new theory of what it is to owe someone a duty, a theory that complements the accounts examined so far. Recall that my overall aim in this book is to assess our use of the language of rights. To do this, we need to know what rights are. Directed duties lie at their heart (see Section 1.2 and Chapter 6), yet we have seen that extant theories of duties' direction fail as non-circular analyses of the concept. The new theory I develop here is not viciously circular, though it draws on concepts within the reason/direction family in a non-reductive way, and I investigate this in Sections 4.3–4.4. The new theory has payoffs beyond its success simply as an account of directed duties. In Chapters 5 and 7, we will see that if directed duties are constituted as outlined in my new theory, then duties that are *naturally* directed (and hence potentially *natural rights*) must be morally justifiable by the good of those to whom they are owed, along the lines of Raz's Interest Theory in its radical version.[1] This has major implications—explored in Part II—for our conception of human rights as natural rights. We will also see that my new theory of duties' direction implies that the only conceptual limit to the *legal or conventional* rights we can create is that right-holders must be conceivable second-personally. Thus the right-holder's good is not a necessary 'tether' on the rights we

---

[1] See Section 2.2.

can create—see the discussion in Section 2.5. This again has important implications for legal-conventional rights' moral justification, explored in Part III.

The new theory—which I call an 'Addressive Theory'—comes from a perhaps unexpected direction. It focuses on how both the duty-bearer and the party to whom the duty is owed should (truthfully) conceive the action (or inaction) which the duty enjoins: e.g. the action of not killing someone, or of paying money to them, or of marking their essay etc. There are two parts to my analysis. The first part says (i) that it is distinctive of a duty owed to a *capable party* (i.e. an adult, young person, corporation as opposed to, e.g. a baby or a rabbit) that that party is required to conceive the action the duty enjoins in first-personal terms as to be 'done to me'. Thus for example, it is distinctive of the fact that A's duty not to assault B is owed to B that B is required to think, in first-personal terms, of what is to be done as 'not assaulting me'; if she thinks of the duty as demanding merely that A 'not assault B', and fails to conceive B (i.e. herself) in first-personal terms as to be 'not assaulted by A', then she has failed to fulfil a requirement distinctive of the duty's being directed. I realize many concerns and counterexamples will immediately strike the reader. Before I address these, I note the second part of my analysis, which says (ii) that it is distinctive of a duty owed to *any party whatsoever* (including 'incapable' beings such as babies or rabbits) that the duty-bearer is required to conceive the action the duty enjoins in second-personal terms as to be 'done to an addressable party, a being conceivable as "you"'. Thus, to use the same example, it is distinctive of the fact that A's duty not to assault B is owed to B that A is required to think, in second-personal terms, of what is to be done as 'not assaulting a party whom I could address as "you"'.[2]

Both parts of this analysis will immediately seem mistaken if read as saying that duties only *exist*, are *fulfilled* or are *directed* if the duty-enjoined action is conceived in the relevant first- or second-personal way. For I can of course owe someone a duty and fulfil it without either of us realizing this or conceiving each other in any particular way: e.g. perhaps I never assault you but both of us fail to realize this, because we fail to recognize each other as persons; the duty still exists, is fulfilled, and is owed to you in this scenario. But I do not claim that the requirements of first- and second-personal conception of the duty-enjoined action must be met if the duty is to exist, be fulfilled or be directed. Rather, the requirement of first-personal conception (no. (i)) needs to be fulfilled if Chapter 3's powers over the duty—demanding, waiving, resenting, enforcing, etc.—are to be exercised by a party *on her own behalf as the party to whom the duty is owed*. And I will argue that, as foreshadowed by Section 3.6, demanding a duty's fulfilment on one's own behalf is a paradigmatic (or, perhaps, a generic or canonical) action of any capable party to whom it is owed, and therefore fulfilling the requirement of first-personal conception (no. (i)) is paradigmatic (generic or canonical) for any such a capable party. Similarly, I will argue, fulfilling the requirement of second-personal conception (no. (ii)) is paradigmatic for any bearer of a directed duty. So the normativity of requirements (i) and (ii) is the normativity of the paradigmatic.

[2] Many thanks to Adrian Haddock for discussions from which these ideas emerged.

In addition, I will suggest (Sections 4.3 and 4.6) that it is also the normativity of moral virtue (or legal-conventional virtue, in the case of morally unjustified legal or conventional rights).[3] A fully virtuous bearer of a directed duty must conceive the duty-enjoined action as to be done to an addressee conceived second-personally, and a capable fully virtuous party to whom a duty is owed must conceive themselves as to be first-personally affected by the duty-enjoined action. These are requirements of virtue driven distinctively by the *directed form* of the duty. Now, a bearer of an undirected duty might for all sorts of reasons be required by virtue to conceive affected parties second-personally—perhaps this is the only way to save something valuable from a perverse evil demon, or perhaps, less bizarrely, a fully virtuous person should normally think of beings with moral status as potentially addressable 'yous' whether or not they are owed duties. But when a duty is *directed*, such a requirement (to conceive affected parties second-personally) also springs immediately from or, I would say, is constitutive of, that duty's direction. A duty's having a direction is constituted by the duty's form necessarily requiring satisfaction of no. (ii) if its bearer is to be virtuous. When a duty's form requires satisfaction of this condition for virtue, that is both necessary and sufficient for the duty to have a direction; when its form makes satisfaction of (i) required too, that is necessary and sufficient for the duty to be owed to a *capable* party—though we will see that neither claim is a reductive analysis. I recognize that there is much to clarify about this position, and that is the aim of this chapter, before examining its implications in relation to the Interest and Desire theories in the next one. (The relation to the Will Theory will already emerge in the present chapter.)

4.2 Exercising Powers on One's Own Behalf: The Importance of First-Personal Grasp

In the current section, I argue that first-personal conception of a duty-enjoined action is necessary for my exercising Chapter 3's powers *on my own behalf as a party to whom the relevant duty is owed*, rather than my doing so on behalf of another or on behalf of nobody. Let us start with the power to demand. In my view, a party cannot demand on her own behalf, as someone owed a duty to PHI, that this duty be fulfilled, unless she thinks in the first person *that the duty-bearer's PHI-ing is to be done, as she should put it, 'to me'*. Suppose you have a duty not to kill Rowan. Any demand I issue that you not kill Rowan can only be issued on my own behalf (as the person to whom the duty is owed) if I think in the first person that what the duty enjoins (namely, not killing) is to be done to me. If, perhaps due to the strange placement of mirrors or because of some psychological illness, I fail to grasp that I am Rowan, and if I think only that your duty is *not to kill Rowan*, then I will be unable to demand your fulfilment of this duty on my own behalf, as the person owed the duty. Any demand I issue will have the same status as that of a demand made by a third

---

[3] The idea of 'legal-conventional virtue' in parentheses is compatible with my earlier suggestion, in discussing Kramer's theory (Section 2.3) that one has no genuine interest served by being 'purely legally' or 'purely conventionally' virtuous. Only the virtues of *natural* or *morally justified legal-conventional* normativity are those in which we must have something like a status interest.

party on behalf of the person to whom the duty is owed; it is just that in this particular case I will bizarrely issue a third-party demand on behalf of a person who, unbeknownst to me, is me.[4]

There are three preliminary points to note. First, I depend on the premise that first-personal thought is a distinctive mode of thought irreducible to third-personal modes.[5] To put it roughly, in thinking in the first person the thinker identifies herself in an unmediated manner, whereas self-identification via a grasp of oneself initially in the third person (e.g. as 'Rowan', 'the person in the mirror', 'the author of that strange book on rights') requires some mediating step or inference linking the thinker's third-personal identification to their grasp of themselves in the first person ('oh, I am Rowan...', 'I am the person in the mirror...', etc.). It seems clear to me that first-personal understanding is irreducible to third-personal modes, and I will not defend this here.

Secondly, my thesis is not that demanding fulfilment on one's own behalf requires thinking in the first person of the duty as 'owed to me'. Instead, the thesis is that so demanding requires thinking of the duty-enjoined action as to be 'done to me'. I suspect that a party can sometimes manage to demand fulfilment of a duty on their own behalf (as the party to whom it is owed) without explicitly thinking that they are the party to whom it is owed—maybe because they have never encountered the idea of a directed duty; I am tempted to say that this is possible but I will not decide the issue here.[6] Instead, what I am committed to is that a party cannot issue a demand on their own behalf without conceiving the action they demand in the first person as to be 'done to me'. In my example above, I must conceive your not killing Rowan as your *not killing me* if I am to be able to demand this of you on my own behalf as the person owed the duty.[7]

Third, the first-personal thinking that I claim to be necessary for *demanding fulfilment of a duty on my own behalf* goes beyond the first-personal thinking required by any demanding, qua act of communication. Demanding, like any other

---

[4] The not-killing example, like the not-assaulting example earlier, reveals that the duty-enjoined PHI ranges over abstentions, inactions, and omissions, as well as actions. Even for these, the person to whom the duty is owed must grasp the PHI in the first person as to be 'done to me' (not killing me, refraining from attacking me, etc.) if this person is to demand on her own behalf that the duty be fulfilled. Note also that the PHI can include thoughts: duties to think of someone a certain way or hold an attitude towards them.

[5] Its relation to second-personal modes is explored in Section 4.5. The idea of the first person 'I' as an 'essential indexical' is Perry's (1979); see also Anscombe 1981b.

[6] Some directed duties seem demandable on one's own behalf as the party owed the duty only if one explicitly recognizes that one is owed the duty: perhaps promises and contractual duties. But other directed duties—such as the duty not to assault someone, and others that I would categorize as 'natural' or 'recognition-independent'—seem to me capable of being demanded by the party to whom they are owed on her own behalf without that party conceptualizing what she demands explicitly as a 'duty owed to me' (her demand might simply say 'stop!'); but nonetheless the party, in issuing this demand *on her own behalf*, must conceive *the action* (non-assault) in the first person as to be 'done to me'. Compare the discussion of the reach of 'intellectualism' about virtue, in Sections 4.3 and 4.6.

[7] Wenar says that a duty to PHI can only be owed to some party if PHI is conceiveable as 'done to' that party (see Wenar 2013, p. 209 (on his 'clause 1') and p. 211 (on prison warders not being owed prisoners' duties to stay in prison because this action is not 'done to' prison warders)). But Wenar does not specify, as I do, that the duty's recipient ought to conceive the PHI *in the first person* as, as she should put it, 'done to me'.

act of communication, requires that the demander conceive the communicative action first-personally. I will not be felicitously demanding anything of you if, while uttering the words 'Do such-and-such', I think only 'Rowan demands such-and-such' and not 'I demand such-and-such'.[8] But this is as true of demanding as a third party as it is of demanding on one's own behalf. Any act of communication that goes beyond unintended signalling requires the communicator to conceive her communicative act at least implicitly first-personally as, as she should put it, 'mine'.[9] By contrast, my thesis here is different. It is the much more specific claim that demanding some PHI on my own behalf (as the person to whom PHI-ing is owed) requires that I think of the PHI in the first person as to be *done to me*. This is in addition to the requirement that, because it is an act of communication, I must think (at least implicitly) of *the communicative action of demanding* in the first person as mine.

Why believe what I have claimed? That is, why think that to demand PHI on my own behalf, I must conceive PHI in the first person as to be *done to me*—as an action that involves me qua patient? I offer reasons in the argument developed across Sections 4.3–4.5. But in the current section, I simply offer examples. Suppose I try to demand that someone not kill me, or respect my order as their manager, while failing to conceive the demanded action first-personally as to be done to me: perhaps in this scenario I conceive my addressee as 'not killing Rowan' or 'respecting her manager's orders' without realizing that I am Rowan or the manager: I demand 'Do not kill Rowan!' or 'Respect your manager's orders!' but do not grasp that I am Rowan or the manager. I do not see how we could regard this demand as made by me *on my own behalf as the person to whom the duty is owed*.

Interestingly, the condition applies even to duties owed to a party which enjoin actions to which that party seems only remotely related. Suppose you promise me that you will walk the length of Hadrian's Wall, and I accept your promise absent-mindedly, having no special connection to your walking or to the Wall. You are now under a duty, owed to me, to walk the length of the Wall, but this action does not seem to be done 'to me'. Yet there is one important description under which your action is done to me: in walking, you *keep your promise to me*. Now, my claim is that unless I think in the first person that your duty-enjoined action is to be done to me, I cannot demand its fulfilment on my own behalf. Thus if, say, I demand that you fulfil your duty to walk the Wall but never think in the first person that in so doing you will keep a promise to me, my demand cannot be a demand issued on my own behalf as the party owed the duty. I need to find some way of conceiving a duty-enjoined PHI first-personally as to be *done to me* if my demand that someone PHI is to be made on my own behalf as owed PHI.

Of course, thinking in this way is not *sufficient* to make a duty owed to me, nor to make me capable of demanding it on my own behalf: that would allow parties to

---

[8] Similarly, for any demand to succeed as an act of communication, the addressee must conceive themselves first-personally as addressed, and second-personal thinking is also implicated.

[9] Of course there is much more to the distinction between communication and unintended signalling, but the first-personal condition is, I contend, one necessary aspect. For more, see, e.g. Grice 1957.

make themselves into recipients of duties through sheer psychological gumption—by getting themselves to think in the appropriate way.[10] Even *truthful* thinking in this way is not sufficient to make a duty owed to me, for an involved third party could think in this way without the duty being owed to her. Consider again Kramer's example from Section 2.2: a shopkeeper contemplating her customer's employer's duty to pay that customer's salary can truthfully think of the salary payment as 'providing some of *my* earnings by giving my customer disposable income which she spends in my shop'. The fact that the shopkeeper can truthfully think of the employer's dutiful action (the salary payment) in this way does not make the duty owed to the shopkeeper. And that is not my claim.

Rather, my claim is that thinking in this first-personal way (of the duty's action as 'done to me') is *necessary* if a party is to be able to demand a duty on her own behalf. We should note that its being possible *truthfully* to think of an action in this way (as 'done to me') is often a *consequence* of the duty's being owed to one, rather than obtaining independently. This is not always the case: I can truthfully think of your not assaulting me, or your educating me, as actions 'done to me' whether or not they are owed to me as a matter of directed duty. But—except in unusual versions[11]—the Hadrian's Wall case is an example in which I can only truthfully think of the duty-enjoined action (your walking the Wall) as 'done to me' if you owe this to me as your duty. Similarly, when someone obeys a manager's instruction to fold shirts, the manager can only truthfully think of the action (the shirt-folding) in the first person as 'done to me' *because* they issued the instruction; without having created the relevant duty with its direction, the manager would be unable truthfully to think of the action as done to her. But these points are compatible with—indeed complementary to—my claim that thinking in this first-personal way of oneself as the object of a duty-enjoined action is a necessary condition on demanding a duty's fulfilment on one's own behalf, as the party owed the duty. No such thinking is necessary (even if it is sometimes possible) when demanding fulfilment of an undirected duty or a duty owed to another.

Note that the same first-personal condition applies to the other powers listed in Section 3.1: again, it distinguishes exercise of these powers *as the party owed the duty* from exercise of these powers *as a third party*. Thus to waive a duty as the person to whom it is owed, it is necessary that I take what I am waiving to be a duty enjoining an action I conceive in the first person as to be done to me. By contrast, to annul the duty as a third party—for example, in my role as a regulator within the Competition and Markets Authority or CMA (to use Section 3.3's example)—I need not conceive the action the duty enjoins in the first person as an action to be done to me. If, as in Section 3.5's suggestion, we reserve the term 'waiver' for duty-annulment exercised on her own behalf by the person to whom a duty is owed, then the distinction between waiver and third-party regulatory annulment is captured by this first-personal necessary condition. The CMA's relation to businesses'

---

[10] Thanks to a referee for OUP for pressing me to clarify this.
[11] Suppose I was the governor of the Wall, or the builder of the Wall, or suppose you knew that walking the Wall would displease me.

contractual duties-to-merge is in an important sense akin to that of an uninvolved third party's relation to your promise, made to me, to walk Hadrian's Wall. Just as a third party in the latter case cannot truthfully see your Wall-walking as 'done to' that third party, so the CMA cannot truthfully conceive the businesses' merger duties to enjoin an action *done to the CMA*. It therefore cannot truthfully take the duties to enjoin action to be done first-personally to, as they might put it, 'us, the CMA'. So the CMA can only take its power over this duty to be third-party regulatory *annulment*, rather than waiver.

Now there might also be cases in which a party in the role of regulator *could* truthfully take a duty to enjoin action done first-personally to that party, yet where the duty would nonetheless not be waivable by that party, but only 'annullable', because the duty was not owed to them. We might think of parents' control of duties that their children owe to each other in this light: a parent can sometimes 'annul' a promissory duty undertaken by one child towards her sibling, and the child's action in such a case can perhaps truthfully be conceived as 'done to' the parent ('keeping promises [including those made to my sister] for dad'), without the duty in question being owed to the parent. I realize this is a debatable case, and one might similarly quibble about the CMA: perhaps there is *some* sense in which the businesses' merger duties really are 'done to' the CMA ('contributing to merger activity within the CMA's jurisdiction'?); in certain moods, I can get myself to think that almost any event can be truthfully conceived as done to almost anyone ('a clock's ticking in Australia alters *my* universe in a small way').

But the latter issue is beside the point. My claim is that in the regulatory 'annulment' cases, the regulator *need not* think of themselves as first-personally affected by the actions enjoined by the duties they regulate, even if they *can* think in this way. By contrast, to 'waive' a duty in the sense entailing that one is owed it, one *needs* to think in this first-personal way of oneself as affected by the duty-enjoined action. Thus I cannot *waive* someone's duty not to attack Rowan (e.g. by consenting to take part in a boxing match) without thinking in the first person that the relevant not-attacking was to be done to me. Such a requirement of first-personal conception of the duty-enjoined action as to be done *to me* must be met if the annulment is to count as a waiver performed by the person to whom the duty is owed. But such first-personal conception is not necessary for a regulatory annulment of this duty (suppose as king I decide, for public policy reasons, to annul your duty not to attack Rowan, while failing to notice that the duty required an (in)action to be done to me).

And the same goes for resentment. To resent a violation *as the victim*, I must conceive the violating action in the first person as done to me. If I claim to resent someone's action, and when pressed on what was done to me I reply 'oh, the action was done to Rowan and I do not know whether I am Rowan', or, less bizarrely, I reply 'oh, the action was done to so-and-so, not me', it is impossible to conceive my resentment as the personal resentment of someone to whom the duty was owed. It can only be conceived as the kind of third-personal response to wrongdoing that is better described as 'outrage'. I must think the action was done to me if I am to conceive myself as wronged and hence able to resent it. Otherwise I will be stuck with, at best, a third-party attitude to the wrongdoing.

By now it should be clear that I want to say the same thing about forgiveness. To forgive some duty-violating action on one's own behalf, as the party to whom the duty was owed, I must conceive the action in the first person as done to me. If I fail to achieve such first-personal grasp of my involvement in the action—if I think it was done to someone else, or I think it was done to Rowan but I fail to realize that I am Rowan—then, like a third party, I will be incapable of forgiving the violation personally on my own behalf. Such forgiving on one's own behalf will be impossible for me: it is an activity that requires thinking of oneself first-personally as having had an action done to one that was forbidden by duty.

Note that the point above is meant to apply as readily to 'artificial' and plural first-personal thinking as to the singular first-personal thinking of a natural person. For a corporation or a national people to demand a duty's fulfilment on their own behalf, or to forgive its violation, etc., the corporation or the people must conceive the relevant action in the first person as, as they should put it, done to 'us'. My own view is that the conditions on such plural and 'artificial' first-personal thinking are fairly easy to satisfy in principle, and can in appropriate cases be met by almost all corporate entities and social groupings that include members with a capability for first-personal thinking, including such groupings as cyclists, the working class, Microsoft, and even humanity; I return to this in Sections 4.5, 9.3, and 10.1.

There is an important misreading to avoid, one that I have already mentioned but that bears repeating. My thesis is not that *whenever* someone can truthfully think in the first person that a duty-enjoined action is to be done, as they should put it, to 'me' or 'us', then the duty is owed to the party in question and this party can then engage in demanding, waiving, resenting, etc. on their own behalf. This would be hugely over-inclusive: for instance, as noted earlier it would make an employer's duty to pay its employee's salary into a duty owed to the employee's local shopkeeper. The fact that the employer's fulfilling its duty could be truthfully conceived in the first person by the shopkeeper as an action done to her should not make such a duty owed to her, nor enable her to demand or waive fulfilment of this duty on her own behalf. Even though the duty-enjoined action is graspable by the shopkeeper in the first person as, as she should put it, done to 'me', she can still only engage in third-party demanding in relation to the duty.

What this tells us is that, as noted before, first-personal conception of a duty-enjoined action as to be 'done to me' is *necessary* but not *sufficient* for the conceiver to be able genuinely to demand, waive, resent, etc. in relation to the duty on her own behalf. To engage in these actions *as the party to whom the duty is owed*, the agent needs to conceive the duty-enjoined action first-personally as 'done to me'. Because—we shall see in Section 4.4—the ability so to engage is both paradigmatic of a capable party to whom a duty is owed, and is necessary for full virtue for such a party, the requirement to conceive the duty-enjoined action as 'done to me' is distinctive to a duty's direction. In Sections 4.4–4.5, I develop this as a necessary and sufficient condition on directedness. Beforehand, the next section (4.3) changes tack, introducing a different condition that, together with the point from the current section (4.2), will be useful in establishing the full analysis of Sections 4.4–4.5.

4.3 Duties as Formally Requiring First-Personal Thinking by their Bearers

This section sets aside *directed* duties for a moment, to focus instead on reasons and duties in general. I suggested in Section 3.6 that *any* duty (directed or undirected) is a form of reason: a categorical, remainder-triggering, demandable reason.[12] My purpose in this section is to strengthen the case for Section 4.1's addressive analysis of directed duties by showing that any reason requires that the agent for whom it is a reason think in the first person that the action enjoined by that reason is to be 'done by me' (as that agent should put it). This formal requirement need not be satisfied for the reason to *exist*, nor for it to be *fulfilled*. For example, I can have a reason not to destroy a forest, and I can do what this reason asks (i.e. not destroy the forest), whether or not I think in the first person that what the reason asks is that *I* not destroy the forest; I might just get on with my life without ever thinking about it. Nonetheless, the *obtaining* of the requirement of first-personal conception—the fact that the reason-enjoined action *ought* to be conceived in this first-personal way by the party for whom it is a reason—is part of what it is for the entity in question to be a reason. I shall offer two bases for this claim: first, that the paradigmatic reason is so conceived, and secondly, that the virtuous agent with a reason to act satisfies this requirement. Then, from this premise combined with the discussion of demanding, waiving, resenting, and so on in Section 4.2, I shall infer (in Section 4.4) that *duties owed to someone* carry an *additional* formal requirement of first-personal thinking: the action they enjoin must be conceived in the first person both by the agent (duty-bearer) and by a formally passive party on whom the action is performed (the right-holder), if the latter party is capable of the requisite thought. I shall then in Section 4.5 develop this in a second-personal direction to yield a fuller account of being owed a duty, one that accommodates duties owed to 'incapable' parties.

First, though, I introduce and explain my premise about reasons and duties in general: a reason or duty enjoins an action that ought to be conceived in the first person (as 'mine' or 'ours', to be done by 'me' or 'us') by the bearer of the reason or duty. Someone who has a reason to PHI and who performs PHI, and who fully comprehends their reason to PHI in the third person ('There is a reason for Rowan to PHI'), but who fails to think in the first person that, as they should put it, 'There is a reason for *me* to PHI', has failed to fulfil a condition whose obtaining is constitutive of the reason's being a reason. This person has failed to conceive their action *as it is meant to be conceived, qua enjoined by this person's reason*. The same is true of duties because duties are one form of reason.[13]

Of course, people frequently fail first-personally to grasp their place in the world in certain respects. I might have third-personal knowledge of my height ('Rowan is 1.85m tall') but fail to realize that I am the person of whom I have such knowledge. In this case, my failure to grasp the relevant fact in the first person means that, in a sense, I am missing a piece of knowledge about how the world is: I fail to realize that I,

---

[12] See also Section 7.2.   [13] See Sections 3.6 and 7.2.

the knower, am 1.85m tall.[14] But this is no failure to grasp *my height as it is meant to be grasped*, in the way that—so I claimed in the previous paragraph—failure to think in the first person that an action for which I have reason is 'my' action is indeed failure to grasp the reason as it is meant to be grasped.

But this will no doubt seem controversial. I claim that someone with a reason to PHI is thereby meant to think of PHI-ing in the first person as, as she should put it, 'my' action, to be done by 'me'. Failure to think in this way constitutes not merely the person's failure to grasp her place in the world (as in the height case), but her failure to fulfil a condition constitutive of her reason-to-PHI's form as a reason. The person has not conceived her reason in the way it was meant to be conceived qua reason by its bearer (namely, as a reason for *me* to PHI). The person might well still *fulfil* the reason, doing the PHI it asks for; and the reason might well still *exist* although misconceived by its bearer. But she has failed a formal condition constitutive of her reason's being a reason. What do I mean by this idea of 'conceiving PHI as it is meant to be conceived, qua action enjoined by reason'? Surely I cannot mean that a reason-to-PHI *wants* PHI to be conceived in the first person by its bearer? Surely I cannot mean that the person who has a reason to PHI, and who performs PHI, but who fails to conceive PHI in the first person thereby makes her reason in some sense *a failure as a reason*? Reasons (including duties) do not have wants, and if we can make any sense of their succeeding or failing this must be solely in terms of whether the PHI they enjoin is performed or not.

I offer two explanations of what I mean. First, I claim that the *paradigm* (or generic or canonical)[15] reason or duty to PHI involves its bearer conceiving PHI in the first person as 'my action'. This paradigm is built into our very concept of reasons (and hence of duties): it is, I propose, entailed by reasons' and duties' logical form as having bearers ('so-and-so's reason', 'her duty'), as opposed to values or goods which lack bearers in this sense.[16]

The bearer of a reason or duty to PHI is whoever, *in the paradigm case*, that reason or duty moves to PHI in the right way—where such motivation by reason or duty in the right way involves, *in the paradigm case*, conceiving PHI in the first person as 'my' action enjoined by reason or duty. If I have a reason to PHI, and even if I am somehow motivated to PHI because I think that 'there is a reason for Rowan to PHI', but I fail to think first-personally that what there is a reason to do is for *me* to PHI, then I fail to be motivated in the manner paradigmatic to a reason to PHI. The case will be non-paradigmatic. The paradigmatic case requires that I take the reason to PHI in the first person as enjoining an action for me. We can define the *bearer* of a reason (including a duty) as the party who must, if the case is to involve a reason in its paradigmatic guise as a reason, conceive the reason-enjoined action in the first person.

[14] Compare Perry's (1979) sugar-dropper.
[15] I recognize that there are differences between being paradigmatic, generic, and canonical, but I set these aside here.
[16] There are, I venture, no 'bearer-less' *reasons* or *duties*, reasons or duties that take the form of Broome's 'unowned oughts' like 'life ought not be so unfair' (Broome 2013, p. 18). By contrast, the *value* or *goodness* of something need not be 'owned' like this.

A second explanation is more controversial. This is to claim that in the case of morally justified reasons and duties (as opposed to, e.g. unjustified legal duties) the agent who is *morally virtuous* must conceive the reason-enjoined action in the first person as, as she should put it, *my* action.[17] This claim adds a first-personal twist to a position called 'intellectualism':

INTELLECTUALISM: It is characteristic of the fully morally virtuous person that she explicitly grasps why her action is right and she can always explain the reasons why it is right.[18]

This position has come in for attack. It entails that agents with a strong intuitive or inexplicit grasp of their moral reasons, but who misconceive them or cannot articulate them, cannot be fully morally virtuous. In the literature, discussion has focused on an example taken from a morally controversial, problematic text: the example of Huckleberry Finn when he does not turn in Jim despite thinking that he is morally required to. Huckleberry is in the grip of the norms of a society that legalizes slavery, yet Arpaly claims that Huckleberry also grasps, intuitively but inexplicitly, that 'Jim is a full-fledged human being', and acts on the latter basis against his socially-generated judgement about what morality requires of him. Arpaly argues that he therefore does the right act for the right reasons despite misconceiving his reasons (and his act) as immoral.[19] My own view is that intellectualism is correct, and hence that Huckleberry does indeed fall short of full moral virtue, even though in some sense he does the right thing for the right reasons. Baldwin denies that Finn should be conceived as in a 'moral predicament': I take from Baldwin's thought that there should be no question of turning Jim in, and that Huckleberry's failure consciously to realize this marks a shortfall in his virtue—as well as in the racialized structure of his society.[20] I am persuaded by Hills's argument that full moral virtue requires a 'full responsiveness to moral reasons that goes beyond the sensitivity required to do the right action for the right reasons, and includes the ability to respond consciously, with awareness'.[21] Hills highlights the centrality, to moral virtue, of articulating reasons, giving advice, justifying and explaining oneself—activities that require the intellectualist's grasp of reasons by their bearers.[22]

Now, observe that if intellectualism is correct, the kind of conception that the fully morally virtuous person must have of the reasons (including duties) that make her action right cannot be simply third-personal. To use the definition of intellectualism given earlier, even if I 'explicitly grasp[...] why [Rowan's] action is right and [I] can always explain the reasons why it is right', I will surely fall short of full moral virtue if

---

[17] And in the case of morally unjustified reasons and duties, the agent who is 'virtuous' in a system-relative sense (legally, conventionally virtuous) must grasp the reason-enjoined action in the same way.

[18] Hills 2015, p. 14.

[19] See Arpaly's discussion in her 2003; the quotation about Huckleberry's conception of Jim as 'full-fledged' is from p. 10. See the original discussion in Bennett 1974. For a range of moral concerns about and assessments of Mark Twain's *Huckleberry Finn*, see Leonard, Tenney and Davis 1991, and Mensh and Mensh 2000.

[20] Baldwin 1979.   [21] Hills 2015, p. 34

[22] Ibid., p. 33. This defence of intellectualism is compatible with the plausible view that Huckleberry-style intuitive-emotional ('non-intellectual') grasp of what is to be done is *also* necessary for full virtue, *alongside* the requisite intellectual grasp.

I fail to take the relevant reasons as enjoining *my* action, but see them simply as enjoining *Rowan*'s action—without realizing that I am Rowan. Even if I perform the required actions, and do them on the basis of a full understanding of the reasons Rowan has to do these actions, nonetheless if I somehow fail to see the reason-enjoined actions as mine (perhaps because I fail to realize I am Rowan: I perform the actions because I want to do what Rowan ought to do even though I do not realize I am Rowan), I must fall short of full virtue.

Further, the activities whose importance Hills uses to motivate intellectualism—advising, justifying, explaining—require that the relevant reason-bearers identify the reason-enjoined actions first-personally: advising you that you have reason to PHI fails if you do not conceive this PHI first-personally; justifying one's own PHI-ing by appeal to one's reason to do so fails if one did not grasp this first-personally, and so on. Intellectualists should therefore conclude that a fully morally virtuous person must take whatever PHI is required by their reasons or duties in the first person as 'my' PHI, to be done by 'me'.[23]

As noted, intellectualism is subject to debate. It seems correct to me, but I do not want to have to rely on it. I propose, instead, to distinguish two conceptions of the normativity of the requirement that reason- and duty-bearers conceive their reason-enjoined action in the first person: satisfying the requirement is, if intellectualism is true, necessary for *full virtue* but even if intellectualism is false it is also necessary if the relevant reason or duty is to be a *paradigm* of its form (i.e. a paradigmatic reason or duty).

I pause to bring out the non-reductive but non-circular nature of these claims as accounts of part of what it is for something to be a reason (or duty). Consider first the version involving the idea of a paradigm: I say that a party has a reason to PHI if and only if it is paradigmatic for that party to conceive PHI in the first person as 'to be done by me'. But it might be paradigmatic to megalomania that the megalomaniac grasp *every* potential PHI, including those that others might perform, in the first person as 'to be done by me' (as she would put it). Further, I might have a reason to do some rather specific PHI—e.g. telephone my neighbour's milk-delivery service—without it being paradigmatic to university lecturers, and hence without it being paradigmatic to *me as a university lecturer*, to conceive such telephoning in the first person as 'to be done by me'. Now, the idea of a 'paradigm' on the right-hand side of the biconditional should not be read in these ways: it should not be indexed to irrelevant concepts like megalomania or university lecturing. Rather, we should read the biconditional's right-hand side as true only when a party's first-personal conception of PHI as 'to be done by me' is paradigmatic to that party *as a reasoner or agent*, and is paradigmatic to them *because of the form of the normative entity enjoining PHI*, that is, *because of the type of normative entity that it is*, i.e. a reason rather than a value. The 'because' here is not causal but constitutive: part of what it is for a

---

[23] For morally unjustified reasons and duties (e.g. in law or convention), a parallel thesis would specify the relevant conception as necessary for full *legal or conventional* virtue. Compare Babb 2016 on the essential indexicality of intentions. My claim is that reasons for action—reasons to form intentions on the basis of such reasons—are similarly ineliminably indexical, and to grasp one's reason in the way 'intellectualists' require for full virtue (moral or legal-conventional) is to grasp it in this indexical way.

normative entity to be a reason is for that entity's form to make first-personal conception of PHI as 'to be done by me' paradigmatic for some reasoning party. This idea of normative entities coming in different forms or types that are differentiated by *how and from whom the entity demands first- or third-personal apprehension of potential actions* is central in what follows, including when we turn to distinguishing directed from undirected duties.[24] An analysis of the idea of a reason in terms of what its form makes paradigmatic for a reasoner—like the biconditional above—is non-reductive in that it fails to offer an account of the concept in external, reason-independent terms. But it is also not viciously circular: the precise idea of 'a reason' does not feature in my proposed reading of the right-hand side.

A similar non-reductive non-circularity is evident in the 'virtue' version of my claim. We can express this version of the claim with another biconditional, this time stating that a party has a reason to PHI if and only if for that party to be fully virtuous, she must conceive PHI in the first person as 'to be done by me'. Again, one might think that in certain special (non-paradigmatic) cases, a party might have a reason to do something that she can best achieve in an unreflective manner, without thinking anything about what is to be done: an example is Railton's tennis player who has reason to win and best achieves this by 'play[ing] tennis more for its own sake [rather than in order to win]'.[25] Conversely, it might seem possible for virtue to require first-personal conception of some PHI as 'to be done by me' without my having a reason to PHI: suppose an evil demon has threatened to destroy the world unless I conceive some trivial action (e.g. grinding my teeth) in the first person as 'to be done by me'. A response similar to that offered in relation to the 'paradigm'-focused biconditional can work here too. The response says that there are various sources of the demands of virtue, and that we should read the 'virtue' biconditional's right-hand side as true only when a party's conception of PHI in the first person as 'to be done by me' is required, for that party to be virtuous, by the *form* of the normative entity enjoining PHI. That is, we should read the right-hand side as true *when it is because of the form of the normative entity enjoining PHI* that the relevant first-personal conception of PHI-ing is virtuous for its grasper. The case for such form-driven virtue can be outweighed if the relevant thinking would be distracting (as in the tennis example), and there can be alternative, consequence-driven cases for the relevant conception (as in the demon example). On this approach, the biconditional is read as saying that a party has a reason to PHI if and only if a normative entity's form or nature makes it the case that virtue requires that party to conceive PHI in the first person as 'to be done by me'. Again, I am tempted to see the 'case-making' here as constitutive rather than causal: part of *what it is* for something to be a reason rather than a value is that it requires some party, for full virtue, to engage in a first-personal conception of some potential action as 'to be done by me'. If this is correct, then my earlier claims that intellectualism supports this first-personal-grasp requirement should not be taken as purely instrumental: it is not merely that a virtuous person should possess the first-personal conception outlined because this is a

---

[24] By referring to 'normative entities', I do not here intend to beg metaethical questions. I hope these entities could be equally taken in 'realist', 'subjectivist', 'quasi-real', or alternative metaphysical ways.
[25] Railton 1984, p. 144.

necessary or useful means for successful advice-giving, justifying, explaining, and so on. In addition, such a conception is simply part of what constitutes virtuous reason-possession (and virtuous reason-possession is a part of virtuous advice-giving or advice-receiving, of justifying, explaining, and so on).

In my view, the account just sketched does not explain what a reason is in terms external to the realm of reasons, but nor is it viciously circular. I do not claim these biconditionals as full analyses of the concept of a reason: they show us *part* of what it is for something to be a reason, but the truth of these biconditionals (suitably read) must hold alongside further biconditionals illuminating other aspects of the reason concept—such as the aspect theorists try to capture when they say a reason is a *consideration in favour* of an action. I have not touched directly on this aspect in my points above.

Let me summarize the points defended in this section. I have argued that when there is a reason to PHI, a formal condition on this being a reason is that someone (the party whose reason it is) should think in the first person that the PHI enjoined by reason is, as they should put it, 'my' (or 'our') action to be done. To put this another way, a normative entity with the form of a *reason* to PHI (as opposed, e.g. to PHI's being *valuable*) obtains if and only if some party is required to conceive PHI-ing in the first person as 'to be done by me' (or 'us'). We saw in the last paragraph that this is only one of various aspects to something's being a reason. Nonetheless, we should note that because duties are one type of reason, the condition sketched is also a formal condition on some party's being duty-bound to PHI: namely, that the party in question should think in the first person that the duty-enjoined PHI is, as they should put it, 'to be done by me' (or 'us').[26] As I have stressed several times, these requirements can go unmet even though the relevant reason or duty *exists* and is *fulfilled*: for example, I can fulfil my duty not to kill you without ever conceiving my not-killing in the first person as 'my' action to be done. But the requirements still *obtain*, generated by the reason's form as a reason (or duty's form as a duty). Satisfying the requirements is *paradigmatic* to reasons and duties, as having bearers; intellectualists should add that satisfying these requirements is also necessary for full practical virtue.

4.4 Directed Duties and the First Person

The previous section argued that *any duty* (whether directed or undirected) is such that if the duty-bearer is to fulfil a condition definitive of it as a duty, then she must think in the first person that the action it enjoins is, as she should put it, 'to be *done by me*'. This condition does not have to be *fulfilled* for a duty to exist, but it *obtains* in virtue of the duty's form as a kind of reason. Now I add that if a duty is *owed to* some

---

[26] An interesting question asks whether the requirement of first-personal thinking is itself a reason/duty. If so, every reason would seem to generate a regress of further reasons (to think in the first person of the action enjoined by the reason at the 'lower level'). The intellectualist position seems more suited to this reading (for don't I have a reason to be fully virtuous, and hence a reason to fulfil whatever conditions are necessary for full virtue?) than the 'paradigm' one (do I have any reason to be, or for my reason itself to be, paradigmatic in the relevant sense?).

capable party (e.g. an adult human rather than a rabbit), then that party to whom it is owed must, if they are to fulfil a condition constitutive of the duty's form as directed, think in the first person that the duty-enjoined action is, as they should put it, 'to be *done to me*'—where this involves conceiving oneself as a formally passive party affected by or involved in the duty-bearer's action.[27] We can represent these claims schematically thus:

> (from Section 4.3):   A's duty to PHI formally requires first-personal conception of PHI by A as to be 'done by me'.

> (from Section 4.4):   A's directed duty to PHI owed to B formally requires both first-personal conception of PHI by A as to be 'done by me' and, if B is a capable party, first-personal conception of PHI by B as to be 'done to me'.

The normativity of both formal requirements is—as sketched in Section 4.3—the normativity of the paradigmatic, and also of virtue. That is, I claim first that for a directed duty to be a paradigm (or generic, canonical) instantiation of its directed form, any capable party to whom it is owed must think in the first person that the action it enjoins is to be done, as she should put it, 'to me'. We can support this with the Feinbergian thought, bolstered by the ideas outlined in Section 3.6, that *demanding fulfilment of a duty on one's own behalf* is the paradigmatic action of someone capable to whom a duty is owed. If this is correct, then it should be no surprise that the paradigmatic capable party owed a duty must conceive the duty-enjoined action first-personally as to be 'done to me'. For Section 4.2 showed us that *demanding on one's own behalf* requires conceiving the action in this first-personal way. Of course this is not to say that capable parties cannot be owed duties unless they demand their fulfilment on their own behalf, and hence cannot be owed duties unless they take the duty-enjoined action as first-personally affecting them. It is just to say that such cases will be non-paradigmatic. The paradigm case of a duty owed to a capable party involves this duty's being demandable by that party on her own behalf, and this involves satisfying the first-personal condition outlined (as 'from Section 4.4') above.

But, as in Section 4.3, we should go beyond this and claim also that a capable party to whom a duty is owed, who fails to think in the first person that the duty-enjoined action is, as she should put it, 'to be done to me', falls short of full practical virtue. In what way does such a party fall short? It is not that a fully virtuous capable party to whom a duty is owed must always demand that duty's fulfilment on their own behalf, or resent its violation, etc. But they must be *able* to engage in such actions, and they must be *ready* to engage in such actions in appropriate circumstances. Otherwise they will be unable to stick up for themselves when this is appropriate. A party who could not demand, on their own behalf, fulfilment of duties owed to them, or who could not personally resent being wronged, or could not attempt to offer personal forgiveness, cannot be fully virtuous: they would lack the important Feinbergian

---

[27] Note that the passivity is purely formal. One can be involved in or affected by a duty-bearer's action while being active, for example as a demander or waiver. Note also that the idea of 'done to' invoked here should be taken broadly—as in my Hadrian's Wall example in Section 4.2. It is sufficient that the party owed the duty can find *some* truthful way of conceiving themselves first-personally as affected by, as the grammatical object of, as acted on by (etc.) the duty-bearer's action.

ability to press or waive claims on their own behalf when appropriate, and to engage in Strawson–Darwall-type personal reactive attitudes.[28] That is, given what was established in Section 4.2, someone to whom a duty is owed who does not think in the first person that the relevant action is 'done to me' will be unable to be fully virtuous.[29] This is not simply the 'theoretical' failing of the person who fails to grasp her own height in the first person.[30] Those who dispute this reading can take instead the 'paradigm' conception of my condition's normativity.[31]

What does the requirement of first-personal conception of a duty as to be 'done to me' imply about cases in which a duty-enjoined action is done to a party but not owed to her? As noted at the end of Section 4.2, a shopkeeper contemplating a local employer's duty to pay its employees' salaries can truthfully conceive the duty-enjoined action in the first person as, as she should put it, 'done to me', without her being owed the duty. My account will not erroneously make the duty here owed to the shopkeeper. But what distinguishes the shopkeeper from the employees? The answer is, first, that for the duty to be a *paradigm* of its directed form, the shopkeeper is not required to think in the first person that the employer's action is to be done, as she would put it, to 'me'—even though she would be accurate if she thought this. The employees, by contrast, are required to think in the first person that the salary-paying action is to be done, as each should put it, to 'me', if the duty is to be *paradigmatic* of its directed form, and if the employees are to be *paradigm* capable parties to whom it is owed. Secondly, if the shopkeeper fails to think in the first person that the employer's action is to be 'done to me' (as she would put it), this need mean no shortfall in the shopkeeper's practical *virtue*—at least if we focus simply on the attitude that the duty's directed form makes virtuous. Again by contrast, the employees will *necessarily* fall short of full practical virtue if they fail to think in the first person that the employer's action is to be 'done to me' (as they should put it). Such thinking is made necessary, for these employees' full practical virtue, because the directed form of the duty makes such activities as demanding-on-one's-own-behalf possible for the employees, and a fully virtuous party must be capable of engaging in such activities. Of course the duty can still exist, be fulfilled, and be owed to her if an employee fails to conceive the enjoined action as first-personally affecting her, but the duty will then fail to fulfil a condition met by the paradigmatic directed duty owed to a capable party, and the employee will fall short of full practical virtue.

An objector might press a charge of circularity here, akin to those considered in Section 4.3. The objection would be that these points do not really help someone who

---

[28] Feinberg 1970, Darwall 2012.

[29] Tom Sinclair has pointed out that a virtuous person might often 'turn the other cheek' or 'love the sinner', where this is a long way from demanding and resentment, though perhaps close to forgiveness. I agree, but I do not see this as incompatible with what I say. The virtuous person should 'turn the other cheek' when this is appropriate, but should also be *capable* of personal demanding and resentment, in order to engage in it when *this* is appropriate. My claim involves denying that someone congenitally incapable of anything other than cheek-turning can be fully virtuous, and that seems the correct diagnosis to make.

[30] See p. 52.

[31] Perhaps the 'virtue' reading will seem problematic when applied to morally unjustified legal or conventional duties. But even there I think we can make sense of a notion of *legal or conventional virtue* of which the capable party failing my first-personal conditions falls short. See note 17.

is trying to find out whether or not the employer's duty to make the salary payments is owed to the shopkeeper as well as the employees. For my account to help them, this inquirer needs some independent understanding of what would be paradigmatic to the duty in question (the employer's duty to make the salary payments), and some independent understanding of what first-personal conception this duty's form makes necessary for full practical virtue on the part of the shopkeepers and the employees. The inquirer needs this so that without yet knowing to whom the duty is owed, the inquirer can use her understanding of what would be paradigmatic in this case, or her understanding of what the duty's form makes necessary for full moral virtue for the parties in question, in order to come to realize that what she has encountered is a duty owed to the employees and not the shopkeepers. Yet surely, the objector will press, if the inquirer knows these things—if she already knows what pattern of first-personal thinking would be paradigmatic to the duty's form, or is required by virtue due to this form—then she already knows to whom the duty is owed. The account fails to make a duty's direction depend on factors on which an inquirer could get some independent handle from which to infer the direction without already knowing it.

Now in my view, the objector's points are importantly correct, but they fail to sustain the charge of circularity. To know whether something is a vixen, an inquirer needs to know whether it is a female fox; but the inquirer cannot come to know the latter—that it is a female fox—independently of (implicitly) knowing the former— that it is a vixen. This does not make the analysis of vixens as female foxes circular. What *would* make it circular would be if an animal's being a female fox was somehow caused or generated by, or dependent on, the logically prior fact of its being a vixen. This, I suggested in Sections 2.4–2.5, is the kind of circularity afflicting Kramer's Interest Theory: the only interest officers have in being saluted in the heat of battle is a status interest created by the logically prior fact that the duty to salute is owed to them.[32] By contrast, the fact that the employer's duty formally requires employees and not local shopkeepers to engage in the kind of first-personal thinking outlined is in my view not caused or generated by the logically prior fact of its being owed to the employees and not local shopkeepers. It is, rather, *constitutive* of this fact.

Yet the objection shows how non-reductive my approach is. It says that a duty's direction is constituted by the formal requirements of first-personal conception outlined. But we humans can construct norms wherever we wish, and this includes constructing formal requirements of the type constituting directedness. The approach therefore allows a duty's direction in principle to float free of direction-independent factors in an untethered way: *created* (e.g. *legal* or *conventional*) direct-edness need not supervene on anything other than our say-so. I say more in defence of this in Section 5.1: we can make duties conventionally owed to anyone, so long as we hold an appropriately authoritative or convention-generating role.[33] *Morally*

---

[32] Must Wenar's Kind-Desire go similarly viciously circular to accommodate our leeway to create directedness wherever we want? I am not sure: see the initial discussion at the end of Section 2.5.

[33] Compare MacCormick's (1982, p. 164) claim that we should be ready to find rights whenever law says they exist: 'When the legislature confers a right *eo nomine* [...], it is in effect left to the courts to effect a structure of duties and remedies sufficient to secure the right in question.' Note that this is a way of supporting my suggestion that rights language should be relatively 'untethered'.

justified directedness need not supervene on anything other than our morally justified say-so.[34] We should therefore not expect to be able to infer whether a given duty is directed, or to whom, on the basis of our knowledge of direction-independent features of the parties involved, such as their direction-independent interests or powers (as in the Interest or Will theories); the objector was wrong to ask for this. For if we could do this, that would be inconsistent with the freedom we have to create conventional directedness wherever we choose.

Nonetheless, I argue in Section 5.2 and at length in Sections 7.3–7.6 that the addressive first-/second-personal analysis of directedness developed here entails that *natural* directedness—i.e. a duty's being owed to someone independently of whether anyone ever recognizes this—supervenes on a duty's being morally grounded by the good of the person to whom it is owed (along the lines of Raz's analysis of rights in general; see Section 2.2). So, by investigating its moral ground in parties' good, we can indeed get an independent handle on whether a duty's *natural* paradigm is directed, and to whom.

But we should expect no such independent access to *created* conventional or legal directedness, even when this is morally justified, such as the directedness of the employer's duty in the example earlier. We cannot come to know to whom this duty is owed via our grasp of direction-independent facts. Some such facts might give the inquirer useful pointers: facts about who can demand the duty's fulfilment, whose interests it serves, and what authoritative legislative acts create and sustain it. But unless the inquirer knows things that already entail the duty's direction—e.g. facts about who can demand the duty's fulfilment *on their own behalf as the party to whom it is owed* (to put it viciously circularly), about whose *status interests as right-holder* the duty serves (again to put it viciously circularly), or about *what pattern of first-personal thinking the duty paradigmatically requires* or *what first-personal thinking is required by the duty's directed form for full virtue* (to put it non-circularly but non-reductively)—she cannot accurately infer its direction. This free-floating aspect of created directedness is appropriately reflected in the difficulties of the inquirer sketched four paragraphs ago: an inquirer who understands the analysis I have proposed but does not know to whom a given duty is owed.

Before exploring these points further in Chapter 5, we need the vital next section (4.5) in order to pursue a crucial development of the first-personal condition introduced in the current section, a development that accommodates duties owed to incapable beings—followed by a brief section (4.6) discussing counterexamples.

4.5 The First Person and the Second Person

The previous section (4.4) argued that (a) because *demanding, waiving, etc. on one's own behalf* is both paradigmatic to a capable party owed a duty, and necessary for virtue for such a party, and because (b) Section 4.2 showed that such demanding or waving on one's own behalf requires conceiving the duty-enjoined action as to be

---

[34] Though see Sections 5.3–5.4 for the limits moral justifiability places on our ability to make duties owed to parties independently of their holders' interests.

'done to me', we should conclude (c) that a duty's being owed to a capable party is constituted by its form requiring (for paradigmaticness and for virtue) the party to conceive the duty-enjoined action as to be 'done to me'. Section 4.3 told us that all duties (directed or undirected) in a sense carry one logical place for the first person as agent: the duty-bearer is a party who is required by the normative entity's form-as-someone's-duty to conceive the duty-enjoined action first-personally as to be 'done by me'. Section 4.4's conclusion ((c) just above) shows that directed duties in a sense carry *an additional logical place for a first person as 'acted on'*: namely, for a party owed the duty, who is required by the normative entity's directed form to conceive the duty-enjoined action first-personally as to be 'done to me'.

One obvious problem for the thesis of Section 4.4 is that it says nothing about duties owed to incapable parties, such as non-human animals (compare Section 3.2). A second problem is that as so far explained in Sections 4.3–4.4, the two parties formally brought together in the first person by a duty's direction need not apprehend *each other* in any particular way. According to the thesis of the preceding section (4.4), when your duty is owed to me I am required to see the relevant action first-personally as 'to be done *to me*'; but you are allowed to see me simply as a separate party, a party that could—for all the duty's directed form requires you to grasp—be an unaddressable machine or a rock from your perspective.

This section addresses both criticisms at once, by arguing that there is a distinctive way of thinking about the party to whom a duty is owed that the *bearer* of a directed duty is formally required to engage in, whether or not the party to whom it is owed is a 'capable' being. We start to get a grip on this condition by considering a bearer of a directed duty who is faced with a demand that the duty be fulfilled, issued by the party to whom the duty is owed on her own behalf. Section 4.2 tells us that such a demand must tell the duty-bearer to perform an action which the party to whom the duty is owed conceives in the first person, as to be done '*to me*'. For example, when I demand that someone fulfil a promise made to me, I must understand the demanded action first-personally: as to be done to me.[35] Now, we should observe that the *duty-bearer* only accurately grasps whatever I have demanded if she thinks, *in the second person*, that the duty-enjoined action is to be done, as that duty-bearer should put it, 'to you' (referring to the person to whom the duty is owed). If instead she hears the demand and takes it simply as requiring action done 'to Rowan' (rather than 'to you', addressed to me as demander), then she has failed to take up my demand on the terms in which I issued it. Her third-personal uptake is appropriate to the demand's having been issued by me on behalf of another or nobody, rather than on my own behalf as a person owed the duty (and hence as a party who conceives myself as first-personally affected by the duty-enjoined action).

This is because 'you' is the term we should use when we want our addressee to take up our reference to them in the first person; by contrast, naming them, describing them, or pointing at them does not carry this implication that the person so picked out should conceive our reference to them first-personally.[36] On this basis, it follows

---

[35] See the discussion of walking Hadrian's Wall in Section 4.2.

[36] The relation between 'you' and 'I' is not wholly captured by this fact (see, e.g. Rödl 2014), but this will suffice for my purposes. Note that I here ignore the modern variant in which 'you' means 'one'.

that where a demander must use 'I' (as Sections 4.2 and 4.4 have shown is necessary for demanding on one's own behalf as the party owed a duty), to grasp the demand on the demander's own terms the duty-bearing demandee must use 'you'.

We might be tempted to conclude that the paradigmatic, fully virtuous bearer of a directed duty must always conceive the duty-enjoined action second-personally, as to be done 'to you' (referring to the party to whom the duty is owed). This looks like the flip-side of the condition defended in Section 4.4. But this would be too hasty. It is not paradigmatic to the bearer of a directed duty that they actually face a demand to fulfil it. Recall my claim (Section 4.4) that the paradigmatic, fully virtuous capable party to whom a duty is owed will be *able and ready* to demand that duty's fulfilment on her own behalf; but she need not actually engage in such demanding. The paradigmatic, fully virtuous *bearer* of a directed duty should therefore similarly be able and ready to understand the duty-enjoined action second-personally, as to be 'done to' the party to whom the duty is owed taken as 'you'. But she need not actually so understand the relevant party. It would be quite odd to think that she should, for a thought containing 'you' always addresses someone, even if only internally: as I wander through the streets, if I think to myself about those I pass and do not attack, 'I am not attacking you', and if I think to myself of those on whose gardens I do not trespass, 'I am not trespassing on your property', I am internally addressing the relevant parties even if this address is not expressed. The parties addressed need not be present or known to me, but my thoughts will address them nonetheless.[37] Yet surely the bearer of a directed duty has not failed to conceive her action in the manner in which she is meant to take it given the duty's direction, if she fails actually to address the party to whom the duty is owed, even in thought alone. A bearer of a directed duty who fails actually to address the party to whom it is owed is not therefore non-paradigmatic, nor short of full virtue. For example, I am not short of full virtue when I fail actually to *address* the many fellow road users (including many unknown to me) to whom I owe a duty to exercise due care as a driver; nor do I count therefore as a non-paradigmatic bearer of directed duty.

Instead, our discussion favours the following conclusion: a duty's directed form requires its bearer to take her duty-enjoined action as to be done to parties who *could* be addressed: to conceive such parties as one's *potential* or *possible* addressee, as potential or possible 'yous'. This is how I must think in order to fulfil a condition definitive of the directed form of the duties I owe to the people I pass in the street without attacking, or the duties I owe to the (unknown) owners of what I avoid trespassing on: I must conceive my actions as *done to these people as beings I could address, beings I could refer to with 'you'.*[38] If I fail to think in this way, I have not

---

[37] This marks a real distinction between thoughts containing 'you' and those containing 'I', 'he', or 'they': the latter need not address anyone other than the thinker, while thoughts containing 'you' always address another (except when one talks to *oneself* using 'you').

[38] Theorists of property have prominently claimed, correctly, that one can *fulfil* one's trespassory duties while knowing nothing about the identity of owners (e.g. Ripstein 2013, p. 159); my claim in the main text goes beyond this in stating that one can *conceive one's trespassory duties as they are meant to be conceived qua directed* while knowing nothing about, and failing to address, those to whom they are owed. One must, simply, conceive these parties in the abstract in a second-personal way as potential addressees. For further discussion, see the start of Section 4.6 and the end of Section 11.3.

violated the duty, nor caused the duty to cease to exist or cease to be directed; but I have made the duty and my relation to it *non-paradigmatic as a directed duty*, and I have fallen short of *full practical virtue*.

We can place the newly developed condition alongside the conditions of Sections 4.3 and 4.4 thus:

(from Section 4.3):   A's duty to PHI formally requires first-personal grasp of PHI by A as 'done by me'.

(from Section 4.4):   A's directed duty to PHI owed to B formally requires (if B is capable of this) first-personal grasp of PHI by B as 'done to me'.

(from Section 4.5):   A's directed duty to PHI owed to B formally requires A to grasp PHI as 'done to B', where B is here conceived second-personally by A as a potential addressee or 'you'.

The normativity of each of these formal requirements is the normativity of the paradigmatic and, if one can accept the intellectualism, of full practical virtue. I have already noted one way to motivate the new condition: unless I conceive a capable party to whom my duty is owed as a potential 'you' that my duty-enjoined action will affect, I will be unable to understand on her terms any demand she might make on her own behalf that I fulfil it. Such an inability to take her claims as made by her on her own behalf would surely be a failing in virtue on my part.

But we should also observe that the new condition ('from Section 4.5' above) can be fulfilled by duties owed to incapable parties such as non-human animals, as well as by duties owed to capable parties. It is possible for me to be formally required to conceive my duty as enjoining action 'done to my dog, taken as an addressable "you"'. Some might respond that while it is *in some sense* possible to hold addressive attitudes towards animals, babies, or dead people (to *say* 'I owe you a walk' to my dog), it is not genuinely coherent to do so. One might think it only coherent to hold such attitudes towards parties who could fulfil my earlier condition from Section 4.4, or perhaps towards parties who could take up in the first person whatever complex thing one might say if one were to call them 'you'. But this would be too strong. Address requires the possibility of first-personal uptake by the addressee, but this can include the way my dog first-personally takes up what is addressed to it when it responds to 'Walkies!' or 'Dinner time!', or the way a cow takes up first-personally its being herded in for milking, or perhaps even the way addressable machines like 'Siri' or 'Alexa' respond to our addressing them. I recognize that there are various important distinctions to be drawn here: e.g. between parties capable of replying to my address linguistically (i.e. most post-baby humans) and less linguistically capable parties that nonetheless naturally possess a first-personal perspective (e.g. babies, dogs, dolphins, bats);[39] between parties with a natural first-person perspective (humans and other animals) and parties for whom first-personality is in some sense a construction (business corporations, robots including machines like 'Alexa' or 'Siri'); between parties with a current, actual first-personal perspective and parties with only a counter-factual or past first-personal perspective (people in a coma or

---

[39] See Nagel 1979.

dead, of whom we can only know what they did or would think); the status of the first-personality of groups is of course another issue. I return to these distinctions and the questions they raise at several points in this book (e.g. Chapters 8–10), but here my claim is simply that it is unjustifiably parochial to restrict coherent address to cases in which two-way linguistic communication is possible; instead coherent 'you'-thoughts can include those whose possibility for first-personal uptake by the addressee is distant from those in communication among capable adults. Denying this would generate an implausibly sharp distinction between our communication with capable parties and our communication with others.[40]

So in my view the new condition ('from Section 4.5') can be fulfilled by duties owed to incapable parties as well as duties owed to the capable. Furthermore, I will argue in a moment that the new condition is both necessary and sufficient for directedness. But why think this? And does this move make the condition from Section 4.4 superfluous?

One approach—which I reject—concedes that the *core or canonical* bearer of a claim-right is one who can demand a duty's fulfilment on their own behalf as the party to whom it is owed, personally resent its violation, forgive, etc. The primary function of the directed duty (or claim-right) concept on this Feinbergian approach is to make such personal demanding and resentment possible by picking out certain capable parties as those to whom the duty is owed: those who should, given the duty's form, conceive themselves as first-personally affected by the duty-enjoined action. From this premise, the approach motivates the new condition ('from Section 4.5') on the basis of the reasons given earlier: that to understand *on her own terms* the personal demands, resentment, forgiveness of a party to whom a duty is owed, the duty-bearer must conceive her second-personally as 'you, on whom my duty enjoins me to act'. The approach claims that once this idea of a duty governed by the conditions from Sections 4.4 and 4.5 has taken root, we *extend* the concept so that something like it—captured by the condition 'from Section 4.5' alone—enables us to see duties owed to incapable parties. This is possible because the duty-bearer can conceive such a party as 'you' in the way that would be required if that party did (*per impossibile*) demand this action on her own behalf.

I reject this because it makes the directedness of duties owed to incapable parties non-core: an extension to unfamiliar ground of a concept at home in the idea of *demanding on one's own behalf, personally resenting*, etc. The ways in which duties are owed to dogs, cows, dead people, or young babies is on this approach less than the full, core directedness of the condition from Section 4.4.

A better approach starts with the idea of a world populated with addressable parties—potential 'yous'—of *all* sorts including capable peers but also animals and babies whose capacity for first-personal uptake is not that of an adult human,

---

[40] Some might doubt especially my openness to the possibility that we can construct an addressable status for machines like 'Siri' or 'Alexa'. This status would make it *possible* for them to be owed duties, but note that whether it would be justifiable to construct duties owed to such parties is a further question. Note that because such parties' good lacks moral importance in itself, and hence cannot make a duty exist independently of legal or conventional creation, no duty could be *naturally* (as opposed to constructedly) owed to such parties (see Section 5.3, and Chapter 7).

machines ('Siri', 'Alexa') for whom such capacity is a construction, and dead and incapable humans for whom such uptake is wholly counterfactual ('what she would think if she were conscious' or 'what she would think if she were not dead'). The function of the directed duty (claim-right) concept on this approach is to require the duty-bearer to conceive her duty-enjoined action as to be done to another 'you', to another first-personality among the many with whom we live. Just as Section 4.3 tells us that my *duties* (like all reasons) call on me first-personally, my *directed* duties address my enjoined action to other 'first persons' by requiring me to conceive those who are to be acted on second-personally.

This approach does not make the condition from Section 4.4 superfluous. When the condition from Section 4.5 pertains to a *capable* party in the B position, that party's capability makes possible a first-personal conception on her part (conception of the duty-enjoined PHI as to be 'done to me') that matches the second-personal conception required of the duty-bearer (conception of the duty-enjoined PHI as to be 'done to a party conceiveable as "you"'). This 'matching' first-personal conception by the party in the B position is required if she is to claim her due on the terms that make it her due: first-personal terms matching the second-personal terms in which the duty-bearer is required to conceive it in virtue of its being the party's due.

On this approach the idea of *demanding on one's own behalf* is not at the heart of the directed duty concept, although such demanding is made possible by it for capable parties. The heart of directedness is the notion of being duty-bound to *act on others who are to be conceived second-personally, as other 'first persons'*. We should be unsurprised to have a concept with this function: it seems to me obviously intuitively important sometimes to be able to require recognition of other parties' first-personality, and it should be unsurprising that we have a concept— directedness– that functions to require this in relation to duties enjoining actions done to others. Further, given the many forms of first-personality with which we live, we should not be surprised that this directedness concept allows duties to be owed to (rights held by) animals, babies, and other 'incapable' beings even though they cannot fulfil the condition from Section 4.4.

Notice that the condition from Section 4.5 does not say that *whenever* a duty can be coherently conceived by its bearer as enjoining action done to an addressable being or 'you', then it is owed to that being. It is only owed to whomever the duty-bearer is *required as a matter of virtue and paradigmaticness by the duty's form* to conceive in this way. Thus—to reuse Section 4.4's example—the employer's duty to pay its employees' salaries is not owed to the shopkeeper who benefits from such salary-payments because the duty-bearer (employer) is not required by the duty's form to conceive the action (issuing salary payments) in a way that construes it as to be *done to the shopkeeper taken as a possible addressee or 'you'*. The employer can take their duty as it is meant to be taken—virtuously, and in a manner paradigmatic to the duty's form—without having this thought. By contrast, the employer is required for virtue and paradigmaticness to take their salary-paying action as to be *done to the employees, conceived as potential addressees*.

What is the shortfall in virtue of the employer who does not think like this? The possibility of this shortfall was created by the employer's and employee's decision to enter the employment contract, and by our wider decision to create employment contracts with a directed duty structure: in taking this decision we *decided* to make it a shortfall in virtue for an employer to fail to conceive her duty to her employees as duties to potential addressees or 'yous', and we could have decided otherwise (see the end of Section 4.4, concerning our leeway to create directedness wherever we wish). But in other cases the implications for virtue are not a construction: in Sections 5.2 and 7.3–7.6, I argue that if someone's good *naturally* makes a duty exist (as the importance to me of not being tortured naturally makes you duty-bound not to torture me), then the duty is naturally owed to that party. The current section (4.5) tell us that if this is correct, then a duty-bearer falls short of virtue, independently of our construction, if they fail to conceive a party whose good naturally grounds their duty as an addressable potential 'you'.

I end this section by comparing my notion of second-personality to Darwall's. Darwall introduces the idea of a *second-personal reason*: one 'whose validity depends on presupposed authority and accountability relations between persons and, there-fore, on the possibility of the reason's being addressed person-to-person'.[41] For Darwall, both directed and undirected duties are second-personal reasons: *both* can be 'addressed person-to-person', *both* can be claimed by anyone with 'representative authority [. . .] as a [. . .] member of the moral community'; what distinguishes directed duties (claim-rights) is that they can also be claimed by parties with distinctive 'individual' authority.[42] While I reject Darwall's Will Theory account of 'individual' authority,[43] my position is consistent with his claim that directed *and* *undirected* duties are second-personal in his sense: addressable by one capable party with authority to another capable party with equal authority. 'Second-personality' and 'address' play a different role for me: my conditions from Sections 4.4 and 4.5 distinguish directed duties by the fact that *the action* they demand from their bearers should be conceived addressively: as an action done to a potential 'you'; by contrast the action demanded by undirected duties need not be addressively conceived by the duty-bearer.

This focus on whether a duty-enjoined action should be conceived addressively is different from Darwall's focus on the addressing of reasons. For my purposes, 'addressive' actions encompass any action conceived as done to a 'you', including the action of addressing practical reasons, but also pure information-giving (one party tells another something) and other activities (calling a dog for 'Walkies!', loving someone, herding a cow, walking Hadrian's Wall as fulfilling a promise). In this sense, incapable beings like animals can have a duty-enjoined action 'addressed' to them—and hence can be owed the relevant duty—even though they cannot be given reasons in anything like Darwall's sense. Even if Darwall is correct that second-personal reasons and duties are to be 'addressed' interpersonally in his sense, and that this presupposes 'that [those who give and receive such reasons] share a common second-personal authority, competence, and responsibility simply as free and rational agents',[44] nonetheless bearing a duty that is owed to some party and hence 'addressive' in my sense does not require its addressee to share authority or

---

[41] Darwall 2006, p. 8.   [42] Darwall 2012, p. 348.
[43] Ibid., pp. 346–7: see the 'discretionary' aspect of 'individual authority'.   [44] Darwall 2006, p. 5.

other capacities with the duty-bearer: it simply requires the party to be coherently conceivable by the duty-bearer as 'you on whom I am to act'. Capable, authoritative agents including third parties can 'address' this duty to its bearer Darwall-style, demanding that she fulfil the duty, but the party to whom it is owed—the 'you' the bearer must conceive her action as to be done to—need not be capable or authoritative in order to be, in my sense, 'addressed' by the duty-enjoined action.

4.6 Counterexamples

By rejecting the idea that duties could be owed to parties to whom the duty-enjoined action is not 'done' (Section 4.2), by endorsing Hills's arguments for intellectualism (Section 4.3), and by rejecting the idea that duties could be owed to unaddressable parties (Section 4.5), I have already dismissed some putative counterexamples to Section 4.5's condition as a *necessary* condition on a duty's being directed. Some might worry about duties owed to unknown parties, such as a president's duty not to bomb a city whose inhabitants she does not know, or my duty not to walk on gardens whose owners are unknown to me. But the addressive attitude required by Section 4.5 can be held in abstract fashion, towards parties known in no other way than as *potential 'yous' my duty-enjoined action is to affect*: fulfilling this condition is therefore possible for the president or me in relation to unknown parties.[45]

Yet one might think that there are counterexamples to the conditions from Sections 4.4–4.5 as *sufficient* conditions. For instance, one plausible theory maintains that when a community has a moral duty to punish a wrongdoer, this is a duty to communicate censure to the wrongdoer.[46] For this to succeed as communication, the wrongdoer must conceive herself first-personally (and her punishers second-personally) as 'I, who is being punished by you', and the community must conceive the wrongdoer second-personally (and themselves first-personally) as 'you, who we are punishing'. Such grasp of the situation is necessary if the punishment is to constitute communication. But is the duty to punish therefore owed to the wrongdoer, perhaps giving her a right to be punished, as Hegel suggested?[47]

Because my account is meant to encompass morally unjustified legal and conventional directed duties as well as moral directed duties, more putative counterexamples appear. For instance, the legal system of a fascist regime might place some officials under a duty to oppress or dominate a particular group. To constitute true oppression or domination it might be that the oppressed or dominated group must conceive themselves first-personally as 'we, who are being dominated by the regime', while it might be that the regime must conceive their victims second-personally (and themselves first-personally) as 'you, who we are dominating'. Without such first- and second-personal grasp, it is not clear that the relevant acts will qualify as genuine oppression or domination: they will be harsh acts, but—let us suppose—not oppression or domination of the kind intended, a kind that involves some communication of contempt expressed to addressable victims, and grasped as such by these victims.

---

[45] See note 38 above.   [46] See, e.g. Duff 2001.
[47] Hegel 1991 [1821], section 100. Compare Tierney on Villey on Ulpian's conception of the punishment of a parricide, in this volume, Section 2.2 (Tierney 1997, p. 16).

But surely we do not want to conclude, on the basis of the first- and second-personal comprehension required, that the victims are owed a legal duty to be dominated and oppressed, even if a mere morally unjustified legal directed duty?

We can reply to both putative counterexamples in the same way. In both cases, the requirements of first- and second-personal grasp spring from the nature of the action enjoined by the duty (what we might call its 'content', the 'PHI', what the duty requires the duty-bearer to do if the duty is to be respected), not from the duty's directed form. In both cases, the duty is *not wholly fulfilled* if the requirements of first- and second-personal grasp are not met: the punishers fail to do what they are morally duty-bound to do, by failing to punish *as communication*, and the oppressors fail to do what they are legally duty-bound to do, by failing to oppress *in the appropriate contempt-expressing way*. But this leaves it open that the form of the duties could be undirected, or at least not owed to the relevant victims. Has an oppressor who fails to conceive those she oppresses as addressable failed to respond to her legal duty's form in the way it is meant to be responded to? Has she fallen short of legal virtue by making the duty *non-paradigmatic as a directed duty*? She has failed to do all that is required by its content but if there is no defect in *her conception of her action qua enjoined by duty*, but only in her performance of its content, then the duty is not owed to those it oppresses. Similarly, has a victim of the legal oppression outlined who fails to conceive in the first person that, as she should put it, 'I' am being oppressed, failed to respond to her oppressor's legal duty in the way it is meant to be responded to *given its form*—or has she simply made it the case that its content is unfulfilled? If her thinking shows no deviation from the paradigm required by the duty's form, then even though she has misunderstood the duty's content, it is not owed to her.

This response to the counterexamples will, I suspect, only reinforce concerns in those who are sceptical of the approach. For my response reveals how much turns on the notion of a requirement generated by or constitutive of a duty's form: a requirement whose fulfilment is necessary if the case in question is to be a *paradigm* case of directed duty, and if the parties involved are to be *fully virtuous* in the sense of conceiving the duty-enjoined action in the way it is meant to be conceived, qua action-enjoined-by-directed-duty.

But we have seen in Chapters 2–3 that the alternative, more reductive analyses of directedness offered by the Interest, Desire, Will and Demand theories fail as biconditional analyses. And in several sections (e.g. 2.5, 4.4), we have seen one reason why they fail: analyses that try to make a duty directed simply in virtue of its relationship to some direction-independent factor (such as direction-independent interests or direction-independent powers) fail to respect the leeway we have, as law- and convention-creators, to make duties owed to whomever we wish them to be owed to. I expand on this in the next chapter.

Before closing, it is worth noting that in one respect the Addressive account of directed duties developed here demands significantly more than its reductive rivals. Unlike the Interest, Desire, Will or Demand theories, the Addressive approach implies that the party who meets all the conditions generated by duties held by and owed to her has not done enough if she simply goes through life conceiving herself, as Section 4.3 requires, in the first person (as 'I, who must PHI') in relation to the duties bearing on her—and conceives others as no more than third parties in relation to whom she is sometimes duty-bound to act, and herself as no more than a happenstance beneficiary of others' dutiful actions. Instead, the very form of her duties as owed to others, and others' duties as owed to her, requires her as a matter of virtue sometimes to conceive herself in an 'I–you nexus' with these others conceived second-personally as 'you, on whom I PHI' and with herself conceived first-personally as acted on, as 'I, on whom you PHI'.[48] On my account this connected, unalienated thinking is required by the very form of duties as owed to others by her, and as owed to her by others. Their directed form is defined by such non-alienating requirements. Such formal requirements of connected thinking are overlooked by the Interest, Desire, Will and Demand theories.

---

[48] For the idea of a 'propositional nexus' involving two parties (as opposed to a single party's propositional *attitude*), see Thompson 2012. For cognate thoughts on the relationality of rights, see Zylberman 2016a.

5

Rights and Interests Revisited

5.1 Legal-Conventional Directedness Depends on Our Thinking It So

Chapter 4 developed a new account of what it is to owe someone a duty. This Addressive approach says that a duty is owed to a party whenever the duty-bearer is required, by the duty's form, to think of the action it enjoins as to be *done to that party, conceived as an addressable being or potential 'you'*. Failure to fulfil this formal requirement does not mean that the duty ceases to exist, or is violated, or lacks a direction; it simply means that the duty is non-paradigmatic as a directed duty, and its bearer falls short of full practical virtue.

In the first sections of this chapter (Sections 5.1–5.2), I take up a question that recurred throughout Chapter 4: what direction-independent factors does a duty's direction, as analysed Addressively, supervene on? In Section 4.4, I briefly defended the way that the Addressive account makes directedness relatively untethered, but there must be some things we can say about what makes one duty generate the formal requirements constitutive of directedness, while another duty does not. As prefigured in Section 4.4, I argue (Section 5.1) that *socially created* (e.g. legal or conventional) directedness supervenes on nothing but authoritative people's belief in it or authoritative texts' and actions' creation of it while, interestingly, it turns out (Section 5.2) that if the addressive account is correct then *natural* directedness is generated when a duty is grounded, as in Raz's theory, by the good of the party to whom that duty is thereby naturally directed. The wide-ranging implications of both claims in these initial sections are explored in detail in Parts II and III, so I am fairly brief here. I end by taking up the two further questions left hanging at the close of Chapter 2: why (Section 5.3) a morally justified directed duty always generates a circular status interest in its own satisfaction, and (Section 5.4) why in *most* cases morally justified socially created directed duties also serve their recipients' interests and kind-based desires in a less circular sense.

First, let us recall Section 1.3's distinction between socially created duties (legal, conventional, etiquette-based, game-based, promissory, etc.) and natural duties, which I take to be duties that exist independently of anyone's recognizing their existence.[1] Let us also distinguish between duties whose direction (the fact that

---

[1] Note that natural duties on this account could include some of Hart's 'special' duties—duties created by particular actions (Hart 1955, section II). It is just that, when actions create *natural* duties, the relevant actions create these duties whether or not anyone notices this. Thus, for example, if Locke is correct about labour creating property rights, we might take this to mean that labouring on unowned items can create

they are owed to someone) is socially created and duties whose direction is natural, in the sense of being recognition-independent. There might be some duties whose existence as duties is natural, but whose directedness is socially created.

If the Addressive account of duties' direction developed in the previous chapter is correct then, I suggest *socially created* direction depends on whatever social mechanisms can generate the formal conditions sketched in Sections 4.4–4.5 as socially created conditions bearing on a given duty. In my view, there is nothing distinctive to directedness about the possibilities here. Whatever mechanisms can create social, conventional or legal *duties in general* can also create directed versions of these duties. Such mechanisms might involve, simply, many social agents thinking of duties as directed, where this means thinking of them implicitly as generating the formal conditions sketched in Sections 4.4–4.5. Or they might involve authoritative people (e.g. lawmakers) thinking in this way. The relevant mechanisms might also involve canonical legal texts referring to rights and directed duties, and they might involve legislative intentions, further language used in statements of the law or rule, related beliefs of those living within the system, and interpretations of the law or rule that might appeal to the instrumental value of people's conceiving themselves as right-holders, for example.[2] We should be open to the possibility of cases in which it is brutely indeterminate whether a given duty is owed to someone or not, because the factors just mentioned do not settle the duty's form either way. But the essence of my thesis here is that our say-so—where that might mean any among the factors just listed—can make a duty conventionally, socially, or legally directed, just as in the same sense our say-so can create a conventional, social, or legal duty.

This means that any duty could, so long as its bearer can coherently make sense of the action it enjoins as 'done to' someone conceivable second-personally, turn out to be directed, if the aforementioned factors made this the case. Thus it is *possible* for the legal duties in the oppression and the punishment cases of Section 4.6 to be owed to the parties in question. For example, suppose legislation makes clear that failure to oppress the relevant parties legally wrongs them; perhaps legislation specifies that a remedy is owed specifically to the parties in question if they are not oppressed.[3] That is, suppose Sections 4.4–4.5's formal Addressive requirements hold in the way that makes this true. My point in discussing the counterexamples earlier was just that the duties' content (what they require from the duty-bearer) does not *suffice* to make the duties directed.

'natural' trespassory duties, duties generated by the labour whether or not anyone including the labourer realized that they had thereby created duties. Various forms of communication might also create natural duties by setting up expectations that 'naturally' ought to be met, whether or not the communication was intended to create such duties; my own view is that promising and contracting, by contrast, require *explicit recognition as involving the creation of duties* if they are to create them.

[2] On interpretation, see Dworkin 1986; theorists who highlight the instrumental value of people's thinking of themselves as holders of legal rights include classical liberals such as David Hume and Adam Smith (see discussion in Part III). See also again MacCormick's (1982, p. 164) claim that (almost) any piece of legislation that uses the term 'a right' will successfully establish a right (see also reference at Chapter 4, note 33, in this volume).

[3] Recall that *being owed a remedy on one's own behalf as the party to whom the duty is owed* is distinct from simply being a party who should receive remedial payment even though the duty was not owed to one. See Section 3.5.

If this is correct, and we can therefore make any duty owed to someone by deploying the appropriate social mechanisms to generate the conditions outlined in Sections 4.4–4.5, the question arises as to when we should do this. We might think that because of directedness's pesky complexity, why should we bother giving any duties a direction, when undirected duties can seemingly do just as good a job at serving the values for which we might want them?

Suppose, for example, that we accept Nussbaum's thesis that the importance of securing for a person the 'Central Capability' of political control over one's environment grounds that person's human right to political participation.[4] Nussbaum writes:

> [B]y defining the securing of rights in terms of capabilities, we make it clear that a people in country C don't really have an effective right to political participation, for example, a right in the sense that matters for judging that the society is a just one, simply because this language exists on paper; they really have been given the right only if there are effective measures to make people truly capable of political exercise. Women in many nations have a nominal right of political participation without having this right in the sense of capability: for example, they may be threatened with violence within the home. In short, thinking in terms of capability gives a benchmark as we think about what it really is to secure a right to someone. It makes clear that to do this involves affirmative material and institutional support, not simply a failure to impede.[5]

I endorse Nussbaum's important thesis that the right to political participation requires more than nominal legal endorsement, and more than simply 'allowing' such participation. It requires an end to violence against women in the home, along with a range of 'positive' measures including the provision of public spaces for debate and voting, education and, I would venture, an end to patriarchal, neo-feudal and capitalist power structures. A threshold level of political participation for all requires these measures.

But notice that these measures could be required as a matter of *undirected* rather than *directed* duty. If our end is to ensure that each person is, in Nussbaum's words, 'truly capable of [a threshold level of] political exercise',[6] it is unclear that achieving this end requires or indeed is even assisted by the complexity of directed duties, that is, by duties linked in the manner outlined to demanding on one's own behalf, to the first and second person. We might think that Nussbaum's end can be most easily achieved as a matter of simple undirected duty.[7] As Section 3.5 showed, even powers to demand, trigger enforcement, waive/annul these duties, and powers to trigger rectificatory duties in case of violation, could be held by parties without the duties being owed to anyone—that is without the powers being exercised by the relevant parties *on their own behalf*, and hence without the duty-enjoined actions having to be

---

[4] See, for example, Nussbaum 2011, p. 34, for the place of political control among Nussbaum's ten 'Central Capabilities'.

[5] Nussbaum 2006, p. 287.

[6] The insertion in square brackets is suggested by Nussbaum's discussion of a threshold level for each capability (Nussbaum 2011, pp. 40–2).

[7] Similar points could be made about Griffin's agency-focused ground for human rights (Griffin 2008), or Miller's need-focused approach (Miller 2007, ch. 7): are *undirected* duties just as good, or better, at than *directed duties correlating with rights*?

conceived first- and second-personally, and thus without the parties personally qualifying as wronged by the duties' violation. This is because of the point, gleanable from Section 3.5, that the switch from undirected to directed duties (and hence from powers to demand etc. exercisable on behalf of nobody or, perhaps, on behalf of the moral community at large to powers exercisable on behalf of a particular party owed a duty) makes no *extensional* difference to what ought to happen. It makes no difference to whether a government ought to supply polling stations, for example, or to whether I ought to be paid compensation if they are not supplied. The difference is only *intensional*: a difference in whether what ought to happen is *owed to me*, and in whether demands I can make in relation to the duty can be '*on my own behalf*', etc.

Now, I think we still have good reasons to make legal and conventional duties in the area of political participation directed. For example, we might think that legal duties in this area are founded on or give legal form to natural duties that are themselves naturally directed, and that even though their natural directedness makes no extensional difference, it should still be reflected in their legal form—I come to this in a moment (Section 5.2) and at more length in Part II.[8]

Alternatively, we might find instrumental reasons for creating a direction for the relevant legal duties. I argued in Chapter 4 that if a duty is directed, then its form requires the person to whom it is owed, if she is to demand its fulfilment on her own behalf, to conceive the action it enjoins first-personally as to be 'done to me', and it requires a matching second-personal thought from the duty-bearer. We might well find that making such first- and second-personal thinking paradigmatic, and required as a matter of practical virtue, is extremely useful for securing particular goods. For example, we might think that political participation is most likely to be protected if people ought to consider their government's and their fellows' participation-securing actions as to be 'done to them', and hence as duties owed to them. People might best police the provision of goods which they consider 'theirs' in this sense—actions which they ought given the form of the duty to take in the first person as to be 'done to them'—rather than simply owed as a matter of undirected duty.[9]

Instrumental considerations of the type just mentioned might be good reasons for us to create legal or conventional directedness. They would be reasons that could morally justify the use of the direction-creating mechanisms mentioned earlier in this section: e.g. authoritative decisions to create directedness, or conventional emergence of beliefs that give a duty a direction, and so on. Sometimes the reasons to make a duty directed might be outweighed by its costs, where these could include costs created by people's considering it to be directed. In Part III, I will argue that significant costs tell against the socially created directedness of the trespassory duties constituting most of our individual private property rights. But at present I note simply that this kind of cost–benefit analysis focused on the value of a duty's being

---

[8]   See especially Chapter 9 where I defend the view that legal human rights should give institutional form to, specify, or be grounded in, prior natural rights (compare Buchanan's rejection of this view—or his 'Mirroring' version of it—in his 2013).

[9]   Compare 'tragedy of the commons' arguments for property rights (Hardin 1968); for discussion, see this volume, Section 13.3.

directed, including the value of the consequences of making it directed, is wholly appropriate to the moral assessment of socially created directedness.

By contrast, we should note that such instrumental considerations—considerations of the value (for or against) of a candidate duty's being directed—can have no weight in determining whether a duty is *naturally* directed, that is, in determining whether a duty is owed to someone independently of anyone's recognition of this. For I will argue in Part II, Section 7.4, that it would be a category error to claim (as Nagel and Kamm seem to) that a duty was naturally directed because of the value of its being directed, or was naturally undirected because of the value of its not being directed.[10] When a duty is naturally directed, this obtains independently of our making it so, and hence—I will argue in Chapter 7—cannot depend on whether it would be a good idea for us to make it so; thus it cannot depend on the value of its being so.

5.2 Natural Directedness Depends on Interests

What, then, determines whether a duty is naturally directed—that is, whether it naturally or recognition-independently carries the formal Addressive requirements outlined in Chapter 4? I think we get a clue to the answer in the third of the three points listed in Section 2.6. I believe Raz's account gives a sufficient condition for a duty's being owed to someone because—at least if 'interest' is taken broadly enough—it is an accurate account of duties that are naturally directed; it just fails to accommodate the further directedness we can create through law or convention.

That is, in my view a duty naturally carries Sections 4.4–4.5's formal requirements of first- and second-personal thinking iff it is grounded—in the sense of being *made to exist*—wholly or primarily by the good of a particular addressable party (a party that might be individual or collective). The rough idea is that when a particular addressable party's good manages largely on its own to place me under a duty, independently of any social conventions, and independently of whether this would serve the good of others beyond the party in question, the form of the duty must address me to that party by carrying Section 4.5's formal requirement of second-personal thinking (and, if the party is capable of satisfying it, Section 4.4's formal requirement of first-personal thinking). Failure to carry these formal requirements would mean that the duty's form failed to register its distinctive basis as moving one addressable party to act for the sake of another.[11] A fully virtuous agent moved to action by an addressable party's good should regard their action as for the sake of that

---

[10] Nagel and Kamm claim that the value of our having rights—as distinct from the value of people's behaving as these rights require—makes them exist in Nagel 2002, pp. 39–42 and Kamm 2007, ch. 8; the argument from rights-status's value to their existence is perhaps more obvious in Nagel; Kamm highlights its value but does not so explicitly press that rights exist *because* the status they constitute is valuable. For more discussion, see this volume, Section 7.4.

[11] If one thinks *all* rights (including non-natural social creations) move one addressable party to act for the sake of another, one should think again. The prime minister's right to declare war moves citizens to refrain from impeding this declaration in certain ways; but they do not here act for the sake of the prime minister, but rather for the sake of other citizens. This is one reason why Raz's account fails to encompass non-natural rights. See Section 2.2.

party, where this—I will suggest—means, among other things, taking the action as 'done to' the party as an addressable 'you'.

Furthermore, I see no other basis for natural directedness. When some good (a party's good or an independent value, or the collective good, for example) naturally enjoins action from me by naturally placing me under a duty, I can see no basis in this natural duty-generation for the duty to place me under Sections 4.4–4.5's Addressive requirements in relation to *some further party* beyond the party, if anyone, whose good it is. The potential value of the duty's being owed to such a further party could at best give us reason conventionally or legally to *make* the duty owed to such a party; it could not make it the case that the duty is *naturally* so owed. My duty can only naturally, recognition-independently place me under the Addressive requirements constitutive of its being owed to some party if that party's good grounds it.

I recognize that this is simply a statement of my view that Raz's account explains natural directedness, not a defence of it. The defence must await Chapters 7–8 in Part II, where I will show that a duty's being grounded in a party's good can take a variety of forms, and is also a scalar matter: some duties are partially but not fully so grounded. Thus a duty's naturally being owed to someone can similarly be a matter of degree—an issue I explore in the sections of Part II just mentioned. But we have two more issues to tidy up before Part I's concluding Chapter 6.

5.3 Morally Justified Directedness (Legal-Conventional or Natural) Creates Status Interests and Desires

Any morally justified directed duty, whether socially created or natural, defines the sphere of moral respect owed to the party to whom the duty is directed. When someone violates morally justified duties owed to me in my role as manager, I am not simply the occasion for wrongdoing committed against the values that justify the structure of the organization in which I am manager. Rather, if the duties owed to me as manager are morally justified, then even though the duties and their directedness are socially created, the wrong committed is a wrong done to me, one which shows me disrespect. I argued in Section 2.4 that this does not extend to *morally unjustified* duties, but the point obviously applies to all naturally directed duties as well as those whose direction is justifiedly socially created. Further, any directed duty, morally justified *or morally unjustified*, sets up a circular kind-based status desire for its own fulfilment, a desire-qua-party-to-whom-the-duty-is-owed that the duty be fulfilled.

The first question on my list in Section 2.6 asks why these points hold. I focus on the claim about interests: why should my being owed a morally justified duty necessarily make it the case that my well-being is enhanced, in a status way, by the duty's fulfilment? The account of duties' direction developed in Chapter 4 lets us say something on this.[12] My suggestion is that when a morally justified normative entity's form (as, say, a reason, a duty, a directed duty) requires first-personal conception of

---

[12] I suggest that a related point can explain why given how kind- or role-based desires are independent of their bearers' psychology and their well-being (see Section 2.3), and rather simply come with the kind or

an action, whether as done by me or to me, this always registers as part of what it is morally to show me respect. To adapt Darwall's terms, 'appraisal respect' is earned by me to the extent that I respond to morally justified normative entities that specify actions that I am formally required to conceive as to be 'done by me': reasons and duties bearing on me. And 'recognition respect' is owed to me by others satisfying morally justified normative entities that specify actions that I am formally required to conceive as to be 'done to me': duties owed to me.[13] Both forms of respect are conceptually tied to my good or interests. The first form delineates and reflects my interest in doing what morality (or morally justified law or convention) asks me to do. We will see in Part III that this is a pervasive and essential human interest, emphasized for example by Socrates' focus on the essential harm to the wrongdoer in doing wrong.[14] The second form is, in a sense, the flip-side or converse of this interest in responding to reason and doing one's morally justified duty: the interest in others doing what morally justified duty requires them to do to me, where this duty is owed to me in the Addressive sense that I am formally required to conceive the duty-bearer's action in the first person as done to me. To call this a *status* interest, as I did in Section 2.4, registers that the interest is necessarily created by the duty's being owed to the person in question. This is what I mean by its being the flip-side or converse of the Socratic interest in doing one's duty or responding to reason. The fulfilment of a duty that is owed to me need not make me happy, or serve my good in any other way, in order to satisfy the status interest in question: the interest is constituted simply by the fact that morally justified duty asks someone to do something to me, and the form of this duty requires me—in the sense of 'require-ment' involving the normativity of the paradigmatic and of practical virtue outlined in Chapter 4—to conceive the action in the first person as 'done to me'.

5.4 Non-Circular Desires or Interests in Legal-Conventional Directedness?

I argued in Section 2.5 that the fulfilment of a morally justified duty owed to me need not serve my interests in some separate, non-circular sense beyond the serving of the status interest just mentioned. Nor need it serve my kind-based desires other than a circular status one. But cases demonstrating this—such as my example of a perverse duty owed to officers to salute them only in the heat of battle, justified as necessary to pacify some third party who would otherwise produce separate ill effects—seem rare.[15] The fulfilment of a morally justified duty owed to someone normally seems to serve their independent interests, or at least normally seems to place them in a position that would typically serve the independent interests of a person so placed (to put it in Kramer's terms). And it also normally seems to fulfil that party's independent kind-based desires (to put it in Wenar's terms)—desires beyond the status one

---

role, it follows from bearing the role 'party to whom a duty is owed' that one will in a role-based sense desire its fulfilment. This will be what I called a 'status desire'.

[13] For the appraisal vs recognition distinction, see Darwall 1977.   [14] See Chapter 14.
[15] See Section 2.5, p. 27.

that each party holds circularly in virtue of being owed a duty. Why is this so? Isn't it incompatible with my form of legal positivism which claims that whether a duty is directed or not should be untethered to the interests or desires of the party to whom it is directed?

In answering this, we should note first that no link to interests obtains for *morally unjustified* directedness: we really can, horrifically, make legal duties to oppress others owed to their victims (see Section 4.6). All we need is to set up the appropriate conditions of first- and second-personal grasp in relation to these duties, using the social mechanisms referred to in Section 5.1.

I suggest the following speculative answer to why in most cases, fulfilling *morally justified* socially created directed duties serves the independent interests or desires (including kind-based desires) of the parties to whom they are owed. Chapter 4 tells us that, when morally justified duties are owed to a capable being like me, then full practical virtue requires me to think of the actions they enjoin as to be *done to me*, and to be ready when necessary to demand these actions as to be done to me. Seeing such actions as at the same time *in no sense good for me or wanted by me*, other than in the circular status senses outlined in Section 5.3, seems, I suggest, in tension with other practical virtues such as the virtue of self-respect. A morally justified duty owed to me which does nothing for me (beyond serving a status interest or status desire it creates) is something I must, if fully practically virtuous, be ready to demand in a way that foregrounds in my thinking *its being done to me* even though it does nothing independent for me. I would suggest that my proper self-respect is in tension with such demanding: that is, with my *demanding something that does nothing for me (in desire or interest terms), while thinking of it as being done to me*.

To return to the example of a perverse but (for consequentialist reasons) justified saluting system, in which private soldiers owe a duty to officers to salute them in the heat of battle: Chapter 4's Addressive analysis tells us that the duty's directed form means that when demanding that she be saluted, a given officer must think first-personally of the saluting as to be 'done to me'. This, I suggest, is in tension with the officer's proper self-respect, given that the action demanded does nothing whatsoever for the officer's independent interests or desires (including kind-based desires). Now I am not saying that the officer's self-respect disallows her from demanding actions that serve further goods and not her or her role; she—like all of us—can of course engage in self-sacrificing demanding which serves others, and she can do this while showing appropriate self-respect. But in demanding such actions that serve others, I believe proper self-respect sits best with the officer focusing on the further goods which justify the duty in question (e.g. the goods for whose sake we set up the perverse saluting system), rather than her focusing on the action's (saluting's) effect on her—an effect which by hypothesis is non-beneficial to and undesired by her. To require the officer to focus on the saluting as to be 'done to me'—as the duty's directed form requires—seems to require the officer to engage in a distracting form of self-puffery, when the duty's ground is the good of others and the saluting does nothing for the officer's independent interests or desires (including kind-based desires).

Another way of putting this speculative point is to start with the idea that there is truth in a weak or defeasible 'guise of the good' thesis about virtuous morally justified demanding. The relevant 'guise of the good' thesis would be that *virtuously demanding some PHI that is required by morally justified duty involves conceiving PHI as independently good or desirable.* We then add that when PHI is, as a matter of virtue, to be demanded in the first person as 'done to me', the relevant good that the demander should see in PHI should include their own good, in some very broad but direction-independent sense (perhaps specifiable in Kramer's 'typical' or Wenar's 'role/ kind' or broader terms). We can then note that a demander who fails to fulfil this condition—who demands PHI in the first person as 'done to me' *without* seeing PHI as good to herself or desired by herself or her kind—arguably violates an attractive principle of self-respect, namely that virtue need only require a demander to focus on a demanded action's beneficial or desired effects on that demander when these effects are in some way part of the action's justification or essentially implicated by that action. The directedness of the duty to PHI seems to ask from the demander a distracting or unwarranted self-focus, if the duty is not justified by nor even in any way serves the independent good or desires (even kind-desires) of the party to whom it is owed.

But I think the flexible range of situations in which we can create morally justified directedness makes the 'guise of the good' thesis at best a weak, defeasible thesis, or makes the proposed principle of self-respect one that we must sometimes see violated. Odd scenarios—like my officers' right to be saluted only in the heat of the battle— morally justify the creation of duties with Chapter 4's directed structure, requiring demandability involving first-personal thinking, but whose fulfilment does not serve any non-circular or directedness-independent interests or desires (including kind- based desires) of those to whom they are owed. We should be willing to see such social-conventional creation of directedness as sometimes justifiable morally on broadly consequentialist grounds—even if it thereby requires people to demand an action as 'done to them' when the action's justification is entirely distinct from any benefit to them or desire of theirs. Nonetheless, we can explain the rarity of such cases by the tension they create with the principle of self-respect outlined above. There is (defeasible) moral reason to avoid making duties directed in a way that creates this tension: to avoid making duties owed to parties who in demanding their fulfilment will have to engage in a self-focus that is inappropriate because the duties do not serve any independent interests or desires of such parties. This moral reason can be defeated on consequentialist grounds, but it explains the rarity of the cases in question

The two principal points to glean from this chapter are, first, that we can set up social or legal conventions to make any duty owed to someone addressable (including parties for whom we might *construct* addressability). One implication of this is that sometimes we will have strange cases in which moral reasons support making duties owed to someone that serve no direction-independent interests or desires of hers. And the second point is Section 5.2's claim, to be developed in Part II, that whether a duty is owed to someone as a *natural, recognition-independent* matter is much more limited or 'tethered': it turns entirely on whether and to what extent that party's good is the moral ground for the duty. We will see in Part II that this can vindicate a broadly 'naturalistic' conception of human rights, but we will also see in Part III that it greatly limits those property rights that are 'natural' or human rights, and indeed throws doubt on much property's status as a right. Before getting to this, we need a final chapter on the relation between directed duties and rights.

6

From Directed Duties to Rights

6.1 Separating Directed Duties from Rights

Despite their titles, Chapters 2–5 focused on directed duties rather than rights. Of course, as Section 2.1 maintains, rights are centrally composed of directed duties, so the titles are not misleading. In this chapter, I consider how exactly rights relate to directed duties, focusing first (Section 6.1) on directed duties as Hohfeldian claim-rights, before (Section 6.2) considering other Hohfeldian positions.

I have assumed that being *owed* a duty and being *wronged* by its violation stand and fall together, and that both are analysable by the Addressive account of direct-edness in Chapter 4, which sits alongside the complementary thesis that duties owed to a party are *ceteris paribus* demandable (by someone, not necessarily the party owed them) on behalf of the party to whom they are owed (Section 3.5), plus the complementary links to interests and desires outlined in Chapters 2 and 5.[1] What needs to be added to these features (my being owed a duty whose violation wrongs me) for me to hold a right? Practices like gratitude suggest that *something* needs to be added: recall (Section 2.1) that if you owe me a duty of gratitude, this duty will be directed to me, your ungratefulness will wrong me, but it is not clear that I therefore hold a right to your gratitude.

My suggestion is that the term 'right' becomes more or less appropriate depending on which and how strong are any additional powers, from Section 3.1's list, beyond demandability associated with the relevant duty: powers exercisable in appropriate circumstances either by oneself on one's own behalf or by others on one's behalf. These might be powers to enforce fulfilment of the duty, to demand or enforce

---

[1] In a recent article, Cornell challenges the assumption that being owed a duty and being wronged by its violation stand and fall together (Cornell 2015). For Cornell, (i) one's *holding a right to someone's PHI-ing* is equivalent to one's *being owed a duty that someone PHI*: both mark one as a party whose importance generates reasons (pre-violation) for an agent to PHI. By contrast for Cornell (ii) *being wronged by that person's not-PHI-ing* marks one as a party who can, in my terminology, complain post-violation on one's own behalf and potentially be owed compensation for the not-PHI-ing. Cornell supports this division by claiming that parents of a child killed by a drunk driver are wronged by the driver but neither hold a right here, nor are owed a duty by that driver. Similarly, he argues that overhearers who are harmed by relying on a lie they overhear are wronged by this but neither hold a right to the speaker's truthfulness nor are owed a duty with this content. I think we can resist Cornell's claims, partly by questioning Cornell's Razian assumption that rights and directed duties must be grounded by the importance of the party owed the duty (consider the rights protecting the prime minister and other offices discussed in Section 2.2), and partly by noting that even pre-violation, demands can sometimes be appropriately issued on behalf of the parents or the overhearer (rather than only on behalf of the child or the speaker's addressee). There is more to say in relation to Cornell's ingenious argument, but I leave this for another occasion.

compensation, to waive the duty or resent its violation, among others. I argued in Section 3.6 that any duty, whether directed or undirected, is demandable in appropriate circumstances, and that this is part of what distinguishes it as a *duty* rather than a non-duty reason. A *directed* duty is demandable, in appropriate circumstances, *on behalf of* the party to whom it is owed—either by that party herself or by someone else. My suggestion now is that the more additional powers are exercisable on behalf of the party to whom a duty is owed, the more apt it becomes to see the duty as her right.

In the gratitude case, the person owed the duty plausibly has powers to waive it in appropriate circumstances ('really, there's no need for you to thank me'), but not to enforce it or demand compensation for its violation. Resentment at its violation might sometimes be morally justifiable, and perhaps the person owed the duty has power to forgive it. Demanding its fulfilment seems to my mind always morally inappropriate when performed by the person to whom gratitude is owed, though third parties can demand its fulfilment on behalf of that person. By contrast, the directed duty not to torture someone is, although not waivable, accompanied by a range of stronger powers held both by the party to whom it is owed and by third parties: permissibly to call on extreme force to ensure it is respected, to demand and extract compensation for violation, as well as powers of resentment and forgiveness shared with the gratitude case.

I suggest that these varied powers underpin our hazy intuitions about whether the duty of gratitude counts as a right for the party to whom it is owed, and also underpin our non-hazy intuition that the duty not to torture counts as a right for the party to whom it is owed. The powers in the torture case permit major costs to be imposed on the duty-bearer via their exercise and this, I suggest, makes the directed duty its addressee's right. The powers in the gratitude case permit fewer costs to be imposed on the duty-bearer, and this leaves its status as a right hazy—even though it is clear that it is a directed duty. Note that this haziness is reflected in theorists' more general uncertainty about whether 'private' directed duties are rights: some claim that there are rights to one's romantic partner's fidelity, not to be lied to by one's friends, or to have one's views listened to by one's family.[2] Other theorists question the language of 'rights' in this context, but nobody denies that the parties in question are owed directed duties with the content in question. I would suggest that one reason why the language of 'rights' can seem inapt here is precisely because the 'private' character of the duties is partly constituted by the absence of strong powers—on the part of the person to whom the duty is owed, or on the part of third parties—to enforce the duty, to insist on compensation if it is violated, to demand a public justification explaining its violation, or to punish its violation. But there remains some attraction to referring to rights in these cases, and this I suggest reflects the scalar nature of the considerations that make it apt for us to refer to a directed duty as a right.

One might wonder whether enforcement has a special role here. For Wenar, *being owed a duty* and *being wronged* involve having one's role- or kind-based interests

---

[2] See Tasioulas 2012, pp. 40–1, for qualified support for the idea that one has a human right not to be personally betrayed; Gewirth 1982, p. 56 regards the right not to be lied to by one's friends as a human right, and Sen 1999, p. 229, says the same about a right to a say in family decisions.

served by the duty's fulfilment, while *holding a right* involves both being owed a duty and that duty's being enforceable in appropriate circumstances. Skorupski similarly makes enforceability central to rights and this is a common move, taken in a different way by 'rights externalists' like Darby, Geuss, or James: theorists who make *actual enforcement* (rather than *permissible enforceability*) a necessary condition on a duty's being a right.[3]

I think we should resist making either actual enforcement or permitted enforceability necessary for a directed duty's being someone's right. Why are theorists tempted to make enforcement so central to rights? Unlike the other activities listed in Section 3.1, enforcement in certain forms compels behaviour from the duty-bearer independently of her will. Waiving a duty, demanding its fulfilment, demanding compensation, or forgiving its violation and so on might alter or threaten to alter the reasons which the duty-bearer should heed; but whether the duty-bearer will heed them is left up to her. (Note that if demanding was requesting backed by *force*, then matters would be different; but I argued in Section 3.6 that force is not essential to demanding.) By contrast, enforcement can—although it need not always—involve making the duty-bearer behave in a certain way by overpowering or ignoring her will, e.g. if the police march her to prison.[4] Enforcement is thus, one might think, characteristic of the public realm of law and state action. For state action through policy, regulation, law, is action by the body that monopolizes the legitimate use of force, to paraphrase Weber. A power to enforce, when exercised by an individual in a state rather than a state of nature, therefore has to be conceived as a power to generate state actions or legal actions, rather than as a power to operate purely 'privately'. The other actions listed in Section 3.1—waiving, forgiving, demanding—can be performed privately even though they will often also take public, legal forms. If we place the preceding observation alongside the view that rights are a distinctively legal notion, then we can generate the thesis that what distinguishes duties correlated with rights from other duties is something to do with enforcement. And I think this is what is going on in the authors listed.[5]

But in my view matters are muddier than the neat 'rights as enforceable directed duties' thesis suggests. The thesis gains support from those 'private' duties that seem directed but that we hesitate to call 'rights' precisely because their enforcement (e.g. by the police, the judiciary, or other state bodies) seems inappropriate: duties of fidelity to one's partner or sibling, or duties of gratitude. Yet, as I noted before, it is not incoherent to refer to rights within private relationships, nor indeed to see the

---

[3] Geuss 2001, p. 144; James 2003; Darby 2004; Skorupski 2010, pp. 307–13; Wenar 2013, p. 214, n. 24.

[4] Enforcement does not always do this: it can involve coercion in which an effect is achieved *via* the duty-bearer's will. A stern letter from an official might qualify as enforcement even though it is simply the threat of imprisonment (outlined in that letter) that generates the action via the duty-bearer's will. But it seems characteristic to enforcement that it could, in certain cases, involve overpowering or ignoring the will of the person subject to force.

[5] Compare also the sharp Kantian distinction between the realms of right (involving coercively enforceable external action) and of virtue (involving the morality of the will). My Addressive analysis of directed duties in terms of when it would be virtuous to think first- or second-personally gives an account of right-qua-directedness in which virtue is central; I thereby 'bridge' or 'violate' this Kantian distinction. I would suggest that this is because directed duties (or indeed rights) need not always be enforceable: see main text.

very cases just mentioned as rights.[6] Nor, as Kramer has shown, is it incoherent for there to be firmly 'public' legal rights that are legally unenforceable.[7] We do better, then, to proceed with the looser thesis that enforceability is not necessary if a directed duty is to qualify as its addressee's right but is, rather, one among the range of possible powers exercisable on behalf of the person to whom the duty is owed which can make that duty qualify as its addressee's right. The more and the stronger are such powers exercisable on behalf of the person to whom the duty is owed, the more apt the language of rights becomes. The duty of gratitude is accompanied by comparatively few such powers, but because it formally requires first- and second-personal thinking in the manner outlined in Chapter 4, it is clearly a directed duty *owed to* the benefactor. But its status as the benefactor's right is hazy.

6.2 Rights Beyond Claims

In the previous section, I argued that when a duty is owed to someone, it becomes more appropriate to call it 'a right' the more powers (among those listed in Section 3.1) are permissibly exercisable in appropriate circumstances on behalf of the person to whom the duty is owed. But, as Hohfeld's framework shows, there are forms of right beyond that constituted by duties owed to one—beyond the Hohfeldian claim-right.[8] The Hohfeldian privilege is defined by its bearer's not owing a directed duty to someone else. Consider my privilege-right to use my property as I wish (within obvious limits). This is defined by my owing nobody a duty to use it in any particular way. The Hohfeldian power is defined as the ability to create or remove duties (directed or undirected), or the ability to create or remove further powers or immunities. Consider my power-right to give my property away as a gift, thereby placing myself under new duties not to use the item, and redirecting others' duties not to use it so that they are now owed to the gift's recipient. The Hohfeldian immunity is defined as another's inability to create or remove certain duties for me.[9]

Once we have an account of what it is for a duty to be owed to someone, that account can be deployed to make sense of the other positions on Hohfeld's framework, each of which is defined partly in terms of its relation to a directed duty.[10] This is one of the ways in which the Hohfeldian claim is 'primary'. Another, perhaps more fundamental way, as noted in Section 1.2, is that Hohfeldian privileges, powers, or immunities can only qualify as rights if their bearer is owed some directed duties. A being who was not wrongable would, I think, not have her Hohfeldian privileges, powers, or immunities aptly designated as rights; her relation to these positions would be akin to that of a third-party regulator rather than a right-holder.

A further way in which claim-rights are fundamental is that they are the only rights on Hohfeld's table which are violable. For example, bare Hoheldian privileges

---

[6] See references in note 2 above.   [7] Kramer 2001, pp. 74–8.
[8] Hohfeld 1964; see also my Cruft 2004, or Wellman 1995, or Wenar 2005b.
[9] Hohfeld 1964, pp. 38–64.
[10] So: I hold a Hohfeldian privilege vis-à-vis you to PHI iff you hold no claim against me that I not PHI; I hold a Hohfeldian power if, e.g. I hold the ability to make you duty-bound to me to PHI, etc. Note that Hohfeldian powers and immunities can involve control over *undirected* duties.

are constituted simply by the absence of directed duties, and hence are not violable or infringeable. Insofar as we talk of the violation or infringement of a privilege right (such as my right to walk on a beach), we are referring to violation or infringement of the Hohfeld claims protecting it (e.g. my claim that you not eject me from the beach), not the privilege itself (which in this case is simply my owing no duty to you to keep off the beach). Similarly, neither Hohfeldian powers nor immunities are violable or infringeable. If somebody stops you from giving a gift to someone else, they do not violate or infringe your Hohfeldian power to give gifts. For your having the power does not specify any action that someone else must or must not perform—only a Hohfeldian claim does that. You might well have a claim that people not prevent you giving gifts, and this claim would be violated or infringed in the case outlined. But you retain your Hohfeldian power: your ability to alter the normative situation by normatively transferring the trespassory duties previously owed to you with regard to the gift, so that they are now owed to somebody else.

It is more controversial to claim that immunities are not violable or infringeable. But consider a standard immunity, such as the right under the US constitution to freedom of religion. This legal right centrally involves a legal immunity, because it is centrally constituted by the fact that within US law the government cannot, *ceteris paribus*, alter or remove citizens' privileges to pursue or not pursue any particular religion—thus, for example they cannot place citizens under a duty to be Christian, say, or to attend specific religious services. Now suppose the government attempts to do this by introducing a law requiring US citizens to be practising Christians. Does this law, or the government introducing it, violate citizens' legal immunity to freedom of religion? As with Hohfeldian powers, Hohfeldian immunities specify no action which a party must or must not take—that is the job of Hohfeldian claims. So the best interpretation of the government's action here is as a violation of a claim not an immunity—perhaps a moral or perhaps a legal claim not to attempt to introduce the relevant law. With regard to the immunity, if the government's action turns out to be legally acceptable (and hence to create a genuine new duty of citizens to be Christians), then surprisingly it will turn out to have been the case that citizens did not hold a legal immunity to religious freedom as they thought they did in the first place. If the outcome—as is more likely—is that the government's actions fail to institute the purported new legal duty (perhaps it is struck down as unconstitutional), then the immunity will not have been violated or infringed because there will have been no legal change. A similar analysis would apply to any moral immunities, such as the fundamental human immunity from being sold into servitude. Any apparent violations or infringements either prove that there was no immunity in the first place, or else fail to constitute a genuine normative alteration—because the immunity makes such an alteration impossible.

In what follows, I will assume that all the standard positions on Hohfeld's table that are normally taken to be capable of being rights—namely, claims, privileges, powers, and immunities—can indeed be rights, but I will retain my focus on the Hohfeldian claim, the position whose possession makes one violable and that Section 6.1 tells us qualifies as a right if supported by enough powers of waiver, enforceability, etc. on the relevant party's behalf.

6.3 Conclusion of Part I

In Part I, I have offered a new Addressive Theory of directed duties, and hence of claim-rights. To understand this account fully one must note how it illuminates the truths and the problems in the earlier theories (the Interest, Kind-Desire, Will, Demand, and Hybrid theories). In Chapter 5, I claimed that my account entails the truths gleanable from the Interest and Desire theories: namely, that Raz's account is correct as a theory of *naturally* directed duties (see more discussion in Chapter 7), that all morally justified directed duties (whether natural or socially created) generate status interests and status desires in their own fulfilment, and that in most but not all cases morally justified directed duties (natural or socially created) serve the independent good, and independent kind-desires, of those to whom they are owed. And in Chapters 3–4, I showed how my theory illuminates and enhances the Will and Demand theories' insight that, as I would put it, all duties are in principle demandable, but directed duties are distinctively demandable *on behalf of the party to whom they are owed*. All these points are integrated by the Addressive account in which a duty's direction depends on form-driven requirements of virtue, requirements to conceive the duty-enjoined action first- or second-personally as to be 'done to me/you'.

In what follows, I use this Addressive account of the nature of rights to develop a new theory of *human rights* in which both natural and legal rights play centre stage (Part II). I start (in Chapter 7) by expanding on Section 5.2's claim that the requirements of relational first- and second-personal thinking which the Addressive Theory tells us are constitutive of a duty's direction are only naturally generated (as opposed to socially or legally constructed) when a party's good grounds the duty in question; the relevant first-/second-personal requirements then make the duty owed to the party whose good grounds it. This is a conception of natural rights independent of the idea of divine natural law in the natural rights tradition; rather, my conception of natural rights—as generated by the Addressive Theory—embraces the truth in both good-based and relational approaches (what might be seen in contemporary terms as the rival approaches of Raz and Darwall): the fact that natural rights are rights that exist naturally for the sake of the right-holder. I go on to defend the thesis that the modern 'human rights' concept is broadly continuous with this idea of natural rights. In particular, their nature as *duties grounded primarily by the right-holder's good—* and whose direction-constituting relational requirements are thereby grounded primarily by the right-holder's good—is one of the defining features of *human rights*. Many legal and politically created norms implement and uphold such duties, and I explain why (and when) many of these norms can also be called 'human rights'. I shall argue that the resulting naturalistic—as opposed to 'political'[11]—conception of human rights is a broadly vindicating one: we can see our use of the rights concept in relation to human rights as playing a justifiable role in our thinking, a role justified as a way of signalling that human rights mark duties whose ground can be traced ultimately to the good of the individual to whom the duties are owed. This is an

---

[11] See the debate examined exhaustively in Etinson 2018; see also my discussion and references at the opening of Chapter 8, this volume; for one broad way in which my account of human rights is 'political', see this volume, Chapter 10.

individual's good that succeeds in generating duties without needing to be aggregated with others' goods in order to do this (although we will see that the degree to which a duty is grounded in an individual's good is a scalar matter). The rights concept, with its relational requirements of connected, unalienated first- and second-personal thinking bringing together agent and party-acted-on, is justifiable as enabling us to comprehend the nature of duties morally grounded in this way; the rights concept is also an appropriate way of distinguishing legal and socially created structures protecting such duties.

In Part III, I then use the Addressive Theory to develop a new account of those socially created rights—such as rights of office and property rights—that are not justified primarily by the right-holder's good but rather by the common good and further values. While much of this use of rights language can be justified as valuably serving important ends, it turns out that many property rights—those that are justifiable only by how as a system they serve the common good—emerge as an outlier whose status as an individual right should be questioned, because the use of the individual rights concept here is potentially misleading rather than useful.

Rights thinking, it will turn out, can be vindicated in many of the contexts in which we find it, including in what is sometimes disparaged as the 'proliferating' realm of *human rights*; but its pervasive role in property thinking is problematic.

PART II

Human Rights for the Right-Holder's Sake

7

Teleological Groundings of Rights and Duties

7.1 Introduction to Part II: Human Rights as 'Rights for the Right-holder's Sake' which are 'Everyone's Business'

The phrase 'human rights' can be used to refer to all rights humans hold—from someone's basic moral right to life, or to political participation, to their right to their spouse's fidelity, to their legally constituted right to be notified of building works on properties adjacent to their own, to their game-constituted right to a penalty when fouled in football. But I will follow standard usage in taking 'human rights' to refer to an important *subset* of our morally justified rights, a subset reflected in international human rights law, in many aspects of constitutional law, and in bills of rights such as the Universal Declaration of Human Rights or the French 'Declaration of the Rights of Man and the Citizen'.[1]

These are normally taken as the rights humans hold *in virtue of being human*. Whether this means rights distinctive to humans alone, or whether instead it means rights held by humans among others, is a matter for debate.[2] But if humans hold some rights simply in virtue of their humanity, then it seems that these rights exist even when they go unrecognized, unrespected, and unlegalized—unless being human in the relevant sense is itself a property that depends on recognition, respect, or legalization. In my view, a full theory of human rights requires a theory of the human or, perhaps, of the person. Many theorists offer this, but I will not do so.[3] Instead, Part II of the book focuses on two formal features of human rights that are often overlooked: human rights are (i) rights that are morally grounded primarily 'for the right-holder's sake' (or that give legal, conventional, or institutional form to rights so grounded) and (ii) rights that are 'everyone's business' in the sense of being rights that anyone anywhere can, *ceteris paribus*, permissibly demand on behalf of the right-holder. I argue for the thesis that much of what is morally distinct about human

---

[1] Note that (unlike Moyn 2012) I do not see human rights as a concept that was distinctively shaped in the 1970s, nor (like Nickel 2007) do I see the post-war declarations as distinctive; instead I share with Griffin 2008 and Simmons 2015 the view that the human rights notion is continuous with earlier bills of natural rights.

[2] See, e.g. Gardner 2008. See also this volume, Section 10.1.

[3] See, e.g. Gewirth 1982, Griffin 2008, Nussbaum 2011. I return to the importance of a theory of the human in Chapter 9 and again at Section 10.6.

rights turns on these two formal features—including much about the relation between legal and pre-legal or recognition-independent natural human rights, and much about human rights' public political role.

First, in Chapters 7–8, I argue that—as prefigured in Section 5.2—a right's metaphysical status as recognition-independent or natural entails and is entailed by its existing for the right-holder's sake. It is worth highlighting (as stressed in Section 1.3) that 'natural rights' in my usage here need not depend on divine creation, nor be rights that would obtain even in some asocial 'state of nature'; they are, rather, rights whose existence—as duties taking the directed character of rights—is independent of whether anyone recognizes that they exist. This recognition-independence entails and is entailed by a right's existing for its holder's sake, I argue. Yet I also show (Chapter 9) that legal and conventional rights whose *existence* is independent of their moral justification, and whose creation and maintenance is (in most cases) *morally justifiable* only by the good of many beyond the individual right-holder, can nonetheless give legal, conventional, or institutional form to their natural right cousins, where the latter exist for the right-holder's sake.[4] I argue that when creating and sustaining law that institutionalizes natural rights, the naturally directed structure of the rights that are to be institutionalized gives us a strong reason to make the relevant legal structures similarly directed or rights-type in form—rather than creating and sustaining them simply as undirected legal duties. Without natural *rights* to institutionalize, we would have significantly less reason to constitute human rights law in a rights-type way. Particularly practically important natural rights to institutionalize, I will argue (Section 9.4), are the natural—i.e. recognition-independent—rights that people in the modern world hold against their states.

In Chapter 10, I argue that not all rights with the moral importance encapsulated by condition (i) (natural rights grounded for the right-holder's sake, or legal-conventional rights giving the latter institutional form) qualify as human rights: human rights must also be 'everyone's business'. I argue that this rather broad condition captures the truth in the recently popular narrower 'political' views of human rights, views which in different ways define human rights as the international community's business.[5] I shall defend the idea that human rights are distinctively public, but I reject narrow conceptions of this 'political' condition. In my view, human rights are the proper business of every human. The aim, by the end of Part II of the book, is to demonstrate the insights we can generate by characterizing human rights' distinctiveness in terms of conditions (i) and (ii), and hence as continuous with the natural rights tradition.

One conclusion will be that the values served by human rights as an idea and as a set of institutions are justifiably characterized with the rights concept: thinking of certain fundamental human values as human *rights* is justifiable, given the kind of values they are, namely (i) individuals' goods that work largely on their own to ground duties, which are (ii) everyone's business. My defence of the human rights

---

[4] For criticism of a 'mirroring' picture of the relation between human rights and law, see Buchanan 2013. This issue is discussed in detail in this volume, Chapter 9, where I defend the view that human rights law (and related branches of law) institutionalizes pre-legal natural human rights.

[5] See, e.g. Rawls 1999, Beitz 2009, Raz 2010.

concept as intellectually respectable—as *appropriately* focusing attention on individual right-holders in relation to certain fundamental values—has an important limitation: I do not provide a full defence against the kind of communitarian who would deny that any individual's good can be important enough in itself to work largely on its own to generate duties in others (see Section 8.3). In addition, my defence of the human rights concept should not be mistaken for a defence of the ideological (mis)uses to which it is put in contemporary politics (e.g. as a reason for military intervention aimed at 'regime change'); I return to this point in the concluding Chapter 15. Before then, in Part III, I turn to rights that are morally justified, but that cannot be justified by how they serve the right-holder, nor give legal or conventional form to rights that can: hence, rights that cannot qualify either as human rights or as recognition-independent or natural.

Part II's contention (in thesis (i)) that at the core of the idea of human rights is the idea of *rights justifiable primarily by what they do for the right-holder* might seem discontinuous with, or perhaps even inconsistent with, the Addressive conception of rights developed in Chapter 4 of Part I. This tension or discontinuity might seem to upset the Razian account of natural directedness mentioned in Section 5.2 and developed later in the current chapter. What is this tension? It is, at first glance, historical-bibliographical: my Addressive view of rights has some affinity with Fichte's view of the foundation of natural rights in first- and second-personal apprehension, Forst's view of all rights as grounded in a right to justification, Darwall's view of directed (or, as he calls them 'bipolar') duties as one species of authority-implicating 'second-personal reason', and perhaps more loosely with Kant's and Kantian conceptions of our rights as a matter of non-dominating social relationships.[6] Such authors tend to oppose teleological approaches on which rights are grounded on goods (see, e.g. Darwall's sharp dichotomy between second-personal reasons and reasons of well-being). Instead, they place a single foundational right, for example the right to non-domination (Fichte, Ripstein's Kant, Zylberman) or to justification (Forst), at the heart of their theories.[7] But a teleological approach is, I will show, central to my distinction between rights which exist primarily for their holder's sake and those which exist for the sake of others beyond the right-holder, and I have already mentioned (Section 5.2) that a certain kind of teleological grounding is, in my view, *required* for duties that *naturally* take a directed form.[8] Now, there seems no need for an Addressive account of the *nature* of rights to require a non-teleological nor a monist conception of their *grounds*. One of my aims is to show—contra Fichte, Forst, Darwall, or Ripstein's Kant—that this is correct: an Addressive conception of the nature of rights fits neatly with a pluralist, teleological conception of their grounds. The Fichte/Forst/Ripstein/Darwall account drives too sharp a wedge between rights and values, failing to give the diversity of goods (e.g. well-being, needs, freedom, beauty, wisdom) their proper non-derivative place at the

---

[6] Kant 1996 [1797], Fichte 2000 [1796–7], Ripstein 2009, Darwall 2012, Forst 2012, Zylberman 2016a.
[7] See references in note 6.
[8] Note that I have already (at the end of Section 5.1) said that this teleological grounding is not *instrumental*. For more discussion, see Sections 7.4–7.6.

heart of our rights. Their account also errs in taking certain core rights as basic—as rights which cannot be grounded by values.

Nonetheless, the teleological view to be defended in the current chapter diverges in two significant ways from the simple theses that what is good is determined entirely independently of what is right, and that such a right-independent good itself then determines what is right.[9] First, my teleological account of the grounds of rights and duties is independent of the claim that the good is metaphysically prior to the right. The defining commitment of my teleological account is simply that we avoid invoking any basic premise to the effect that certain deontic entities (reasons, duties, rights) exist. Such entities require explanation, and on my account their existence—at least when they are natural rather than legal or conventional entities—is explained by their relation to goods, as when the good of helping someone makes me duty-bound to do so. But such explanations might be compatible with and perhaps even more accurately redescribable in terms other than the good.[10] Furthermore, I intend my approach to be compatible with 'reverse' explanations in which the nature or existence of a value is entailed by the nature or existence of some reasons, duties, or rights. For what it is worth, my own uncertain hunch is that there is some metaphysical priority to the evaluative over the deontic, and that this makes most such reverse explanations fail as grounding explanations. But a proper defence of this would require a different book, and I hope to avoid relying on it in what follows. My aim will simply be to show how we can explain duties and rights in terms of the good rather than having to assume as a starting assumption that some duties and rights exist.

The second way in which my claim about goods grounding reasons, duties, or rights diverges from a traditional teleological picture is that in my view, when an action's goodness grounds a *directed duty* to perform it or a *right* to its performance, as opposed to merely a non-duty *reason* or *undirected duty* to perform it, the existence of the directed duty or right thereby gives the action's goodness a further distinctive character it would not otherwise have: it possesses what I will call a 'deontically-infused' goodness. I explain this in Section 7.3.

In Sections 7.2–7.6, I develop my account of the teleological grounding of duties and rights. This will then be used in Chapter 8 to underpin the distinction between rights that exist primarily for the right-holder's sake and rights which exist primarily for the sake of others beyond the right-holder. I go on to show how *human rights* are best conceived as among those which either *exist* primarily for the holder's sake (natural human rights) or are justifiable as giving institutional form to such natural human rights (legal and conventional human rights). The way in which the former is

---

[9] This proto-consequentialist assumption is, I venture, evident in Raz 1986, and in a sense in Gould 1988 (in which freedom and participation are the rights-independent goods that determine our human rights), in Griffin 2008 (evident especially in his idea of a 'threshold' of normative agency to which one has rights—see Griffin 2010, pp. 747–8), in Nussbaum 2011, and perhaps in the grounding place for interests in Beitz 2009; compare also the role of a good life in Liao 2015, or the role of needs in Miller 2007 and Renzo 2015. I realize these are controversial interpretive claims which I cannot say more to defend here.

[10] I have in mind here Kantian groundings for deontic entities, including, e.g. Engstrom's sophisticated cognitivism (Engstrom 2009; see also Kant 1997 [1785]).

a *teleological but non-instrumental* view of the grounds of human rights, while the latter is instrumental, is outlined.

7.2 Duties Grounded in Goods

It will be helpful to start, rather artificially, with undirected duties whose contents do not affect humans. For example, suppose one has the opportunity to destroy an uninhabited planet in a distant galaxy. Or suppose one has the opportunity to disfigure a beautiful rock formation in a forest glade, a formation that will in any case crumble to dust soon, before anyone else has a chance to see it. The artificiality of the examples reflects the fact—noted in Section 2.1—that it should be controversial whether there are any genuinely undirected duties.

Nonetheless it seems to me that in the cases outlined, the value or good at stake in the opportunities presented generates or constitutes a *duty* for the agent. I endorse the standard view that this means that, say, the beauty of the rock formation does not simply give the agent a defeasible *reason* not to disfigure it, a reason engagement with which is optional for the agent. Rather, the beauty of the rock formation constitutes a *categorical* reason for the agent, a reason with which the agent *must* engage (at least minimally and implicitly) whatever her particular concerns. Furthermore, this reason *excludes, silences or in principle outweighs* some potential countervailing reasons.[11] Fulfilment of this reason is in principle *demandable* by those suitably placed (though because the duty is undirected, any demands issued are not made on behalf of someone to whom the duty is owed). And failure to respect it would, *ceteris paribus*, trigger some 'secondary' or 'remainder' duties and reasons, for example to feel regret or to make amends.[12] Duties, whether directed or undirected, in my view just are categorical, exclusionary-or-weighty reasons that are demandable and whose non-fulfilment can trigger 'remainders'.[13]

Now in the cases in question, the value or goodness of the planet on the one hand, or the beautiful rock formation on the other, places the agent under duties. Because a certain action—or in these cases inaction—by the agent constitutes a contribution to or respect for a non-optional good, and this (in)action is (*ceteris paribus*) demandable and remainder-triggering, the agent is duty-bound to engage in the relevant action (inaction). This idea that an action's goodness can make one duty-bound to pursue it is the core of a teleological account of duties and rights.

Some goods can be non-optional yet seemingly fail to ground duties. For example, suppose I could delay the crumbling of the rock formation for half an hour by working hard to move some stones out of the way. It is not clear I have a duty to do

---

[11] For the idea of exclusionary reasons, see Raz 1975, ch. 1; for reasons that silence, see McDowell 1998, pp. 91–3. Raz's idea of exclusionary reasons has spawned a large literature; I will not engage with this or choose between the available options; something like excluding, silencing, or simply in-principle outweighing is sufficient to distinguish the kind of reason (see also the idea of certain reasons as 'non-maximizing' constraints (Kagan 1998, p. 72; Cruft 2004, pp. 352–5) or as marking discontinuities in value (Griffin 1986, pp. 85–9)).

[12] For the idea that duties to apologize or make amends need not be owed to anyone in particular (though they often are!), see Section 3.5.

[13] See Section 3.6.

this. The formation's beauty gives me a duty not gratuitously to destroy it, and I think it gives me a reason to preserve it, but given its relative place among other values (as determined, among other things, by the fact that nobody else will see the formation), it is doubtful that it gives me a *duty* to put in the work to preserve it for an extra half hour. The reason it gives me to preserve it is categorical, binding on me whatever my concerns, but it is not (or perhaps only minimally) exclusionary or weighty: the countervailing importance of the burdensomeness to me of moving the stones can weigh against, and indeed outweigh, my reason to preserve it. Its lowly place among other values makes demanding the relevant preservatory action impermissible, and means that non-performance of the relevant action requires no regret or other remainder.

What seems to be going on here is a claim about the relative *importance* of the good in question: it is important enough to generate some duties but not others. The question of what makes a good important enough to generate a duty rather than a reason, and in what circumstances, might seem irritatingly inaccessible. Tasioulas writes—focusing on how interests generate duties correlative with *human rights*— about the relevant threshold of importance:

> It is doubtful [...] that there is a great deal that can be helpfully said, at the abstract level at which philosophers customarily operate, about the threshold at which [...] interests give rise to duties to deliver the objects of putative rights. As we should expect, philosophy is best confined to articulating the variety of considerations that bear on the question of the threshold and the relations among them, rather than striving to offer a litmus test that would enable us to dispense with any resort to contestable judgements. Moreover, we should acknowledge that at the level of pure moral reasoning, there may be ineliminable indeterminacy in the deontic content of any given right, even one we are confident exists, so that the formulation of a practically workable standard will require us to supplement such reasoning with positive legal norms or social conventions.[14]

This indeterminacy in the relationship between something's being good and its being a matter of duty might seem very worrying for the teleological account: when is a good important enough, relative to countervailing considerations, to generate a duty? How can I be sure that what I take to be mere non-categorical, non-exclusionary, undemandable reasons are not duties? There are three reasons not to be disturbed by this.

First, although a reason's categoricality (or a good's optionality) is a binary matter (a reason either is or is not categorical; engagement with a good either is or is not optional), its exclusionariness, overiddingness, or silencing quality is a matter of degree, as is its demandability and its triggering of 'remainders'. Some reasons exclude many more countervailing considerations than others; some reason-enjoined actions are permissibly demandable more frequently, by more people, or by demands imposing greater costs on the demandee, than others (see Section 6.1); and non-performance of some reason-enjoined actions triggers more duties of regret and recompense than others (again see Section 6.1). In my view, the more exclusionary,

---

[14]   Tasioulas 2015, p. 57.

demandable, and remainder-triggering a categorical reason is, the more apt it is for the label, 'duty'. But this of course means that whether a good teleologically generates a duty will similarly be a matter of degree: a non-optional good which gives an agent reason to pursue it, reason which excludes some but only a few countervailing reasons, and which possesses minimal demandability and remainder-triggering (perhaps merely permitting requests for explanation of non-fulfillment, and requiring mere minimal regret), will generate something whose status as a duty is vague, and not in a purely epistemic sense. I would suggest that the good of my preserving the rock formation can be like this: given an appropriately 'medium' level of natural beauty encapsulated in the formation, the question of whether my reason to move the stones in order to preserve it for an extra half hour is a duty will be vague because it will exclude or silence a wide but not enormous range of countervailing considerations, and it will be demandable and remainder-triggering but only in minimal ways—and that vague answer seems the right one in this case.

A second reason to be unworried by the indeterminacy in the grounding of duties in values or goods arises from how 'grounding' in my approach does not mark strong metaphysical priority for the good. My view is that the specific way in which anything which is good is good determines its deontic role in relation to the other reasons, duties, and rights springing from further—including countervailing—goods. Hence the indeterminacy lies not in the relation *between* on the one hand a fully determined good and on the other an incompletely determined deontic entity (an entity on the borderline between reason and duty) which the fully determined good grounds. Rather, the indeterminacy really concerns the nature of the particular good, conceived as in part a matter of its deontic implications. That is, in asking how *important* the rock formation's beauty is, we are not asking for something that can be settled separately and prior to settling the precise circumstances in which we have a reason or a duty to preserve it.

Third, it is not clear that what we have is indeterminacy as opposed to epistemic inaccessibility. There seems no algorithm that can be applied to tell us whether and when exactly a good's importance constitutes a duty to preserve it as opposed to a mere reason, or a duty to do something else. But this is not to say that there is no determinate answer to these questions; they are simply difficult questions that we can only approach with judgement.[15]

These points might still seem disturbing. But I think they are true to the phenomena. In certain circumstances, some goods just do generate or constitute reasons to do certain things; in other circumstances, they generate or constitute duties; and I will argue below (building on the claims in Part I) that in other circumstances still, certain goods generate or constitute rights. To talk of their 'importance' is to talk of their specific deontic generative capacity across different circumstances. Epistemic access to this is often difficult, but that seems to be the way things are—and of course it is

---

[15] Compare neo-Aristotelian debates about the non-algorithmic nature of moral judgement (e.g. O'Neill 1996, chs 1–2).

also often not difficult: it is very clear that in normal circumstances, the good of life presents duties not to kill.[16]

Before shifting to directed duties and rights, I draw attention to the components of my account of duty, and to the non-instrumental character of my teleological account. First, the components of a duty. Does the fact that a reason is categorical *make it* weighty, exclusionary, or silencing, *make it* demandable (*ceteris paribus*) by someone, and *make it* trigger a remainder (*ceteris paribus*) if unheeded? No, as shown by the example of the categorical reason to put in work to preserve the rock formation for an extra half hour. But categoricality is *necessary* for demandability and the triggering of moral remainders. It would be an odd moral system that permitted parties to demand actions enjoined by reasons which, as non-categorical, their bearers were permitted to ignore; it would equally be an odd moral system that subjected agents to compulsory 'remainders' for non-respect for optional, non-categorical reasons. Requests for an agent to explain her non-engagement with non-categorical reasons might be permissible, but not requests with the illocutionary force of a demand. Similarly feelings of regret might be permissible at the non-fulfilment of non-categorical reasons, but surely not required. I am tempted, how-ever, by the further thesis that categorical reasons that are also weighty, exclusionary, or silencing to some degree will be to that degree demandable and remainder-triggering. This thesis—which I offer as a conjecture to be defended on another occasion—maintains that a reason's *weight* relative to other reasons, including any exclusionary or silencing effects it has, in combination with its *categoricality*, together make demanding sometimes permitted and remainders sometimes required.

It is notable that the grounding of duties on the good, in the manner I have sketched, is not instrumental. On my account, the duty not to destroy the rock formation does not owe its existence to its usefulness as a means—in the way that a traffic light might specifically have been created because of its usefulness in prevent-ing accidents. This is not simply a consequence of my attempt to avoid an account which gives metaphysical priority to the good. Even on a strong teleological account which gave the good (of the beautiful rock formation) metaphysical priority over the duty (not to destroy it), the duty would not exist *because* it was going to be useful for securing the good. For even such a strong account would make me duty-bound not to destroy the formation *whether or not I was going to respect the duty*. Something's value can make me duty-bound to respect it even if I am the sort of perverse person who is more likely to damage it if I think I am subject to a duty to respect it. Putting this in general terms, someone P's duty to PHI does not come into existence because it would be good if a *duty requiring P to PHI* existed; instead, P's duty to PHI comes into existence because it would be good if *P were to PHI*.[17] Or at least, this is the general form of the teleological grounding of *recognition-independent* duties: the (appropriate type of) value of an option I could pursue makes me duty-bound to

---

[16] Note that my talk of access to deontic entities need not be read in a realist way. The entities might be quasi-real or have some different metaphysics.

[17] This is the truth in the 'instrumental' label for teleological approaches. But note that the duties-to-PHI are not themselves *means* to the occurrence of PHI, and the goodness of PHI-ing itself need not (though might) be its goodness as a means. See the further discussion at Sections 7.4–7.7.

pursue it. Matters are different for recognition-dependent, created duties (e.g. legal duties), because their existence is itself an option I could pursue (i.e. I could decide to create such duties, to respect or dismantle those I encounter). But teleological grounds for recognition-independent or natural duties cannot be instrumental. Such grounds make me duty-bound to PHI because of the value of my PHI-ing, not because of the value of my duty to PHI. I return to this crucial point in Sections 7.4–7.7.

A final note before turning to rights. Sometimes a set of duties borne by a plurality of people can be grounded, in my sense, in a single good. For example, if two of us find the rock formation and can through joint action preserve it long enough for our third fellow to arrive and see it, then we might as a duo be duty-bound to do so, with each of us duty-bound to play a particular part in preserving the formation. In this sort of case, whether I am duty-bound to do my part will depend on whether you do your part. It is not that we decide to *create* the duty as a pair—as we would if we were legislators creating a new law for ourselves—but rather the jointly held duty is generated naturally by the value of the rock formation, and this joint duty in turn generates specific duties for each party dependent on whether the other party does their bit.[18]

7.3 Natural Rights Grounded in Deontically Infused Goods?

If Raz, Kramer, Steiner, Sreenivasan, or Wenar were correct about the nature of directed duties and rights, then the next five sections (taking us almost to the end of this chapter) could be just one very short one: it would simply say that when duties, grounded by goods in one of the manners outlined in Section 7.2, bear an appropriate relation to someone's interests, desires, or powers (they are grounded by her interests (Raz), place her in a position that would necessarily serve the interests of the typical person so placed (Kramer), are governed by waiver powers of hers (Steiner) or governed by a level of control grounded in her interests (Sreenivasan), or necessarily serve her role- or kind-based desires (Wenar)), then these duties are directed duties that potentially (see Section 6.1) correlate with rights. Nothing more need be said about the teleological grounding of rights.[19]

But Part I tells us that more must be said. As suggested by the discussion of Nussbaum in Section 5.1, one might wonder whether *directed* duties or *rights*—duties with the Addressive form outlined in Chapter 4, requiring first-personal and second-personal conception of the duty-enjoined action as to be done by 'me' to 'you' and vice versa—are really groundable by a teleological account. There might be an instrumental case for sometimes creating legal and conventional structures with this rights-type, directed form, and I discuss this in Section 7.7. But, first, does a teleological account ground recognition-independent, natural types of this form? What kind of goods naturally require directed, rights-style duties?

---

[18] See Gardner 2002.
[19] See Chapters 2 and 3 for analysis of the advantages and shortcomings of the theories listed.

Before—in Section 7.6—filling out the Razian answer to this question already sketched in Section 5.2, it is instructive in the preceding sections to pursue three mistaken answers that take us close. One, discussed in the current section, observes that protection by rights seems essential to the character of certain goods. For example, it can seem attractive to say that a person cannot realize the good of *independence* simply by being left alone to make their own choices, following an effective autonomy-enhancing upbringing and education; instead, independence requires that the person be unimpeded *as a matter of right*. Being unimpeded by chance, or even being unimpeded on the basis of undirected duties or duties owed to others (perhaps I let you make your own choices because I owe it to your boss to do this), is not enough for independence for you. True independence requires being unimpeded by others on the basis of your own right.[20] This might seem plausible whatever one's analysis of rights: either my Addressive account or one of the rivals discussed in Part I.

Similarly, it can seem attractive to say that the distinctively human good of *human life* which grounds a person's right to life is again a rights-infused value: it is not the bare, rights-independent good of continued living, but the more specific goods of not being killed unjustly, not being left gratuitously to die in a way that violates a duty owed to one, and so on: not dying in a way that involves one's rights being violated. Again, this claim might seem plausible whatever one's analysis of rights.

Generalizing from these cases, a teleological theorist might try to explain why certain goods require *rights or directed duties*, as opposed simply to reasons and duties *simpliciter*, by observing that rights or directed duties seem essential to the goods that ground them: as noted, such rights and directed duties are essential to the goods of independence and life, when construed in the manner outlined above.

This approach fails for two reasons. It correctly notes that certain important goods, such as independence and life, can be conceived in ways which presuppose the idea of specific rights or directed duties and hence are what I shall call 'deontically infused'.[21] But appealing to deontically infused goods as teleological grounds of rights or directed duties is viciously circular: the characterization of the goods themselves already assumes that the relevant rights or directed duties exist. That is, grounding rights as required by the rights-infused nature of the values which ground them is, on closer inspection, a return to the idea in Fichte, Forst, Kant, and Ripstein that some rights are basic, separate from any good-based grounding.[22] It thereby violates my weak teleological requirement: that any rights' and directed duties' existence be explainable rather than presupposed.

Furthermore, the approach also wrongly assumes that a teleological explanation of a given right must ground it on some good which respect for that right *guarantees*, and which violation or infringement of that right *necessarily destroys*. Now respect for someone's right to life does not guarantee that that person will continue living, for

---

[20] Ideas of this sort can be found in Ripstein 2009, esp. pp. 34–5, and in Zylberman 2016a.

[21] I should use the term 'dikaiologically infused', following Thompson's 2004 characterization of directed duties as 'dikaiological' where undirected duties are merely 'deontological'. But this term has not caught on.

[22] See note 6 above, and accompanying main text.

some natural disaster or disease might kill them even though their right is respected; similarly, violation of that person's right to life necessarily involves something like killing them, or gratuitously leaving them to die, rather than failing to make some enormous, supererogatory sacrifice to save them. Therefore, *the person's continued life* is as such not a good that respect for that person's right to life guarantees, nor a good that violation of their right to life necessarily destroys.[23] Rather, something like 'life insofar as the person is entitled to it' or, most obviously and circularly, 'life as protected by the person's right to life', looks like the good which respect for their right to life guarantees. More generally, respect for one's human rights overall need not guarantee one a good life, nor need violation of these rights condemn one to an unsatisfactory life.[24] But if we think that teleological grounding for a right on a good must guarantee the good which grounds it, then this phenomenon will be hard to explain—and we will be driven to the circular argument sketched two paragraphs above and then rejected.

My favoured conception of teleological grounding does not work in this guaranteeing way. The relation between a duty and a good—as explained in Section 7.2—is not that respect for the duty *guarantees* the good that grounds it, nor that any violation or infringement of the duty *must necessarily* destroy the relevant good. So, for example, my refraining from destroying the rock formation does not guarantee that an unexpected volcanic eruption will not emerge to destroy it; similarly, my violative destruction of it leaves open the possibility that a bizarrely benign eruption will overturn my destructive activities, restoring the beautiful formation. Indeed on my teleological account, a right or duty need not even be *promotive* of some result for the results' goodness to ground that right or duty. Rather, in my style of teleological grounding of a given duty to PHI, PHI-ing's *aptness* to the good in question is *reflective* of the nature of the good in question—but PHI-ing need not guarantee the relevant good. Sometimes it will, and often it will *promote* the good without *guaranteeing* it. But sometimes PHI-ing will merely *respect* or partially *instantiate* the good in question without promoting it. To say that PHI-ing must promote or guarantee the good which grounds a duty to PHI is, I think, only a temptation if one is drawn to an excessively instrumental conception of teleological grounding.

Before looking (in the next two sections) at two alternative mistaken accounts of the way certain goods ground rights and directed duties, I say a little more to explain why and how values get deontically infused. This happens because of the general status interest, mentioned in Sections 2.4 and 5.3, in respect for any morally justified natural or conventional duties owed to one.[25] This interest is created by one's status as permitted (*ceteris paribus*) to demand one's rights (or duties owed to one) on one's own behalf (or for others to do this on one's behalf), and as owed any 'remainder'

---

[23] The latter clause might be doubted, but I would argue that, for example, being shot and buried alive violates one's right to life even if one manages to survive the attack. An instance of this from the Second World War is self-described in 'A Man's Story' in the oral histories in Alexievich 2016, pp. 298–302.

[24] See Cruft 2015.

[25] A similar point can be made about the effect of the kind-based status desire that, *qua party owed a duty*, the relevant duty be fulfilled. See Section 5.3.

duties. As a result of this interest, any good guaranteed by a morally justified duty owed to one, or a morally justified right of one's own—whatever the ground for the existence of this duty or right—is a good in which one has an interest qua right-holder. This status interest gives a special character to the goods respect for which is *guaranteed* by one's morally justified rights (and indeed by duties owed to one): homing in on these goods involves isolating goods whose character is determined partially by the fact that one has a right to them or is owed them by directed duty. Given the status interest in having one's morally justified rights and duties owed to one respected, goods so characterized gain a special character from this right-generated or direction-generated interest.

But as noted earlier, such deontically infused goods—goods an attack on which is necessarily an attack on one's deontic status—cannot, on pain of circularity, themselves ground the rights or directed duties with which they are infused. Rather, we still need to make sense of what sort of *non-deontically-infused goods* teleologically ground rights and directed duties, rights and directed duties which then go on to generate deontically infused goods.

7.4 Natural Rights Grounded in their Own Non-Instrumental Value?

An alternative but related approach might focus not on the deontically infused goods rights protect for the right-holder—such as the good of 'life as protected by rights' or 'independence as constituted by respect for rights'—but instead on the bare non-instrumental value of the rights themselves: the value that the existence of directed structures and rights brings to the right-holder and to the world independently of its relation to other goods such as life or freedom.

Kamm characterizes this non-instrumental value of rights in terms of the value of a status of inviolability:

[T]here may be a type of good that already exists but that would not exist if it were permissible to transgress the right of one person in order to save many lives. This is the good of being someone whose worth is such that it makes him highly inviolable and also makes him someone to whom one owes nonviolation. This good does imply that certain of one's interests should not be sacrificed, but inviolability matters not merely because it instrumentally serves those interests. [...] Inviolability is a reflection of the worth the person.[26]

Nagel follows Kamm:

What actually happens to us is not the only thing we care about: What *may* be done to us is also important, quite apart from whether or not it *is* done to us.[27]

Kamm and Nagel understand inviolability as a normative requirement that must sometimes be fulfilled even if that means failing to minimize violations of that very type of requirement. For example, my inviolability means that you cannot kill me to

---

[26] Kamm 2007, pp. 253–4.   [27] Nagel 2002, p. 38.

prevent three people from suffering similar killings.[28] Now, my arguments in Part I should lead us to observe that inviolability in this sense can be secured for an individual *without their possessing rights or being owed duties*: others could simply hold *undirected* duties not to kill me to prevent three similar killings, or they could owe all such duties to god as the right-holder, for example.

But we might develop an alternative version of Kamm's and Nagel's idea focused not on the value of *inviolability* independently of its effects, but on the similar non-instrumental value of the *directedness* at the heart of rights: that is, the non-instrumental value of directedness as captured by my Addressive account.

Imagine that there were no rights or directed duties, that all duties were undirected, as in Feinberg's 'Nowheresville'.[29] Recall my Addressive account of duties' direction in Chapter 4: a person in the imagined directed-duty-free scenario would go through life never being required by the *form* of her duties to think of her actions as to be performed on another conceived second-personally as a potential 'you' (and hence would go through life never required in this formal way so to conceive them for full practical virtue). Nor would she be required by the form of others' duties to conceive their dutiful actions first-personally as to be done 'to me'.

Now the person in this world might be subject to undirected duties which, as a matter of *content*, ask for actions whose successful performance requires conceiving another second-personally. For example, she (P) might have an undirected duty to let someone Q know that a mutual acquaintance R requires help. Successful performance of this undirected duty will require that P conceive the recipient of the communication (Q) as an addressable 'you'. Such a conception is part of what distinguishes (both attempted and successful) communication from simply speaking in front of someone without communicating to them. But in the example P will not be required to conceive the party whose good or welfare underpins the duty (i.e. the acquaintance in need: R) as 'you, on whom I act', nor will this party (R) be required to conceive the duty-bearer's action first-personally as doing something to (helping, putting in a good word for, taking up the case of) 'me'. If the duty here were directed to R, then Chapter 4 tells us that its form would require this. But in this scenario without directed duties, no duty's form can require this.[30]

I suggested at the end of Section 4.6 that the person in a world without directed duties would be alienated in a certain way from her fellows. Even though actions of hers motivated by duty might need to be addressed to other 'yous' (as in the case above), and she might take herself as an 'I' receiving duty-enjoined communication from others, the *form* of her own or someone else's duty will not be what requires this. Hence, as Chapter 4 shows, others will not be able to claim or demand of her on their own behalf (in the sense of being a party who is formally required to recognize the duty-enjoined action as to be 'done to me') that she fulfil her duties. The needy

---

[28] Thus inviolability is what Kagan calls a 'constraint' and what I have elsewhere called 'non-maximizing'; for references, see note 11 above. As noted there, non-maximizing inviolability is one possible form of the exclusionary or silencing aspect of duties.

[29] Feinberg 1970.

[30] Although the example is inspired by Feinberg's Nowheresville (ibid.), he does not take demanding on someone's behalf to implicate first- and second-personal thinking as outlined in this volume, Chapter 4.

acquaintance R in the earlier example will be able to remind the person P of her duty to take up her case with their mutual friend Q; she will even be able to *demand* this, but her demanding will be like the demands of any other third party.[31] Even if the needy acquaintance R demands of the duty-bearer P that she 'help *me* by speaking to our mutual friend Q', this 'me' will not have been required or made apt by the form of the duty; it will simply be a piece of self-identification performed by the needy acquaintance. It will not give her demand the character of one made on her own behalf as the person owed the duty.[32]

One conclusion that I think we can draw from the above is that it would be a non-instrumentally good thing if some duties were directed to or owed to parties with natural first-personality (and hence, when appropriately demandable etc., were rights for such parties (see Section 6.1)). This is not the simple points that it would be good if parties with natural first-personality were recognized as such, or if capable such parties had their 'I'-thinking matched by others' 'you'-thinking. These latter goods could be achieved without directed duties and rights: even in Feinberg's 'Nowheres-ville', each agent could have an *undirected* duty to try to spot natural first-personality wherever it occurs, and an *undirected* duty to engage in matching 'I'- and 'you'-thoughts about each other's behaviour. What directed duties or rights add is a distinctively formal requirement that, in my view, marks out a distinctive form of practical reason: a duty whose enjoined action is, in virtue of the duty's form, to be conceived second-personally as to be 'done to you' and (if the relevant party is capable of this) first-personally as to be 'done to me'. Section 4.3 told us that *practical reasons in general* (where this includes duties, whether directed or undirected) are distinguished from values and goods by the fact that they are 'for' someone qua agent: they tell someone to act, and that 'someone' is picked out by a formal requirement to conceive the action first-personally as to be 'done by me'. In a sense, all practical reasons (and duties) speak to first-personality in its agential guise, specifying that someone should conceive a potential act as 'mine to be done'.[33] What Sections 4.4–4.5 showed is that directed duties or rights constitute a distinct type of this form of practical reason, a type that speaks not simply to first-personality in its agential guise, but to a specific version of first-personality's agential guise: first-personality as 'acting on others-conceived-second-personally'. This type of practical reason at the same time speaks to the relevant 'others' first-personally as 'acted on'. The *formal* requirements of second-personal and (where possible) matching first-personal thinking distinctive of this type of practical reason (i.e. distinctive of directed duties and rights) are different from the *substantive* requirements constituted by, say, epistemic reasons to think first-personally that someone is or ought to be acting on one, or similar

---

[31] Compare May ms, for the related claim that Nowheresville can involve demanding, just not demanding issued by right-holders or others *on behalf of right-holders*.

[32] I think there is an interesting analogy to pursue between *the alienation of parties-qua-agents from parties-qua-patients in a world without directed duties* (a world lacking the requirements sketched in Sections 4.4–4.5) and *the alienation of parties-qua-agents from values in a world without duties or reasons*: a world lacking Section 4.3's requirement of first-personal conception of valuable actions as 'mine'. Without Section 4.3's requirement, goodness and badness need not formally require any effect on anyone's practical will.

[33] Note that this requirement of first-personal conception is defeasible. See the discussion of Railton's tennis example in Section 4.3.

epistemic reasons to think second-personally—e.g. reasons, based on my perception or on your testimony, to believe that someone is hitting me or that I am hitting you or that my job entitles me to your parking space. As formal requirements separate from the requirement to perform the action enjoined, the requirements constitutive of a duty's direction mark out directed duties as a distinct form of practical reason.

Even if one agrees with this, one might dispute the sentence that opens the previous paragraph: namely, the claim that the relevant distinct form of practical reason is a non-instrumentally valuable one: the claim that it is a good thing that the world contains directed duties, independently of whether direction has any valuable effects. Many areas of moral philosophy, such as the utilitarian tradition or the more deontological elements of the Kantian tradition, seem not to need the distinctively directed form of practical reason constituted by directed duties and rights, and we saw in Chapter 3 (and noted at the start of the book) that we do not need this form in order to make an extensional difference to how people ought to behave—a difference to the overt behaviour we can require of them.[34] Nonetheless it seems clear to me that it is a good thing that the world contains this form of reason: a non-instrumentally good thing akin to the good Kamm and Nagel find in the existence of inviolability independently of whether it is respected. But rather than defend this further in the current section, we should note that for two reasons this fact—directedness's non-instrumental value—is insufficient on its own to ground natural rights.

The first reason is that if we could see directedness as generated by its non-instrumental value, that would seem at best to require that *some* duties were directed, without telling us anything about *which* duties should be. On this approach, one might simply look at the range of duties grounded teleologically in the manner sketched in Section 7.2, and decide randomly that some of them should be dir-ected.[35] Such an approach is clearly unsatisfactory because it matters which duties, with which content, are directed; this is not something determined at random.

Further, secondly, the bare fact that it would be a good thing for some duties to have a direction (and hence to be able to qualify as rights if accompanied by enough powers) cannot itself confer a *natural, recognition-independent* directedness on any duty. The value of directedness could justify us in creating and sustaining legal or conventional directedness. But the fact that it would be a good thing if some duties were directed can no more *make them* directed naturally—i.e. independently of any conventional or legal direction-creating—than the fact that it would be a good thing if there were life after death can simply make there be such an afterlife.[36] The value of

---

[34] See also Gilbert 2018, ch. 12, section 8.1, for the claim that moral theory's main conclusions would survive whether or not there were moral *rights*.

[35] Wenar and I have (in two separate articles) claimed that this is one problem with Kamm's and Nagel's defence of rights/directed duties as conferring a valuable 'high status' on their bearers (Kamm 2007, pp. 253–4; Nagel 2002): if we hold rights/directed duties simply in order to have this high status, it seems irrelevant what particular content these rights/directed duties have, because for Kamm and Nagel their formal quality as rights or directed duties is sufficient to confer the valuable high status (Wenar 2005a, Cruft 2010). See the similar claims in Kagan and Lippert-Rasmussen, where a range of example rights with unusual structure and content are developed as conferring the same high status as those we naturally favour (Kagan 1991, Lippert-Rasmussen 1996).

[36] This is Nagel's analogy in his 2002, p. 39; see note 48 below for further discussion.

a potential post-death life can perhaps justify technological efforts such as cryogenic freezing, but it cannot in itself magically make an afterlife happen. To think that the value of directedness could just make certain duties directed naturally (i.e. independently of any efforts on our part to make them directed) seems to be an error: a form of wishful thinking or a category error.

It is important to get this point clear. Section 7.2 showed us that the value of *an action* can naturally make us have a reason or be duty-bound to perform it, independently of any conventional or legal construction of this reason or duty; this natural duty- or reason-generation does not involve the error identified in the previous paragraph. It is not wishful thinking that makes a natural, recognition-independent duty to do PHI exist when the value of PHI-ing is what makes someone duty-bound to PHI. The value of your not torturing me really does make you naturally duty-bound not to torture me, independently of any legal or social construction of this duty. This is because you can *choose* whether or not to torture me, and the good of your not doing so naturally makes you duty-bound to choose not to. By contrast, wishful thinking and category error are involved if we say that *the value of the natural duty itself* (i.e. not the value of PHI-ing but the value of there being a natural duty to PHI) makes it exist; similarly, wishful thinking and category error are involved if we say that *the value of a duty's being naturally directed* makes it directed. These are category errors because if it is a natural duty or naturally directed then nobody can *choose* whether this duty exists or is directed; and it is only the value of options we can choose (i.e. PHIs) that can create natural duties—duties to choose these options. This means that Nagel's and Kamm's strategy of focusing on the non-instrumental value of the existence of rights cannot—even when focused on the value of directionality rather than inviolability— explain why natural rights exist. At best, it can give us a reason for creating directionality and rights through law and convention.

7.5 Natural Rights Grounded in the Good of Connected, Unalienated Thinking?

Where does this leave the possibility of natural rights or naturally directed duties? The final paragraph of Section 4.6 shows us that rights and directed duties are valuable for requiring connected, unalienated thinking between agents and those on whom they are duty-bound to act. Is this a good that teleologically grounds natural rights and directed duties—that is, that makes them and the actions they enjoin necessary or apt independently of our construction of them?

We saw above—and will explore further in Section 7.7—that the value of the existence of the formal Addressive requirements constitutive of directedness cannot itself make any duties naturally directed. But we might wonder whether the value not of the requirements themselves but of *the first- and second-personal thinking* that they require could naturally generate these very requirements to engage in the relevant thinking. That is, we might focus on the value of *thinking of* or *conceiving* a duty-enjoined action second-personally as to be 'done to (a potential) you', or the value of *thinking of* or *conceiving* a duty-enjoined action first-personally as to be 'done to me'. These are actions we can choose whether or not to engage in, and we might ask whether the value of the relevant thinking itself generates natural reasons or natural duties to choose to engage in it, reasons or duties that will constitute the requirements that Chapter 4 told us are constitutive of directedness.

As it stands, though, this idea is problematic: simply generating natural reasons or natural undirected duties to engage in the relevant first- and second-personal thinking is not right for our purposes. That is, the value of the relevant first- and second-personal thinking might well naturally give us reason or make us duty-bound to engage in it; but this makes such thinking *the content* (i.e. itself the enjoined action) of natural reasons or undirected duties, rather than making it a (natural) *formal requirement* of a duty to do some *other action PHI*.

Further, we could not say that every time the value of *thinking of a duty-enjoined PHI second-personally as to be 'done to (a potential) you'* naturally gave someone a reason to or made them duty-bound to engage in such thinking then that person's duty to PHI was therefore directed. For we saw in Sections 4.1–4.5 that there can be ways in which such second-personal (or similar first-personal) thinking might be valuable and naturally generate duties to engage in it, *without* the duty to PHI therefore being directed. For example, perhaps we ought always to think of other humans as potential 'yous': then the employer first introduced in Section 2.2 has a natural reason or duty to think of their duty to pay their employees-who-will-spend-their-salary-in-the-local-shop as to be done to the local shopkeeper conceived as a potential 'you'. But this does not make the employer's duty owed to the shopkeeper. Similarly, there might always be a duty to consider convicts second-personally when punishing them, but again—as Section 4.6 observes—this should not make a punisher's duty to punish therefore owed to the convict. We need some way of capturing the distinctively *formal* aspect of the Addressive requirements of first- and second-personal thinking, as features of the form of a duty to PHI, rather than as required for more substantive reasons (in the way the PHI itself is required). It is not clear how generating the requirements in Section 7.2's manner from the value of the thinking they enjoin can make them part of the *form* of a duty to PHI like this.

Nonetheless, we will see in the next section that there is a kernel of truth in the thought that the requirements of first- and second-personal thinking outlined in Sections 4.4–4.5—the requirements that make a duty to PHI directed—exist because of the value of engaging in the thinking they ask for. It is just that the value of the PHI and the value of thinking of the PHI as to be 'done to (a potential) you' or 'done to me' are entwined rather than distinct values, so the 'accompanying' is not simple conjunction. Rather, the values of PHI and of first- and second-personal thinking about PHI are entwined in a manner to be explained in the next section.

7.6 Natural Rights as Duties to Act for the Sake of the Right-Holder

In essence, my view—to be defended in the current section—is that when the good of a party with natural (i.e. unconstructed) first-personality naturally brings a duty into existence (rather than through legal or social construction), then—and only then—is the duty naturally owed to that party. This is the thesis, outlined at Section 5.2, that

Raz's account of rights in general is, actually, an account specifically of *natural recognition-independent* directedness (at least if 'interests' in Raz is taken broadly to mean 'good'), as opposed to the created directedness of law, convention and promising. The central thought is that when a party (i) with a good (e.g. with well-being, interests, needs, projects, for whom possession of freedom, agency, capabilities, wisdom or perhaps other things are good) and (ii) with natural first-personality (unlike, say, 'Siri', Microsoft, or a car or other artefact that can nonetheless do 'better' or 'worse') is such that an action's being good for that party naturally makes someone duty-bound to perform that action in the teleological manner sketched in Section 7.2, then the duty in question must carry the second-personal (and, where applicable, first-personal) requirements of Sections 4.4–4.5 that make it owed to the party whose good makes it exist.

Let me unpack the components in this scenario in which a naturally directed duty exists:

- Some party's good makes a duty exist naturally, where this is not a matter of conscious or intentional duty-creation (as in law, convention or promising).
- What is created by the party's good is a *duty*, where this means a categorical reason of notable (exclusionary, overriding, silencing—perhaps inviolability-defining or 'non-maximizing' constraint-style) weight, that is demandable and whose violation triggers remainders (see Section 7.2).
- The party possesses a form of natural first-personality, so is coherently address-able with 'you' (in the manner outlined in Section 4.5) independently of our construction of an addressable status for her: this can include animals, babies, dead people, and groups as well as individual adult humans, but it cannot include legally created corporations or addressable machines like 'Siri'.[37]

One way to read these claims is along the lines rejected in the preceding section. This mistaken approach says that on the one hand we have *the party's good* working to create a natural duty to promote, respect or instantiate it in Section 7.2's manner, and on the other hand we have *the good of recognizing the party's natural first-personality* working again in Section 7.2's manner to create a separate natural duty to engage in the second- and first-personal thinking outlined in Sections 4.4–4.5. The trouble with this 'separate duties' reading, as noted in Section 7.5, is that all it gives us are two undirected duties, and the second one—enjoining Addressive thinking—is not an aspect of the form of the first one, but is a distinct substantive duty.

A different way to describe the problem with the mistaken 'separate duties' reading is that it requires the duty-bearer to act for the sake of *a particular good* (such as the good of not torturing the party in question), a good that happens to be borne by the party in question, rather than asking the duty-bearer to act for the sake of *that*

---

[37] Whether plants or planets have appropriate first-personality will determine whether duties can be naturally owed to them; see Section 4.5. Corporations and, perhaps, addressable machines like 'Siri' can possess constructed first-personality but their good cannot itself make someone naturally (as opposed to legally or conventionally) duty-bound—see Chapter 9 and Section 10.1.

party.[38] Then separately it asks the duty-bearer to recognize the addressable status of the party in question. In such a scenario, duties ask the duty-bearer to act for a particular good, and then as it were add 'oh, and remember that it is the good of an addressable party!'

Compare, similarly, how problematic it would be if Section 4.3's requirement— that the bearer of any reason or duty to PHI should conceive the enjoined PHI-ing first-personally as to be 'done by me'—were taken as a separate reason or duty, existing *alongside but separate from* the independent value or to-be-doneness of PHI-ing. It is unclear in what sense PHI-ing can be 'to be done' at all unless it is to be done *by someone*, who is picked out by Section 4.3's requirement. The 'separate duties' reading makes no sense in this case.

By contrast, the 'separate duties' reading is *coherent* with regard to the scenario at the outset of the current section, because there might indeed be independent duties to conceive parties with natural first-personality as addressable (e.g. standing duties to conceive others as 'one of us'), duties that sit alongside other duties to serve such parties' good. But the 'separate duties' reading fails to make a single duty demand action at one and the same time for the sake of a particular *good* of a party and for the sake of *that party*, as it were. My central claim in the current section is that when a duty is naturally grounded by the good of a party with natural first-personality—as sketched at the outset of the section—such a duty must demand action for the sake of that party's good in a way that is at the same time for the sake of that party: party-qua-first-personality and good-of-that-party should be entwined as that for which the duty asks the agent to act, rather than separable. For example, when your need not to be tortured naturally places me under a duty not to torture you, my refraining from torturing you should be at one and the same time for the sake of the need you possess and for the sake of you. This is achieved if my duty not to torture you formally requires me to conceive you second-personally (in the manner outlined in Section 4.5) while substantively requiring me not to torture you. It is not achieved if my duty not to torture you is accompanied by a separate substantive duty that requires me to think of you second-personally.

To put this another way, when a duty is naturally generated in the manner outlined at the outset of this section, the intellectualist's virtuous agent who under-stands the duty on which she acts will not merely think 'I am acting for the good of this third-personally-conceived party' *while separately* thinking 'this party is address-able, a potential "you"'. Rather, she will think 'I am acting for *your good*' or 'I am acting for *the good of this party who I conceive second-personally*'. The requirement to think like this (possibly in the abstract, without knowing who 'you' are)[39] is Section 4.5's requirement of second-personal thinking, constitutive of directedness. Only if such a requirement is part of the form of the duty made apt by the party's good, rather than a separate duty, is the virtuous agent required to think of the duty as enjoining action for the sake of a *party's good* conceived as comprehending that

---

[38] This is Katrin Flikschuh's concern with the Razian approach, as expressed in a workshop on an early draft of this manuscript: she thinks the approach grounds duties for your good rather than for you.

[39] See the opening of Section 4.6.

party's first-personality. Duties grounded on the good of naturally first-personal parties surely should take this form. Further, it should be unsurprising that we have a concept, directedness, that enables us to distinguish such natural duties from natural duties grounded on 'unowned' goods (goods that are not goods *of* specific parties).[40]

One might wonder whether merely having one's good *necessarily served* by a natural duty—rather than (as I have claimed) one's good being the source of the duty—is enough to make the duty in question naturally owed to one (i.e. generating Chapter 4's formal Addressive requirements of second- and first-personal thinking). And one might wonder about refining this contention in the manner of Kramer or Wenar (as in Chapter 2). But this would be a mistake. To see this, suppose that person P's interest in not being tortured, or need not to be tortured, plays no role in grounding my duty not to torture P.[41] But suppose nonetheless that I am under a duty not to torture P, grounded naturally by the importance to P's family or the wider community of my not torturing P. And suppose also that P holds a strong non-contingent interest in not being tortured. In this situation, my fulfilling my natural duty not to torture P necessarily serves P's good, even though the duty does not exist for the sake of P's good. In such a situation, must I as a fully virtuous agent think of my not torturing P as to be (not) 'done to P, conceived second-personally as an addressable "you"'? I believe I should think this way, but only as a matter of *substantive* duty: because P is a person, to be fully virtuous I should *ceteris paribus* think of them as addressable in all my dealings with them. In the case in question, I should think this *alongside* thinking of my non-torturing actions as to be done for the sake of P's family and the wider community. But because, in this example, P's good is not the source of my duty, I can see no reason—absent social construction of such a reason through justified law or convention—why as a virtuous agent I should be *formally* required by the nature of my duty not to torture P to think of this (in)action second-personally, as to be 'done to P as an addressable party or "you"'. The duty's natural source in the good of others means that there is no natural reason for me to think of the relevant (in)action as to be done for P's sake, and hence no natural formal requirement that in thinking of the not-torturing as to be done to P, I must think of it as to be done to P-qua-addressable-'you'.[42]

---

[40] Similar points apply to the first-personal requirement on capable parties outlined in Section 4.4. We saw in Section 4.5 that when the bearer of a duty to PHI is subject to the formal requirements of second-personal thinking constitutive of directedness, this triggers—in parties capable of this—formal requirements of matching first-personal thinking for the party of whom the duty-bearer should think second-personally. These requirements must be formal aspects of a duty to PHI, rather than distinct duties. If, as claimed in the main text, the relevant second-personal formal requirements are naturally generated when a duty is naturally grounded by the good of a party with natural first-personality, then matching first-personal formal requirements will be similarly generated if the party in question is capable of fulfilling them.

[41] I might here be supposing the impossible. See note 49 below for discussion.

[42] Note that in this case I *will* be formally required to conceive my not-torturing-P as *for P's family's sake* or *for the wider community's sake*; and this will require me to conceive my not-torturing-P as to be done to P's-family-conceived-second-personally or to the-wider-community-conceived-second-personally. See the related discussion of cases like that of walking Hadrian's Wall, in Chapter 4.

It is worth stressing this final point. My claim is not merely that when a naturally addressable party's good naturally makes someone duty-bound, that duty is naturally owed to the party in question (in my Addressive sense developed in Chapter 4). It is also that there is no other source of natural, recognition-independent directedness. This is rather controversial. For example, it is common to defend what are taken to be natural civil rights—to freedom of speech, for example—on the ground that they constitute an open society, where this basis for such rights gives no special place to *the right-holder's good* as opposed to the collective or common good (including, e.g. the good of babies and other members of society who lack the right).[43] My view is that even though the duty in question—to allow and facilitate speech in certain circumstances[44]—serves many goods beyond the right-holder's, nonetheless unless it would exist even while doing little to serve these further goods but simply or primarily because of its relation to the good of the speaker, the duty's status as *owed to* the speaker cannot be natural or recognition-independent. When someone's good naturally places someone else under a duty, that duty's form cannot naturally require the duty-bearer to think of *some further party* second-personally in the manner outlined in Section 4.5, nor naturally require the relevant further party to think of themselves first-personally as outlined in Section 4.4. For it is unclear what basis there could be for this, if these requirements are formal rather than substantive. A duty's being directed to X cannot be naturally appropriate if Y's good *and not X's* is the duty's source. (We will see in Chapter 9 and Section 10.1 that this should not lead us to reject the idea of a natural right to freedom of speech; rather, we can find a source of the relevant duty in the speaker's own good.)[45]

We have, I think, now found an attractive teleological explanation of the existence of duties that are naturally (as opposed to conventionally or legally) owed to others. We will see in Chapter 8 that just as whether a directed duty is a right (Section 6.1) and whether a reason is a duty (Section 7.2) are matters of degree, similarly a duty's being grounded by a naturally addressable party's good is a scalar matter, and hence whether a duty is naturally directed is again a matter of degree. Note, further, that as in the case of undirected duties in Section 7.2, the ground given for duties' natural direction is not based on its value (i.e. the value of the direction itself). Duties are naturally directed when an addressable party's good grounds them whether or not they will be respected, whether or not they will be thought of as directed, and hence whether or not they or their directedness instrumentally serves the good that grounds them. And we saw in Section 7.4 that its non-instrumental value could not make it exist. I take these points up in the next section, where I compare natural with created directedness.

---

[43] Raz 1994, p. 54. Compare Wong (2004, p. 39) for the view that rights are grounded in the value of relations between individuals, rather than in the relevant individuals' own good; compare the views rejected in this volume, Sections 7.4 and 7.5.

[44] My focus here is on the claim-right, not on the privileges or powers also central to free speech. See Section 6.2.

[45] This does not rule out the way goods borne by a community generate duties naturally owed to its members qua members. See Section 8.3.

7.7 Teleological Groundings of Natural vs 'Non-Natural' (Legal, Conventional) Rights

My focus so far has been on natural directedness. Before the final sections of this chapter, I here develop further an important point about the difference between grounding natural (or recognition-independent) and created (legal, conventional, promissory) duties and rights. I argued in Section 7.2 that some duties can exist independently of whether they are created, owing their existence simply to values that obtain whether or not they are recognized, such as the beauty of a rock formation; then I argued in Section 7.6 that some such natural duties can also possess a natural direction—if and only if they are naturally grounded in the good of a being with natural first-personality, a good such as my interest in not being tortured. But other duties and rights are created intentionally: by law, convention, the rules of a game, promising.

For clarity, we should note that some duties or rights might be *created unintentionally* by human action in certain contexts. If a log falls on your leg and I am unable to move it on my own, then I have no duty to attempt to do so (though I have other duties—to call for assistance, say). But if a log falls on your leg and somebody else comes along with whose assistance I could lift it, and that other person shows themselves willing to take part in the joint lifting effort, the context then creates a duty for me to attempt to lift the log in conjunction with the other person.[46] This is not what I have in mind by the current section's idea of the creation of duties. What I mean, rather, are duties we create intentionally through systems like law or activities like promising. What distinguishes these latter created duties, I suggest, is that their existence depends on their recognition as duties. Even if both you and I and everyone else failed to notice that your willingness to help me lift the log placed me under a duty to do so, the duty would still exist. By contrast, there can be no legal, conventional, or promissory duty which goes forever unrecognized by everyone; such duties depend for their existence on being recognized at least sometimes somewhere by someone. (Note that in my terms, 'recognition' for a duty does not mean respect for it. A duty is recognized when someone believes truly that the duty exists; but they might recognize it and go on to violate it.)

Now, the teleological approach developed so far in this chapter maintains that the value of a course of action PHI can ground a recognition-independent duty (perhaps directed or not) to perform that action. I stressed in Sections 7.4 and 7.6 that this is not an instrumental grounding of the duty or its direction. But this bears repeating because recognition-*dependent* (legally or conventionally created) duties and their directions can be grounded in a more straightforwardly instrumental way. In his early work, Scanlon sketches an instrumental approach to moral (or what I would call natural or recognition-independent) rights, and we should note how this goes awry:

The view that there is a moral right of a certain sort is generally backed by something like the following: (i) An empirical claim about how individuals would behave or how institutions

---

[46] I am grateful to David Owens for discussion of this sort of case and its relation to promising. See also the final paragraph of Section 7.2, and Gardner 2002.

would work, in the absence of this particular assignment of rights [...]. (ii) The claim that this result would be unacceptable. This claim will be based on valuation of consequences [...]. (iii) A further empirical claim about how the envisaged assignment of rights will produce a different outcome.[47]

This approach looks fine for socially created, recognition-dependent rights. We would expect to do a cost–benefit analysis before creating them, assessing how the creation of the rights—both as duties and as directed—'will produce a different outcome' to the situation in which they are left uncreated. And post-creation we would expect to do continual cost–benefit analyses to justify sustaining them. But such an instrumental conception is mistaken regarding the grounding of *recognition-independent* rights and duties. For these rights and duties exist and possess whatever direction they have even when they and their direction are wholly unrecognized, and thus even when they do not 'produce a different outcome'.

As Nagel points out, a Scanlon-style instrumental conception of the teleological grounding of recognition-independent rights and duties 'has the form that P is true because it would be better if it were true. That is not in general a cogent form of argument: one cannot use it to prove that there is an afterlife, for example.'[48] Yet Scanlon does indeed seem to ground recognition-independent moral rights on the fact that it would be instrumentally valuable if they existed.[49] Similarly, for Kamm and Nagel, the *non-instrumental* value of my being duty-bound (in a right-type way) makes it the case that the relevant directed duty exists.[50]

---

[47] Scanlon 1984, p. 146.

[48] Nagel 2002, p. 39; see my earlier discussion in Section 7.4. Oddly, Nagel himself goes on (pp. 39–40) to suggest that, exceptionally and in my view incorrectly, inferring P's truth from its value might be acceptable in the case of rights and duties. Nagel here draws on Quinn 1993.

[49] Note that one might raise questions about the very claim of value here: if I hold a recognition-independent right not to be a serf, then I seem to hold this *necessarily*. If (*per impossibile*) I did not hold this right then I would not be human and would not be me. But in what sense then is my holding this right of value? A similar question can be raised about Kamm's claims about the value of necessary human inviolability (Kamm 2007, pp. 253–4; see also discussion in this volume, Section 7.4). It can seem to make no sense to say, as Kamm implies, that my life would be less valuable—because of less worth—if I lacked a natural right. For the scenario in which I lack this right is an impossible one. Recognition-independent or natural rights are rights I hold necessarily in the contexts in which their grounds obtain, and the fundamental human ones are held necessarily in virtue of essential features that make humans human. Claiming (as Kamm does) that recognition-independent rights confer non-instrumental value on humans which they would otherwise lack, or (as Scanlon does) that such rights instrumentally achieve results that we would otherwise miss, thus looks a bit like claiming that squares having four sides is intrinsically better than or instrumentally more useful than squares being round. But on balance my view is that the latter concern—that it is nonsense to refer to the value (instrumental or not) of recognition-independent rights or duties—is rebuttable. We do seem to be able to think coherently about the value of necessary features of the world: the value of our being embodied, of the passing of time. I would suggest that at least part of what it is for these necessary things to be non-instrumentally valuable is that they should inspire awe and respect, and that we can perhaps also coherently see our embodiment and time's passing as instrumentally useful. We need not maintain that their value must be captured by what they add to the world vis-à-vis their (impossible) nonexistence.

[50] Compare also Raz's rarely noticed Kamm/Nagel-style view at his 1986, pp. 191–2. Here Raz allows that a right be grounded by an interest in its (i.e. the right's, not the action it secures) existence.

As noted in Section 7.4, moves of this type involve a category error because the 'outcome' here—the existence of a duty or right—is not under my control. The value of something my will can influence can naturally create a reason for me or make me naturally duty-bound to act in a certain way, and thus can naturally make a reason or duty exist (and Section 7.6 showed that if the relevant action's value is of the right type—its good *to a party with natural first-personality*—then the relevant duty will naturally be a directed, rights-correlative one). But the value of something my will cannot influence, such as the existence of recognition-independent duties or rights, cannot work in this way: it cannot naturally make any duties exist for me. Things that are independent of our wills (such as recognition-independent rights, or the passing of time, say) might inspire awe and respect, or be valuable in other ways including instrumentally. But their value does not make them obtain.[51]

But this is only a category error about natural or *recognition-independent* duties and rights. By contrast, recognition-dependent duties and rights are under the control of our will: we can choose to create them through promises or legislation or in other ways, and once they have been created we can choose whether to sustain or dismantle them. So their value simply as rights or duties independently of the value of the actions for which they ask can play a role in determining whether we create or sustain them and hence in whether they exist. In addition, their role in bringing about the actions for which they ask—whether their existence will make such actions more likely or will instead perversely disincentivize such actions—can also play a role in determining whether we create or sustain them and hence whether they exist. And further effects of these rights—e.g. the symbolic value of directed structures as things that are recognized or believed in—can also play such a role.[52] Thus, unlike in the case of recognition-independent rights and duties, far more than simply the value of the action they enjoin (the PHI) is relevant to whether they exist or not, and to whether they take a directed, rights-type form. It is only recognition-independent rights and duties whose ground (i.e. that which makes them exist) is limited to the values of the actions for which they ask, and cannot turn on the value of the right or duty itself.

---

[51] Nagel and Kamm are drawn to make this error because of their aggregative-maximizing conception of how teleological grounding would work for rights. This makes it difficult for them to see how the value of my not being assaulted could ground a right that I not be assaulted even when assaulting me would minimize assaults overall (see esp. Nagel's 1986 discussion of deontology (pp. 175–80)). For such a right forbids the maximization of value (in Kagan's terms, it is a 'constraint' (1998, p. 72)). Nagel and Kamm appeal to the value of the right independently of its results as a way of explaining how the right can serve value even though the results it secures fail to maximize value. By contrast, my teleological approach—like Raz's—is not maximizing; I do not think that the value which grounds a duty or right must generate a duty or right justified respect for which maximally serves the relevant grounding value. So I am happy to allow that some values make duties or rights exist when these duties or rights are Kaganian constraints— compare also Finnis 1980, Gould 1988, Griffin 2008, Nussbaum 2011, Tasioulas 2015, for non-maximizing but teleological grounding of human rights; such a non-maximizing teleological approach avoids Zylberman's objections in his 2016b. Others who, I think, assume one can only be teleological if one is aggregating or maximizing include Darwall 2006, p. 37 and Ripstein 2013, p. 175.

[52] Compare Raz 1986, pp. 250–5 on the value of rights as creating an open society; and see especially Harel 2014 on the non-instrumental value of constitutional rights.

7.8 Notes on the Literature

We should note some points on the literature before closing. First, we might wonder why Scanlon, Raz, Kamm, and Nagel are tempted to make what Section 7.7 identifies as an error. One explanation might be that a putative natural reason's, duty's or right's value is an *epistemic* reason to infer the existence of the reason, duty, or right. It is not that reasons, duties, or rights come naturally into existence simply because it would be good if they did. But (1) a putative natural reason's, duty's or right's *instrumental* value is defeasible epistemic reason to infer that the natural reason, duty or right exists. Why? Because reasons, duties, and rights are in principle graspable by the person whose action they enjoin, and we have epistemic reason to take as our default, defeasible position the thesis that they will be so grasped and acted on.[53] Of course often this default is defeated—for example, if we discover that the feudal aristocracy were motivated, by their serfs' natural rights, specifically to maintain their serfdom rather than free them. But it seems to me that if in the appropriate context we discover, as Scanlon envisages, that the valuable result of PHI's occurring would be made more likely by the existence of some putative natural reason, duty or right, this gives us defeasible *epistemic* reason to infer that the relevant natural reason, duty, or right exists. Such epistemic reasoning is defeated in a variant on the aristocrats-and-serfs case: suppose that we discover that the counter-suggestible aristocrats are most likely to free their serfs if they judged them to have a natural right not to be freed; we cannot infer that they therefore have such a natural right, even though it would be a great instrument for securing their freedom.

In addition, (2) a putative natural reason's, duty's or right's *non-instrumental* value is again defeasible epistemic reason to infer that the natural reason, duty, or right exists. This is because, as Geoffrey Sayre-McCord observes in a draft paper, a necessary condition on a moral norm's existing is that it be non-instrumentally morally good that it obtain.[54] There cannot be a moral requirement whose existence is in no respect non-instrumentally morally good. If this is correct, then again we can take the goodness—this time non-instrumental—of a putative natural reason, duty, or right as defeasible epistemic reason for inferring that it exists. But none of this means that the non-instrumental value or goodness of a putative natural reason, duty, or right is, as Nagel, Kamm, and Raz suggest, *what makes the reason, duty, or right exist*. Even though its non-instrumental value can give us (defeasible) epistemic reason to infer that it exists, it cannot be what makes it exist. That would be to get things the wrong way round. That PHI-ing would be good for a suitably first-personal party can make me duty-bound to PHI in a manner that is owed to the relevant party, and the fact of my being directedly duty-bound might well then be itself non-instrumentally good for the party in question, in a way that underpins the party's status interest as outlined in Sections 2.4 and 5.3. But neither *the status*

---

[53] This default is generic or paradigmatic rather than statistical: the generic or paradigmatic reason, duty, or right is acted on, just as (see Section 4.3) the action it enjoins is conceived in the first person by its bearer. This is true even if most reason- or duty-bearers fail to act on their reasons and duties.

[54] This goodness is, I suggest, conceptually linked to our status interest in the fulfilment of any duties owed to us. For cognate but separate points, see Kramer 2009.

interest nor *the good of being owed a duty* nor *the good of the duty's existence* can be what make the duty exist or be owed to the relevant party.

Finally, Stephen Darwall opposes not only the erroneous teleological groundings for duties and rights rejected here, but also the approach I favour in Section 7.6. He writes:

> However desirable it might be from some external perspective that someone do something, this is a reason of the wrong kind to support a demand that he do it, and hence to support the claim that he would do wrong if he didn't. Unlike considerations of desirability (even moral desirability), demands are second-personal reasons; their validity depends not on the value of any outcome or state, but on normative relations between persons, on one person's having the authority to address the demand to another.[55]

Darwall is correct to think, with Strawson, that a demand for PHI cannot be morally justified simply by the good of *demanding PHI*; whether it is justifiable will depend also on whether what is demanded is enjoined by a duty, whether the demander has standing to demand, and other factors.[56] But in my view whether a 'natural' duty to PHI exists does indeed depend, contra Darwall, on *the good of PHI-ing*. From one perspective, this seems rather obvious: the badness of someone's treading on my toe is surely a reason of the right kind to support my and others' demanding that the agent not do this. If it were not bad under some description to tread on my toe, it is hard to see how demanding that the agent not do this could be justifiable—at least in natural morality as opposed to the morality of created laws and conventions. If this is bad in the right kind of way, that is, weightily bad enough to be demandable and to trigger remainders in the manner sketched in the conjecture in Section 7.2, then this is surely the right kind of reason to license issuing a demand.

I recognize that the points above do not do justice to Darwall's careful arguments, but simply report my opposing position. Further, Darwall's view has affinities with my own point developed in the preceding section (7.7). Just as the value or good of a putative natural reason, duty, or right to PHI cannot, on pain of category error, make this reason, duty, or right exist, so the value or good of demanding PHI, feeling gratitude at PHI, resenting failure to PHI, forgiving this failure and so on, cannot, again on pain of category error, on its own make such actions permitted or required. But in my view the value or good of PHI can make an agent naturally duty-bound to PHI, as outlined in Section 7.2, and when this is the case then some ways in which demanding PHI, feeling gratitude, and so on would be good can—against the background of the existence of the natural duty to PHI—permit or require such actions. Permission or justification for demanding, feeling gratitude, and the other 'second-personal' actions or attitudes is parasitic on the existence of a duty to PHI. (And, we saw in Chapters 3–4, demanding, feeling gratitude, etc. *on behalf of the person owed PHI* are parasitic on the existence of a directed duty to PHI.) These

---

[55] Darwall 2006, p. 103.

[56] One might add that whether it even *qualifies as a demand* depends on these factors. If PHI is not enjoined by a duty, the attempted demand for PHI will fail to be backed by the potential 'remainder' duties (of apology, recompense, etc.) that give the demand part of its illocutionary force as a demand. See Section 3.6.

'second-personal' or 'reactive' actions and attitudes cannot be justified solely by reference to the value (or 'desirability') of their being performed; rather, they presuppose appropriate authority relations between demander and demandee. But this important point stressed by Strawson and Darwall is compatible with the good-based teleological account of the foundation of duties (both directed and undirected) developed in Sections 7.2–7.6.[57]

7.9 Implications

If the argument of this chapter is correct, then when some action would be good in an appropriately important kind of way, this makes the agent naturally (i.e. recognition-independently) duty-bound to perform it, and if the duty-making goodness is *good to a party with natural first-personality*, then the relevant duty will be naturally owed to that party. But I suggested at the end of Section 7.6 that the extent to which some-one's good naturally grounds a duty can be a matter of degree, and hence whether something is a natural right can similarly be a matter of degree. I explain this in further detail in Chapter 8. I also claimed (in Section 7.1, and to be defended in Chapters 8–9) that a duty's being morally grounded by a party's good was one hallmark of its constituting a *human right*; this in combination with the thesis of Section 7.6 might seem to make all human rights natural rather than created rights. But I show in Chapter 9 that while legal and conventional rights' existence conditions turn simply on whether they have been created and sustained, some of them can be morally justified as giving institutional form to natural, recognition-independent rights. I suggest that our human rights concept encompasses (i) both natural rights and legal-conventional rights instituting such natural rights, which are (ii) also 'everyone's business' (to be outlined in Chapter 10).

Why does any of this matter? It matters whether there are any natural rights or natural duties, and if so what they are. Without natural (recognition-independent) duties and rights, there can of course still be created (e.g. legal) duties and rights, such as the rights of human rights law or criminal law. And there might well be natural reasons to create, sustain, and respect these constructions. But with no natural *duties*, respect for these natural reasons could not be recognition-independently demand-able (though we might have reason to create legal structures enabling such demand-ing), nor would failure to act on such reasons trigger natural remainders. Failure to act on such reasons would therefore not be a naturally condemnable wrong. And without naturally *directed* duties, nothing would be naturally *owed to* any party;

---

[57] One conclusion to infer from this, I suggest, is that any PHI's goodness is in a sense 'first- and second-personal from the start', in that when it generates a reason it calls on first-personal apprehension of PHI by the reason-bearer as 'my action' (see Section 4.3), and when it generates a demandable reason (i.e. duty) it legitimates second-personal apprehension of the PHI-er by the demander (as 'you of whom I demand PHI'). And of course in Sections 4.4–4.5 I add that a *directed* duty (i.e. those demandable *on someone's behalf as owed it*) is constituted by additional requirements of first- and second-personal grasp. But it seems to me that all of this is in a sense already encapsulated in the varieties of ways that an action can be good; there is no such thing as an action's being good without generating at least Section 4.3's requirements of *first*-personal apprehension constitutive of reasons—though the good of a *thing* or a *state of affairs* might be able to be independent of any first- and second-personal grasp requirement (see Bykvist 2009).

failure to create any duties or rights which we had natural reason to create would therefore not naturally, recognition-independently *wrong* anyone in particular; it would not be naturally personally resentable. Some—like Bentham—might celebrate this result.[58] But in my view this approach is inconsistent with what many human rights practitioners (activists, lawyers, as well as philosophers and 'ordinary citizens') think they are doing, and inconsistent with the continuities between human rights legislation (international and domestic) and the natural rights tradition. I believe most users of the 'human rights' concept think people would hold certain human rights even if they had not been legalized and, further, that the failure to create legal human rights—and violation of such legal rights when they have been created—is violation of natural directed duties: people are naturally morally wronged by such failures independently of whether anyone notices this, and independently of our creation of directed legal duties that make people legally wronged.

My argument in the current chapter is one step on the road to vindicating this conception of human rights.[59] For I have argued that there are some duties that exist naturally—independently of whether anyone recognizes this—and that when they are grounded in the good of naturally first-personal parties, they are naturally (recognition-independently) owed to those parties. Contra Bentham, natural rights are not nonsense but are rather natural reasons (of a certain kind) generated by a party's good. Human rights laws and institutions are justified, along with criminal law and other areas of law, in important part as the state's and the international community's recognition and specification of a significant subset of these natural rights.[60]

But we might wonder why natural rights need legal recognition, or why particular departments of law (e.g. criminal law, human rights law) should institutionalize particular natural rights. These questions are tackled in Chapters 9–10. We might even wonder whether—having established that there are some recognition-independent rights and duties—these natural normative entities deserve our attention at all. Perhaps they are like some gender concepts which, arguably, refer but to which we would not draw attention if we lived in a just world.[61] We might think that a focus on how violating a naturally directed duty harms everyone, rather than the specific wronged right-holder, would be more appropriate or helpful.[62] A proponent of this view says 'here are some duties naturally grounded in a way that Section 7.6 tells us makes them owed to someone; but let's not tell others about this or reflect it in our legal or quotidian practice; instead let's—say—create undirected legal duties that

[58] Bentham 1987 [1789]; see also 'rights externalists' like Darby 2004 or Geuss 2001. The result is also compatible with Buchanan's 2013 view that human rights are fundamentally international legal rights that can be morally justified in a variety of ways, including ways that appeal to no natural duties or rights.

[59] What Tasioulas (2015) calls the 'orthodox' conception: see discussion in next chapters.

[60] The subset is those natural rights that are everyone's business: see Chapter 10.

[61] We might see differential intelligence or reasoning-ability concepts as similar: referring but not deserving our attention. This is one way of reading Carter's (2011) conception of a *respectful* attitude as one that treats its subjects as *opaque*—an attitude that treats individuals identically, without modifying itself in response to differences in the individuals' levels of intelligence or ability.

[62] For arguments in broadly this direction, see Marx 2000, Ihara 2004, and the discussion at the opening of this volume, Chapter 1.

serve these natural rights without drawing attention to their rights-type, directed character.' My response to this view is that while particular circumstances might sometimes justify individually ignoring or collectively failing to institutionalize natural rights as rights (e.g. if there would otherwise be terrible consequences), someone who genuinely believes that there are such things cannot honestly maintain that they or their directed, rights-type nature are to be ignored in all contexts: that would be inconsistent with their character as forms of practical reason. I pursue this further in relation to law in Chapters 9–10. Beforehand, we need to say more about the varying roles someone's good can play in grounding a duty that, depending on these roles, might or might not naturally be owed to them as their right. That is the task of Chapter 8. In pursuing this, we bring out the individualism of the natural and human rights concepts.

8

The Individual's Place in the Grounding of her Rights

8.1 Human Rights as 'Rights for the Right-Holder's Sake'

There are many accounts of what is distinctive about human rights: some say they mark the moral limits of sovereignty,[1] or are international legal rights protecting minimal well-being and equality,[2] or are rights to be treated with the attitude of respect owed to a human,[3] but many (often called 'orthodox' or 'traditional' theories) start with some account of what is distinctively important about humans—perhaps human needs, important human interests, capabilities, autonomy or normative agency—and assert that human rights protect these things.[4] There is, I suggest, less to distinguish many of the latter positions than meets the eye: in particular, needs and interests are not relevantly independent concepts, nor are autonomy and capability.[5] An assumption shared by almost all these diverse conceptions both political and orthodox (though rejected explicitly by Buchanan and not in Rawls) is that human rights, perhaps like some other rights, are held by the right-holder for their own sake, rather than for the sake of others beyond the right-holder.[6] But the claim that human rights are *distinctive* partly because of this right-holder focus in their justification, and that this underpins their continuity with the natural rights tradition, has received little attention. I defend and elaborate this claim in the current chapter and the following one: In Chapter 9, I show how legal and other socially created rights, although rarely owing their *existence* to nor *justifiable* by how they serve the individual right-holder, can nonetheless give institutional form to rights so grounded (i.e. natural rights); and I argue that their doing so gives us a strong reason in favour of creating rights-type, directed legal structures of institutionalisation (as opposed to

---

[1] See Rawls 1999, Beitz 2009, Raz 2010 and 2015.   [2] Buchanan 2013.   [3] Dworkin 2011.

[4] See, e.g. Gould 1988, Fabre 2000, Sen 2004, Miller 2007, Griffin 2008, Nussbaum 2011, Liao 2015, Renzo 2015, Simmons 2015, Tasioulas 2015. I venture that Sangiovanni's recent (2017) cruelty-focused, equal status approach is structurally similar; it certainly takes human rights to exist fundamentally for the right-holder's sake.

[5] The contrast between teleological approaches (as referenced in the last note) and transcendental ones (as in Gewirth 1982, O'Neill 1996, or Flikschuh 2015) is a stronger one than contrasts between different accounts of the relevant telos (needs, interests, etc).

[6] See Buchanan 2013, pp. 61–2; Rawls 1999. Note that Buchanan *asserts* that human rights exist for the sake of the right-holder (Buchanan 2013, p. 23)—but his view that many human rights are not justifiable by how they serve the right-holder is inconsistent with this. See this chapter, note 44 below.

merely creating undirected legal duties). Before then, I pause on the different degrees to which a right might owe its existence to a party's good (Section 8.2), and I show that a right can exist for the right-holder's sake in surprisingly communitarian, non-individualistic ways (Section 8.3); but it will be important to recognize the individualism at the heart of human rights, and the limits this places on the concept's universal accessibility. By the end of Chapter 9, I hope to have demonstrated both the plausibility and the fruitfulness of focusing on human rights as 'for the right-holder's sake'. Coupled with the further idea of human rights as 'everyone's business' (Chapter 10), we will by the end of Part II be in a position to assess and defend the rights concept as it features in human rights.

The claim that human rights' distinctiveness turns at least partly on their existing or being justifiable for their holders' sake is challenged implicitly by Raz and explicitly by Buchanan. In motivating his own political account of human rights, Raz writes that human rights, according to orthodox accounts, are 'thought to combine exceptional importance and universality. Even though various writers have offered explanations of the first element, that of importance, none seems to me successful.'[7] I suggest that Raz fails to notice that his own account of rights in general (as grounded (or made to exist) by what they do for the right-holder) is better taken as a theory of natural, recognition-independent rights, and hence as a theory of part of the importance distinctive to human rights. They are important because—unlike, say, most property rights or rights protecting duties of office—human rights either exist for the right-holder's own sake as natural rights, or are legally or conventionally created rights justifiable as protecting such natural rights.

Buchanan by contrast specifically denies that human rights need be justifiable for the right-holder's sake (or in his terms, 'subject-grounded') or institutionalize natural rights. He takes what he calls the 'heart' of human rights to be *international legal human rights*. And he notes that many international legal human rights have 'corresponding duties the fulfilment of which requires large-scale social investment and limitations on the liberty of large numbers of people'.[8] As examples, Buchanan mentions the legal human right to health, which requires governments to set up vaccination programs to deliver herd immunity, and the legal human right to democracy, which entails duties on governments to hold fair elections with appropriate nationwide logistics in place.[9] Buchanan claims that such legal human rights, with their demanding corresponding duties, cannot be justified simply by what they do for the individual subject. As he writes, 'To put the point bluntly: No matter who you are, you are not important enough to justify a set of duties that correlate with the panoply of legal rights [protected by international human rights law]'.[10] Buchanan concludes that international legal human rights must in most cases be justified by how they serve 'the interests and autonomy of large numbers of people', and he thinks this means that these rights cannot be grounded in what they do simply for the right-holder.[11] Buchanan goes on to conclude that international legal human rights cannot be seen as reflecting or operationalizing pre-legal moral rights (what I would

---

[7] Raz 2010, p. 39.   [8] Buchanan 2013, p. 62.   [9] Ibid., pp. 61–2.   [10] Ibid., pp. 63–4.
[11] Ibid., p. 64; Buchanan's argument follows Sreenivasan 2012.

call 'natural' rights)—because he thinks such pre-legal, recognition-independent natural rights must be grounded by what they do for the right-holder.

My account in Section 7.6 supports Buchanan's view that pre-legal, recognition-independent natural rights must exist for the right-holder's sake. But in Chapter 9, I argue that legal rights—including international legal human rights—can, contra Buchanan, give legal form to such natural rights, even when the legal rights in question entail legal duties requiring large-scale social investment: these legal rights can legally specify or operationalize pre-legal natural rights that exist simply on the basis of the individual right-holder's interests—even though the latter natural rights do not require the large-scale social investment required by the legal rights that give them institutional form. I further argue that the case for the relevant legal duties taking a rights-type structure would be significantly diminished if they did not specify or operationalize natural rights in this way.[12] We thus need not accept Buchanan's claim that if international legal human rights are (at least part of) the heart of human rights, then human rights cannot either be or institutionalize natural rights justified primarily for the right-holder's sake. Indeed we should conclude that if this were the case, then there would be little reason for international legal human rights to be *rights* rather than undirected duties.

Beforehand, in the current chapter, I lay out in Section 8.2 a schematic taxonomy of the extent to which a right might exist for its holders' sake, and in Section 8.3 I explore the individualism this implies. In earlier work, I refer to rights that exist for the right-holder's sake as 'individualistically justified', and Buchanan calls them 'subject-grounded' rights.[13] We will see that subject-grounding can be a matter of degree.

8.2 Rights for the Right-Holder's Sake vs Rights for the Sake of Others

The following taxonomy distinguishes stronger and weaker parts that the good to a party (the party's interests, freedoms, needs, capabilities or 'good' in some broader sense) might play in making some agent duty-bound to perform some action PHI. Note that the taxonomy below focuses on an agent's being naturally or recognition-independently duty-bound to PHI, and hence—see Sections 7.4 and 7.7—only the values (and disvalues) of the agent's *PHI-ing* can play a role in making the agent duty-bound. The values of the agent's *being duty-bound to PHI* cannot play such a role.

The taxonomy distinguishes seven roles that *the agent's PHI-ing's being good to a party* can play in making that agent duty-bound to PHI:

(1) STRONGEST: In all contexts, what the agent's PHI-ing does for the party, independently of extra benefits that the agent's PHI-ing brings for others or costs the agent's PHI-ing imposes (on the party, the agent or others), makes it the case that the agent is duty-bound to PHI. That is, what the agent's PHI-ing does

---

[12] See Sections 9.2–9.3 and 9.5 for argument.   [13] Cruft 2006, Buchanan 2013.

for the party on its own always makes it the case that there is a categorical, weighty-silencing-exclusionary, demandable and remainder-triggering reason for the agent to PHI.

For example, one might think that for any given human, the value of her not being tortured is a categorical reason for all agents not to torture her, a reason of significant (perhaps exclusionary) weight, whose fulfilment can permissibly be demanded and non-fulfilment of which triggers duties of recompense etc. One might think that this reason (a duty not to torture) exists simply in virtue of the good to the party of not being tortured, no matter how any further goods line up either for or against torturing that party. This can seem especially plausible when one remembers that the *existence* of the duty is in principle compatible with its being justifiably infringeable in certain horrible extreme circumstances. I return to this point immediately after completing the taxonomy. For now, we should note that when good to a given party plays this STRONGEST role in making another duty-bound, Section 7.6 tells us that the relevant natural duty will be naturally owed to the party whose good grounds it.

A second prominent role for good to a party in making an agent duty-bound is as follows:

(2) STRONG A: In contexts with *normal* countervailing considerations against the agent's PHI-ing, what the agent's PHI-ing does for the relevant party on its own makes it the case that the agent is duty-bound to PHI. That is, what the agent's PHI-ing does for the party on its own *normally* makes it the case that there is a categorical, weighty-silencing-exclusionary, demandable and remainder-triggering reason for the agent to PHI. But in circumstances with exceptional countervailing considerations, the good to the relevant party fails to do this. In the face of such exceptional considerations, additional values in the agent PHI-ing must be conjoined with what it does for the relevant party, to make the agent duty-bound to PHI.[14]

I am wary of presenting an example of this structure. Some have suggested the right to political participation, but I am not convinced that even in extreme circumstances in which significant costs attach to allowing someone to participate (suppose the person in question is a popular fascist, racist, or hate-monger), the reason to allow the relevant party to participate thereby loses its duty-type status or vanishes altogether; it seems to me more plausible to characterize such circumstances as involving the exceptional, justifiable infringement of the relevant right. One might perhaps be

---

[14] 'Normal' should be understood modally rather than statistically. Even if my interest in being brought a cup of tea happens, due to the strange absence of countervailing considerations and further happenstance factors which make it categorical and remainder-triggering, always to place others under an appropriately categorical, weighty duty to bring me a cup of tea, this will still not be a STRONG A grounding for a right for me, because tea's unimportance vis-à-vis alternative possibilities means that likely countervailing factors are modally nearby even if, in the odd scenario under consideration, these possible factors are never actualized. At best, this scenario involves an ACTUAL grounding in my interests of the duty to supply me with tea—see main text in a moment. Thanks to Joseph Bowen and Kieran Oberman for each pressing me on this. For careful discussion of the modal relation between rights and interests, see Bowen ms. Bowen thinks all directed duties and their correlative rights are grounded in their safely protecting rights-holders' interests across relevantly close worlds.

tempted by the idea that a right to free higher education (rationed to those with a certain ability level) fits the STRONG A model. If we define 'normal' countervailing considerations as those obtaining in the modern world, such as 'normal' opportunity costs for alternative public spending and macro-economic stability, then it can seem that the good of higher education to the student makes the state duty-bound to offer such education in the face of these 'normal' costs. But in exceptional contexts—war, famine—perhaps such a duty vanishes, or becomes a mere ordinary, undemandable reason. Against this, one might make the same claim I made about political partici-pation: perhaps in exceptional circumstances the right does not vanish or revert to an ordinary reason, but is simply justifiably infringeable. Or, arguing in a different direction, one might take up Buchanan's idea that no individual person's good is sufficient to make a state duty-bound to offer them higher education, given the costs involved; only the good of many can generate such a duty.

My own perhaps surprising view—to be defended in Section 9.3—is that we can take higher education, and almost all the other rights on standard lists of human rights, as either natural rights fitting the STRONG A or even the STRONGEST model, or as legal institutionalizations of such rights. But if instead we side with Buchanan, we might think higher education could fit the following model:

(3) STRONG B: What the agent's PHI-ing does for the relevant party, in conjunction with *normal* further grounds for the agent's being duty-bound to PHI—such as the fact that PHI-ing will involve creating or participating in an institution or practice from which many others also benefit—together make it the case, in the face of any or at least most (and more than simply *normal*) countervailing considerations, that the agent is duty-bound to PHI.

Many will take the right to higher education, and further human rights of the type Buchanan cites, such as a right to the herd immunity that can be secured by a vaccination programme, to fit the STRONG B model. Notice that on this model the good to any individual human (a particular potential student, or potential beneficiary of the vaccination programme) seems to play a comparatively small role in making the agent duty-bound. In light of Section 7.6, we might then wonder whether the duty in question can be naturally owed to the relevant individual human as her right. We should perhaps see this as a vague matter: the moderate but not dominant role played by the individual's good in generating the duty means that the duty is somewhat but not predominantly owed to her. Perhaps we should expect 'humanity' as a joint party to be its more natural recipient.[15] I will suggest in Section 9.3 that we can distinguish different versions of the STRONG B model, some of which involve a fuller role played by the individual's good than others. But individual parties whose good can play a STRONGEST or STRONG A role in making the agent duty-bound are more fully naturally owed the relevant duties, Section 7.6 tells us. All this is of course compatible with *legal* or *conventional* duties justifiable in something like the STRONG B manner

---

[15] See Tasioulas and Vayena 2016, p. 378, for excellent critical discussion of Gostin 2014's conclusion that the human right to health is fundamentally held by the community not individuals. This sort of conclusion is to be expected if we pursue versions of the STRONG B model focused on a duty's benefit to many. See Section 9.3 for more discussion.

being fully legally-conventionally directed to individuals, correlating with legal or conventional rights held by individuals.

There are also weaker roles that good to a party can play in making an agent duty-bound:

(4) MEDIUM: Given both *normal* countervailing considerations and *normal* further grounds for the agent's being duty-bound to PHI, what the agent's PHI-ing does for the relevant party is sufficient in conjunction with these normal further grounds to make it the case that the agent is duty-bound to PHI. (Unlike in the STRONG B case, in the MEDIUM case the combined normal grounds for the agent's being duty-bound to PHI, including the relevant party's benefit, cannot together defeat stronger-than-normal countervailing considerations.)

(5) ACTUAL: In the actual context, what the agent's PHI-ing does for the relevant party constitutes a fully sufficient positive case for the agent's being duty-bound to PHI—albeit a case that would be easily overridden or silenced in many likely alternative scenarios. (Such ACTUAL cases are rare, I think, because if the good, to the relevant party, of the agent's PHI-ing is a factor that would be easily overridden or silenced, then it would often need support from other factors if it were to succeed in making the agent duty-bound to PHI. That is, the good to the party would most often play a STRONG B, MEDIUM, or WEAK role in grounding the duty in question, rather than succeeding in grounding the duty on its own as in the scenario I have called ACTUAL.[16])

(6) WEAK: In the actual context, what the agent's PHI-ing does for the relevant party plays a necessary but small role in one grounding account which makes it the case that the agent is duty-bound to PHI.

(7) NONE: What the agent's PHI-ing does for the relevant party plays no necessary role in any grounding account which makes it the case that the agent is duty-bound to PHI.

Section 7.6 tells us that duties in whose grounding good to the relevant party plays no role (as in NONE) cannot be naturally owed to that party to any extent—though we could make them so owed through legal or other created conventional structures.

Note that positions (1)–(7) comprise a taxonomy of the degree to which a duty or right is 'subject-grounded' in Buchanan's sense: that is, of the degree to which value to the potentially right-holding party plays an important role in grounding the duty or right—in making it exist.[17] It is therefore, Section 7.6 tells us, also a taxonomy of the degree to which a duty can be naturally owed to a party. It is not a taxonomy of the importance of the duty or right itself. Some duties, and indeed some *legal* or *conventional* rights, can be justified in my WEAK or NONE ways, yet nonetheless be extremely important: consider the earlier example from Chapter 2 of the duty (within limits) to allow the prime minister to declare war. Similarly, perhaps some duties and rights can be grounded in my STRONGEST sense yet not be very important.

---

[16] See Section 12.1, note 8, for an example of this argument for the rarity of the ACTUAL structure.

[17] Buchanan 2013, p. 58. It is at the same time a taxonomy of the ways in which one might construe 'sufficient' in Raz's claim that a right exists when an interest is sufficient to ground a duty (Raz 1986, p. 166).

Perhaps my parents' interest in being visited in all contexts grounds a right that I visit but this right is frequently justifiably infringeable.

This latter point highlights an important aspect of the taxonomy above. Being duty-bound to PHI does not mean that all things considered one must PHI. In some contexts it might mean just that, but in other contexts it might mean instead that even though all things considered it is not the case that one must PHI, some 'remainder' obtains, such that one should apologize or offer redress for failing to PHI even though PHI-ing was not what one all things considered should have done. (This, of course, is not to say that to be subject to a duty to PHI is to be able to *choose* between PHI-ing or offering redress: the context will determine whether the duty ought to be infringed or not.[18]) Remembering this bolsters the hypothesis that any natural *human right* is grounded in my STRONGEST sense by its value to the right-holder. For even human rights that one might think are quite frequently justifiably infringeable—such as, perhaps, the human right to holidays with pay,[19] or a human right to IVF treatment[20] or to Internet access[21]—can plausibly be seen as protecting interests of the right-holder which are sufficient on their own to ground the right *as something quite frequently justifiably infringeable*.[22] That is, when we remember that we are looking at the grounding of a right or duty to PHI, as opposed to an all things considered case for PHI, this can make plausible the idea that certain interests or freedoms *always* ground such rights or duties no matter the context. The context just determines that sometimes these rights or duties are justifiably infringeable.[23]

It is also important to notice that a duty or right can be grounded in any one of my seven senses while at the same time being groundable in parallel ways. For example, in saying that my right not to be tortured is grounded, in my STRONGEST sense, on my interest in not being tortured, I do not exclude the plausible claim that even if my interest in not being tortured failed to ground such a right (perhaps because I had no such interest), there would be further values, independent of my-not-being-tortured's good to me, that would make agents duty-bound not to torture me: for example, agents are plausibly so bound for the sake of my friends and family, and for the sake of wider society.[24] Grounds for a right in the right-holder's good, where they exist, do not exclude alternative grounds. But my claim in Chapter 7 is that the extent to which a duty is *naturally directed* (and hence, if naturally demandable as outlined in Section 6.1, then a natural right) depends on the extent to which grounds in the right-holder's good work to make it exist in my STRONGEST or one of my other STRONG senses—and hence any natural human rights will need to be grounded in this way. And in Chapter 9, I will show that legal human rights can give institutional form to such natural rights even though their *justification*, qua legal rights, depends on the

---

[18] So we are not in the realm of the simplest 'law and economics' conception of legal norms as simply attaching extra costs to certain behaviours.

[19] In my view, this right is much maligned. See Waldron 1993, pp. 12–13, for important defence of this right.

[20] Tasioulas 2015, p. 62.   [21] Fellmeth 2016 cites this and similar cases at p. 8.

[22] Thanks to Christina Dineen for pressing this.

[23] For opposition to this view, see 'specificationists' about rights: Oberdiek 2004 and 2008, and Zylberman 2016b; I side with Judith Thomson (1990, ch. 3) and Jeremy Waldron (1993, ch. 9) instead.

[24] See Raz 1994, ch. 3, and also Nickel's linkage arguments in Nickel 2007, pp. 129–31, and as further developed in Nickel 2008.

good of many, and their *existence*, qua legal rights, depends on legal creation. In my view, existing for the right-holder's sake or giving institutional form to rights so grounded are among the formal hallmarks of a human right.

Sometimes theorists and practitioners identify human rights with the values that ground them. For example, they fail to distinguish between the human interest in not being tortured and the human right not to be tortured.[25] The account I have sketched can explain this impulse, for on my account, natural rights are simply a certain species of natural reasons: categorical, weighty, remainder-triggering, demandable reasons constituted or generated solely or predominantly by a particular naturally addressable party's good (and hence taking an Addressive form). In the STRONGEST case, this good or value always in some sense constitutes the reason which constitutes the right.[26] If natural human rights fit this STRONGEST model, then we have an explanation for the impulse just mentioned, because in such cases the value grounding the right in a sense constitutes it. Note that such an approach neither should nor does appeal in relation to duties in whose grounding good to a particular party plays only one of my weaker roles. We should have no impulse to identify the prime minister's personal good with her right to be unimpeded in declaring war. This is because her good is not what constitutes our reason not to impede her declaration.[27]

8.3 Individual, Communal, and Other Goods as Grounding Rights for the Right-Holder's Sake

The preceding section presented a spectrum of roles a party's good might play in making a duty exist. As a party's good slips down to 'weaker' roles along my spectrum, it becomes progressively less appropriate to see the relevant duty as naturally (rather than constructedly through convention, law, promising) owed to that party—where a duty's being naturally owed to one means that one is recognition-independently the formal addressee of the duty-bearer's action (see Section 4.4). I claimed in Section 8.1 that *human rights* must either exist for the right-holder's sake (as natural rights) or legally-conventionally institutionalize rights that so exist, where this 'for the holder's sake' is explicated by the spectrum in Section 8.2. I say more to defend this view of human rights in the next section (8.4), and in relation to law in Chapter 9. Further, we will see (in Chapter 10) that some duties are natural rights but are not human rights.

But before defending this conception of human rights, I must address a concern: isn't the picture too individualistic? Why assume that human rights must be justified by the good of the individual human? Why not construe individually held human rights as, for example, justified by the good of humanity collectively, or the good of specific human communities? My approach to *natural rights* in Sections 7.6 and 8.2 implies that some party's good cannot play a major role in naturally making a duty exist without that duty being naturally owed to the relevant party, and it implies that when a party's good fails to play a major role in making a duty exist naturally, that duty could not naturally be owed to that party. My claim introduced in Section 8.1

---

[25] This is the 'Reductive View' that Tasioulas finds in aspects of Griffin 2008 and Nussbaum 2002: see Tasioulas 2012, pp. 21–6.

[26] The same is true of STRONG A cases in normal contexts.

[27] Compare the discussion at Section 1.2.

(and defended further in Section 8.4) that *human rights* are 'rights for the right-holder's sake' implies that rights that can only be morally justified by what they do for people or values other than the good of the right-holder, and that do not institution-alize prior rights justifiable by the good of the right-holder, cannot be human rights. This might seem to make both the natural and human rights concepts unavailable to those who endorse communitarian claims that the community's good is the ground for any rights we have, or that an individual's good is largely constituted by common or communal goods.[28]

My aim in the current section is to explore how far my account of human rights, and of natural rights on which it depends, are compatible with communitarian conceptions of the good. We will see that while many communitarian insights can be accommodated by my picture, there are nonetheless important limits to human rights' consistency with some forms of communitarianism.[29]

One response to the communitarian concern is the common observation—developed in Section 10.1 in discussion of communal aspects of human rights law—that among the individual human's goods which can ground her natural and human rights are socially shaped interests and interests in living a socially embedded life, interests far more extensive than those that the individual would, *per impossibile*, hold in an asocial 'state of nature': for example, interests in loving relationships, in social play, in speaking one's native language, in forming a trade union, in doing one's duty by one's various communities including friends and family, in many further forms of political and wider social participation. One way to interpret some communitarian claims is as a reminder that (almost?) all our interests are socially shaped and embedded in this way. My taxonomy in Section 8.2 can accommodate this straightforwardly by including what PHI-ing would do for a party's socially shaped features or her interests in living and fulfilling social aspects of life among the STRONG grounds for making others duty-bound.[30]

Another quick response to the communitarian is Tasioulas's observation that the goods which ground human rights are holistically interrelated such that, for example, the good of my freedom depends in part on its relation to others' goods: freedom to

---

[28] There are many forms of communitarian claim, and one might debate whether 'communitarian' is a label that can catch them. Among the claims I have in mind I would include e.g. Taylor's 1985 rejection of 'atomistic' views of the self, or Sandel's arguments against Rawls (Sandel 1982); I also have in mind Mbiti's claim that 'I am, because we are; and since we are, therefore I am' (1970, p. 141) and Menkiti's thesis that 'as far as Africans are concerned, the reality of the communal world takes precedence over the relative individual life histories, whatever these may be' (1984, p. 171); see the discussion of Mbiti and Menkiti in Gyeke 1998. Compare also the Confucian picture sketched in Ihara 2004 and Wong 2004, as well as aspects of Finnis on how the common good constitutes individuals' good (1980, ch. VI). I feel I still need to do a lot of work to engage with and come fully to understand the variety and nature of these distinct communitarian claims—so the current section is a promissory note with much more to be done.

[29] Buchanan (2013, ch. 7) engages in a similar examination, with broadly similar conclusions—though Buchanan's denial that legal human rights need reflect natural rights grounded in the individual's good allows him to locate the inconsistency with what he calls 'valid collectivist moralities' in 'the [specific] implementation of some rights in the existing [international legal human rights] system' (p. 271), rather than in the very concept of human rights, as I do.

[30] Moves of this type can be found in Nickel 2007 and Griffin 2008, and perhaps more explicitly in Gould 2004, p. 63 and pp. 94–102, Parekh 2004, ch. 4, Nussbaum 2011, and most recently in Gould 2015 and Brownlee 2016.

wrong others is not a right-grounding good of mine.[31] Again, my approach can accommodate this straightforwardly: by making whether what PHI-ing would do for a party generates duties in others (and rights for the party in question) dependent partly on how PHI-ing would affect further parties. The freedom secured for me by your allowing me freedom of movement, to adapt Tasioulas's example, only places you under a duty to allow me movement that would not affect others in certain ways. Now, this might look like a step away from the idea that my right to freedom of movement (constituted by your duty to allow it) exists wholly *for my sake*. But notice that with a suitably specified 'PHI' (specified as *your refraining from impeding my movement in circumstances X, Y, Z, but not in circumstances which would, say, involve me assaulting others*) it is still the case that, in Section 8.2's STRONGEST sense, you are made duty-bound to PHI simply by the importance of my freedom of movement, independently of whether this would bring costs or benefits to others or serve other goods.[32] We can thereby accommodate Tasioulas's insight without denying that your duty to allow me freedom of movement (and my correlative right) is grounded on the basis of the importance of my freedom of movement—and hence is a duty (and right) that exists for my sake.

But I think a certain kind of communitarian theorist would claim that these points do not go far enough: they do not accord ontological priority to the community's good, from which its members' interests derive, nor do they make the individual's self-conception fundamentally or primarily a conception of oneself as a community member.[33] How much space does my account of natural and human rights allow for those committed to communitarian claims of this type? I think the answer is 'some limited space'. This space, and its limitations, derive from the formal rather than substantive character of the individualism at the heart of my conception of natural directedness. I will take two paragraphs below to explain this space, and then seven paragraphs on its limitations before concluding the section.

First, the space my approach has to accommodate the communitarian point mentioned. To qualify as grounded in one of my STRONG ways and (hence as a duty that is naturally someone's right, a right existing 'for their sake'), a duty must be grounded predominantly by the relevant party's good. Any grounding predominantly on some factor that is *genuinely the relevant party's good* will do. We might then

---

[31] Tasioulas writes that 'one way of enhancing people's freedom is by increasing the number of the options that are valuable in these various ways [i.e. as instantiating justice, beauty, knowledge, friendship...]. By contrast, multiplying trivial or morally depraved options does not enhance their freedom. [...]Second, freedom is often implicated in our engagement with other values, transforming their nature [...] Even something as rudimentary as the conditions for preserving one's animal being—such as our interest in adequate nutrition—acquires a different character through the exercise of our capacity to choose what and how to eat and with whom' (Tasioulas 2015, pp. 52–3).

[32] This is reflected in the fact that we do not think that you have a *justifiably infringeable* duty to refrain from preventing me assaulting another; rather, in these special circumstances you have no such duty to refrain from impeding me.

[33] The points made so far seem, to my mind, to accommodate aspects of the claims made by communitarians like Sandel who stress the socially constructed nature of our interests, but perhaps not radical communitarians like Mbiti or Menkiti (for the 'radical communitarian' label, see Ajei 2015, p. 497, and Gyeke 1997, pp. 52–61), nor perhaps those like Wong (2004) for whom the character of the relations between individuals, rather than the good of the individuals, is what should ground our rights.

observe that often the good or flourishing of a morally justified group of which I am a part is in itself good for me. I say 'in itself' to rule out empirical or causal claims: often when my group does well, this has knock-on causal effects that benefit me personally, but these are not what I am referring to here. Instead, my focus is on the sense in which whenever my morally justified group does well, I benefit necessarily *simply in that my group is doing well*. The benefit 'to me' need not be constituted by anything over and above the fact that my group is doing well. This is the sense in which, for example, my academic department's flourishing benefits me even if I personally do not experience any of the benefits: perhaps the intellectually active, insight-generating members of the department make it flourish even though I never interact with them, nor gain extra pay or further benefits from this; nonetheless, in a sense I benefit simply qua member of the department.[34]

This kind of individual benefit is ontologically derived from the group's benefit. Yet it looks as though even goods to an individual of this communitarian kind could, in principle, sometimes function in one of my STRONG subject-focused ways as a natural ground for others' duties. Against this, one might think that any purported such grounding will be based ultimately on the communal good on which the individual good is ontologically dependent, and hence the right in question will not really exist primarily for *its holder's* sake, but rather for the sake of the relevant group or community. But this overlooks the intensionality of grounding and justification, that is, the fact that statements of grounding or justification, of 'for whose sake' a duty exists or is justified, are, in the jargon, 'opaque contexts'.[35] This means that there is a genuine distinction between, for example, a right's being grounded or justified by how it allows my nation the good of self-determination and its being grounded or justified by how it allows me the good of my nation's being self-determining, even if the only sense in which my nation's self-determination is good for me is the ontologically derivative sense sketched earlier: as a member of the nation for which self-determination is good, I benefit simply qua member (and, let us assume in this case, in no further way). Now *if* such an individual good based entirely on good to the group of which the individual is a member can function in a STRONG way as ground for a duty, then my account says that that duty is naturally owed to the relevant

---

[34] An interesting question which I cannot pursue concerns how my wholly-group-based interests compare with or relate to Wenar's idea of 'role-based or kind-based wants' (see this volume, Section 2.3). Note that individual interests in independent non-personal goods are not at all unusual. A mathematician's discovery of a new theorem might be something she wants to pursue, something she has made her life's work; but the value to her of discovering it or simply of coming to learn it need not depend on her wants or projects; its intrinsic importance as a theorem confers importance on her belief in it independently of her attitude to this belief. Here, good to the mathematician is derived largely from—and in a sense consists in no more than—good of the theorem believed. Compare Sarah Buss's claim that humanity's value is ultimately instrumental: a means to the development of instrinsically valuable knowledge, for example (Buss 2012). The term 'instrumental' seems misplaced here, and Buss does not share my focus on good to individuals. But her idea that values beyond individual flourishing are often what confer value on the individual is consonant with my claim that participation in values primarily conceivable in terms beyond an individual's good is often in a sense what that individual's good consists in.

[35] Compare Kramer's claim that one can distinguish the value of a downward slope (as viewed from the top) as justification for undertaking earthworks from the value of the logically equivalent upward slope (viewed from the bottom) for the same works (1998, p. 3).

individual. For it is the individual's good that grounds the duty: it is just a wholly group-dependent individual good, an individual interest in the group's good.[36]

But I find it hard to think of a fully plausible example that fits the structure just sketched. The national self-determination case mentioned does not seem like a good fit: I believe I do indeed have an interest in my nation's self-determination that is not dependent simply on how this is good for me in other ways; but that interest of mine—in the good self-determination brings for the nation of which I am a member—does not in itself seem important enough to play a STRONG role in making anyone (or any institution) duty-bound to respect my nation's self-determination. To ground such a duty, we seem to need to look beyond simply my own interest here, even my interest in my group's good. We seem to need to look either to the good of my nation as a whole, or to the good of the many people who comprise it (or to both, or to some other good). While my own interest in my group's good is not *logically* unsuited to grounding the relevant duty, it seems substantively implausible to claim that it could do this on its own: can other nations' duties to respect my nation's sovereignty, and other individuals' duties to do so, be grounded solely on my own group-focused interest in my nation's self-determination? This seems doubtful.

The latter paragraph is an assertion, not an argument. Some might disagree, and I think other examples can be found of rights that better fit the proposed structure: might my right of political participation be groundable in a STRONG way not only by my interest in participating, but also separately by my interest in my group's constituting a valuably inclusive group (an individual interest of mine in my group's good)? Might my right not to be tortured be groundable in a STRONG way not only by my interest in not being tortured, but also separately by my interest in my group's not torturing its members (another individual interest of mine in my group's good)? I confess that I am uncertain about these claims: I am unsure that my interest in itself in my group's good often works in such a STRONG way (unbolstered by others' interests or further goods) to ground others' duties. Perhaps this doubt reflects my failure to learn communitarian lessons: it is a doubt about the relative duty-generating power of individual interests in group goods (e.g. in my group's being inclusive, forgoing torture, determining itself on the international stage), when compared to individual interests in more personal though still relational matters (such as my being educated, receiving health care, my participating politically, my not being tortured). Qua individual interest, the latter seem more likely to play a STRONG role in natural duty-generation than the former; the former seem to need supplementation by others' similar interests, or by the goods themselves (inclusivity,

---

[36] It is worth noting that the approach sketched in the main text is different from Raz's attempt to squeeze rights that are ultimately grounded by how they serve goods beyond the right-holder's interests into a model in which they exist or are justified for the right-holder's sake (see Section 2.2). My approach considers the possibility that an individual's interest in their group's good can sometimes itself be important enough to play a STRONG role in grounding a duty, a duty which is then naturally owed to the individual. Unlike Raz, I claim that this way in which duties can be grounded is *distinct* from scenarios in which duties are grounded directly by how they serve the group's good—even though the good of the individual which grounds duties in the former case is simply an interest in the group's good. Raz, by contrast, I think has to make *any* case in which a group's good grounds a duty which necessarily serves someone's interests into a case in which the relevant interests 'ground' the duty (Raz 1994, pp. 48–52).

self-determination, etc.) independently of my individual interest in them, in order naturally to generate duties. Perhaps my doubt here is a symptom of individualistic indoctrination—but I cannot shake the doubt.

One reason for this doubt is that if, say, my *interest in my group's being an appropriately inclusive group* were to play a STRONG role in grounding duties in others to allow me to participate politically, it would seem therefore also to ground *a lot* of further duties: not just duties to allow me to participate, but duties to allow everyone else to participate too. For that is what is needed if my interest in my group's inclusivity is to be served.[37] It seems to me that the interest *I* hold in such a group good is not enough on its own to play a STRONG role in grounding all these duties; it needs supplementation by others' similar interests, or by the group interest, or by the value of inclusivity itself. If this concern is well founded and generalizes, then even though there is logical space for an interest in one's group's good grounding natural rights for one (which legal-conventional human rights could then institutionalize), such space is not actually (or perhaps only rarely) filled.

A deeper communitarian concern is that the isolation of 'an individual's good', and the role I say it should play in grounding a duty (as in Section 8.2), are inconsistent with the inseparability of individual and community—even when the 'individual's good' in question is an individual interest in the group's good, as in the cases above.[38] This problem is not that the strategy sketched above fails to give enough weight to the community's good. My general approach can recognize significant weight in a community's good because it implies that when the good of a community or group with first-personality is sufficiently important naturally to ground a duty, then that duty will be naturally *owed to the relevant community or group*, potentially (see Section 6.1) as their right—and I think we can add that in such a case the relevant duty will also be naturally owed to the community's or group's members qua members. I suggest that such an approach can plausibly characterize the grounding of natural rights of national self-determination—i.e. rights whose existence is recognition-independent, grounded in a STRONG way by the nation's important interest in self-determination. Further group rights might similarly fit my human rights picture, and I return to this in Section 10.1.[39] The deep concern mentioned at the outset of this paragraph is, rather, that the distinction between the individual's and others' (including the community's or group's) good at the heart of my account of natural directedness in Sections 7.6 and 8.2—the distinction that allows both for individual *and* group natural rights, some of which qualify as human rights—is problematic. Should we draw this distinction in the way that Sections 7.6 and 8.2 do, by isolating the contribution of the right-holder's interests from other contributions to the natural generation of the duty in question? Is such isolation and distinction really possible?

[37] A potential response might claim that my interest in *my group's including me as a participant* grounds others' duties (rather than my interest in my group's *inclusivity in general*)—but this is not then really an interest in *my group's* good.

[38] Thanks to Katrin Flikschuh for pressing related concerns.

[39] Some will question my claim that groups can have natural first-personality; I return to this in Chapters 9 and 10.

Suppose it is not really possible. Suppose there is something illegitimate in pointing to 'your good' as the ground, or a major part of the ground, for someone's having a duty: this illegitimately distinguishes 'your good' from other goods in a way that is misleading or mistaken. If this were correct, then I think we would have reason to abandon the idea of natural rights (and therefore, I will argue in the next paragraph, the idea of legal-conventional rights too).[40] For Chapter 7 showed us that the only basis for a duty's naturally, uncreatedly bearing the formal Addressive requirements constitutive of its being owed to someone is if it is grounded in their good. If we cannot consider goods as 'attached' to specific people or groups in such a distinguishing way (as my good, or ours or theirs), then I do not see how goods could naturally require directed duties. I argued in Chapter 4 that a duty's direction is constituted by formal requirements that the duty-bearer think of the relevant action as to be done 'to someone addressable as "you"', and that capable parties to whom duties are owed think of the relevant action as to be done 'to me'. I do not see how duties involving formal requirements of this type can be naturally grounded (i.e. grounded independently of our creation of them) by goods that are not distinguishable as 'a party's': mine, yours, so-and-so's. We saw in Section 7.4 that the value of such requirements themselves cannot naturally make them exist. And we saw in Section 7.5 that the value of thinking of others second-personally—which could be an undifferentiated value rather than such thinking's good 'to someone'—need not naturally ground directed (as opposed to undirected) duties to engage in the relevant thinking. Within my broadly teleological perspective, I cannot see how duties with a directed, rights-type structure (X's rights; duties owed to X) could be naturally grounded, if we cannot make sense of 'someone's good' (X's good) as grounding them.[41]

Suppose we did think that isolating certain goods as 'someone's' in the required way was illegitimate—and hence we concluded that no duties were naturally directed and there were no natural rights. We might still think there could be reasons to create legal, conventional, and promissory directedness and rights. But the reasons for creating legal and conventional directedness are very weak, in the absence of natural directedness to which legal-conventional institutions might give institutional form. Sections 3.5 and 5.1 showed us that we can achieve most of what we might want from legislation or institutionalization using undirected duties alone. For example, we can create undirected legal-conventional duties whose violation triggers undirected legal-conventional requirements to apologize and rectify, and we can create legal powers to forgive or waive such undirected duties. I argue in Chs. 9–10 that the best reason for creating legal-conventional *rights* and *directed* duties is to reflect the naturally directed structure of natural rights which they institutionalize (see especially Section 9.5). And I then argue in Part III (especially Chapter 14) that against this background in which the rights concept is justifiably in legal-institutional use,

---

[40] To be precise, we would have reason to abandon the idea of natural (and hence also legal-conventional) *claim*-rights; we could keep other Hohfeldian types of rights such as power-rights; see Chapter 1, note 13 and main text.

[41] Now of course there might be non-teleological options here; for discussion of my teleological assumption, see Section 7.1.

it becomes acceptable—though optional rather than compulsory—to use the directedness concept to apply also to legal duties that do not institutionalize natural rights, when these legal duties nonetheless protect important interests of a party and there are no further costs of using the concept here. But with no natural rights underpinning our usage, the reasons for creating legal-conventional directedness are not strong, given how much we can achieve with undirected duties (see also Section 13.3).

Matters are different in the case of promissory duties. Promissory duties are created through an act in which one party addresses another, and it seems to me that a duty so created will bear the Addressive requirements constitutive of directedness simply in virtue of the addressive nature of its creation, largely independently of the interests of the parties involved.[42] Thus the possibility of promissory directedness (and promissory rights) seems not to require that we can make sense of one party's *good* as distinct from the good of another or of the community. If we cannot draw this distinction, then the idea of natural rights, and thus I suggest also of legal-conventional created rights, is threatened; but promissory rights are perhaps not.

Nonetheless, it should be clear that those who think it illegitimate to regard 'someone's good' as a coherent concept, or who reject the way I isolate the contribution 'someone's good' can make to a duty's existence, must reject the account of natural rights given in Sections 7.6 and 8.2, and this will undermine many uses of the rights concept—including in 'human rights'. This marks a limit to the universal accessibility of the concept. I cannot pretend to know whether the authors cited at note 28 would press this complaint. But it is important not to forget this limit. Those committed to moral schemes in which the relevant distinction is not drawn might rightly resist wholeheartedly embracing the concept. Nevertheless in what follows I mostly set this concern aside. Its relation to the rights concept is too radical to be addressed fully here. The attractions of the view developed in Chapter 7 might go some way towards addressing it, as might the further attractions outlined in the next section (8.4). But rather than pushing these points as an *argument* against those who would reject the relevant distinction and isolation, I will instead largely *assume* that we can make sense of the taxonomy in Section 8.2 as genuinely distinguishing different roles for a party's good in naturally grounding a duty—and commensurately different degrees to which that duty is naturally owed to that party, potentially (see Section 6.1) as their right. The early parts of the current section show that this taxonomy is compatible with some communitarian claims but, we have seen in the later parts, not with all.

8.4 Why See Human Rights as Existing or Justified for the Right-Holder's Sake?

At the outset of this chapter, I claimed that a necessary condition on a right's being a *human right* is that it either be grounded for the right-holder's sake, or legally-conventionally institutionalize a right so grounded. Section 8.2 laid out a taxonomy

---

[42] See Section 12.3.

of degrees to which a duty might owe its existence to the good of a particular party—that is, be grounded for that party's sake—and hence naturally (recognition-independently) be owed to that party.[43] Legal and other created rights and duties by contrast owe their *existence* to acts of creation and (in most cases) continued maintenance. We could develop a taxonomy similar to that in Section 8.2 mapping the degree to which the good of a particular party can *morally justify* creating, maintaining, and respecting any such legal right. I sketch the implications of such an approach in Section 9.2, where we will note the extreme rarity of cases in which creating and maintaining a legal right can be justified primarily on the basis of an individual's good. We can also observe that many legal-conventional rights morally justified by how they serve many people or, perhaps, by how they serve 'the generic citizen' or 'the generic human', protect, operationalize or specify prior natural recognition-independent rights grounded in the right-holding party's good. I argue in Sections 9.3–9.4 that most legal human rights qualify as human rights in virtue of bearing this type of relation to natural rights grounded for the right-holder's sake. And I argue in Section 9.5 that this is the strongest ground for giving human rights law a specifically *rights*-type, directed structure.

Beforehand, in the current section I say more about the attractions of seeing human rights in this general way—despite the limitations sketched in the previous section.[44] Of course, the idea of human rights is perhaps unusually malleable, so any suggested condition or account of the concept will feel overly determinate. But there is much to recommend the idea that for something to be a human right, it is necessary that it be a right which either exists naturally for the right-holder's sake, or institutionalizes such a natural right.[45]

First, this makes the idea of human rights continuous with though different from the concept of natural rights, and I think that is itself a benefit of the approach, cohering with how activists and practitioners conceive their actions, and—we will see in Chapter 9—giving fairly strong grounds in favour of human rights law's *rights*-based, directed structure.[46]

Secondly, from a certain perspective the very idea of rights that exist for the right-holder's own sake is attractively radical. It goes beyond the idea of a list of *undirected* duties such as the Ten Commandments—which, in form at least, simply specify types of behaviour without making this behaviour (e.g. 'not coveting', 'not killing') owed to anyone. It also goes beyond the idea of a *system of duties owed to right-holders that is*

---

[43] The relevant party here could be an individual human or a group or, indeed, a non-human animal.

[44] Note that even a theorist like Buchanan who makes international legal rights the heart of human rights, and who goes on to argue that such rights cannot be morally justified by what they do for the individual right-holder, nonetheless maintains that 'the basic idea of the system of international legal human rights is to develop a regime of international law whose primary function is to provide universal standards for regulating the behavior of states towards those under their jurisdiction, *for the sake of those individuals themselves*' (Buchanan 2013, p. 27). But Buchanan fails to see how this falsifies his claim that legal human rights cannot be grounded as institutionalizing recognition-independent rights. For argument on this, see Sangiovanni 2016 and 2017, pp. 212–20.

[45] Recall that I say there is another major condition on something's being a human right as well: it must be 'everyone's business', so not all natural rights are human rights; see Chapter 10.

[46] For concerns that such continuity with the natural rights tradition downplays the statist, political aspects of contemporary human rights practice, see Chapter 10.

justified because the system as a whole is good for the community: compare the classical liberal view of property in Hume, Smith, and Hayek, in which the duty not to use a given item is owed to you because a system of duties of this type serves the common good (see Part III, and the doubts I raise there about the strength of the case this approach can make for the relevant duties being directed, rights-correlative ones). By contrast, the idea of human rights as grounded for the right-holder's sake in one of my STRONG senses is the idea of duties being owed to the right-holder grounded in *what they do for that right-holding party*.[47] Even if sometimes the relevant good to the right-holder is an interest in their group's good (see Section 8.3), on this model the focus of justification or grounding is always primarily on the right-holder.

This is a radical idea, a version as I see it of the same idea Rawls tries to capture with his notion of the moral significance of the 'separateness of persons'.[48] The idea is that each human person—and, potentially in the same way, certain animals or appropriate groups—generates the existence of non-aggregating reasons for behaviour that serves or respects aspects of that person's (or animal's or group's) good: reasons that are categorical, exclusionary-weighty-silencing, in principle demandable and remainder-triggering (Section 7.2), and that are owed to that person (Sections 7.6 and 8.2). The idea that each person's good on its own plays a primary role in generating such duty-type reasons protecting that good, rather than duties emerging only from an aggregating process (as in utilitarianism), or only from the importance of communal goods (as in one version of the classical liberal case for property), is a distinctive and significant idea. It is an idea that gives centre stage to what we might call 'formal individuality': not individuality in Mill's sense of the particular interests or practices that distinguish me from others, but in the sense of my and your and others' being distinct sites of subjectivity (or first-personality) for whom life can go better or worse, and whose resultant duty-generating status reflects the bare importance of parties of our type having a good.[49] The idea is that for appropriate parties with subjectivity, simply having a good can generate or justify duty-type reasons in itself. This idea, captured by the notion of 'rights for the right-holder's sake', is, I suggest, the radical heart of both the idea of natural rights and the idea of human rights as continuous with the natural rights tradition.

At first glance, human rights *law*—if taken as a mixture of the rights on international documents and those basic rights in relevant national constitutions and other basic rights aspects of national laws—seems to contain a range of counterexamples to my claim that human rights either exist primarily because of what they do for the right-holder, or institutionalize rights so grounded. One set of problem cases includes parental rights, rights to protection of the family, language rights and group rights to self-determination including national self-determination.[50] The individual right-holding party does not look like the main ground of these rights. Other cases include rights to the public goods bound up with some canonical human rights:

---

[47] And Chapter 7 showed us such duties are naturally owed to the right-holding party.
[48] Rawls 1971, p. 27.   [49] See Mill 1991, ch. 3.
[50] Thanks to Christopher McCrudden for pressing these complaints forcefully. Recall that these are at the same time counterexamples to Raz's general account of rights (see this volume, Section 2.2).

rights to nationwide polling stations or to vaccination programmes to deliver herd immunity. As noted, Buchanan and Sreenivasan have argued that the individual cannot be the ground for these rights.[51] One also sometimes encounters the claim that rights to equal treatment should be seen as grounded in the value of equality, rather than in the importance to the individual of being treated in the same way as others. And rights to equal treatment have a central place in human rights law.[52] A different line of attack claims that my model assumes that individual agents are duty-bearers—but isn't the state the primary duty-bearer in relation to legal human rights, and can state duties be justified in the manners sketched in Chapters 7 and 8? I discuss the point about state duties in Chapter 10, along with some of the earlier-mentioned problem cases. First, though, it will be helpful to show, contra Buchanan and Sreenivasan, how specifically *legal* rights that cannot be justified by the good of the individual right-holder can nonetheless often give institutional form to natural rights that exist for the right-holder's sake—and that this justifies human rights law's rights-type structure. These points will emerge in the next chapter's discussion of the models of the human whose good grounds human rights.

---

[51] Buchanan 2013, p. 61; Sreenivasan 2012.   [52] Buchanan 2013, pp. 28–31.

9

The 'Human' in Human Rights and the Law

9.1 Generic Humans and Concrete Individuals

My claim is that a necessary condition on something's being a human right is that it either be grounded predominantly on the basis of what it does for the right-holder—where 'predominantly' can come in the degrees outlined in Section 8.2—or it institutionalize or legalize rights so grounded. Human rights are thereby held by the right-holder for the right-holder's own sake.[1] In this chapter, I explain what this implies for human rights law, including (Sections 9.3–9.4) addressing the serious concern that many 'positive' or socio-economic legal rights seem to lack subject-grounded pre-legal natural right counterparts which they could institutionalize, and (Section 9.5) showing how the view of human rights law as an institutional realization and specification of prior natural rights can offer a powerful justification for the directed, rights-type structure of the relevant law. But to get clear on the relation between the natural rights of the previous chapter and their legalizations we need to start, in the current section, by asking how should we interpret the idea of the 'party's good' that grounds her natural human rights (and that her legal human rights institutionalize).

We can distinguish three ways of conceiving the features of the right-holder which ground her human rights, ways that constitute rival conceptions of 'the human' at the foundation of human rights. In the current section I focus on these alternatives as grounds for *natural* (i.e. recognition-independent) human rights, and I begin an examination of the alternatives' implications for human rights *law* that continues through Sections 9.2–9.5. The three alternative conceptions of the right-holder's features which ground her human rights are:

1. Varied Specific concrete features: features specific to the particular, idiosyncratic embodied right-holder ground her rights.
2. Shared Specific concrete features: features which the particular, idiosyncratic embodied right-holder shares with all other humans ground her rights.

---

[1] I also noted my view that most human rights on standard lists are either groundable as natural rights *by what they do for the right-holder in my* STRONGEST *sense*, or are institutionalizations of such rights. The defence of this thesis emerges in Sections 9.3–9.4. It depends on my controversial claim that there are natural 'positive' rights to goods and services, held against humanity as a whole. If one rejects this, one might still believe in natural 'positive' rights grounded in a STRONG but not STRONGEST way—while leaving natural 'negative' rights with a STRONGEST subject-based grounding. See the aforementioned sections.

3. Generic Human features: (some of) the right-holder's generic features 'as a human' ground her rights.

The first approach takes seriously the fact that what is good for a particular person is specific to that person: it need not be what they think is good for them, but nor need it reflect some 'standard' account of the good life. Rather, each particular person, with their particular biological, social, and cultural make-up, could be benefited by rather different things. According to the Varied Specific approach, one powerful ground of our human rights will be what is good for us 'as an individual with a concrete history, identity and affective-emotional constitution'.[2]

This could in principle generate different human rights for different individuals. Perhaps there are some cases in which some lack the 'standard' right-grounding interests. For example, it seems at least in principle possible that I might have no interest in political participation—not in the sense that I am not interested in it, but in the sense that political participation really would do nothing for me. I will be a very rare case: far rarer than is often imagined, and there is a real danger here of wrongly imagining that someone lacks such an interest.[3] But such a case is maybe not impossible in principle.

Perhaps less rare—though still unusual—are people for whom 'non-standard' freedoms are as important as those on the standard list. Controversial examples can be found in claims made in debates about human rights and cultural diversity. One claim made in this context is that one's cultural and institutional heritage can determine the kind of old age care to which one has a right—care by one's children or family *versus* institutionalized care funded by the state. The potential for inappropriate stereotyping here is enormous, but the 'children/family'-based care approach has been associated with East Asian (e.g. Chinese, Japanese) and Southern European (e.g. Greek, Italian) cultures and institutions, while the 'state' approach has been associated with North American (e.g. Canadian, US) and Northern European (e.g. British, Swedish) cultures and institutions.[4] Whether the claims in question are true or not, the possibility of cases of this type—in which some humans hold important right-grounding interests which others lack—is opened up by the 'specific individual' approach.

Note that to get this kind of variation going it is not enough to invoke cases in which *on balance* someone's interests are not served by the standard array of rights, or would be better served by some new right. Instead, we need a case in which someone's standard interest, need, freedom, or capability, etc. is missing or lacks

---

[2] Benhabib 1992, p. 159. I see some affinities with this approach in Gould's anti-essentialist, Marx-inspired focus on the 'many-sided individuality' of the agency and interdependency that, for her, ground human rights (Gould 2015, p. 193); Gould infers that 'the list of human rights can be thought of as somewhat variable for different social and historical contexts', (p. 195). However, as she put it in correspondence with me, Gould 'certainly would resist the idea that human rights vary for each individual'—contra my 'Varied Specific' view in the main text. Gould favours the view that there is a fairly substantial set of human rights as conditions of agency that are widely shared.

[3] Some might think that children and those with severe mental health problems are candidates for parties to whom political-participation-by-that-party offers nothing. But I am unsure: participation imaginatively construed and creatively delivered seems possible for almost any human, I venture.

[4] See Chan 1999, pp. 235–6; Parekh 2004, p. 138; Owens 2017, pp. 561–3.

right-grounding importance, or a case in which someone else holds an extra such right-grounding feature beyond the standard array.[5]

It is notable that any case of the type sketched can always be interpreted as involving rights grounded in specific interests, freedoms, or needs which are them-selves generated in context by more abstract interests, freedoms, or needs *which all humans share*. For example, the variations in rights to old age care sketched earlier can be seen as contextually necessitated versions of a universally shared right—grounded on a universally shared interest—in being cared for in old age in a manner that secures one with minimal self-respect. The claim would be that in certain societies such minimal self-respect requires familial attention, while in others it requires state institutional attention. Somewhat similarly, Nickel has argued that a group-differentiated right (like my right specifically to *familial* care in old age) can legitimately be called a human right 'if it is derivable (using plausible additional premises) from a universal human right'.[6] On this basis, Nickel suggests that we should take, for example, women's rights to prenatal care as human rights because '[s]tanding behind the right to prenatal care during pregnancy is the universal right to basic medical care. The right to prenatal care necessary to the health and survival of mothers and babies is derivable from that general right.'[7]

The fact that such universalist interpretations of apparently varied specific, con-crete grounds for varied, specific human rights are available does not imply that we should always make such interpretations. Nor, if we *do* make such interpretations, would this make the Varied Specific view collapse into the Shared Specific view that we have not yet discussed (the second on the list at the start of this section). Before we get to the latter point in two paragraphs' time, note first that we might resist the universalist interpretative approach on the basis that it makes the wrong derivation. For example, some feminist theorists question the derivation of women's rights to prenatal care from universal rights to health care. Peach outlines the general position: 'Cultural feminists generally stress the significance of differences between men and women and among women. [...] Cultural feminists are, then, skeptical about the value of subsuming all "women" under the concept of "human" as the latter has been defined in international human rights law.'[8] If the understanding of the human in international human rights law is patriarchally structured—as is inevitable given world history—then we should take Peach's point about deriving 'women's interests' from this concept. (Note that Peach's target—the derivation of specific rights for women from the idea of 'the human' *in international law* is not what Nickel proposes, for his abstract 'universal right to basic medical care' is, I take it, meant to be natural and pre-legal.)

---

[5] See Section 2.2, p. 15.   [6] Nickel 2007, p. 163.

[7] Ibid., p. 162. Similarly, against Raz's concern that aspects of the international legal human right to education make no sense as timeless rights held by Stone Age people, one might suggest that the 'aim of the human right to free elementary education—the high-level, basal universal right standing behind it—is to ensure that human beings acquire the knowledge necessary to be adequately functioning individuals in their circumstances. In this regard, it does not seem odd to say such an aim or high-level right was relevant, important, and applied in the context of cavemen' (Cruft, Liao, and Renzo 2015, p. 8).

[8] Peach 2005, p. 90. For doubts about rights 'related to reproduction and childbearing' in particular, see Peach 2005, p. 91. Compare Gould 2004, p. 57.

Secondly, we might also go on to claim that there are some rights grounded by interests, needs or freedoms in one of my STRONG senses for which we cannot find *any* universal abstract roots: interests, needs, or freedoms of right-grounding importance which are idiosyncratic 'all the way down'. I am doubtful about this latter claim: while misderivations of specific interests or needs, etc. from purportedly 'universal' goods are dangerously commonplace, it seems to me that promotion, reflection, or respect for the right-holder's *well-being* or *freedom*, taken in the broadest senses (which encompass interests, needs, desires, capabilities, projects, autonomy), are the only interpretations of what a right 'does for' its holder (the 'holder's good' that it serves) that could constitute grounds for it for the right-holder's sake. That is, we cannot escape the duo of well-being and freedom in conceptualizing at the fundamental level how a right could be grounded in how it serves its holder's good.[9] Therefore, we cannot avoid seeing all natural human rights—rights which exist for the right-holder's sake—as grounded on interests, needs, or freedoms which are interpretable as concrete versions of the right-holder's very general interest in well-being or the right-holder's very general freedom. *These* universal human goods—a person's well-being and freedom—cannot be escaped as abstract grounds for abstract human rights from which, qua grounds or qua rights, more concrete rights and grounds are generated in context.

Some might take my commitment to well-being and freedom as universally shared abstract right-grounding goods as the claim that the Varied Specific approach collapses into the Shared Specific approach. But this would be a mistake. Even if I am correct in seeing the Varied Specific approach as depending on one or two highly abstract goods (well-being and freedom) that all humans share, such an approach supports far fewer universally borne rights than the standard bills of natural rights, and the standard legal and constitutional schedules. Even if the universalist interpretative strategy underpins the Varied Specific approach's array of varying rights for different people, it starts from a very short list of *universally borne* rights. We will see that the Shared Specific approach, by contrast, assumes that *many* rather specific, concrete goods are of right-grounding importance for each and every person.

By opening the possibility of individual variation among human rights, my first approach—the Varied Specific one—might immediately seem to make international universal legal human rights at best an inaccurate attempt to 'mirror' varying natural human rights, because the law, especially an international law applying across the globe, cannot reflect widespread variations. But I am not sure this is correct. Law can be structured to reflect such variations to some extent, for example through the use of waiver clauses and exceptions. We already find such structures in the legal treatment of children and other exceptions.[10] I return to the legal implications of the Varied Specific approach in Section 9.2.

---

[9] I here assume that needs and well-being can be explained in terms of each other and are not fundamentally distinct concepts, while freedom and well-being are fundamentally distinct in this way.

[10] Compare also the highly context-specific discriminating capacity required to distinguish whether legal concepts such as 'mens rea' have been instantiated. Law can and does discriminate between varied individual cases.

What I called the Shared Specific approach (no. 2 at the start of this section), like the Varied Specific one, grounds human rights on the specific features of concrete individuals, but it homes in on those right-grounding concrete features shared by all humans (or at least by all humans at a given time).[11] The Shared Specific approach differs from the Varied Specific by denying that the concrete right-grounding interests, needs, or freedoms which are genuinely universal—those from which the specific ones are generated in context—are likely to be few. Instead, the Shared Specific view is that there is a broad range of shared concrete interests, freedoms, or needs of STRONG right-grounding importance which deliver for everyone the natural rights that are (broadly speaking) given legal and constitutional form by current human rights law.

The Shared Specific view maintains that *all* the features—interests, freedoms, needs—of a given human which function on their own to make rights exist for her sake are those universal human features which for any other human again function on their own to make the same rights exist for that human's sake. This can seem attractive: my features which are most likely to constitute STRONG grounds for rights for me look like my interests in minimal autonomy, in absence of severe pain, in social interaction, in play—roughly, the types of thing Nussbaum lists as the ten central capabilities.[12] Wouldn't any other adult human similarly need these things for a 'life of dignity', and hence wouldn't these features for any other adult human similarly ground rights for them in one of my STRONG senses? Consider Fabre's claim about the preconditions for autonomy, preconditions which, she assumes, apply for any human:

If we are thirsty, cold, hungry, and ill, if we are homeless, then we do not have the personal intellectual and physical capacities to frame and revise a conception of the good life, let alone pursue it. We thus need money to buy food, liquid, and clothing, as well as medical treatment and shelter. Besides, in order to have some intellectual capacities we need some education.[13]

Isn't this correct? Don't we each have a powerful autonomy-based interest in not going thirsty, cold, hungry, ill, or homeless? To accuse such claims of liberal imperialism, and to maintain that some humans in all their specificity will lack interests in avoiding thirst or hunger or illness, etc. looks like a dangerous roman-ticization of what Benhabib calls '"the otherness of the other" [...] their irreducible distinctness and difference from the self'.[14]

But I confess that I do not know what to think on this issue. Claims of the type proposed by Fabre, Nussbaum and similarly Nickel and Griffin (see Nickel's 'four secure claims' and Griffin's universal three 'highest-level rights') strike me as highly

---

[11] The Shared Specific view is probably the most common view in the pro-human rights analytic literature, shared in some form by Donnelly, Fabre, Finnis, Griffin, Liao, Nickel, Nussbaum, Raz, Renzo, Tasioulas—even Beitz via the role in his theory for 'urgent individual interests' (2009, p. 109); but we will see that Nussbaum and Tasioulas sometimes seem instead to favour the Generic Human view; and we should note Raz's and Tasioulas's commitment to the merely *synchronic* universality of human rights, rather than their universality *across time* (Tasioulas 2012, pp. 31–6; Raz 2015, p. 225). More references follow in subsequent notes.

[12] Nussbaum 2000, pp. 78–80; Nussbaum 2011, pp. 33–4.   [13] Fabre 2000, p. 19.

[14] Benhabib 1992, p. 167.

attractive.[15] But I worry that this might be a failure of imagination on my part, that what Benhabib calls '"the otherness of the other"' should give me pause, and should push us towards the more restricted view, sketched in discussing the Varied Specific approach, that only very abstract goods like well-being and freedom can be seen as universally shared interests, and that their specifications will vary across contexts in ways that, for example, Fabre's discussion fails to consider. But on the other hand that can seem ridiculous: *surely* health and education are importantly good for each and every one of us? Rather than take a stance on this very important issue dividing the Varied from the Specific view, I return to it throughout the current chapter—for the issue turns out to have significant implications for how we conceive human rights as law.[16]

By way of contrast, let us consider the Generic Human approach (no. 3 in the list at the start of this section). This approach does not assume that some things—e.g. health, education, not being tortured or attacked—are good for anyone whoever they are in their specificity. But nor does it, like the Varied Specific approach (no. 1), see the human rights as varying between individuals with their specific, concrete variations. Instead, the Generic Human approach grounds each individual's human rights in her *generic* important features—roughly, the features they hold as *standardized* humans:

The universal interests referred to [as grounds of an individual's human rights...] are *standardized* [...where this means] that in their specification one may abstract from some variations among individuals by focusing on the standard case of an ordinary human being living in a modern society. Hence, for example, we can regard personal achievement—engaging in difficult activities in such a way as to merit admiration—as a universal human interest, notwithstanding the fact that some individuals may not share this interest, such as those whose idiosyncratic psychological make-up effectively precludes them from engaging in challenging enterprises.[17]

Sesha's entitlements are not based solely upon the actual basic capabilities that she has, but on the basic capabilities characteristic of the human species. [...] Such entitlements would not exist were capabilities based only on individual endowment, rather than on the species norm.[18]

[15] See references to Fabre and Nussbaum in notes 12 and 13 above; see also Nickel 2007, pp. 61–9; Griffin 2008, p. 149; compare Finnis 2011, pp. 4–8; Liao 2015; Renzo 2015. Compare, on the other side, American Anthropological Association 1947 and the response to it in Nickel 2007, ch. 11; see also Donnelly 2003.

[16] Note that a variant version of the Shared Specific approach accepts that some important right-grounding features might vary between individuals, but reserves the concept 'human rights' for rights grounded in *shared* important features. Like the first form of the Shared Specific view, this approach contains the challenging yet attractive claim (which I attributed to Fabre, Griffin, Nickel, Nussbaum) that many goods or ways of behaving are importantly good *for any adult human, whoever they are*. For the variant under consideration, these goods generate human rights for the right-holder's sake while *equally important yet individually varying* other goods can generate equally important but varying rights for the right-holder's sake which, because they are non-universal, we do not call 'human rights'.

[17] Tasioulas 2015, p. 51.

[18] Nussbaum 2006, p. 285. For cognate issues and moves, see Wenar 2013, pp. 223–5 on our unclarity over what humans qua humans want, and Thompson 2004, pp. 376–9, for the Aristotelian idea of our human life-form as the basis of our rights.

This approach grounds a person's human rights in that person's important *generic* 'features as a human'—features that will in some cases not map precisely onto her particular interests and needs as a specific embodied being.

One implication of this Generic Human approach is that all humans will hold the same natural human rights, *not*—as in the Shared Specific approach—because each and every human has certain concrete shared interests (in housing, health, and education, say), but rather because *the human qua human* has such interests, and these interests qua human will ground natural human rights for me, whether or not I as a specific, embodied human in context have such concrete interests. The thought would be that even political participation could be seen as something all humans qua human need—even those in a coma, say. *As a human*, I need to participate, even if as an embodied being in a coma I do not.[19]

There are two oddities about the Generic Human approach. First, it seems odd to claim that when someone S's *generic interest qua human* places someone else under a duty to PHI, this duty exists genuinely for S's sake. Is it really S, rather than humanity or 'the human', for whose sake the duty exists? Against this charge, the defender of the Generic Human approach can claim that because S's generic interest qua human is a genuine feature of S, a feature whose right-justifying importance does not have to be explained in terms of how serving it serves further values, it follows that duties grounded by this generic interest of S's really are grounded for S's sake.[20] The defender of the Generic Human view could here draw on the same point—about the intensionality of rights' grounding—that I used in Section 8.3 to sketch out the idea that an individual's interest in a group good could ground a right for that individual's sake. Similarly, the defender of the Generic Human view can claim that grounding a right primarily on *an individual's* interest-qua-human in X is grounding a right for that individual's sake—where grounding it on *'the'* human interest in X would not be. The intensionality of grounding, as highlighted in Section 8.3, tells us

---

[19] See note 3 above on imaginative ways to give the voiceless a voice. We should pause to note a contrast between different ways of expressing the Generic Human view: the one I will use most refers to the 'generic' human but earlier I also, following Tasioulas, referred to the 'standardized' interests of a standardized human. Using *'generic* human' to pick out the important interests or other important right-grounding features of a person isolates those interests or features that are characteristic to a human given her humanity. 'Characteristic' here need not mean 'necessary', nor even 'typical': the generic lion has four legs and eats meat even if—perhaps due to disease or injury—the majority of lions do not. While 'generic human' features are, I think, features characteristic to a human because of her humanity, the alternative 'standardized human' concept suggests features that some norm or standard specifies that humans should possess (compare Nussbaum's reference to 'the species norm') (2006, p. 285). Again, the typical human need not be the standardized human, but unlike the 'generic' idea, the 'standardized' notion does not imply that the relevant standards or norms are internal to the concept 'human'. It is conceptually open for the standards or norms defining the 'standardized human' to be external standards or norms. This is a reason why I favour the 'generic human' construction: someone's generically human features must be features characteristic to her as human directly in virtue of her humanity, rather than features she should qua human possess potentially in virtue of externally imposed standards—such as standards chosen for humans by some particular ruler or state.

[20] By contrast, the defender of the Generic approach might note, we do have to explain the right-justifying importance of a person's generic *interests as prime minister*—unlike her generic *interests as a human*—by referring to how serving such interests in turn serves the interests of the people or citizenry.

that these could be two separate ways of grounding a right, even if the relevant individual's interest-qua-human in X is identical to 'the' human interest in X.

But this response looks suspicious in light of the second oddity, namely the idea that PHI could be *good for S as a human* without being *good for S simpliciter*. The latter distinction is crucial to the strategy of the Generic Human approach, as sketched in the quotations from Tasioulas and Nussbaum, for ascribing human rights from standard lists to 'non-standard' or non-generic humans. It seems to me that we really can draw the relevant distinction, allowing that, say, a lion might have an interest qua lion in eating meat even if as an experimental subject (the first lion successfully weaned off meat) it has no interest in carnivorous consumption. Aristotelians will question whether this makes sense, perhaps especially in the case of 'human': can we really make sense of the idea of something's being good for me qua human without being good for me *simpliciter*? And perhaps more problematically still, if we *can* draw the distinction between my good *simpliciter* and my good qua human, it might then seem, *pace* the previous paragraph, that duties constituted by reasons to respect my good qua human will not be duties that exist for my own sake—for surely such duties should be grounded in what is really my good (my 'good *simpliciter*') which, it has turned out, is not what is good for me 'qua human'.

The points above might seem to favour either the Varying Specific or Shared Specific over the Generic Human approach. But each has its problems, and we can learn much from the implications which the distinct approaches carry for the idea of human rights as created *legal* or *conventional* entities. This will occupy Sections 9.2–9.5.[21]

9.2 Human Rights as Law: Natural-Legal Isomorphism and the Generality of Law

Each of the preceding section's three approaches gives a model of the grounding for the right-holder's sake of recognition-independent or natural human rights: grounding in the right-holder's Varied Specific, or Shared Specific, or Generic Human interests, needs, freedoms. By contrast, legal and other created (e.g. conventional or promissory) rights cannot owe their *existence* solely to the right-holder's interests or freedoms in the way that natural rights do. For created rights' existence depends on people creating them and, often, maintaining them in existence. But we might think

---

[21] The Varied Specific approach can be taken as interpreting 'being human' in roughly an existentialist way: on this view, what is distinctive of humanity is that it has no essence, and so the most important goods for a given human will be distinctive to that particular, embodied, and specific human (Sartre 1958 [1943] and especially 1948). The Shared Specific approach by contrast is roughly liberal: what is distinctive of humanity is that certain goods including freedom, absence of pain, and several specific freedoms (of speech, political participation, etc.) and capacities (being educated, fed, etc.) are important goods for all of us. Finally the Generic Human approach is perhaps roughly Aristotelian: each of us is such that certain things are good for us as a human whether or not they reflect our specific needs and interests as a particular embodied being. In the two paragraphs above in the main text, I introduced worries which should already make the 'Aristotelian' label seem inapt for the Generic Human approach, and we might similarly question whether 'liberal' properly captures a Shared Specific approach in which freedom or liberty need be only one shared value among others. The labels are less important than our choice among the approaches.

that some legal and conventional rights can be *morally justifiable*, if not grounded or made to exist, in a manner that is directly isomorphic to the grounding of natural rights for the right-holder's sake. This would involve *the legal right-holder's good* giving the agent all (in Section 8.2's STRONGEST sense) or most (STRONG A) of the case for creating, maintaining or respecting-qua-law the legal right in question. In this section, I show that such right-holder-based justification for legal rights is extremely unusual.[22] This is most evident if one adopts the Varied Specific view, but the point holds also for the Shared Specific and the Generic Human views.[23]

Law is general; it cannot in its canonical formulations place one under a duty specifically *not to assault Sarah* or any other duty with a proper name in it.[24] Instead, it must use general roles or kinds: perhaps a duty *not to assault citizens* or (in morally problematic jurisdictions) *not to assault special citizens* or *not to assault the prime minister*. This is part of what it means for positive law to be a *system*. The specific, idiosyncratic, and non-universal good of the particular right-holder Sarah—her good as picked out by the Varied Specific view—cannot in most cases constitute a moral reason *sufficient on its own*, nor constitute simply our *predominant* reason (STRONG A in Section 8.2's taxonomy), to justify our creating something so systematic, involving rights borne by all people who fall into specified roles or kinds, constituted by a wide array of duties. Nor is the specific, idiosyncratic, and non-universal good of the particular individual right-holder Sarah a moral reason sufficient on its own in most contexts to justify our *respecting* such rights because they are law. It is a reason to respect our duty not to assault Sarah, but rarely a reason to do so because it is the law.

Why not? Because Sarah's good—the good of *just one person*—is insufficiently important, and perhaps simply the wrong kind of good, on its own in normal circumstances either to justify creating or sustaining such systematic rights and duties or to justify respecting them because they have been created. As a retort, critics might direct me to the various laws named in honour of particular victims whose experiences generated the campaign that created the law. But consider a particular person's rights under such a law. Suppose the law is named for person X whose experiences triggered the campaign that created the law. Suppose that Y now holds a right under this law. Was X's good sufficient reason on its own (as in Section 8.2's STRONGEST model), or a major and rarely defeasible part of the reason (STRONG A), to justify creating, sustaining, or respecting the law encompassing Y's right alongside rights for many other people and their correlative legal duties? Was X's good sufficient or major reason to justify my respecting the law qua law—that is, the law wherever it holds, in its application to X, Y, and others Z and so on? Perhaps

---

[22] Thus I agree broadly with Buchanan on the following: 'No matter who you are, you are not important enough [I would add 'normally'] to justify a set of duties that correlate with [...] legal rights' (2013, pp. 63–4). But we will see that *sometimes* you might be important enough, and in Section 9.3, I will show that even when you are not your legal rights can still operationalize natural rights grounded for your sake.

[23] Thanks to Andrea Sangiovanni and Leif Wenar for pressing me on this.

[24] The proper name 'God' is, I think, admissible for use in law—but this is because in relation to mortals it also marks a role or kind.

sometimes the answers to these questions are 'yes'.[25] But I do not see how this can be a frequent response, even in relation to our most important human rights. What the law against assault does for one person is, I venture, insufficient to justify creating and maintaining this law without a significant justificatory role being played by the good of others who will also fall under this law (both as right-holders and duty-bearers). Creating and maintaining the right not to be assaulted which this law confers on one person cannot, I venture, be justified simply or primarily by what this law does for that person. This is especially clear when we remember that on the Varied Specific approach, the person in question's right-grounding interest in not being assaulted (which, we are assuming, is meant to justify creating and respecting the law) will not be shared by many of the other people on whom the law confers a similar right. The points above leave open the possibility that in rare cases (e.g. laws specifying roles filled by only one person) a particular individual's idiosyncratic interests *could* ground a whole law or convention. But this is rare. Furthermore, when such rare cases involve legal rights for more than one person, most bearers of the relevant legal rights under the law will not be the person— the X—for whose sake the law is created and maintained; only X will be. So most bearers of the relevant legal rights will bear them for X's sake rather than their own.

The Shared Specific approach is as unsuited as the Varied Specific approach to right-holder-based justifications for the creation and maintenance of legal rights, and for respecting such rights qua laws. Unlike the Varied Specific approach, the Shared Specific approach maintains that X's interest or need or freedom etc. is one which other potential right-holders under the law (Y, Z, . . .) share. But despite this fact, it still seems very unlikely that X's own interest, need or freedom could always (STRONGEST case) or normally (STRONG A) on its own constitute sufficient reason to create or maintain a law conferring rights on Y and Z, etc. as well as X. Similarly, it seems very unlikely that X's own interest, need, or freedom could always or normally on its own constitute sufficient reason to respect such a law qua law wherever it applies (i.e. including with regard to Y's and Z's rights under the law).[26]

But the Shared Specific approach opens the possibility of what I called STRONG B justifications for human rights laws. (The Varied Specific and Generic Human approaches can also deliver similar STRONG B justifications, but it is easier to see this in the Shared Specific case.[27]) Recall that a recognition-independent or natural duty owes its existence in a STRONG B way to a particular party's good in the following circumstances:

STRONG B: What the agent's PHI-ing does for the relevant party, in conjunction with *normal* further grounds for the agent's being duty-bound to PHI—such as the

---

[25] Perhaps sometimes the considerations in Section 8.3 might support this. X's interest in the group good of *its member's not suffering as X did* might be a feature of X that could—in a STRONGEST or STRONG A way—justify creating a law. But I suggest that this will be unusual.

[26] Note, however, that in the rare cases where X's own interest constitutes sufficient reason to create and maintain a law conferring rights on Y and Z as well, the Shared Specific view tells us that even though Y and Z will bear their rights for X's sake, they will also bear them for their own sake (i.e. Y's, Z's). For the Shared Specific view says that each person will share the kind of interest sufficient on its own to ground a system of rights for all. Compare the final sentences of the previous paragraph for the difference with the Varied Specific view.

[27] See note 30 below for the Varied Specific view's version of a STRONG B justification for human rights laws. The Generic Human view's version is discussed in the main text shortly.

fact that PHI-ing will involve creating or participating in an institution or practice from which many others can also benefit—together make it the case, in the face of any or at least most (and more than simply *normal*) countervailing considerations, that the agent is duty-bound to PHI.[28]

I claimed in Section 8.2 that because to play a STRONG B role in making a natural duty exist is not to play a *predominant* role in making it exist, a party whose good plays this role only satisfies to some extent Section 7.6's condition necessary for the duty naturally to be *owed to* the relevant party (as her *right*). But we can also make sense of the parallel notion of a particular party's good (interest, need, capability, freedom) functioning as STRONG B justification for creating, maintaining, or respecting some *legal* duty: the party's good will do this when what the relevant law or respect for it qua law would do for that party, in conjunction with normal further grounds for creating, maintaining, or respecting this law, are together sufficient to silence or outweigh most countervailing considerations. And Sections 5.1 and 7.7 tell us that if there are also good reasons—springing from the party's good or from other factors— to create and maintain this legal duty *as a right*, then it can be a legal right even though the right-holder's good's STRONG B role in justifying the legal duty in question is not a dominant role.

STRONG B justifications for laws allow us to place the individual's concrete, specific interest in PHI (say, in not being assaulted or in access to food) alongside what the Shared Specific approach tells us will be similar concrete, specific interests in PHI borne by other individuals, in order to generate the case for creating a law conferring rights to PHI on all relevant individuals, and for respecting that law as law. It seems to me that many laws can be grounded in this STRONG B way. Even if my interest in not being assaulted is insufficient on its own to justify our creation of a general law against assault, or to justify respect for this law as law in every case where you encounter it, nonetheless when my interest is placed alongside your identical interests and the identical interests of the many others who gain from not being assaulted, my interest can play a STRONG B role in justifying the creation of the law and our respect for it as law.[29] Exactly similar reasoning applies to the role my interest in having food can play in justifying the creation of, and respect for, a welfare system which will ensure I receive some subsistence supplies.[30]

---

[28] See Section 8.2.

[29] Note that in this example, I am treating a criminal law right—the right not to be assaulted—as a human right. For defence, see Section 10.2.

[30] We should note that if some laws function as roughly what Rawls called 'primary goods', that is, as laws that would serve the parties living under them even if the relevant parties had highly varied interests, laws that would serve a party *whatever* her good is, then creation, maintenance, and respect for such laws can be grounded in a STRONG B way by what they do for the right-holder even under the *Varied* Specific approach (Rawls 1971, p. 62). For such an approach could place humans' varying interests alongside each other in order to justify the creation of and respect for the relevantly universally useful laws. Personally, I am unsure whether (and if so, which) certain laws play such a function. If the Varied Specific view is taken in its more radical form—as the idea that only welfare and freedom in their most abstract sense are good for each human, with highly varied forms of welfare and freedom being goods for different humans—then I doubt many laws could helpfully serve enough varied humans to be justifiable in this way.

The Shared Specific approach thus enables us to conceive human rights law as justified for the right-holder's sake in a manner broadly similar to the right-holder-based ground for moral or natural pre-legal human rights. But the 'broad' in 'broadly similar' merits further attention. The approach does not allow that legal human rights (international or domestic) could be created, or respected as laws for reasons in which the particular individual right-holder's interests, needs, or freedoms, etc. play a STRONGEST or STRONG A role. The largest role, in their justification, for what legal human rights do for the right-holder, is the STRONG B one: a reason deployed alongside similar reasons generated or constituted by the important interests, needs, etc. of other people. Yet I suggested in Chapter 8 that many natural recognition-independent human rights will be grounded simply (STRONGEST) or primarily (STRONG A) on the basis of what they do for the right-holder.[31] So the Shared Specific approach, like the Varied Specific approach, drives a wedge between the recognition-independent, pre-legal, or natural human rights and those which are legally created: what they do for the right-holder plays a differing sort of role in their grounds.

The Generic Human approach, by contrast, seems prima facie to allow what legal human rights do for the right-holder to play a primary (e.g. STRONG A) role in their justification, just as it does for recognition-independent natural human rights. For what is special about the Generic Human approach is that Sarah's generic interest-qua-human in political participation is numerically rather than qualitatively identical to Joe's generic interest-qua-human in political participation. This is one and the same interest *not* in the sense that there are different right-grounding interests for each person and these interests are qualitatively identical in that they have the same content (that would be the Shared Specific approach). Rather, Sarah's generic interest-qua-human in political participation just is *the* generic interest-qua-human in political participation. All members of the relevant class—in this case, 'human'—partake in this one, numerically identical interest.

This seems to imply that when Sarah's generic interest-qua-human in political participation (which is *the* one and only interest-qua-human in political participation) functions on its own in a STRONG A or STRONGEST way to ground pre-legal rights that others enable her to participate, it can at the same time function in a similar STRONG A way to ground the creation of and respect qua law for legal rights with the same content. For surely it is attractive to see *the generic human interest in political participation* as itself, without the need for further support, a sufficient ground *both* in favour of a recognition-independent natural right borne by each human to political participation (constituted by directed duties to allow and facilitate such participation) *and* in favour of creating and respecting a *legal* right (constituted by parallel legal directed duties) borne by each human to political participation, a ground sufficient to override normal countervailing considerations.

But on closer inspection, the Generic Human approach to the justification of legal human rights turns out to be like the Varied and Shared Specific approaches after all.

---

[31] Natural 'positive' socio-economic rights might seem to be an exception, but see Sections 9.3–9.4 for defence of such rights, and their intricate relationship to my STRONG B conception.

This is because of the point mentioned in sketching the problems for the Generic Human approach at the end of Section 9.1: there is a genuine distinction between justifications based on 'the' generic human interest in political participation and justifications based on *Sarah's* generic human interest in political participation, even though these are numerically the same interest.[32] Defenders of the Generic Human approach must draw this distinction in order to preserve the idea that rights grounded or justifiable by the right-holder's generic human interests really are grounded or justifiable for the right-holder's sake. But once this distinction has been drawn, a gap opens up between how the approach handles natural and how it handles legal rights: the same gap encountered by the Varied and Shared Specific approaches. For even if *Sarah's* generic human interest in political participation is sufficient largely on its own to make us duty-bound to allow and encourage her participation, it will not be sufficient to justify our creating a systematic law allowing and encouraging such participation for her and all others: for that we need 'the' generic human interest in political participation, rather than focusing on this interest *as Sarah's*. We need this, I suggest, even though Sarah's generic human interest here just is 'the' generic human interest in question. Focused on as Sarah's—like a group's good when focused on as my good (see Section 8.3)—it has the wrong form to justify creating, sustaining, or respecting-qua-law a systematic legal or conventional human right.

To preserve a strict isomorphism between the grounding of natural and the justification of legal human rights, the Generic Approach would instead need to take even natural human rights as grounded not by what they do for the individual right-holder's generic human interests, but by what they do for 'generic human interests' as such—and then the natural bearer of such rights will be *the generic human*, and our own possession of such rights will depend on our participating in the genre 'human'. Such an approach makes natural human rights exist for the *generic* human right-holder's sake, but not for the sake of any particular, embodied human. If instead one wants to make the Generic Human approach conceive natural human rights as grounded for the concrete right-holder's sake, it looks as though one will need roughly the position sketched in the previous paragraph, in which natural and legal human rights' groundings diverge. I return to this, and the other problems of the Generic approach, in Section 9.6.

I think we have sufficient materials to be wary of the idea that most legal or conventional human rights could be morally justified in exactly the same right-holder-focused way that Chapter 8 tells us natural human rights are grounded. Each of Section 9.1's three approaches seems to make the justification of human rights law only distantly related to a given individual's good (e.g. in the STRONG B manner, for the Specific approaches), when compared to the major (STRONGEST or STRONG A) role played by such good in grounding the individual's pre-legal recognition-independent human rights.

But this does not mean we should follow Buchanan in seeing human rights law as sharply distinct from any prior natural rights. While we should abandon the idea that

---

[32] See p. 142, drawing on the intensionality of statements of justification.

justifications for legal and natural human rights can often be strictly isomorphic, we can still recognize that frequently a law is introduced specifically to give legal form to a prior natural human right held by many—and that at other times a law might succeed in doing this even if it has not been introduced for this purpose.[33] In either case, the creation and maintenance of the law, and respect for it as law, is likely to be justifiable only in a STRONG B manner by the specific interests of many parties together (e.g. interests in political participation), or, perhaps, justifiable in STRONG A manner by the generic interest of the citizen or the human. But it will give institutional form to a prior recognition-independent natural human right groundable for each particular, concrete right-holder in a STRONGEST or STRONG A manner by what it does for that individual. For example, the good to me of political participation is *sufficient* all on its own naturally to place my peers under a duty (owed to me as my natural right) to allow me to participate, and is *insufficient* on its own to justify creating a legal system of universal suffrage involving nationwide polling stations; but the latter system (creation, maintenance, and respect for which is justifiable only by the good of many (or some other good beyond that to the individual right-holder)) gives institutional form to my aforementioned natural right of political participation. Despite its STRONG B collectivist or STRONG A generic justification, the law and its institutions are in this case my community's way of giving public, legal form to pre-legal natural rights of each of its members which exist simply for each member's sake. (It is worth adding that the law in such a case need not be a mere means to enforce exactly what the pre-legal right already requires; it might also be a *determination* or *specification* or *extension* of this right, and an *expression* of it.[34])

9.3 The Foundational View, the Mirroring View, and Socio-Economic Human Rights

The previous section outlined two relations that legal human rights might bear to natural rights justifiable for the right-holder's sake. Most of the section focused on examining whether and when legal rights could be justified for the right-holder's sake in the same manner as the 'STRONGEST' or 'STRONG A' right-holder-focused groundings sketched for pre-legal natural rights in Section 8.2. Such justifications for legal human rights turned out to be unlikely to succeed. But the final paragraph of Section 9.2 introduced a different option: perhaps some legal human rights, while not justifiable for the right-holder's sake, nonetheless give legal form to natural rights that are so justifiable. This latter position looks like what Buchanan calls the 'mirroring view', but I shall argue that the best way to conceive pre-legal natural rights' relation to legal human rights is as a foundation rather than a mirror.[35] In the

---

[33] Consider, for example, the causal role that fears of revolution played in justifying the British nineteenth-century Reform Acts which extended the property franchise; these laws, I suggest, gave legal form to a natural right to political participation, even though this natural right, and the interests underlying it, were perhaps not the main reasons driving lawmakers: instead, arguably, fear of revolution was. (Note also that the reformed franchise laws were, of course, still unjust, exclusionary, and patriarchal.)

[34] See Harel 2014.   [35] Buchanan 2013, p. 17.

current section, I defend a place for legal human rights as legal determinations or operationalisations of pre-legal natural human rights.[36] It is important to make this defence because we will see in Section 9.5 that human rights law's relation to natural rights—and hence its relation to duties grounded for a particular party's sake as in Section 7.6—constitutes the strongest reason for such law to take a rights-type, directed structure, as opposed to a structure involving merely *undirected* legal duties.

There are several versions of what I call the 'foundational view' that legal human rights give institutional form to recognition-independent natural rights. We can quickly dismiss the crudest version which maintains that *whenever* a pre-legal natural right is grounded by its holder's good, we must create, sustain, and respect a legal right protecting it. As noted in Sections 5.1 and 7.7, the justification of recognition-dependent rights and duties, including all legal rights and duties, can turn on more than simply the value of the action they enjoin. Indeed I think recognition-dependent rights' and duties' justification is *always* partially instrumental: we should only build, maintain, or respect these human creations if so doing will generate good empirical results.[37] It follows that there is no natural right that must be legalized even if the heavens will fall. For example, even though duties to allow people freedom of worship are grounded as recognition-independent natural rights by the importance to the right-holder of such freedom, certain monoreligious societies might on balance have reason to refrain from legalizing this if, in Tasioulas's words, so doing would create 'grave social unrest and a steep decline in people's confidence in the legal system'.[38]

However, I believe that the existence of a pre-legal, recognition-independent natural *human* right—one (i) grounded by its holder's good (by its holder's human features taken in one of Section 9.1's three ways) and one (ii) that is everyone's business—always constitutes a defeasible *reason* for some form of legalization or institutionalization (perhaps non-legal) of its primary duty.[39] This is because of my view, defended in Sections 10.3–10.5, that human rights are necessarily 'public', necessarily in a certain sense everyone's business, demandable by anyone on the right-holder's behalf—and law and related institutions are the structures in which to enact such public demands. But we will see that this is compatible with there being rights that exist as natural rights for the right-holder's sake (on the basis of their important human features) yet that are not everyone's business; these natural rights (perhaps to one's partner's fidelity, or not to be lied to by one's friends) which fail to qualify as human rights need generate no reason whatsoever for their own legalization.[40] Furthermore, even recognition-independent or natural *human*

[36] Versions of what I call the foundational view are, I think, evident in Griffin, Nickel, Tasioulas, and even in Raz's 'political' account of human rights.

[37] By contrast, a *recognition-independent* duty to PHI is generated by the value of PHI, even if PHI's being a matter of recognition-independent duty has no effects or is counter-productive. See Chapter 7.

[38] Tasioulas 2007, p. 85.

[39] By 'primary duty', I mean the duty whose violation constitutes violation of the right: denying someone access to a polling station violates their right to political participation; failing to educate children about the political process does not violate that right's primary duty, though it plausibly violates secondary duties related to that primary duty (see Section 10.3).

[40] See Chapter 10 and Section 6.1. The examples are from Tasioulas 2012, pp. 40–1 and Gewirth 1982, p. 56.

rights (that are therefore everyone's business) need generate or constitute no reason for institutionalization through *international human rights law*. Again, we will see later (Section 10.2) that human rights on my account encompass many departments of law beyond international human rights law, including domestic criminal and welfare law.

The last paragraph's claim that recognition-independent, natural human rights must always (defeasibly) count in favour of laws or institutions protecting them is less common than the claim that any human rights law must have at its foundation prior recognition-independent natural human rights. I endorse both views, so long as we remember that the latter makes human rights law protect, determine, and operationalize recognition-independent human rights, without having strictly to 'mirror' such rights. Buchanan introduces what he calls the 'mirroring view' in order to attack it:

The Mirroring View holds that to justify an international legal human right typically involves defending the claim that a corresponding moral human right exists. The qualifier 'typically' is designed to accommodate the fact that some who hold this view acknowledge that in some cases a justified international legal right does not mirror a moral human right, but rather is either (a) a specification of a moral human right [...] or (b) something that is instrumentally valuable for realising a moral human right.[41]

Read in a certain spirit, this statement of the mirroring view seems true. But the spirit in which it should be read is, it seems, probably not Buchanan's.[42] First, one should take the view as maintaining that the best way to justify a legal human right—*whether international-legal or domestic*—is to begin by establishing that a corresponding recognition-independent, natural human right exists, and then to go on to examine whether the costs of legalizing this right are outweighed by its benefits. Secondly, one should read 'corresponding' broadly, so that a legal right can 'correspond' with a recognition-independent right on which it is founded without thereby having precisely the same content as that right: thus a legal right to an accessible polling station can 'correspond' in the relevant sense to a recognition-independent, natural right to political participation. Third and relatedly, clauses (a) and (b) in the quotation above should be taken not as rare exceptions but as commonplace: cases in which legal human rights are justified as specifications of or as instrumentally valuable for realizing recognition-independent rights. Read along the lines of the three points just listed, the statement quoted above makes the mirroring view attractive. But I am not sure that Buchanan takes the view in this expansive spirit (see e.g. his attribution of the mirroring view to Griffin on the basis that he sees international legal human rights as 'simply moral human rights in legal dress').[43] For this reason, I suggest we use the term 'foundational view' to capture the relation between legal and natural human rights that I endorse: legal human rights give institutional form to recognition-independent and hence 'natural' human rights, and the relevant legal institutionalizations need not have the same content as the natural rights on which they are based: the latter might be more abstract.

---

[41] Buchanan 2013, p. 17.   [42] It is certainly not the Buchanan portrayed in Tasioulas 2017.
[43] Buchanan 2013, p. 19.

Now Buchanan himself resists the 'mirroring view' he outlines, and I think he would want equally to resist what I call the 'foundational view'. His thought is that, first, as Section 9.2 tells us, my legal human right to the wide provision of polling stations (to return to that example) entails legal duties that are too costly to be justifiable by my good alone; but secondly, Buchanan infers from this that my legal human right to such polling stations cannot operationalize or specify a prior natural human right grounded predominantly in my good (in Section 8.2's sense).[44] So stated, Buchanan's inference seems implausible. I do not see why my costly legal right to a polling station, justifiable only by the good of many, cannot be an institutionalization or operationalization of my cheaper prior natural right to participate, grounded predominantly by my good. The legal right in question will at the same time institutionalize *others'* natural rights of participation too. But this kind of relation between the legal and the natural seems frequently encountered—and unthreatened by the differing relation that the legal and the natural bear to the right-holding party's good.[45]

O'Neill deploys a different argument to reach a conclusion that threatens my foundational view. She claims that while there are good reasons to institute legal human rights to 'goods and services' (to use her phrase), there are no natural pre-legal such rights because prior to institutionalization the duties correlative to such purported pre-legal rights would not be claimable from anyone in particular: their pre-legal indeterminacy means that they cannot exist as pre-legal right-correlative duties. She writes:

[T]he correspondence of universal liberty rights to universal obligations is relatively well-defined even when institutions are missing or weak. For example, violation of a right not to be raped or a right not to be tortured may be clear enough, and the perpetrator may even be identifiable, even when institutions of enforcement are lamentably weak. But the correspondence of universal rights to goods and services to obligations to *provide or deliver* remains entirely amorphous when institutions are missing or weak. Somebody who receives no maternity care may no doubt *assert* that her rights have been violated, but unless obligations to deliver that care have been established and distributed, she will not know where to press her claim, and it will be systematically obscure whether there is any perpetrator, or who has neglected or violated her rights.[46]

O'Neill concludes that while institutional or created human rights to goods and services are of great importance and should be created, they do not reflect or institutionalize pre-legal natural human rights. We should note that O'Neill's argument is targeted only at rights *to the provision of goods and services*, as opposed to rights to 'liberty' or 'non-interference': as she notes, 'the correspondence of universal liberty rights to universal obligations is relatively well-defined even when institutions are missing'.[47]

---

[44] Ibid., pp. 63–4.

[45] Similarly, to take another of Buchanan's examples, surely my expensive legal right to a vaccination programme can be an institutionalization of my cheaper prior natural right to some health care.

[46] O'Neill 2000, p. 105; see also O'Neill 2015, p. 77.

[47] Buchanan's argument, by contrast, is targeted at any legal right constituted by or generating legal duties that cannot be justifiably created, maintained, or respected qua law simply on the basis of an

I resist O'Neill, while—at Section 9.4—acknowledging an important limited truth revealed by her claims. O'Neill's distinction between rights to provision and liberty rights is reminiscent of Vasek's famous division of human rights into 'three generations': first, civil and political rights; secondly, social rights; and thirdly, solidarity rights including group rights and rights to peace and development.[48] It is also reminiscent of those who distinguish 'positive' from 'negative' rights.[49] Like many theorists, I am wary of these distinctions: while there is indeed an analytical distinction to be drawn between rights whose violation involves doing something active to the right-holder (e.g. rights against assault) and rights whose violation involves failing to do or provide something for the right-holder (e.g. rights to care), there are important cases that do not fall clearly on one side of it or the other. For example, do participants in global free trade actively impose poverty on those left starving in the context of such trade, or are they simply not assisted by it? I suspect there might be no determinate answer here.[50] Further, institutionalizing either kind of right famously involves costs and positive action.[51] And neither kind is morally more important than the other.[52] I will not argue for the points just mentioned. Instead, my aim is to show that both legal human rights to *provision* (O'Neill) and more broadly to *costly institutional action* (Buchanan) are plausibly founded on—and determine or operationalize—natural or recognition-independent human rights with more abstractly specified content. Without such an argument linking human rights law to duties grounded naturally for a particular party's sake (and hence to rights grounded for the right-holder's sake, to natural rights), we will see in Section 9.5 that we would have relatively weak reasons to endorse the rights-type, directed structure of human rights law: we could do as well with merely undirected legal duties.

My favoured way of rebutting O'Neill is to claim that any given human's important human interests, needs, or freedoms—whether conceived in a Specific or a Generic way—place *humanity* under demandable, categorical duties: duties that are owed naturally, recognition-independently, by humanity to the relevant specific human because they are grounded wholly (STRONGEST) or primarily (STRONG A) by her interests, needs, or freedoms. Often certain human interests ground duties for specific others: for example, Joseph's interest in not being tortured places each other

---

individual right-holder's interests—and Section 9.2 shows us that this will include the vast majority of legal human rights.

[48] Vasek 1977, pp. 29–30. For an excellent more recent taxonomy, see Nickel 2007, pp. 93–5.

[49] See libertarians such as Narveson 1988. Recall also that 'doing to' in the sense used in this volume, Chapter 4 (the sense in which any directed duty enjoins action done to the party to whom it is owed) is defined differently; it includes inactions. See Section 4.2, at note 4.

[50] See, e.g. Young's idea of 'structural injustice' (Young 2011); compare Ashford's and Shue's related work on the interrelation between apparently 'negative' and 'positive' violations (e.g. in Ashford 2015 and Shue 1980). See also Fellmeth 2016, pp. 221–5 for doubts about the action/inaction way of drawing the positive/negative distinction applied to rights correlating with *state-borne* duties. Fellmeth develops an alternative version of the distinction, focused on whether a duty-forbidden harm originates with the state or not (2016, p. 241).

[51] Holmes and Sunstein 1999.

[52] See, e.g. Rachels 1979, Singer 1972, or more recently in relation specifically to *human rights*, Jones 2013.

human under duties not to torture him. This was the model I worked with in Chapter 7 but we need not see individual humans as the only parties subject to natural duties.[53] I think that every relevantly important interest, need, or freedom also places duties on humanity at large. Thus, for example, I claim that Joseph's subsistence needs are sufficient on their own to place humanity under a duty, naturally correlating with a right for Joseph, to supply these needs. Humanity bears this duty naturally even though, as O'Neill tells us, prior to institutionalization it is not clear whether any specific individual human has a duty to feed Joseph, or to supply some proportion of his food or to work to institutionalize a property system in which he could feed himself, and so on. Nonetheless, in my view humanity has a duty to ensure that Joseph can meet his subsistence needs. And if Joseph is unable to meet these needs, he can permissibly demand that humanity do something about this, a demand which if unmet leaves a 'remainder' duty also borne by humanity. He can similarly demand an education, medical care, or political participation.

Now, my claim that humanity is the bearer of the relevant duties—or indeed any duties—is extremely controversial. It raises many issues that are matters of debate, such as whether humanity is an agent and if not, whether it can still bear duties, and what the implications are for individual humans of duties borne by humanity.[54] I cannot address these issues here, and hence I cannot here fully defend the position I favour. But I will outline my reasons for it before—in the next section (9.4)— sketching alternative positions that also go some way towards addressing O'Neill and Buchanan.

My primary reason for saying that we all hold recognition-independent, natural human rights, for example to subsistence, education, medical care, or political participation, constituted by duties owed to us *by humanity*, is simply that when someone's important interest, need, freedom, or capability goes unmet or unrespected—for example, when someone dies of starvation in our wealthy modern world—it strikes me as obvious that humanity has let this person down (other things being equal).[55] It seems to me that we should see this not simply as a metaphorical way of saying that something regrettable has happened, nor even as a metaphorical way of saying that some people have failed to fulfil undirected duties and hence

---

[53] See the final paragraph of Section 7.2.

[54] On collective agency and the difficulties and possibilities for duties borne by uncoordinated groups like 'humanity', see, e.g. Wringe 2005 and 2010, List and Pettit 2011, Collins 2013, Schwenkenbecher 2013, Lawford-Smith 2015, and Dietz 2016; my view is close to Dietz's and (even more so) to Wringe's except that I see 'humanity' as a highly distinct collective, neither random nor corporate but *sui generis*—as discussed shortly in the main text.

[55] Should we add that the relevant important interest must go unmet despite humanity's being able to meet it *with some ease*? Probably yes, if we are describing a *violation* of a human right. But justified *infringement* might occur when someone is left to starve even though saving them would incur unjustifiable costs (Thomson 1990, ch. 4). If there is a natural human right not to starve, this I think is infringed— though not violated—even when someone starves because a fair system for coping with famine, say, leaves them with the short straw. This is a consequence of regarding the right as justified in Section 8.2's STRONGEST sense by the interest in nourishment. A STRONG A approach instead could say that in such extreme circumstances, the relevant duty (and hence right) vanishes. My aim here does not require the controversial STRONGEST interpretation, though it is the one I would favour.

have done wrong.[56] Rather, we should rather take this at its face value, as saying that humanity has *wronged* the person in question—by leaving one of her important interests, needs, freedoms, or capabilities unmet or unrespected when it had the resources to meet or respect this. Through our social structures, interactions, and attitudes within which context this person died of starvation, we, humanity, have wronged this person, one of our members. In Section 7.6's sense, the person's good has placed humanity under a duty—which it has violated.

'Humanity' here does not mean the particular collective constituted by the set of humans alive at the moment of utterance. It would be odd to say that this particular collective bears duties, partly because this particular collective will cease to exist almost immediately after being referred to, as some members die and new people come of age; for the same reason, the relevant particular collective will only have come into existence at the moment of utterance. 'Humanity' is not a *random* collective of this type.[57] But nor does 'humanity' mean a corporate entity like Microsoft, with an identity distinct from its members' identities, and that can flourish even at the expense of some of its members. So what does 'humanity' mean, when ascribed duties constitutive of natural human rights? I regret to say that I cannot answer this here. It seems to me that its form as a collective or community is distinctive and perhaps *sui generis*—and that the idea of humanity in the relevant sense as a *community* is important.[58] In my view, to fail to conceive humanity as a community which acts, and in whose actions one's own actions participate, is to make a metaphysical error about humans akin to the individualistic 'atomism' condemned by Taylor.[59] Each human has to see herself as part of the human community—of humanity, and as acting as part of humanity's actions—if she is properly to respect other humans. The shared values necessary for communication, coupled with the fact that each human qua human can in principle communicate with any other human, I think entail that humanity is a community in at least one loose sense.[60] But my further claim that this community can act, and that proper understanding by its members of their form as human requires understanding this, of course requires more argument. Nonetheless, it should be clear that on my view making *humanity* a bearer of duties is not to absolve humanity's members from playing parts in fulfilling these duties.

Note that I am attracted to this view partly because I am doubtful about contemporary philosophy's implicit assumption that it is somehow simpler or less

---

[56] This would be O'Neill's diagnosis. See also Hope 2013.

[57] So I would reject Tomalty's attack on this approach by denying her view that humanity is a random collective (see Tomalty 2014, pp. 11–13).

[58] See my Cruft 2010, but there I made the category error I diagnose in Kamm, Nagel, and Raz in Sections 7.4 and 7.8. For a conception of the collective that is neither 'corporate' nor 'random collective', see Haase 2012.

[59] Taylor 1985. Compare also this suggestive passage from Julius 2016, at p. 209: 'I don't just think there are several goats grazing in the same pasture, and I'm one. I see myself as a goat by nature capable of and responsible for co-grazing with the other co-grazers. I know myself to be someone whose nature includes my capacities and responsibility for knowing and valuing other persons capable and responsible for the like knowing and valuing of me. It's because I can know myself to be one of the many, and to act from this knowledge as one protagonist of several lives, that I am one-of-many by nature.'

[60] Davidson 1984.

controversial to start with the *individual human agent* as a bearer of duties, before moving on to more complicated cases like groups, collectives, or non-human agents. It is unclear to me that any particular form of agent is the best starting point—and that is part of the reason for my willingness to embrace what many will regard as the extravagance of humanity as an agent.[61] Any given individual agent seems to me to be composed of a confusing aggregation in many of the same ways that a group, or indeed humanity, is.

I recognize that these are highly sketchy remarks that will not persuade those (no doubt most) readers not already on my side. I stand by the claim. It seems obvious to me that humanity wrongs any human who starves to death, or of affordably treatable disease, or who goes uneducated, just as—through the action of one of its members—it wrongs any one of its members who is murdered or assaulted. Contra O'Neill, I would say that each of the actions enjoined or required by these duties, including 'positive' actions providing 'goods and services', are permissibly demandable from humanity by the human in question, or by others on her behalf. They are naturally owed by humanity, as recognition-independent human rights, to the relevant human whose good grounds them. If this is correct, then legal and institutional rights that supply the goods in question (from the legal rights in the European Convention on Human Rights to the domestic administrative rights conferred by a particular welfare system, including the British right to child benefit payments, say) are legal entities that give institutional form to recognition-independent, natural human rights which constitute their moral foundation—despite Buchanan's and O'Neill's claims to the contrary. The relevant legal rights in this sense institutionalize or give legal form to recognition-independent natural rights, rights that exist *for the right-holder's sake*, even though Section 9.2 tells us that, qua legal rights, their justification normally depends on the interests of many people (or, perhaps, on the interests of 'the generic human'). Nonetheless they are structures operationalizing—giving legal, determinate form to—the duties humanity bears to fulfil natural human rights which themselves exist for the particular right-holder's sake. We will see in Section 9.5 that this is a central part of the case for conceiving such legal, conventional, institutional entities in *rights*-type, directed terms.

9.4 Duty-Generation by the Right-Holder's Good and by Other Values

Readers who know the literature on O'Neill will wonder why I have overlooked the many less metaphysically extravagant proposals for responding to her. Instead of focusing on duties owed naturally by *humanity* to each right-holder, why not appeal

---

[61] This is my response to what Elizabeth Kahn characterizes as the need 'to avoid the arbitrary prioritisation of those requirements of justice that do not require collectivisation to be achieved' (2018, p. 16). In future work, I hope to investigate how my humanity-based approach relates to the approach Kahn draws from Collins 2013, in which 'all people have duties to collectivise in order to achieve the fulfilment of demands of fundamental justice as part of their positive duty to promote and support justice' (Kahn 2018, p. 12); in so collectivizing I would say that humanity is thereby taking its first step towards fulfilling the duties grounded by an individual's good. See note 79 below.

to the fact that the pre-institutional indeterminacy she identifies can be resolved by additional moral principles that allocate specific natural pre-institutional duties *to individuals or to corporate entities like the state*, natural duties the joint fulfilment of which would secure each human with an education, with subsistence supplies, etc.?

Proposals in the literature include Barry's contribution principle (which says agents who 'merely suspect' that they have contributed to the existence of acute deprivations—in terms of health or education, say—bear duties to alleviate them),[62] Kamm's principles about the importance of proximity (which claim that we bear greater responsibility to alleviate suffering the nearer we or our means are to the suffering person or the threat to them),[63] Miller's 'connection theory' of responsibility (which proposes 'six ways in which remedial responsibilities [e.g. duties to provide health care, housing or education] might be identified' and allocated, including to those who cause the deprivation, to those who benefit from it, to those capable of alleviating it, and to those sharing community with the suffering person),[64] Stemplowska's proposal that each individual has a natural claim to assistance (a contribution towards subsistence supplies, education, etc.) from any individual human who has not already met someone else's similar claim,[65] or Wenar's least-cost principle (which says that 'the agent who can most easily avert the threat [e.g. by delivering subsistence supplies] has the responsibility for doing so—so long as doing so will not be excessively costly').[66] If any one of these proposals is correct, then it looks as though an individual human's good (their interest, need, freedom, capability, whether Specific or Generic) will *in conjunction with the relevant principle* 'naturally' generate pre-institutional duties borne by individual humans or metaphysically respectable corporate agents like the state. Don't these correlate with natural rights in my sense: rights (to the relevant behaviour from individuals and corporate entities) that exist independently of whether anyone recognizes their existence? Why not say that *these* natural rights are those that human rights law can operationalize? Why leap instead to Section 9.3's metaphysical extravagance of *humanity's* duties?

But here is what I called the 'important limited truth' in O'Neill's critique. Even if we can identify the relevant principles (among the suggestions just listed) and hence make determinate the allocation and content of natural pre-institutional individually or corporately (e.g. state-) borne duties to supply a party with subsistence or education, it is not the relevant party's good (her Generic or Specific interest, need, freedom, etc.) which performs this determination. The extra principles do this, and because—O'Neill tells us—the party's good does not on its own discriminate between the disjunction of possible specific determinations which would serve or respect that good, it looks as though the resultant duties do not exist for the party's sake in my

---

[62] Barry 2005.
[63] Kamm 2007, chs 11 and 12; see also Kamm 2007, p. 377 for a summary of her claims about our intuitions.
[64] Miller 2007, pp. 99–107.   [65] Stemplowska 2009, p. 482.
[66] Wenar 2007, p. 260. Compare also Tasioulas and Vayena's 2016 suggestion that each individual naturally bears a duty to contribute to each other individual whatever 'fair' contribution would be required by a fair tax system.

STRONG A or STRONGEST senses. Instead, the prominent role played by the extra principles mean that the party's good can at best play a STRONG B role—*alongside the principles in question*—in grounding such duties. If this is correct, then Section 8.2 tells us that the relevant duties will not meet the condition they must meet if they are to be in the fullest sense naturally, recognition-independently owed to the party in question. They might be recognition-independent or natural *duties*, but their status as recognition-independent or natural *rights* will be less than full because the relevant duties do not exist wholly or predominantly for the putative right-holder's sake. Natural duties become progressively less plausibly recognition-independently *directed at* or *owed to* a party as the role of that party's good in grounding them diminishes.

Now the point above might seem to rule out all the proposals listed, as routes to natural *rights* to goods and services (as opposed to *undirected* natural duties to provide goods and services). When compared to the humanity-based approach, according to which a party's good does all (STRONGEST) or the predominant (STRONG A) work in determining 'positive' natural duties borne by humanity, to supply that party with goods and services, the alternative proposals invoke principles other than the party's good as duty-generators, and these principles' role thereby diminishes the natural directedness or rights-correlativity of whatever duties they help ground. But on closer inspection I contend that it turns out that *some* of the proposals that determine who has natural duties to supply 'positive' goods and services to a party do more to threaten the natural directedness of the relevant duties (as rights for the party in question) than *others*. In particular, I suggest that Section 7.6 tells us that STRONG B groundings for a duty in which *the fact that the performance of the duty-enjoined action will serve or respect the good of other parties* plays a major role in grounding that duty do more to threaten the duty's naturally being owed to me than other kinds of STRONG B groundings.

I explain with an example. Suppose that *you* (as opposed to some other person or institution) are naturally made duty-bound to supply me with an education on the basis that your educating me, as opposed to others doing it, both serves my need for an education and serves others who would not be served if you were not to educate me. The role played by my need in the generation of your duty is here diluted by the role played alongside my need by the good of others. The importance, in the generation of your duty, of your action's serving those others, means that if you are fully virtuous you should not think simply of the action as to be done to me, but to 'us' (where this includes the relevant others). The degree to which the duty exists for my sake, and hence is naturally owed to me, is thereby diluted (see Section 7.6).

But I do not think the diluting effect is nearly so great if the role played by the good of others in generating the duty is not that the enjoined action will *serve* or *contribute to* this good. Consider Stemplowska's proposal: that I hold a natural right to be educated (say) which gives me a claim against any individual who has not already met someone else's similar claim.[67] This proposal says that even in contexts with merely 'normal' countervailing considerations, my good—the importance to me of

---

[67] Stemplowska 2009, p. 482. Compare also Tasioulas and Vayena 2016.

my being educated—does not on its own make it the case that you must provide me with the resources for an education. Rather, the fairness-related fact *that you have not already provided the relevant assistance to another* is, on Stemplowska's proposal, an essential and important component working alongside my good in making it the case that you bear the duty in question. My good thus plays neither a STRONG A nor a STRONGEST role in the generation of the duty.[68] Nonetheless, it seems to me that according to this proposal, in the generation of the duty it is only my good that plays the role of something to be served or contributed to by the action enjoined. Your good, and the good of other potential contributors including those who have already assisted other people, do not figure in the generation of your duty *as something to be served by your education-providing action*. Rather, it seems as though the other parties' interests figure in the duty-generation as served by the *allocation* of the duty (in the sense of being treated fairly by its allocation), but not served by the duty's *performance* (in the sense of being served by the action the duty enjoins). I suggest that this is an important difference. STRONG B justifications of duties in which only a single party's good figures as *that to be served* make the relevant action more naturally conceivable as to be done for the sake of that party than for the sake of others whose good might be respected or in some other way acknowledged by the duty's allocation.[69]

This point implies that there is indeed a truth in O'Neill's critique, but the truth is limited. The truth is that any natural duties to supply goods and services for a party, if of determinate content[70] and borne by an individual or corporate entity, as opposed to humanity (see Section 9.3), must owe their existence in significant part to principles beyond the relevant party's good—and must to that extent be less than fully naturally owed to that party as her natural right. The limitation on this truth is that when the additional principles combine with the party's good (to make a duty exist naturally) in a manner that does not make *the serving of others' goods* the purpose of the duty-enjoined action, there is still a natural sense in which the duty exists for the sake of the party in question. Admittedly, under these circumstances the party's good does not work *on its own*, even in 'normal' conditions, to make the duty exist. But when the action is virtuously performed, it will not be for the purpose of serving any others beyond the relevant party. The identification of the agent, and the precise determination of the action required, will depend on such further interests— for example, on what would be a fair (e.g. Stemplowska, Tasioulas and Vayena) or efficient (e.g. Wenar) way to respect such interests. But the action's positive contribution to the world, vis-à-vis its nonperformance by anyone, seems to depend wholly on what it does for the party in question. Because of this, I suggest that the dilution of the contribution of the party's own good by principles of the type in question—even

---

[68] See Section 8.2.

[69] This point should be recalled when considering the distinction between duties grounded as serving some good and as respecting or in other ways made apt by it. See Section 7.3, p. 99.

[70] I think it possible that a given party's good naturally on its own in my STRONGEST sense generates *highly indeterminate* duties to supply goods and services for that party, borne by each individual—but these will be duties 'to do something about' supplying such goods. For more determinacy, we need something like the principles introduced at the opening of Section 9.4—or we need Section 9.3's approach in which humanity is the duty-bearer.

though it makes the relevant grounding a STRONG B one—does not do a lot to reduce the degree to which the relevant duty is naturally owed to the party.

In light of this discussion, we might adopt an appropriate one of the principles which opened the current section, and jettison the humanity-based approach of Section 9.3. We could then, contra O'Neill (and Buchanan), identify quite precise natural 'positive' rights to goods and services, held against individuals or corporate entities such as states, for human rights law to institutionalize. I will not do this, first because I believe in the humanity-based approach which generates natural positive rights in my STRONGEST or STRONG A sense (and thereby generates duties that are in the fullest sense naturally *owed to* the relevant parties), and secondly because I shall not compare the many different possible proposals outlined at the start of this section.

But I do want to sketch one particularly important such proposal, to complement Section 9.3's humanity-based approach. This proposal is that we hold natural rights against the state.[71] In the modern world of states, it seems plausible to maintain that an individual's important good—say, the importance to me of being nourished—naturally, recognition-independently places *her state* under a duty to ensure that this good is respected or provided. If I die of starvation in the United Kingdom, other things being equal the United Kingdom has failed to fulfil a natural duty to see to it that each and every one of its members (citizens, inhabitants?) can feed themselves. Section 9.2 showed us that my good is insufficient on its own to justify creating or maintaining a state-wide law that would secure me against starvation. But it might well seem that my good is sufficient on its own to place the United Kingdom under a natural, pre-institutional duty to ensure that *I* do not starve. Isn't this duty borne by the UK naturally owed to me, grounded in my good?[72] Now, my good does not work all on its own, even in contexts with only 'normal' countervailing considerations, to ground the UK's natural duty here. To generate the duty in question, my good needs to work in conjunction with principles allocating responsibilities for different people to different states, principles that determine whether I am the UK's business (principles that might risk leaving some as no state's business).[73] But this point only indicates a limited reduction in the extent to which the UK bears a duty *naturally owed to me* to ensure I can feed myself. This is because of the point earlier in this section: while my own good cannot work on its own as the sole or predominant ground for the UK's natural duty here, it is the only good that the duty-enjoined action need have as its purpose to serve; the allocation of the duty to the UK depends on further factors, but the duty-enjoined action's performance vis-à-vis its non-performance is necessitated simply by my good.

My claim here is akin to but distinct from various 'political' views of human rights: the right in question is not itself a political *creation*, nor need it define the

---

[71] I am inspired here partly by Dworkin's 2011 work (pp. 332–38) on the distinctiveness of *state attitudes of disrespect*.

[72] Of course it is not a duty that would exist in a stateless 'state of nature', but it is a duty whose existence is independent of whether anyone anywhere recognizes that it exists.

[73] For important wider doubts about the limitations implied by the statism of contemporary liberalism, see Flikschuh 2017, ch. 7—and further discussion in this volume, Chapter 10.

limits of permissible interference with state sovereignty.[74] It is, rather, a recognition-independent, natural right held against a distinctively political entity: the state. Contra Buchanan and O'Neill, such natural human rights are prevalent, including rights that one's state secures one with political participation, education, health care, and so on. Contra Buchanan and O'Neill, legal and other created institutional rights (e.g. within welfare and health care systems) operationalize these natural rights. Admittedly, because the right-holding party's good is not the sole or predominant generator of the natural state-borne duty in question, this duty is not in the fullest (STRONGEST or STRONG A) sense naturally owed to the party as her natural right. But the role played in its grounding by the party's good makes the duty nonetheless to a significant degree (STRONG B in a manner in which the reason for the *performance* of the duty need be only her good) naturally owed to her as her right.[75]

Let me summarize where we are. I have claimed (Section 9.3) that my good works in a STRONGEST or STRONG A way to make humanity naturally pre-institutionally duty-bound to serve it both 'positively' and 'negatively'—and hence the relevant duties humanity is under are naturally owed to me as my natural rights. In the current section (9.4) I have argued that O'Neill's point teaches us that my good requires significant supplementation by further principles if it is naturally to ground pre-institutional determinate 'positive' duties borne by individuals or corporate entities like the state, though it does not require such supplementation to ground 'negative' duties so borne. The previous paragraphs showed us that the relevant kind of supplementation need not go far to diminish the sense in which duties borne by individuals—or, I highlighted, *the state*—might be naturally a party's 'positive' right, grounded for that party's sake and to be institutionalized in human rights law. It is, nonetheless, a notable diminution in their natural rights character.[76]

Before drawing out the implications of these points, I briefly address a concern: have I been forced to opt for *humanity* as the agent of our natural 'positive' rights (Section 9.3), and then to consider the alternative principles involving *individual* and *state agents* (the current Section 9.4), because my Hohfeldian Addressive conception of directed duties (Chapter 4) and my taxonomy of degrees of natural directedness (Section 8.2) necessitate this? Are these conceptions of directed duties and rights with which I am working illegitimately narrow—in their Hohfeldian focus on rights as correlating with *duties for which there are agents*? Now as it happens I think it would be possible to develop versions of my Addressive view of directedness, and of Chapter 8's taxonomy of degrees of subject-grounded (and hence natural) directed-ness, in which the Hohfeldian idea of a *duty with an agent* is replaced by something

---

[74] Compare Beitz 2009 or Raz 2010.

[75] Note that this approach, if taken on its own without my further humanity-based approach, would seem potentially to leave some with different human rights to others, depending on whether they had a state and what that state was capable of.

[76] One might try to develop this line of thinking in relation to the legal rights that Section 9.2 told us could not be grounded for the right-holder's sake. But because legal rights are fundamentally general in form, any particular person's good cannot play the role, in grounding the right, of 'that to be promoted by the enjoined action': this would allow, say, my interest in not being assaulted to play the role of 'that which is to be promoted' in grounding your duty not to assault anyone under the law, whether me or another. Section 9.2 tells us that individual goods are very unlikely to play this role.

less agential, such as a *norm or standard that must be met, or a social structure that must exist*. For example, we could say that a required social structure (that might but need not entail an individual or collective agent to deliver it) is owed to a capable party iff that party is formally required to conceive the changes that would result in the creation of the structure in the first person as 'to happen to me'.[77] And we could run Section 8.2's taxonomy on the degree to which a party's good makes such a requirement for such a structure exist—thus we could say that the structure is some party's natural right (which legal rights could then 'mirror', or on which they could be 'founded') when that party's good plays a predominant role in making it the case that the structure is required.[78] Thus much of my machinery could work without the idea that a right must have a duty-bearing party who will violate the right if she fails to fulfil the duty. My turn to the options in Sections 9.3–9.4 should therefore not be seen as driven by these aspects of my theory. Instead, I turn to Sections 9.3–9.4's agential, Hohfeldian options partly for their own plausibility (as noted, it seems obvious to me that humanity wrongs a party who starves to death), and partly because the idea of a right seems to me closely tied to the ideas of *violation and action* entailed by the concept of a duty: without such ties—that is, without the Hohfeldian idea of rights as constituted by action-enjoining duties held by agents— what we are left with seems insufficiently distinct from the notion of a value (see Section 1.2).[79]

9.5 Vindicating the 'Rights' in Human Rights Law

The main points in the previous two sections are important for showing on the one hand (Section 9.3) that there are natural rights that contemporary human rights law and institutions can be seen as operationalizing or determining, and yet on the other hand (Section 9.4) the very specific individually borne natural duties that are determined by the best moral principles need not be the duties that law and institutions must operationalize or determine, in order to qualify as legalising our natural human rights. Both points deserve more discussion.

The first point is important to a defence of the rights-type, 'directed' structure of human rights law. We saw in Part I (and will see again in Chapter 13) that the

---

[77] We would, however, struggle to find a non-agential parallel of the formal requirement to conceive the right-holding party second-personally as 'you, on whom I am to act'. See Chapter 4.

[78] For work towards this idea, see Cruft 2012.

[79] I recognize, however, that I have not done enough to explore the options in the work of e.g. Young 2011, Collins 2013, Kahn 2018. I am tempted to think that insofar as these take human rights to ascribe duties, the rights in question will be rights against the relevant duty-bearers (e.g. rights that all parties collectivize in order to address the relevant problems); and insofar as they take human rights not to ascribe duties, the rights in question will be akin to values. But this is obviously a place-holder for more work. In Cruft 2012, I try out the idea that what we might call 'subject-grounded values'—values whose existence as values depends in something like one of Section 8.2's STRONG senses on a particular party's good—look rather like 'claim-rights without correlative duties'. *Perhaps* some human rights claims are best conceived along these non-Hohfeldian lines. I have resisted this because it seems to me that use of the term 'rights' (rather than 'values') to refer to such entities will impede rather than aid understanding. And because the approaches in Sections 9.3–9.4 show that we really can find Hohfeldian natural claim-rights at the foundation of the legal-institutional rights in question.

behaviour for which we need legal institutional rights could be equally secured by non-rights, undirected legal duties and similar structures. I believe that the principal reason to structure legal and institutional duties as owed to someone, correlating with their rights, is because this reflects the fact that these structures institutionalize natural duties that are naturally, recognition-independently 'directed' to someone as their rights. In my view, most legal human rights—including domestic constitutional and other rights, and international human rights law—give legal form to natural rights that the individual holds against humanity, other individuals, and her own state on the basis of the importance simply of her own human good.[80] Now sometimes legal structures which operationalize natural human rights fail themselves to take the form of rights, or fail to be conceptualized in right-type ways. We see this, for example, in the thinking which conceives welfare provision or education primarily in terms of its contribution to economic efficiency. Even if this form of thinking is used to justify welfare institutions and educational institutions that deliver excellent services, if the institutions are not conceived as delivering *rights*, then citizens risk being misled into overlooking the fact that the institutions in question are our local legal institutional way of operationalizing prior natural rights. It is for its contribution to our *understanding*—of the fact that certain laws institutionalize natural duties grounded primarily by a particular party's good—that a rights-type structure is required for the relevant laws and institutions. This is our best reason for making human rights law take a rights-type structure.

The second point is that legal and institutional rights can determine or operationalize natural human rights even if they do not involve the precise individually borne natural duties determined by Section 9.4's moral-principles-that-go-beyond-the-right-holding-party's-good (i.e. Barry's, Kamm's, Miller's, Stemplowska's, Tasioulas and Vayena's, Wenar's, etc.).[81] Suppose a society has created certain legal rights and these institutionally realize some natural human right, such as the right that humanity ensure one access to nourishment, a right grounded in a STRONGEST way on one's interest in nourishment. And suppose these legal rights do not at the same time threaten other natural rights or duties. But suppose that among the values-beyond-good-to-the-right-holder that played a major part in lawmakers' and citizens' decisions to create, maintain, or respect the particular legal rights in question were several democratically admissible principles *other than* the favoured moral principles of Section 9.4 (Barry's, Kamm's, Miller's, Stemplowska's, etc.). Indeed suppose the legal rights in question fail to live up to the requirements of the latter principles: perhaps the legal rights in question are somewhat inefficient, fail to respond to historical injustice or proximity, or are to some degree unfair. The relevant legal rights could nonetheless be truthfully taken as our local legal way of giving institutional form to the individual's important natural, recognition-independent rights— natural rights that exist for the right-holder's sake. The latter point should not be taken as underplaying the importance of Section 9.4's moral principles in human

---

[80] See Sections 9.3–9.4 for details of the roles the individual's good can play in generating 'positive' rights against humanity, the state, and other individuals.
[81] See notes 62–66 above.

rights legalization and, in the jargon, 'responsibilization'.[82] We just need to remember that the demands of these principles go beyond the demands of duties generated by the individual's good alone—and get us thereby progressively further from the demands of duties naturally taking the form of rights.

9.6 Conclusion: The 'Human' in Human Rights

This chapter explored the intricate relation between the individual's good and natural and created-legal duties, and their natural or created direction. Does my defence of the 'foundational view' over the previous sections help resolve Section 9.1's question about how to conceive the individual's good at the heart of her human rights—as Varied Specific, Shared Specific, or Generic?

One version of the Generic Human view has the advantage that it allows us, if we wish, to dispense with the 'foundational view', and to regard the metaphysical distinction between posited-legal-created and natural or recognition-independent rights as comparatively unimportant in relation to our concept of human rights. On this version of the Generic Human view, whether a right—legal or natural—is a human right depends straightforwardly on a single issue, namely whether it is grounded or justifiable by the generic human's good (generic human interests, freedoms, needs).[83] The generic human's good can play as significant a part in justifying creation, maintenance, and respect for legal rights as it can play in grounding natural rights. To maintain the closest isomorphism between human rights law and natural rights, we might therefore choose this view. But in Section 9.1, I raised a question about whether this version really takes human rights (natural or legal) to be for the right-holder's sake: they exist or are justified ultimately not for the sake of the concrete right-holder, but for the generic human. Further, I also introduced some serious problems for the alternative version of the Generic Human view which distinguishes natural human rights, grounded by *the particular right-holder's generic human good*, from legal human rights justified by *'the' generic human's good*.

But both Generic Human approaches might still seem moderately attractive. Carter suggests that treating one's fellows generically—as 'human' or 'citizen' without delving into their specific details—looks like a form of respect. Carter puts this point in his claim that treating someone as 'opaque' is central to respect.[84] This means not investigating the specifics of the person's nature, not responding to someone in the knowledge that they are weak-willed, or unusually courageous, or have a family that depends on them—but rather responding to them as a generic citizen (Carter's focus) or generic human (my Generic Human approach). Is Carter right that this is the more respectful attitude? Sometimes responding to someone in their idiosyncratic specificity seems respectful. Consider a student who one knows has had lots of problems (perhaps family and personal problems) but has not applied for an extension to their essay deadline. Is it more respectful—*ceteris paribus*—to apply

---

[82] See, for example, Reinecke and Ansari 2016.

[83] It will also depend on whether the rights in question are 'everyone's business' in the sense explored in Sections 10.3–10.5, but I set that aside here.

[84] Carter 2011.

the rules generously, perhaps giving them extra time without their requesting it (thereby treating them in all their specificity as an idiosyncratic, situated person), or is it more respectful to treat them as a 'standard student' and stick strictly to the letter of the rules (thereby treating them generically)? I often find myself unsure in such cases. Sometimes I am inclined towards the latter approach, and one might see this as weighing at least to some degree in favour of the Generic Human views.

But on inspection, the case above does not really point in favour of the Generic Human views. It is essential to these views that a concrete human's specific good or interests can diverge from her good as a generic human, and that the grounding of human rights follows either *her* generic good or *the generic human's* good—rather than her specific good.[85] By contrast, Carter's suggestion and my intuitions in support of it point towards the view that what is really in the interests of or good for a given individual are often what would enable her to flourish as a human, or as a citizen, or as a student. That is, in deciding to treat the student generically I am not thereby deciding to act against or to overlook her specific contextually determined interests or good; I am rather deciding that these interests would be best served by treating her generically—and underpinning this is the premise that our generic interests often constitute our truest concrete interests. Yet if that premise is our starting point, this can lead either Generic Human view to collapse into a form of, or account of, the Shared Specific view: a version of that view which holds that each individual human shares certain important right-grounding specific goods (interests, needs, freedoms), and which explains *why* each shares this by reference to the fact that to realize the relevant specific goods is to flourish generically as a human.

The Generic Human views need not be taken in this way. One might see Generic Human interests as grounding human rights independently of the thesis that satisfying these interests enables their concrete human bearer to do well. But this seems to involve giving up on the idea of human rights as *for the right-holder's sake*. Instead, they would be rights that exist for the sake of the generic human, or perhaps for humanity or for humanness. Insofar as they are naturally grounded by the good of the generic human, they would be owed naturally to 'the human', and only to individuals as 'participants in the human'. The same would be true even for the view that *my* interests as a generic human are what ground my human rights—for remember that what is good for me as a generic human is meant to be independent of what is good for me *simpliciter*. To keep the Generic Human view genuinely grounding rights for the specific right-holder's sake, we need instead the interpretation in the previous paragraph, according to which it underpins or explains the Shared Specific view.

I remain open to a defence of human rights for the sake of 'the human', rather than for the sake of the right-holder. But suppose we accept that one or other of the Specific views must be correct, because we want human rights law to be founded on duties that are naturally owed to individuals as specific, concrete individuals—rather than as instances of 'the generic human'. We might then, as suggested two paragraphs

---

[85] See the quotations from Nussbaum and Tasioulas, and accompanying discussion, at Section 9.1, pp. 141–43.

above, explain the truth of the Shared Specific view on the basis that shared *generic human* interests define the most important specific concrete good of each human. Or we might offer alternative reasons for the Shared Specific view. Or we might prefer the rival Varied Specific view, perhaps on the basis that the *generic human* interests are few and abstract, or on other bases. Our choice between the Shared and the Varied view will be the important one: on the Shared view, even though legal human rights are rarely justifiable primarily on the basis of what they do for the particular concrete right-holder, most human rights law is—as argued in Sections 9.3–9.4— justifiable as operationalizing recognition-independent natural rights shared by all humans, recognition-independent rights that each human holds for her own sake. By contrast, if the Varied Specific view is correct, this is harder to maintain. It is not impossible: as noted in Section 9.2 one could see human rights law as protecting and determining the *varied* recognition-independent natural rights that different humans hold,[86] and one might see legal exception clauses, legal rights to local self-determination, and legal rights to freedom of choice over one's legal rights as similarly protecting our varied natural rights.[87] But the resulting picture is likely to be messy and difficult, not least because true variation in natural human rights might encompass rights not to be given liberal choices.

Here we reach the limits of the approach I have been pursuing: an approach that avoids developing a theory of the human or the person, and of what it is for them to flourish or do well.[88] I have tried to reveal the implications of regarding human rights as grounded for the right-holder's sake, and one of my central conclusions is that— despite arguments to the contrary from Buchanan and O'Neill, for example—many extant legal human rights, in international human rights law and in domestic laws and conventions including domestic welfare and educational institutions, are plausibly institutional determinations of natural, recognition-independent human rights grounded for the right-holder's sake (Sections 9.3–9.4). But how often these natural groundings succeed, and how often legal-conventional institutions successfully operationalize them—and which parts of extant human rights practice are thereby vindicated—depends on the particular Shared or Varied Specific view adopted: the particular human goods which are of right-justifying importance. I cannot answer that question in this book. My aim is instead to bring out the implications of the structural notions that human rights are (i) rights for the right-holder's sake that are (ii) everyone's business. I say more about (ii) in the next chapter, after addressing apparent discrepancies between (i) and some prominent parts of current human rights practice and law.

---

[86] See the comparison with the idea of Rawlsian primary goods in note 30 above.

[87] See note 10 and accompanying text. See also Ajei 2015 for intellectual underpinnings for the idea of the African Charter on Human and Peoples' Rights as asserting fundamentally a right that Africa determine its own African interpretation of human rights.

[88] See the opening of Part II in Section 7.1.

10

Human Rights as Everyone's Business

10.1 The Diversity and Collectivism of Human Rights Law: Not for the Right-Holder's Sake?

The picture outlined so far lies within what is known as the 'orthodox' or 'traditional' conception of human rights: the conception which takes contemporary human rights practice to be continuous with older natural rights doctrines.[1] As sketched, my view of human rights is that they are, qua *rights*, distinctively Addressive (see Part I), categorical, weighty-exclusionary-silencing, demandable and remainder-triggering reasons (see Chapter 7), and qua *human rights*, they either exist as natural rights (thus grounded solely or predominantly by the right-holder's good), or else they are created legal-conventional rights that institutionalise such natural rights (Chapters 8–9). Values beyond good to the right-holder play at most a minimal role in grounding them in their recognition-independent, 'natural right' forms. I noted in Section 9.5 that legal rights can operationalize such natural rights even when factors beyond simply good to the right-holder (factors such as fairness (as in Stemplowska's approach) or efficiency (as in Wenar's)) play a major role in the case for creating, maintaining, and respecting them, so long as they are nonetheless a polity's—or indeed the international community's—legal or conventional way of instituting one among the disjunction of possibilities required by the right-holder's own (Generic or Specific) interests, needs, or freedoms.

Against this conception of human rights as fundamentally *rights for the right-holder's sake*, two criticisms are frequently made which draw on features of human rights law: (1) the fact that human rights law seems to include many rights which protect individual-right holders for the sake of *others*, or protect *groups*,[2] and (2) the fact that *states* are exclusively or at least primarily the duty-bearers correlative to legal human rights, yet the idea of 'rights for the right-holder's sake' is not statist.[3] I turn to the second point in Section 10.2. In the current section I address the first. (And in later sections (10.3–10.5) I turn to the further idea of human rights as distinctively public, as 'everyone's business'.)

The departments of law which most frequently get categorized as human rights law in contemporary practice are domestic constitutional law, perhaps the

---

[1] See Chapter 7, note 1, above.
[2] Buchanan 2013; this point has been pressed on me in discussion by Christopher McCrudden.
[3] Rawls 1999, Beitz 2009, Raz 2010.

humanitarian law of war, and—most obviously and centrally—international human rights law as derived from specific international human rights covenants and treaties.[4] All these departments of law contain protections for groups: consider the protections of the family in Article 23 of the International Covenant on Civil and Political Rights (ICCPR), the protection of national self-determination in both Covenants, the growing legal tendency to regard business corporations as holders of certain human rights,[5] or the protection against discrimination for specific groups in the Convention on the Elimination of All Forms of Discrimination against Women or the United Nations Declaration on the Rights of Indigenous Peoples. At first glance, it is hard to see how my account of human rights as *rights for the right-holder's sake*, in which legal human rights must institutionalize and determine natural rights grounded primarily in their good to the individual human right-holder, can accommodate such cases.

Two responses to this point which I shall not pursue are to question the relevance of actual human rights law to a philosophical theory of human rights, and to challenge the empirical-interpretive claim that actual human rights law contains many rights which protect groups and parties beyond the right-holder. Given the centrality of human rights law to human rights practice, including the practice of organizations campaigning for the protection of human rights, and the practice of individuals and groups seeking redress, a theory of human rights which ignored extant human rights law would 'talk past' a significant aspect of the practice. And an interpretation of human rights law which drew a sharp distinction between, say, the two International Covenants on the one side, and the Declaration on the Rights of Indigenous Peoples on the other would I think be drawing a sharp line that is not reflected in our thinking about the moral status of such instruments, where any such lines are rightly much more blurred. I must therefore address the concern that much of human rights law seems to contain (or, at the margins, shade into) rights whose creation and maintenance, and respect for which as law, are not justifiable as institutionalizing natural rights grounded for the right-holder's sake in the manner examined in Section 9.3.

My response is to split the purportedly problematic cases into four classes: (I) genuine mistakes where we would do better not to characterize the right in question as a human right, (II) accommodatable cases where the right in question, despite appearances, gives legal form to a natural, recognition-independent right that is grounded by what it does for the individual right-holder, (III) special cases derived from or related to cases of the second type, and (IV) special cases in which a group itself has independent right-grounding status. My defence will be that most apparent problem cases actually turn out to be of type (II)—accommodatable—and that the continuities between cases of type (II) and cases of types (III) and (IV) diminish the force of the latter as problems.

First, there are some legal rights which are currently categorized as falling under human rights law but which, I think, should not have been so categorized.

---

[4] See Neuman 2003, Teitel 2011, Besson 2015, Benvenisti and Harel forthcoming.
[5] See Fellmeth 2016, p. 31, for European and American cases. See also Nicol 2011.

The relevant cases are the rights of business corporations and other artificial bodies (clubs, transnational institutions) whose status as a right-holder can only be justified morally by reference to how their holding rights serves others beyond the right-holder. For example, insofar as the legal rights of a business corporation—perhaps, the Yukos oil company, to take a famous case, or Anheuser-Busch, Inc. or Cassis de Dijon[6]—are morally justified, they have to be justified by reference to how the creation and existence of a right-holding entity like Yukos or Anheuser-Busch, etc. serves others, perhaps in terms of efficiency in the allocation of resources, perhaps in terms of other values including how they serve others' natural rights. No plausible moral justification of the business corporation's legal rights could take them to determine or operationalise *natural rights held by that business*. This is because the business's good (Yukos's, Anheuser-Busch's, etc.) is insufficient on its own to play a predominant role in making others 'naturally' duty-bound, for its good (its interests, needs, freedoms) lacks any moral standing in its own right.[7] The moral case for agents being duty-bound in relation to the business has to turn ultimately on how such duties serve further ends beyond the business's good (such as efficiency, fairness, the serving of others' natural rights). For this reason, the legal rights of a business corporation or similar entity cannot plausibly be understood as reflecting or operationalizing any natural rights of the business. Hence they should not be included under *human rights* law, even though—as Part III will argue—they might well be fully morally justifiable as legal rights of a different category.[8]

Secondly, many claims that particular rights falling under human rights law cannot be legalizations of natural rights justified by what they do for the individual right-holder are, on inspection, false. One such claim is Buchanan's, Sreenivasan's and O'Neill's contention that legal human rights to goods and services including vaccination programmes and nationwide polling stations cannot institutionalize or operationalize natural human rights grounded by what they do for the right-holder, and I have already rejected this argument in Section 9.3. Somewhat similarly, Raz

---

[6] Fellmeth 2016, p. 31, briefly discusses Anheuser-Busch and the European Court of Human Rights's 2007 decision to extend the human right to peaceful enjoyment of possessions to a corporation's enjoyment of its trademark; Nicol 2011, pp. 234–5, discusses the Cassis case considered by the European Court of Justice as a free movement case under the EU rights regime rather than the European Convention.

[7] Compare how, similarly, a moral justification of the prime minister's right to declare war cannot halt simply at how this right serves the interests of the prime minister.

[8] Note that it is only *business corporation's* rights that I want to dismiss here as inappropriate to human rights law. I do not want to follow Griffin (2008, ch. 15) or Wellman (2011, pp. 67–8) in rejecting the possibility of any group holding a natural right as a human right reflected in human rights law; and I certainly do not want to follow Griffin (2008, p. 95) or Wellman (1995, pp. 107, 113) in rejecting the idea of human rights for humans with severe mental health difficulties or young babies. For more critical discussion of corporations as purported holders of legal human rights, see Fellmeth 2016, pp. 31–2. Note also that it is *in principle* possible for some businesses' legal rights to so closely protect the human rights of individuals that we might not object to calling the relevant legal rights 'human rights'; the legal business rights in question would fall under my third heading in the main text, akin to parental rights justified by how they serve children (see discussion, in main text shortly, of 'special cases derived from or related to cases of the second type'). But as it happens I doubt any businesses' legal rights are so closely linked to individuals' human rights.

argues that many of our core civil and political rights—the rights to freedom of speech or to political participation, say—can only be grounded by their role in constituting an open society that serves the common good, rather than by what they do for the individual right-holder.[9] We can reject this argument without denying the common good role of such rights.[10] All we need to note is that *the right-holder's Generic or Specific human interest in free speech or political participation* can on its own in my STRONGEST or STRONG A manner ground recognition-independent natural duties to allow the person in question to speak and participate, and further it can also (in conjunction with similar interests in my STRONG B manner) generate reasons to create, sustain, and respect *legal* duties to allow the person to speak and participate—duties which give legal form to the natural duties that, because of their grounding in the right-holder's good, naturally constitute rights.[11]

The same can again be said about equality and anti-discrimination rights, contra Buchanan.[12] The very great importance *to the right-holder* of not being discriminated against on the basis of their gender or sexuality is in my view sufficient to ground a natural recognition-independent duty not so to discriminate against the right-holder. Note that we do not have to reduce the importance of non-discrimination and equal treatment to their contribution to *pleasure* or *desire-satisfaction* in order for them to generate a 'for the right-holder's sake' justification for natural rights. We simply need to take the sense in which not being discriminated against, or being treated equally, is *good for the right-holder, in the broadest sense*, as the basis of her right. And this seems plausible—more plausible than taking *the value of equal treatment as such* as the basis of such rights.

A further largely accommodatable set of putative counterexamples is rights protecting the family. While most of the legal human rights in this area (to found a family, not to be forced into marriage) serve the institution of the family, they can also be grounded as natural rights by how they serve the individual right-holder, and the legal rights can be seen as protecting these natural rights. Where they cannot—e.g. in the claim (ICCPR, Art. 23) that the family, as 'the natural and fundamental group unit of society', is *itself* 'entitled to protection by society and the state'—they are in my view either special cases of one of the types discussed in the next paragraphs, or else perhaps another of my first, unjustified cases, like the purported human rights of business corporations (e.g. suppose 'the family' is interpreted in a patriarchal or specifically heterosexual way, or indeed if family of any form turns out on further inspection to be unjustified).

What I called 'special cases derived from or related to cases of the second type' involve legal rights of one party justified predominantly by how they serve further rights of some other parties which are themselves *human rights*. These further rights will be either themselves natural human rights (as in Section 8.2) or legal rights institutionalizing natural human rights (Section 9.3). Examples of rights justified

---

[9] Raz 1994, pp. 54–5.   [10] See Section 8.2, penultimate paragraph.

[11] This is consistent with Raz's claim that one should prefer to be denied free speech oneself while living in a society in which others have it, than have such freedom while all others lack it (1994, p. 54). One's own interest in speaking is still on its own of natural right-grounding importance.

[12] Buchanan 2013, pp. 28–36.

predominantly by how they serve such 'further rights' include some parental rights grounded in the interests of their children (e.g. rights to discipline children humanely, protecting the child's human rights to be nurtured and educated), and some educators' rights grounded in the interests of students (e.g. rights to mark work without political interference, protecting the student's right to education). Sections 7.6, 8.2, and 9.4 tell us that because the right-holder's own good (e.g. the good of the parent or educator) does not play a major part in making the rights in question exist, the relevant duties cannot constitute or correlate with natural rights. But we might still find good reason to create and maintain them as legal rights rather than undirected legal duties, and their close relation to prior natural or legal human rights *of others* (rights of the types outlined in Sections 8.2 and 9.2–9.3, held by the children and the students in the cases in question) gives us forceful (but defeasible) reason to classify the former legal rights as themselves human rights, even though they are rights for someone else's sake, rather than the right-holder's. The case for so classifying them as human rights depends on the closeness of their relation to legal or natural human rights that are more clearly 'for the right-holder's sake', and this will—as in other places in this book[13]—be a scalar matter.

My fourth case is especially interesting. One might think that the nation—bearer of the right to national self-determination—is unlike business corporations or other clubs in that its good (its interests, needs, freedoms) *is* an appropriate place at which to halt in giving a moral case for recognition-independent duties (borne by other powerful entities, such as rival nations) to allow it self-determination. Perhaps we do not need to refer to how serving the nation's interest in self-determination serves the good of further individuals beyond the nation itself, in order to get a case for duties respecting national self-determination: perhaps the interests of the nation (taken as a distinct group *or* as a collection of individuals with interests) have moral status in themselves and are enough on their own to ground such duties as the nation's recognition-independent or natural right. This would make the nation's right to self-determination contrast with the rights of business corporations and with cases like the prime minister's right to declare war. One might read the ICCPR's assertion about the rights of the family in a similar way.

In my view, this is a moderately attractive way to understand national self-determination—especially if we take the interests of the nation as simply something like the collected communal interests of its members, rather than focusing on its distinct interests as a separate entity, interests that might diverge from the interests of its members.[14] My favoured approach says that the combined communal interests of the people who make up a nation are sufficient on their own (at least in 'normal' circumstances, so this is a STRONG A structure) to ground a natural, recognition-independent right to self-determination for this nation. And we can add that the

---

[13] Recall: whether a *reason* is a *duty* is a matter of degree (Section 7.2); whether a *duty* is *naturally owed to someone* is a matter of degree (reflecting the scale of degrees to which a duty can be grounded by a party's good) (Section 8.2); and whether a *duty owed to someone* is a *right* is a matter of degree (Section 6.1). Now we have seen that whether a legal right is a human right can also be a matter of degree.

[14] For this distinction, see Jones 1999; for the conception of interests I have in mind at the heart of this argument, see Raz and Margalit 1994.

combined interests of nations together also seem sufficient (in a STRONG B manner) to justify giving international legal status to this right. Such a legal right to national self-determination is a right that is justified for the right-holder's sake in Section 9.3's 'foundational' sense, reflecting an underlying natural right with broadly the same (though more abstract) content. It is just that the holder of the natural right here is not an individual but a community. The very hard question is what exactly makes a group sharing territory into a nation with appropriately important communal interests: not every territorially unified collective has the right kind of or important enough interests (consider a conquered territory that has been 'resettled' unjustly);[15] and it is too much to insist that the relevant group must have been organized into a state.[16]

Can we make the same point about the family? Maybe the collected interests of the set of people who make up any given family are sufficient on their own in 'normal' modern circumstances to ground rights to the unity of this family.[17] Now as it happens, I think we can also justify most of the rights associated with protection of the family by referring to the good (interests, needs, freedoms) of the individuals involved taken separately; but a more communal approach like this might be possible.

The family example reveals something important: 'orthodox' conceptions are often accused of conceiving human rights as ahistorical and timeless, in contrast to the dynamism of the historical development of human rights law and practice. But my approach implies that as the (Generic or Specific) interests, needs, and freedoms sufficiently important to ground duties shift over time, so will both the recognition-independent, natural rights groundable by what they do for the right-holder, and the legal and conventional rights for which we can find a basis in what they do for the right-holder. I suspect that the need for participation in a family—and certainly in a nuclear family based on biological relationships—can and will shift historically in this way.

We should return to the concern driving this section. At first glance, many aspects of human rights law appear to protect rights that are not justifiable for the right-holder's sake. But I have argued that on close inspection, this is a mistake. Most rights falling under human rights law protect, determine, or operationalize natural rights groundable without significant reference to what they do positively for people beyond the right-holder.[18] And this includes the right to national self-determination: a case in which a community's interest (or need or freedom) grounds a right for that very community's sake. We will see in Section 10.5 that the reach of this national interest, and its associated right, is one among several factors determinative of another aspect of human rights law: who should make human rights law enforcement their business. Before tackling this, we must address a closely related question: who bears duties under human rights law.

---

[15] For more on this question, see Stilz forthcoming.   [16] Flikschuh 2017, ch. 7.

[17] We can see such rights as violated—along with the violation of many other rights—by the policy of forcibly separating Indigenous Australian families. See http://www.humanrights.gov.au/our-work/aboriginal-and-torres-strait-islander-social-justice/publications/bringing-them-home-stolen.

[18] To say that they are 'groundable' without this reference of course leaves it open that parallel groundings do also involve reference to the wider good. See Section 8.2's penultimate paragraph.

10.2 The Diversity and Collectivism of Human Rights Law: Beyond the State as Duty-Bearer?

Both domestic constitutional and international human rights law are distinguished by a focus on *states* (and their 'agents', governments) as primary duty-bearers.[19] For example, Beitz writes that contemporary human rights practice consists of 'a set of norms for the regulation of the conduct of *governments* and the range of actions open to various agents for which a *government's failure* to abide by these norms supplies reasons'.[20] My sense is that this analysis overestimates the centrality of states or governments as duty-bearers under what is standardly conceived as human rights law. I endorse Lafont's claim that the human rights encapsulated in current human rights law are better taken as 'rights whose actual or anticipated violation is a defeasible *reason for action against the violator by members of the international community*'.[21] To summarize Lafont's nuanced argument, the contemporary body of human rights law is a project engaged in by the international community, and this means that the idea of rights-promotive and rights-enforcing action—not necessarily military intervention, but attention and censure[22]—by the international community plays a defining role in contemporary conceptions of legal human rights.

Such action is most likely to be morally justified against wrongs committed by *states* rather than by *private individuals*. So a murder committed by one private individual against another single private individual, a murder that is appropriately investigated by the state and that is not motivated by or implicated in misuse of state power, will not qualify as a matter for human rights law on this account because such a private wrong, which has been properly investigated locally, is no reason for action by the international community. Yet although violations of the rights listed in international human rights law are most likely justifiably to trigger the concern of the international community when these violations are committed by *states*, this is merely a contingent result of the fact that states hold great (and comparatively unconstrained) power, and hence that their actions are especially likely to be of international concern. Violations committed by *powerful non-state actors* (e.g. multi-national corporations or 'warlords') can also frequently trigger reasons for the international community to act. Indeed there is nothing in principle to exclude crimes by *individual private actors* from violating human rights law on Lafont's conception of it: *when* such crimes meet the conditions sufficient to generate reasons for the international community to act.[23] Nonetheless, this characterization—which

---

[19] Notice that I here deliberately distinguish states, their agents (governments), and nations. There are states that in different ways encompass multiple nations (Belgium, Canada (including its relationship to First Nations and to Quebec), China (including Tibet), Spain, USA, UK) and there are some multistate nations (China-Taiwan, the Kurdish nation), even though the state–nation distinction is not straightforward. (The examples given are not meant to 'normalize' states whose existence or reach across conquered nations is unjustified.)

[20] Beitz 2009, p. 44, emphasis added. Compare Rawls 1999; Raz 2010; Dworkin 2011, ch. 15. See also Ruggie 2013, pp. xxviii–xxxvi.

[21] Lafont 2012, p. 35, emphasis added.   [22] Compare Beitz 2009, p. 109, no. 3.

[23] Note that therefore on Lafont's characterization, international criminal law will be a further department of human rights law—for the kind of crimes the International Criminal Court tries are crimes

seems to me fairly accurate as an account of standard conceptions of human rights law and practice—will make states a primary bearer of legal human rights duties.

My aim in this section is to make clear that human rights as I have characterized them in earlier sections include but are not limited to the rights of the legal human rights practice outlined above. On my account, ordinary domestic criminal law rights, some tort law rights, and rights in welfare law will be human rights, in that they determine or operationalize natural human rights grounded by what they do for the (Generic or Specific) human interests, needs, or freedoms of the right-holder. This is because a party's good which functions on its own—or with minimal support from other values—to ground natural duties meriting legal-conventional operationalization need not be especially or solely served by *states*, nor are all the duties it generates naturally, or that legally operationalize it, necessarily matters of *international concern*.

This is not to deny that an attack by *a state* on, say, its citizens' human need for nourishment (say) has a distinctive character as a wrong. Unlike a private individual's stealing the subsistence supplies of another, the wrong of a state's doing this has a distinctive character because of the imbalance of power involved. And unlike even a powerful business's stealing such supplies, the wrong of a state's doing this is distinctly affected also by the specific betrayal involved in turning on those to whom one has special responsibilities (as their state).[24] Such points about the distinctiveness of state wrongs also apply as much to official neglect as to attack.

Nonetheless, the human interests, needs, freedoms, and other goods to the individual which can in my STRONGEST or STRONG A way ground natural duties can clearly (in a STRONG B way) justify creating, maintaining, and respecting-qua-law many legal duties borne by *individuals and small groups* as well as states and large corporations—including domestic criminal and tort law duties. In my view, criminal law is distinguished primarily by its function to condemn a wrong *on behalf of the polity as a whole*,[25] while tort law plausibly has the twin functions of condemning *under the control of the victim*[26] and of *fairly reallocating costs* of a wrong.[27] By contrast, international human rights law on Lafont's conception condemns wrongs *on behalf of the international community*. Our human interests in bodily integrity as readily constitute a case for creating, maintaining, and respecting criminal and tort protections of these interests against the actions of private individuals that would be a matter of domestic concern[28] as they do for creating international human rights

---

generating reasons for the international community to act. Note also that what exactly the conditions are which a wrong has to meet to trigger international concern is unclear; mere seriousness is perhaps not enough. See Sections 10.3–10.5.

[24] Compare Nagel 2005 (on the distinctiveness of the wrong of arbitrary inequality between those living together under a single sovereign state).

[25] For a nuanced version of this view, see Duff 2001, 2010, 2011a; Duff and Marshall 2010; this view clearly presents questions for the idea of an International Criminal Court, and I return to these below.

[26] See Goldberg and Zipursky 2010.

[27] See Goldberg and Zipursky, 2010, pt. II, for a summary of these recently 'traditional' tort theories.

[28] And of course also against the actions of states. I am obviously not denying that criminal and tort law can have states as duty-bearers.

protection of these interests against states and non-state actors whose violative actions would be a matter of international concern.

So if human rights are both natural rights grounded for the right-holder's sake by her important interests, freedoms, etc., and legal rights operationalizing or protecting these natural rights, then we should be willing to see domestic criminal and tort law as forms of human right: as laws that protect natural human rights alongside constitutional, humanitarian, and international human rights law.[29] This conclusion prompts two critical questions about the contours of contemporary forms of law, contours which we could change if we wished: first, should we rest content with contemporary conceptions of the legal duty-bearers correlative to legal rights within these different departments of law? Or should we, for example, change international human rights law so that it is violable by private individuals acting in a private capacity—should we take single 'ordinary' murders, say, to merit the concern of the international community? Alternatively should we change international human rights law so that it is violable by large business corporations if not private individuals?[30] Secondly, should we rest content with contemporary conceptions of those on whose behalf these different departments of law condemn? Or should we, for example, change our conception of domestic criminal law so that it condemns violations on behalf of humanity as a whole?

I take up the second question in Sections 10.3–10.5. We can say a little now about the first question, on the allocation of legal duties correlating with the many forms of human rights in different departments of law, though a full answer depends on the discussion to come, as the two questions are interrelated: the allocation of duties within a particular department of law depends partly on the question of on whose behalf that department of law condemns and enforces.[31]

The allocation of the duties constitutive of *natural, recognition-independent* human rights is determined by the nature of the right-holder's good which grounds the right, as it works in context 'naturally' to make agents duty-bound to take any actions it requires: in different cases perhaps the duty-bearer will be a specific individual agent (e.g. a parent duty-bound to care for their child), or all agents (e.g. all agents duty-bound not to assault me), or the state or other institutions or humanity itself (e.g. see Section 9.3 on uninstitutionalized 'positive' rights to goods

---

[29] Compare Fiss 2011, ch. 5, whose concerns about criminal law as a vehicle for implementing human rights are practical-pragmatic rather than principled.

[30] Note that Ruggie's 'Guiding Principles on Business and Human Rights' do not effect this change: they give businesses 'responsibilities' rather than 'duties' under international human rights law (Ruggie 2013; Fellmeth 2016, pp. 34–5).

[31] Note that the term 'allocation' is misleading here, at least regarding Hohfeldian *claim*-rights: such rights simply *are* directed (Addressive) duties that are permissibly demandable and enforceable to some degree (see Part I—contra, e.g. Miller 2007, pp. 99–107; Tasioulas 2007, p. 94). Restated without talk of 'allocation', the first question asks whether current legal rights/duties, with their particular duty-bearers as recognized by contemporary divisions in departments of law—divisions into human rights law as a matter for the international community, domestic criminal law as a matter for the polity and so on—should be altered or preserved. In particular, should the legal duties *constitutive* of given legal rights (the duties whose violation constitutes failure to *respect* legal rights) be allocated as they are currently across departments of law?

and services).[32] When it comes to the contours of *law* as operationalizing or mirroring such natural rights, many more values can come into play, as Sections 7.7 and 9.4 showed. The allocation of duties within the law and within other conventional institutions for the right-holder's sake will be based on its instrumental value in terms of its direct and indirect effects: as likely to generate satisfaction of the relevant individual interests, needs, or freedoms, as likely to serve other interests, needs, or freedoms, as generating other goods including educative and symbolic effects. Given the wide range of values that these facts mean are of relevance to the creation, maintenance, and adjustment of *legal* or *conventional* rights for the right-holder's sake, there might seem little systematic that can be said acontextually about whether, for example, all 'private' murders should be legally of concern to the international community. It depends significantly on what is already in place in context, and on the costs and benefits, for the full range of values, of the proposed change.

Nonetheless, the many instrumental considerations will include and interact in prominent ways with the principle that human rights are justifiable for the right-holder's sake on the basis of her good. For example, recall my argument in Section 9.5 that institutions allocating to individuals various duties that together realize someone's natural human right to (e.g.) education should be framed, at a minimum, as giving the person to be educated a legal *right* to such education. They should also be sufficiently firmly legally entrenched to ensure their immunity from anti-human rights political decisions.[33] Further, I suggest that there is (defeasible) reason in favour of greater unity between the branches of law that directly protect human rights, in recognition of their shared moral significance as legal rights founded on natural rights groundable predominantly by the right-holder's good.

10.3 Public/Private and Solidarity: Human Rights as Everyone's Business

There are also points of moral principle to be made about whose business it is to demand, enforce, or protect different rights (both legal and natural), and these points of principle partially determine the contours of the departments of law. My romantic partner's fidelity to me as a private individual is, in principle, not a matter for the state to enforce, nor a matter for the international community.[34] Can we say analogous things about 'private' murders? About businesses' duties not to bribe?

Let me clarify the topic here. It turns on a distinction between duties *constitutive* of human rights (legal and natural) and what we might call '*secondary*' duties and permissions concerning those primary duties that constitute human rights. It is vital to note that in calling them 'secondary', I am not signalling that the relevant duties are less important in any respect than those I call 'primary': e.g. I am not saying that

---

[32] Note my claim in Section 9.3 that all natural human rights against individuals (e.g. not to be tortured, to education) will also be held against humanity at large.

[33] The rights removed by the 'benefit cuts' made by the UK government on austerity grounds strike me as an example of the kind of legal-administrative-welfare right that should have been more entrenched.

[34] Perhaps the state is allowed to pursue public policies that increase the possibility of fidelity within relationships, but even that is (rightly) controversial (see e.g. Chambers 2013).

they merit less effort at fulfilment, or must be overridden in cases of conflict. Instead, I mean only the following. The primary duties are those directly grounded as recognition-independent natural rights by how they serve the individual, or morally justifiable as legal rights (e.g. in criminal law or welfare law as much as international human rights law) by how they determine or operationalize the relevant recognition-independent natural rights. The secondary duties or permissions include the (natural or morally justified legal) duty or permission to demand fulfilment of a given right, to call a potential violator to answer for their conduct, to condemn this conduct, to enforce fulfilment of a given right, to pursue public policies that will make fulfilment more likely. They also include duties to remedy borne by rights-violators post-violation (what I earlier called 'remainder' duties).[35] All these secondary duties or permissions might, like the primary duties, be grounded 'naturally' by how they serve the individual, or be morally justifiable as legal duties or permissions that legally protect natural duties or permissions—but their existence is logically parasitic on the primary duties which constitute the (natural or legal) rights. Without these primary duties, natural or legal, the secondary duties and permissions would make no sense as protecting or enforcing *rights*, for they would have nothing to protect or enforce. The secondary duties include Ruggie's duties to protect and remedy, and Eide's duties to protect and fulfil, while the primary duties—the duties in whose existence the right inheres—are the duties to respect.[36] (Note that this latter point should add to our sense that secondary duties in my sense are in no way less important than primary ones: often a state's duties to protect and fulfil should be its main focus of human rights resources, because they offer its principal way of realizing individuals' natural human rights.) The secondary permissions include the permission in principle to demand fulfilment of one's own right, alongside the permission that third parties sometimes hold to demand fulfilment of one's right.[37] They also include the permission (and duty) to punish violators.

This section and the subsequent two (10.4–10.5) concern these secondary duties and permissions: who bears them and why? I will suggest that alongside being rights justifiable for the right-holder's own sake (or legal rights operationalizing such prior rights), human rights should also be thought of as distinctive in being 'everyone's business', in that respect for a particular person's human right is—*ceteris paribus*—in principle morally demandable by any human anywhere. The bearer of a duty (natural or legal) constituting a human right is in principle answerable to all humans for her conduct in relation to that duty. But we will see that most human rights are not (even merely as a matter of defeasible principle) *criminally enforceable* or *criminally condemnable* by just any human anywhere, and that there are principled reasons to oppose their being so enforceable or condemnable by just any *state* either. This turns out to be because of the moral importance of national self-determination: the importance of respecting a community's having taken on its own duties of enforcement and condemnation by claiming control of itself and its members.

---

[35] See e.g. Section 3.5.   [36] Eide 1987; Ruggie 2013, ch. 3; for discussion, see Lafont 2012, p. 36.
[37] Recall this distinction in Chapter 3.

Some duties seem to be private matters. Recall again the example of my romantic partner's fidelity. Compare also the duties of fidelity in friendships and among colleagues in professional relationships. These are duties which are not demandable by just anyone anywhere: it would be apt to respond to an external third party, who demanded that one be faithful to one's friend, that this is 'none of their business'. Such a response would be apt even when the friend in question could rightfully demand and condemn one as an unfaithful friend. Similar examples might include a child's right to its parents' assistance with homework, or a spouse's right against unjustifiably callous treatment from their spouse.[38] In each of these cases, it is I think not very plausible—though also not clearly mistaken[39]—to call the rights in question 'human rights', even though the goods which ground them are vitally important human goods of the individual party in question (e.g. the friend, child, or spouse). I think it is illuminating to say that the reason why these are not obviously describable as human rights is because they are private matters: most humans are not permitted to demand their fulfilment or to call the duty-bearer to account for violation; such permission is reserved for those who stand in special relationships to the duty-bearer or right-holder.

As forewarned at the start of Part II (see Section 7.1), this move introduces a new necessary condition on human rights, to supplement my previously developed condition that human rights be groundable for the right-holder's sake (or be institutionalizations of natural rights so groundable). The new necessary condition claims that human rights must be 'everyone's business' in the sense that anyone anywhere is in principle permitted to demand their fulfilment and to call duty-bearers to account for violations. The cases above are not human rights because they fail this condition. Against this move, two alternative explanations might be offered for why the cases above are not human rights—moves that leave us not needing this new claim that human rights must be everyone's business.

First, it might be claimed that it is not correct to regard many such directed duties (e.g. between friends) as *rights* at all, because the ways in which they are morally enforceable and claimable are limited (see Section 6.1). But there are ways in which such duties can be enforced—e.g. through punishment or ostracism within the relationship. And they can clearly be demanded by relevant members of the relationships. Talk of rights here is therefore not absurd, even if Section 6.1 tells us such talk would be even more apt if the directed duties in question were more forcefully demandable and enforceable by more parties.[40]

A second and stronger response claims that the type of rights in question are not human rights because, on inspection, they turn out not to be grounded for the right-holder's sake. The response observes that the examples mentioned—friendships,

---

[38] This is Griffin's example (2008, p. 52) though he uses it—implausibly in my view—to argue that one's interest in avoiding great pain (as caused by the spouse) cannot ground a human right for one. A better explanation of why callous treatment by one's spouse is not a human rights violation—if indeed it is not—is because it is a private matter in my sense: not 'everyone's business'. Compare also Duff on aesthetic matters being none of one's business (2011b, p. 357)—but here there is no often right (e.g. that one's cohabitor decorate one's kitchen tastefully) whose fulfilment is not my business.

[39] This is important: see discussion of Gewirth, Sen, Tasioulas, and Wellman in this volume, p. 182.

[40] See also Waldron 1993, ch. 15.

romantic relationships, collegial relationships—seem to involve duties that are not grounded in my STRONG A or STRONGEST way by what they do for the party in question. Instead, the value of such duties to *both parties*, or to *the group*, appears necessary to ground them. To say otherwise would seem to allow, say, that a person might have a right to their partner's fidelity simply on the basis of their own interests largely independently of the interests of their partner. This kind of lop-sided, potentially patriarchal relationship seems to lack duty-grounding value. Seen in this light, the cases in these examples look closer to duties protecting groups, which depend for their existence on the interests of all members. And Section 7.6 tells us that regarding the cases in this light compels us to conclude that the duties' status as *rights* of, as *owed to*, the relevant individual parties, is not unequivocally 'natural' or recognition-independent but must be in part a conventional creation— for according to the view in question, the right-holder's good does not play a predominant part in grounding the relevant duties.

I have some sympathy with this response. But we can reply to it along the lines developed in Section 9.4: even though principles invoking others' good have to play a role in making it the case that I am duty-bound to listen sympathetically to you, my friend in need, nonetheless only your good plays the role, in grounding the duty, of *good to be served by the relevant action's (i.e. the sympathetic listening's) performance*. My good plays a role in determining that I bear the duty, and perhaps in determining its precise content. But my good does not play a role as *that to be served by the dutiful action*: only your good plays that role. Section 9.4 tells us that there is therefore a powerful—if limited—sense in which the duty is grounded on your good and naturally owed to you.

This kind of retort can concede that whether a friendship develops and persists depends crucially on how it serves the interests, needs, or freedom of both friends (as well as on other things). A friendship that was only ever of value to one party would not be a genuine friendship: it might be a relationship of unequal dependency. For a genuine friendship to be generated and persist, both parties' good must be engaged at least sometimes. The retort can also concede that once a friendship exists its own non-instrumental good as a friendship will sometimes itself be sufficient to enhance both parties' lives independently of any further goods it triggers instrumentally.[41] But the key claim is that even though the friendship's emergence historically as a particular friendship depends causally in part on its being good in further ways for both its parties, nonetheless the friendship itself is partially constituted by and structured by duties (e.g. of care and concern) owed by each friend to the other the grounds for the performance of which are solely or predominantly the good of the friend in question. For example, my duties to listen to my distressed friend seem morally grounded predominantly in how such listening will help my friend, in the sense that the ground for requiring the listening is my friend's good; it seems wrong to say that the way my listening will serve me, or will serve the good of friendship itself, work in this way as grounds for the duty. If they *were* so grounded, they would not be 'duties for my friend's sake' and I suggest that they would therefore seem not

---

[41] Compare Section 8.3.

to be duties of *friendship* (instead, they might be, say, contractual duties resulting from our agreement to help each other). Now it is important to recognize that my good and the good of friendship can play a role in determining that I hold the relevant duties, and in determining their precise content; but only your good plays a grounding role in the duties as *that which is to be served by the duties' performance*.[42]

If this retort is correct, then it turns out that our uneasiness about labelling rights within private friendships and romantic relationships 'human rights' cannot be explained on the basis that such rights are not morally grounded for the right-holder's sake. For they *are* morally grounded for the right-holder's sake, at least in a STRONG B way in which the case for the enjoined action does not turn on the good of parties beyond the right-holder. Further the interests or goods of the right-holder which the duties serve will include (Generic or Specific) important human interests or goods: surely, for (almost?) everyone there is an important human interest in being cared for by one's friends. To block their qualifying as human rights, I suggest there is therefore some attraction to appealing to my new 'everyone's business' condition: they are not human rights because it is not the case that in principle any human would be permitted, other things being equal, to demand their fulfilment and to demand an accounting from their violators.

Waldron writes approvingly of '[t]he idea [. . .] that there is a class of rights such that no human should be indifferent to the violation of any right in that class. These rights are called "human rights" because humans are called on to support them.'[43] I recognize that Waldron's idea—with its focus on being 'called on to support' rather than merely permitted as 'one's business'—is not quite the same as mine. But my 'everyone's business' condition can be seen as a non-political humanistic moral version of Beitz's, Raz's, and Rawls's, or Lafont's, 'political' view of human rights: rather than defining human rights as rights of *international* concern, we define them (in part only: we also need the idea of their being for the right-holder's sake in the manner outlined in Chapters 8–9) as rights of concern to all *humans*, where this means demandable in principle by all and any human, with duty-bearers in principle answerable to all and any human.

This is intuitively appealing. Any individual human who observes an attack on or indifference to a human right is, other things being equal, morally *permitted* as a human to call the attacker or the body showing indifference to account.[44] The kind of calling to account which any human is in principle permitted to engage in in relation to someone else's human right is an act of *solidarity*. One very important aspect of my 'everyone's business' condition can be restated as the condition that human rights are necessarily rights with which it is apt for any human anywhere to show solidarity, where this involves a third party 'sharing' a violated party's wrong.[45] I have quite a precise understanding of solidarity in mind here: Suppose A holds a right that B do

---

[42] Compare Section 9.4. Note that the same point would apply, *mutatis mutandis*, to the duties of romantic partners and work colleagues who form a collegial group (as opposed to a group generated purely through the employment contract).

[43] Waldron 2018, p. 118.

[44] I think this is true even if the relevant attacking or indifferent party is *humanity*—see Section 9.3.

[45] Compare Duff and Marshall 2010.

PHI. In this context a further party, C, acts in solidarity with A when C acts, in relation to B's duty to do PHI, in *some of the ways that would be appropriate if the duty were owed to C as well as A*. This involves 'standing beside' A in demanding fulfilment and condemning violation, *not* on A's behalf as A's fiduciary, but as a human who would 'share' in the wrong if A were wronged by B. On this account, C acts in solidarity with A when C does some of the forms of *demanding in relation to A's right* which A could permissibly do. In so acting, C 'takes on' A's right and the wrong its violation would involve as her own business.

This conception of solidarity is close to but distinct from the idea of a solidary obligation in law. Supiot quotes the following from the French Civil Code:

An obligation is joint and several (solidaire) between several creditors, where the instrument of title expressly gives to each of them the right to demand payment of the whole claim, and payment made to one of them discharges the debtor, although the benefit of the obligation is to be partitioned and divided between the various creditors.[46]

A duty or obligation of this type is such that any party permitted to demand the 'payment' (e.g. A or C in the previous paragraph) from the 'debtor' (B) qualifies as a 'creditor' to whom the duty to make 'payment' was owed. This is not what I have in mind for human rights, for there we want one among the various parties permitted to demand 'payment'—namely, A—to have a special status as the right-holder who would be wronged by the violation. We do not want to have to say that those standing in solidarity with A do so because their own rights are violated when A is attacked, and violated in the same way as A's are. This would fail to preserve A's special status as the wronged victim.

Instead, on my account if A holds a human right, and hence a right with which acts of solidarity by any other human are apt, then one of the central things this means is that any other human is in principle permitted to demand the right's fulfilment, condemn its violation and call violators to account *in some of the ways that A is permitted to on her own behalf*. In this way, any other human will 'share in' the wrong done to A by violation, but the wrong will still be done to A: the duty is not owed to the third-party demanders but to A.

There are many conceptions of solidarity and I do not claim that mine is the best.[47] But it captures some aspects of other conceptions: not that solidarity must involve a commitment to shared values in general, but that it involves acting on and sharing in another's right or sharing in their being wronged, taking their violation as one's own.[48] The account can also offer some explanation for those who claim that solidarity *concerns* justice but is not itself demandable as a matter of justice.[49] On my view, most individual humans are not themselves required to engage solidaristically with a given human right, though they (any human anywhere) are *permitted* in

---

[46] Supiot 2007, p. 208, n. 68.
[47] For a useful summary of conceptions of solidarity in political philosophy, see Gould 2014, pp. 102–15.
[48] See e.g. Gould's discussion of Rippe 1998, p. 357 (at Gould 2014, p. 108).
[49] See Gould 2014, p. 107. See also the final three paragraphs of Section 10.4 for discussion of a stronger sense of something's being 'everyone's business' qua demandable from humanity as a matter of justice.

principle to engage in solidaristic demanding, condemning, and calling to account as outlined—and when they do so their demands are for action as a matter of right.

We should note that there is also a second aspect of human rights' being 'everyone's business' which is not captured by my concept of solidarity. This is the idea of human rights as rights on the basis of whose violation compensation or apology for the right-holder can be claimed or demanded by any human, acting as the right-holder's fiduciary, if the right-holder permits this. Now, this is not *solidaristic demanding as if one were the right-holder*, for that would involve include *claiming compensation or apology for oneself* and one is not permitted to claim that when one is a mere third party. Instead when compensation or apology is demanded by some third party for the right-holder, this cannot but be done on the right-holder's behalf in something like a fiduciary's role. Such an activity is not claiming or demanding solidaristically by sharing the wrong as if one were the right-holder. Nonetheless, this gives a different sense of my 'everyone's business' clause, one that like the solidaristic idea can distinguish seemingly private rights from those we call 'human rights': just as it is in principle impermissible for me as an unrelated party to demand that someone be faithful to her friend, similarly it is in principle impermissible for me to demand compensation or apology on the friend's behalf, even if the duty is violated in a way that imposes compensation-justifying costs. If it is only a duty of friendship (and not also, say, a duty not to assault or defraud), then its violation is not 'my business', even if I am well-placed to demand compensation, acknowledgement, or apology on behalf of the friend.

10.4 Doubts about Everyone's Business

I have argued that human rights are subject to two necessary conditions: not only must they be or operationalize rights groundable for the right-holder's sake, but they must also be 'everyone's business'. I have explained 'everyone's business' as distinguishing rights (natural or legal-conventional) in which any human anywhere can in principle permissibly 'share' by engaging in solidaristic demanding, calling to account, or condemning, and rights regarding the violation of which anyone anywhere can permissibly demand compensation or apology on behalf of the right-holder, if she allows this. Some contend by contrast that seemingly private rights that are not everyone's business should still be classified as human rights. Others contend that the 'everyone's business' clause does no work because all rights are in principle everyone's business.

The first line of response is implicit in Gewirth's, Sen's, Tasioulas's and Wellman's willingness to allow, for example, a right to a say in one's family's decisions, a right to one's romantic partner's fidelity, and a right not to be lied to by one's friends to qualify as human rights.[50] These theorists are happy to admit that such rights are not everyone's business but can only be demanded by particular parties, yet they still regard them as human rights. There is, I think, nothing decisive that can be said in response to this. I refer simply to my linguistic intuitions about the phrase 'human

---

[50] Gewirth 1982, p. 56; Sen 1999, p. 229; Wellman 2011, pp. 36–9; Tasioulas 2012, pp. 40–1. Recall my argument in the previous section that in one sense these rights exist for the right-holder's sake as duties naturally owed to them.

rights', coupled with my sense that the 'everyone's business' clause picks out something importantly distinctive about those rights that fall under it. If the rights that
were not 'everyone's business' were therefore private in every possible way—e.g. by
being ruled off the table as matters of government policy, thereby excluding policies
designed indirectly to support romantic monogamy or family cohesion, say—then
the clause would pick out something highly distinctive, and it could be motivated by
the thesis that theorizing about human rights must aim to illuminate our collective,
governmental, or state actions and rights that are so private cannot illuminate this.
But in my view the privacy entailed by the 'everyone's business' clause does not go
beyond what I have outlined already: it therefore does not rule out private rights as
appropriate objects of government policy in certain ways.

What the clause does do is throw light on debates about whether something is a
human right which seem to turn precisely on whether it is everyone's business. Thus,
for example, a strong argument for the idea that spouses' rights not to be treated
'coldly', or romantic partners' rights to their partner's fidelity, *should* qualify as
human rights is an argument that implicates the relevant right-enjoined actions
within larger structures of patriarchy and gender or age inequalities. These kind of
arguments maintain that—in some cases despite appearances or ideologies to the
contrary—what has been thought of as 'private', *not* a right with which to show
solidarity by sharing the right-holder's wrong or for whom all could claim compensation on the right-holder's behalf, is actually (perhaps because of its structural role
or for other reasons) better thought of as 'public'. I am sympathetic to many
arguments of this type, and if my view of human rights as 'everyone's business' is
correct, then it will explain why a focus on misconceptions of the private sphere can
reveal rights to be human rights that were not previously so conceived.

A second line of objection maintains that *every* right, indeed every *reason*, is in
principle everyone's business. This approach maintains that our reasons *not* to
demand, condemn, or take up seemingly private matters belonging to others are
contingent, rather than principled: we are not best placed to pursue these matters
given contemporary contingencies, but in principle they could become ours if the
situation changed. Thus Gardner writes that '[i]n a sense [...] everyone's conformity
to every reason is everyone's business'.[51] He goes on to clarify that this is 'only in a
sense. For there are plenty of reasons [...] why each of us should attend more to
some reasons and less to others.'[52] Gardner mentions how sometimes my taking up
someone else's reasons (e.g. by demanding their fulfilment of a right-correlative duty)
can be counterproductive, or too time-consuming relative to my other reasons;
Dempsey highlights the way people in different roles can realize different values
and the importance of 'whether the person typically stands in a particularly good
position to realise [particular] values'.[53] These views do not deny that in a specific
context demanding fulfilment of your right to your partner's fidelity will not be my
business; but they see this as contingently determined, say, by my standing in a poor
position to help ensure your partner's fidelity or to help improve your relationship.
This is a matter not of principle but context.

[51] Gardner 2011, p. 89.   [52] Ibid.   [53] Dempsey 2011, p. 264.

I need something more principled for my 'everyone's business' clause. For I do not want to deny that in particular contexts particular people will be morally forbidden from demanding or insisting on accountability for the fulfilment of particular human rights. I am not allowed to demand fulfilment of your right not to be tortured, or compensation for its violation, if so doing would cause the heavens to fall,[54] or perhaps (and more controversially) if I have lost standing to do this by engaging in torture myself. So I should not insist that human rights must in every context be permissibly demandable by any human anywhere. Instead my thesis is that they are *in principle, but defeasibly*, so demandable. (Note that this is compatible with the idea—perhaps implicit in my suggestion about debates about changing conceptions of privacy (see two paragraphs above)—that whether a particular matter is in principle *ceteris paribus* demandable by everyone can itself depend on the context: rights within romantic relationships might be in principle private in certain contexts but not in the modern patriarchal world.)[55]

Dempsey and Gardner claim that *all* reasons (thus including duties and rights) are in principle demandable by anyone anywhere; it is just that such in-principle demandability is frequently defeated. I believe this is a mistake. Duff mentions aesthetic reasons—e.g. not to read trash, or to decorate one's home in certain ways—as examples of reasons that third parties are clearly in principle not permitted to promote or interfere with in relation to those who bear them. In comparing his approach to Dempsey and Gardner, he goes on:

> We face here deep differences about the nature of practical reason and our place as agents in the normative world(s) in which we find ourselves. For Gardner and Dempsey, all values speak to every agent as an agent: to recognise something as a (dis)value is to recognise it as a reason for action, which becomes a good reason if I am well placed to act in a way that might realise that value or avert that disvalue. In that sense any value is everyone's business. Now I agree that values speak to us all, in that they invite appropriate responses from us all, but I do not think that they always speak to us all as agents: sometimes the appropriate response to a value is a recognition with no practical implications, not because I am not well placed to help realise the value, but because it is not connected to me as an agent. The site of agency is not the whole world; my agent is grounded in the more limited, particular forms of life in which I function, and find my reasons for action. Those reasons are sometimes doubly universal in their reach: the desperate suffering of any human gives any other human being reason for action, in virtue simply of their fellow humanity. [...] We might think that every reason is thus universal; but the example of aesthetic reasons casts doubt on that.[56]

---

[54] See Section 9.3, second paragraph.

[55] This might seem to collapse my position into Dempsey's and Gardner's: in the sentences in parentheses, aren't I saying—like Dempsey and Gardner—that any right is demandable by anyone in principle, and context determines whether it is on this occasion? But this is not my claim. Instead, I claim that in a given context, some rights will be in principle demandable and others will not be. Further context then determines whether the demandable ones can on this occasion be permissibly demanded, or whether their demandability is defeated. But principled demandability (by someone or everyone) is prior to this, even though it is also a contextually determined matter.

[56] Duff 2011b, p, 358.

If—as I think he is—Duff is correct, then the 'everyone's business' clause is not vacuous, and we see that solidaristic and fiduciary demanding have principled limits. The human rights are rights with which in principle any human anywhere could engage in solidaristic and fiduciary demanding.

While the sketched conception of human rights excludes private rights, the 'everyone's business' clause nonetheless includes much more than standard 'political' conceptions (including Lafont's broad account which I endorse as an account of what most people mean by international human rights *law*).[57] For example, everyday rights to polite treatment by anyone one encounters are both grounded for the right-holder's sake and everyone's business: any human permissibly can (and often should) 'call out' rude interactions, showing solidarity with victims of rudeness. Even quite trivial cases implicate what we might here call the human right to respect.[58]

In light of this result, those who favour a more political conception of human rights might want to invoke stronger forms of the 'everyone's business' clause: perhaps human rights are not just *permissibly* demandable by anyone anywhere; rather they are distinguished as rights which *must* be demanded, rights of which someone (the community? humanity?) is morally *required* to demand fulfilment, account-giving, or compensation. Or we might go stronger still and say that human rights are rights regarding which someone is morally required in principle to *call violators to account on behalf of the community*, to *condemn on behalf of the community and punish*. The strongest versions would make human rights those for which something like criminal proceedings, or (stronger still) international criminal condemnation are required (or perhaps even for which compensation is owed to humanity, though here we move beyond claims made on behalf of an individual right-holder to the idea of a right held by humanity). Some of the initial strengthening moves in this spectrum would plausibly exclude the everyday right to polite treatment but include rights against assault and torture, and would also include rights to education and access to nourishment, among many others.[59]

My view is that we should work concurrently with both weaker and stronger conceptions of 'everyone's business', and hence with both more and less expansive conceptions of human rights. This reflects the vague edges of the concept of human rights. The stronger conceptions pose some difficult new questions. For example, we will see in the next section that *required, criminal-type* calling to account cannot be seen as the same form of solidarity with the right-holder that the weaker conception of everyone's business involves, but nor can it be seen as a fiduciary action on the

---

[57] See Section 10.2.   [58] Cruft, Liao, and Renzo 2015, p. 34.

[59] See Section 9.3. Sangiovanni's recent suggestion (in his 2017, p. 191) that human rights are 'those moral rights whose systematic violation ought to be of universal moral, legal, and political *concern*' uses one form of 'everyone's business' clause to characterize human rights: not my weakest version in one respect—for Sangiovanni, human rights are those whose systematic violation ought to be of 'legal and political' concern—but very weak in others, with its focus only on 'concern' and only on 'systematic' violations. Sangiovanni's subsequent suggestion (pp. 194–206) that different interpretations of his condition characterize different human rights practices (and the attendant 'context-sensitive' proposal) is consonant with my suggestion that we should be willing to work concurrently with a range of 'everyone's business' conditions. But I differ from Sangiovanni in presenting the 'everyone's business' condition merely as one necessary condition on human rights, not as their central conceptual characterization.

right-holder's behalf. *Required* calling to account by *humanity* or *the community* does not involve doing (either oneself as 'sharer' of the wrong or on the right-holder's behalf as her fiduciary) something that the right-holder is permitted to do.

What are the implications of the 'everyone's business' clause—in either its stronger or weaker senses—for my earlier question about the contours of the departments of law? Should we, for example, take it that any state anywhere is entitled to enforce human rights anywhere in the globe, because the 'everyone's business' clause tells us that individual humans are permitted to demand fulfilment of any such right? Should we take criminalization with universal jurisdiction to be *required* with regard to those human rights that are *strongly* everyone's business? Should we favour an international or global tort law over domestic variants? I think it is a mistake to draw these conclusions, and I explain this in the next section.

10.5 Public/Private and Solidarity: International and Domestic Legal Enforcement

When someone demands fulfilment of a right that is not 'their business', this is (among other things) a form of busybody intrusion: consider a distant third party's demand that I care for my friend. I have argued (in Sections 10.3–10.4) that human rights are distinctive partly because they are 'everyone's business': any human anywhere is *permitted* in principle to demand their fulfilment and to demand compensation for right-holders; and in many cases some body (e.g. the community, the state, the nation) is *required* to call violators to account in a public way. I have also argued (in Section 10.2) that domestic constitutional and criminal law rights, and many rights in tort and welfare law, qualify as human rights (though not as what is standardly called 'human rights law', which Lafont has correctly characterized as the international community's business).[60] But it would look like busybody intrusion (and worse) if the Italian supreme court took it upon itself to declare an American ruling unconstitutional under the US constitution, or if a Russian criminal court took it upon itself to condemn and punish an 'ordinary' murder committed by a British (and non-Russian) citizen against a fellow British (and non-Russian) citizen in the UK. Only a very small set of rights (a subset of international legal human rights and the rights prosecuted by the ICC) can plausibly be permissibly demanded, with the duty-bearers called to account for themselves and potentially punished, by just any court anywhere.[61] But if human rights are everyone's business, why is this the case? Is it a mistake when we think—as I do—that a Spanish criminal prosecution of Pinochet could only have been a suboptimal 'second-best' result, with Pinochet's crimes being ultimately Chile's business?

The first step in an explanation of this phenomenon is to note that criminal punishment, calling to account and condemnation are not a matter of solidarity, in my precise sense, with the victim whose human right was violated. This is because such solidarity with a right-holder I defined as *acting in some of the ways that would be appropriate if the relevant duty were owed to one as well as to the right-holder*. This

---

[60] Lafont 2012.   [61] See the legal notion of 'erga omnes'.

is what is involved in 'standing beside' and 'sharing' the right-holder's wrong in my precise sense. Criminal calling to account and condemnation on behalf of the community, and criminal punishment, are not actions that the right-holder is morally permitted (or indeed conceptually able) to perform, even when they have been wronged. By contrast, there are forms of calling to account, condemnation, and punishment which the right-holder is allowed and able to perform: individual demands for fulfilment, requests for explanation, individual ostracizing, and condemning statements and actions. The solidaristic aspect of the right's being 'everyone's business' in its weak sense means that all humans are permitted to engage in these kinds of actions when a given person's right is violated: the condemnatory, demanding actions which that right-holding person permissibly can engage in. But as an individual human I am neither permitted nor able to condemn or call to account on behalf of the community or on behalf of humanity as a whole. Like the right-holder, I am also morally forbidden from punishing the wrongdoer in ways associated with the criminal law such as incarceration or fining.[62]

As well as these differences between what criminal (and constitutional) law does and what the right-holding individual is permitted to do in terms of demanding and condemning a violation, it is also notable that while the individual right-holder is often permitted to take charge of the 'prosecution' of a non-legal moral right, for example by forgiving the offender and sometimes disallowing others from continuing to pursue or condemn her, in criminal cases the victim rightly has no (or little) such standing.[63] Criminal procedures therefore also differ from fiduciary demands for compensation or apology made on behalf of the right-holder: demands over which the right-holder often has controlling power (demands standardly taken to be given legal form by tort rather than criminal law).

These differences mean criminal and related legal proceedings, including state punishment, involve actions which no individual is morally permitted to perform as an individual, not even the wronged right-holder or on the wronged right-holder's behalf. This is why the solidaristic and fiduciary demanding permitted by the weaker 'everyone's business' clause does not normally licence punishment by one state of crimes committed in and wholly involving citizens of another—for the weaker 'everyone's business' clause licences nothing like state punishment or condemnation. It only licences individual account-holding.

We are still left with the question about jurisdiction. This is pressing with regard to those human rights which satisfy *stronger* versions of my 'everyone's business' clause. These include the moral *requirement* that someone call to account, condemn, and punish violation of a given human right *in a criminal-type way*. This cannot be a requirement that just *anyone* do this, for we have seen that no individual acting as an

---

[62] Perhaps Locke is right that in a state of nature individuals could punish wrongdoers (Locke 1960 [1689], sections 7–8). I am not sure about this, partly because I am not sure that such punishment is really at all the same kind of activity as state punishment with its official condemnation. But even if we go along with Locke, it is still the case that in a world of states with no state of nature, no individual right holder is morally allowed to engage in official condemnatory punishment, incarceration, or the other kinds of hard treatment central to state punishment.

[63] For defence, see Marshall 2014.

individual is permitted to do this. It is, rather, a requirement essentially demanding action from a community[64]—and not just any community will do. In some cases, a right that is 'everyone's business' in my weaker sense might be such that violations of it require criminal condemnation and punishment, yet without the latter requirement (of condemnation and punishment) being in any sense 'everyone's business'. Being 'everyone's business' in the weaker sense would be sufficient to satisfy the necessary condition on its being a human right.

But in some cases a right might be 'everyone's business' in the stronger sense that a requirement in principle to call to account and condemn its violator falls ultimately on *everyone* as a community—perhaps on *humanity*. We could develop an instrumental account of jurisdiction from this: particular states are charged with pursuing and condemning 'their' human rights violations because this is the most efficient way for humanity to discharge its general duty to pursue the violation of human rights. Without the language of 'humanity' and 'human rights', Duff puts this position (which he rejects) thus:

> On such a view, every state has reason to claim jurisdiction over every crime committed by anyone anywhere in the world: criminals need to be prosecuted and punished, and states have the capacity to prosecute and punish. So every state has reason to give its criminal law jurisdiction that is universal or unlimited as to both ambit and venue [...] As with any kind of demand or good, we must ask how it can most efficiently be satisfied or realised, and how we can efficiently assist its satisfaction and realisation; and in a world of nation states, the answer will typically be that the demands or goods related to criminal law are most efficiently satisfied or realised if states prosecute and punish (only) crimes committed within their own territory.[65]

This could be supplemented with the claim that the efficient punishment of *crimes committed by states* will be through international mechanisms. The trouble with this instrumental view of jurisdiction is that it does not explain our sense that when one state has to step in to punish an individual human rights violator who would normally have been assigned to another state—say because the violation will not be fairly punished in the latter state—this is suboptimal in principle; or that when just one lone member of the international community punishes a *state* that has been a violator, this is again suboptimal in principle. These are not just temporary reallocations within systems that would normally be efficient except in these cases. Rather they are regrettable (even if they are justifiable) violations of a (defeasibly) principled allocation. The instrumental account of jurisdiction cannot explain why it seems that *in principle* violations by their own members are particular states' primary business and violations by states are the international community's primary business, even

---

[64] I speculate that the reason for this is that being punished in roughly the criminal sense (more than just the ostracism of a friend; rather public, official condemnation) is so hard on a person who is punished that it is not something that just any individual or any state anywhere can perform in response to a human rights violation. The violator's own community—the community of which she is a member—must, if possible, do the punishing. For only then is she in a sense an active participant in her own punishment: when a community justifiably punishes its member she, by being a member of the community, punishes herself. The harshness of criminal-type punishment requires this for its legitimacy.

[65] Duff 2014, p. 6.

when the states in question or the international community are inefficient callers to account or punishers.

I cannot properly develop an alternative account here: that would require a theory of the justification of both domestic and international criminal and related procedures and punishments. Instead, I simply point out that even if some rights are 'everyone's business' in the strong sense under consideration—rights that it is humanity's business to punish—we need not take jurisdictional allocations to states as a mere *means* to realizing this. Rather, we can see states as *assuming or taking on* humanity's business in relation to their own territory, citizens, or inhabitants. And we can see their permission to take this on—and to do so in their own distinctive ways (e.g. involving an adversarial or an inquisitorial criminal system)—as justified partly by the importance of national self-determination. So one principled reason why a Spanish trial of Pinochet could only be second-best is because a trial at home by a Chilean court would involve greater self-determination by the Chilean people (including Pinochet himself).[66]

There is of course a great deal more to be said here, but this is not the place for it. But we should note that the point above is compatible with the claim that some human rights violations are such that the importance of their being condemned *by humanity* outweighs the self-determination case for leaving them in 'local' hands. Here is a role for the international criminal court. I am not convinced that violations of this kind must be attacks on 'humanity itself'. Further, if the human community were to become closer to the agential status of a state, then I think the principled objections to extensive jurisdiction for an international criminal court would diminish in force. (I have no sense of whether this would be an advance, or whether we should favour current jurisdictional allocations.)

These quick points are also compatible with the claim that when human rights are violated *by a state* (as in most of what is standardly called 'human rights law' even on Lafont's characterization) criminal-style condemnation must be performed by the international community, rather than by other states acting alone. This is, I venture, due to the necessity for punishment to be performed by a community on one of its members.[67] Now perhaps punishments are not really ever permissibly inflictable on states, but even so criminal-type condemnation and censure surely are, and these cannot legitimately be performed simply by one state on another; rather, they require the international community (including the state to be censured) to constitute itself as a community for condemning or censuring its own members. This is one reason among many in support of *international* bodies for enforcing or institutionalizing human rights in law: they enable criminal-style censure of a state by a community of which it is a member.[68] But note that individual states can also act alone in solidarity

---

[66] Compare Harel 2011 on the triadic structure of answerability: one party is answerable to another party for something. I agree with Duff (2011b, p. 354) that this conceptual structure does not in itself guarantee self-determination (either for the party answering or the party answered to), but it is consonant with it.

[67] See note 64 above and accompanying main text.

[68] For a spirited case for UK participation in such institutions, see Gearty 2016. For a moral rather than an empirical argument, and in favour of international human rights law in general, rather than UK participation in any specific international human rights institutions, see Sangiovanni 2017, pp. 220–33.

(in the manner sketched in Section 10.4) with individual and group or national right-holders by demanding or expressing condemnation of violations in the very manner that the right-holder could. This non-criminal type of condemnation really is *ceteris paribus everyone's* business, including states acting alone.[69]

I have focused on a distinction between individual non-legal condemnation of a rights violation (which everyone can permissibly perform) and criminal condemnation (which only either states or humanity can perform): I have therefore said nothing directly to address the question about *tort* jurisdiction, insofar as this asks who or what body can claim *compensation on the right-holder's behalf* for a violation, or can call a violator to account *on behalf of the right-holder rather than acting on behalf of the community or humanity*.[70] I lack the expertise and the space to do this here, beyond repeating that it is criminal condemnation—condemnation in the community's name, rather than simply on the right-holder's behalf and under the right-holder's control—that is sharply distinct from individual solidarity with or fiduciary action for a victim, and that therefore falls primarily to the state(s) bound up with the violation.[71]

There is more to say. But what I hope to have established is simply that some of the stronger ways in which human rights can be 'everyone's business' do not entail that prosecutions of human rights (pursuit of criminal-style answerability and punishment) can be immediately performed by just anyone anywhere on humanity's behalf. In many cases local states have in principle default jurisdiction for criminal-style callings to account and punishment, with back-up 'second-best' duties falling on other states or the international community only when the local states fail to discharge their duties. And I hope also to have shown the appeal of and variety inherent in the notion that human rights are 'everyone's business'. At its weakest, this means that they are rights which any individual human anywhere (and not necessarily the right-holder) is in principle permitted to demand. Getting a little stronger, it can instead mean that they are rights that someone is morally required to demand. Getting stronger still, it can mean that they are rights which should be pursued in criminal ways, but with jurisdiction limited to states acting on their own community's behalf in order to respect the requirements of self-determination. Or it can mean those rights entailing duties for states, which the international community is required to pursue. At its very strongest, it is those rights that humanity is required to pursue—punish, condemn—on its own behalf through institutions acting in humanity's name, such as the international criminal court. I see no reason to limit 'human rights' to those which are 'everyone's business' in the stronger senses, but I think they cannot be *wholly* private: the weaker sense rings true in our conception of human

---

[69] The *ceteris paribus* clause captures, e.g. states who have lost standing to engage even in merely solidaristic demanding, because of their own status as, say, colonists or rights-violators in other ways.

[70] See Goldberg and Zipursky 2010.

[71] This point might seem to favour something like universal tort jurisdiction, as in the most generous interpretations of the US Alien Torts Statute. But of course much more argument is needed to establish this, and one point the argument needs to accommodate is that the legitimate space for local variations (as mentioned in the contrast between adversarial and inquisitorial criminal systems above) is not limited to criminal matters. Note that 'bound up with' in the main text is deliberately vague; much more needs to be said again about the relative place of violator, victim, and location of crime.

rights as rights with which everyone's solidarity and fiduciary involvement is in principle permitted.

10.6 Conclusion of Part II: Vindicating Human Rights

The aim of Chapters 7–10 was to demonstrate the appeal of the idea that human rights are distinctively (i) justifiable for the right-holder's sake and (ii) everyone's business. Chapters 7–9 show that if point (i) is true, then human rights must be natural, recognition-independent rights (Chapters 7–8) or their legal-conventional determinations (Sections 9.3–9.4).[72] Chapter 10 shows that if point (ii) is true, then the idea of human rights picks out a subset of those justifiable for the right-holder's sake: those that are distinctively public, demandable in principle in solidaristic and fiduciary ways by anyone.

As stressed in Section 9.5, this view—and in particular point (i)—vindicates our use of the 'rights' concept in referring to human rights. We could, as outlined at the very start of this book (Section 1.1), require the same range of behaviour using only the concept of a duty and not that of a right.[73] But in doing so we would overlook the fact that some natural duties owe their existence entirely or predominantly to the good of a particular subjective, first-personal party, and are permissibly demandable on that party's behalf. If we refrained from using the 'rights' concept in thinking about duties springing from our important human features, we would overlook either our first-personality (treating one another like the rock formation in Section 7.2) or we would overlook how the individual party's good on its own grounds or constitutes duties, perhaps thereby slipping into utilitarianism. Referring to human *rights* highlights their justification, qua natural rights, in the right-holding party's good, or qua legal rights in their relation to such natural rights.

Now the second half of Section 8.3 revealed an important limitation to the reach of this argument: if one cannot accept any distinction of an individual's good from a group good, one will see no role for natural rights (except in promissory cases, where the right is created and hence not 'natural' in my precise sense); the necessity for the rights concept will thereby be greatly diminished, and the idea of human rights will seem misleading. Because I believe the relevant distinction can be drawn—especially when we remember that it is in a sense 'formal', compatible with the interpenetration of individual and communal interests—I think there is an important place for the human rights concept. But we should remember this potential limit to the concept's universal accessibility and coherence.

In addition, aspects of the account of human rights outlined in Part II might seem problematic in light of the specific Addressive account of rights developed in Part I. In particular, Part II takes nations as natural right-holders alongside individuals, and it takes both states and humanity as duty-bearers. In what sense can these parties (nations, states, humanity) grasp, in the first person, that as they should put it, 'we'

---

[72] Or perhaps in very rare cases, legal rights directly justifiable themselves simply by an individual's good (Section 9.2).

[73] We might decide to do this if we think 'human rights' is a misleading piece of ideology—e.g. a utopian aspiration to avoid politics (Moyn 2012). My view is that the concept is defensible, as outlined.

are acting, or that actions are being done to 'us' (as required by Chapter 4)? We should observe that corporate entities (Microsoft, the University of Stirling, even states (the United Kingdom)) can have a constructed first-personality sufficient to bear constructed legal rights. The nation (as opposed to the state) is perhaps more amorphous but, I suggest, sufficiently first-personal to meet the weaker requirements necessary to be a right-holder (rather than a duty-bearer: see Section 4.5). Humanity is of course more contentious. I believe it is capable of the form of first-personality required for bearing duties, though this has to be understood as distinct from the first-personality of either a collective or a corporate entity (see Section 9.3). If not, we will need to lean more heavily on the arguments of Section 9.4 to defend 'positive' human rights to goods and services, and I think we could successfully do so if necessary.[74] Whatever one's moves in that debate, I hope to have made plausible that many duties (namely, those in whose grounding a party's good plays a predominant role) naturally take a rights-types structure for that party, and thereby bring together the duty-bearer and the right-holding party in the first person (often qua groups or collectives)—and human rights law, along with criminal and aspects of other departments of law are justified as founded on and institutionalizing these natural rights.

As stated in Section 7.1, this part of the book (Part II) has attempted to develop a structural theory of human rights without appeal to any metaphysical or substantive theory of the nature of the human, or of human goods. An account of the particular rights that are human rights—the particular rights justifiable for the right-holder's sake, that are everyone's business—requires such a theory of the human and of human goods. We need such a theory to work out what to list on our bills of human rights. I introduced rival versions of such a theory in Chapter 9. I do not here want to fill in a favoured account; I do not feel well qualified to do this. But I will reminder the reader again that Sections 9.3–9.5 show that human rights can and should include demanding 'socio-economic' rights to goods and services, as well as 'civil and political' rights. I will also voice my conviction, contra Griffin, that the relevant 'filling in' of an account of human rights should include many important right-grounding features (e.g. interests in avoiding pain, in nourishment) that humans share with non-human animals. Perhaps we have linguistic reasons to keep 'human rights' solely for the rights of humans, but the formal idea captured by points (i) and (ii)—rights with whom anyone can show solidarity, justifiable for the right-holder's sake—need not respect this speciesist distinction.

The principal ground vindicating use of the concept 'rights' to refer to human rights is, I suggested above, that so doing is necessary to bring out their natural recognition-independent character as rights, or as legal rights protecting such natural rights. Does it follow that rights independent of natural rights—that is, rights that cannot be grounded for the right-holder's sake and that are therefore legal or social

---

[74] Note that some might think we should infer from point (ii) (the fact that human rights are everyone's business) to their being at some fundamental level held against humanity as the correlative duty-bearer. But this is not so. A child's claim to their parents' care is everyone's business in several of my senses, but humanity is not the duty-bearer—even though in my view humanity holds background duties e.g. to step in where a parent fails.

creations, but that do not institutionalize prior natural rights—would be better described without the notions of 'directed duty' and 'right'? Part III will answer this negatively, finding a proper place for rights language (and the first- and second-personal understandings it implicates) in describing legal or conventional duties whose fulfilment enables someone to perform a morally justified legal or conventional role. But this argument will depend crucially on there being *some* natural rights: against this background (in which there are natural rights), I argue that we can legitimately use the 'rights' concept sometimes to refer to legal or conventional structures that institutionalize natural rights (Section 9.5) *and to refer to legal-conventional structures that are in relevant ways similar to those institutionalizing natural rights* (see Chapter 14). But without natural rights, there would be no point to this usage. Furthermore, we will see (in Chapters 12–13) that my case for referring to legal-conventional duties as 'rights' leaves many *property rights*—which do not protect right-holders in performing a justified role, but in many cases also do not institutionalize natural rights—inaptly described as 'rights'.

PART III
Property Rights for the Common Good

11

Introducing Property Rights

11.1 Introduction to Part III: Rights that are Not Justifiable for the Right-Holder's Sake

In Part I, I suggested that a duty to PHI is *owed to* someone if and only if its form, as a duty, is addressed to that party. I explained this as involving a formal requirement of first-personal apprehension (of 'me' as the party to whom the PHI will be done) on the part of the party to whom the duty is owed (Section 4.4), matched by a formal requirement of second-personal apprehension on the part of the duty-bearer (an apprehension that this PHI will be done to 'you') (Section 4.5). Conceived appropriately, this account can, I argued, encompass duties owed to animals, babies, dead people, corporations, and nations, as well as adult humans. Such a duty owed to another constitutes a *right* when it is enforceable, demandable, or subject to related powers exerciseable on behalf of the party to whom the duty is owed (Section 6.1). Other forms of rights can be grasped using Hohfeld's distinctions, built around this core notion of a duty owed to another (Section 6.2).

In Part II, I argued that for a duty *naturally* to qualify as owed to someone—that is, for it so to qualify whether or not anybody recognizes this—it must owe its existence wholly or predominantly to the good (broadly conceived) of the party to whom it is owed (Section 7.6). But we can also *create* directions for duties, making them owed to particular parties (i.e. making them subject to relevant formal requirements of first- and second-personal grasp) as a matter of social construction including convention and law, whenever so doing would be justified on balance, sometimes independently of the good of those to whom they are owed (Section 7.7). On the basis of these positions, I argued for the appeal of the idea that one of the key, overlooked distinguishing features of *human rights* is that they are justifiable *for the right-holder's sake*: they are either natural rights grounded wholly or predominantly by the right-holder's good (Chapter 8), or they are legal or conventional operationalizations of such natural rights (Chapter 9 and Section 10.1).[1] I was then able to defend our use of the 'rights' concept in reference to human rights, on the ground of the concept's importance for signalling the relevant duties' basis in the good of a particular human party.

This defence of our use of the 'rights' concept in relation to human rights should prompt a question about its use elsewhere. When rights cannot be grounded by what

---

[1] Of course I also argued for the independent condition that human rights are *everyone's business*, where this means at a minimum that they are demandable by anyone anywhere on their own behalf as a matter of solidarity with the right-holder (Sections 10.3–10.5).

they do for the right-holder, Section 7.6 tells us that their status as rights rather than as undirected duties cannot be natural or recognition-independent. We might then wonder why we should create such a status in these contexts. What useful role might the concept of 'rights' play here? This is the topic of Part III: when and how can we justify rights that are not justifiable for the right-holder's sake—rights that Section 7.6 tells us do not bear their rights status naturally?

I stressed in Section 8.2 that duties justifiable predominantly by what they do for a particular party—who thereby naturally qualifies as the right-holder—can often *also* be justified by how they serve others beyond the right-holder.[2] But my topic in Part III is rights that cannot be justified *except* by how they serve others; what they do for the right-holder is insufficient to justify them. In particular, my topic is rights of this type that do not even determine or legalize rights that can be justified by what they do for the right-holder. My topic includes many rights in politics and business, such as the prime minister's right to be unimpeded in declaring war or the business manager's right that her directive to employees be acted upon. These rights seem not to be justified, qua legal or conventional rights, by any personal good of the right-holder, nor to be institutionalizations or legalizations of natural rights grounded by the right-holder's (the prime minister's or the manager's) personal good. Rather, it seems to me that these rights must be justified ultimately by how they serve a wider group of which the right-holder is just a small part: the good of 'the people' (in the prime minister's case) or the business and the economy as a whole (in the manager's).[3] Other examples include a doctor's right to care for patients or a judge's right to be unimpeded in sentencing. Again, the personal good of the right-holder appears not to justify these, although here we might say that the good of *particular others* (the patient, the victim, and the convict) or particular *values* (health, justice) play a prominent part in their justification. In some of these cases, we might think that the good of particular others grounds natural rights borne by the relevant particular others—the patient's right to medical care, the convict's right to a fair trial—which the doctor's or judge's rights serve. But like the political and business cases, the good of the doctor or judge themselves does not in these cases seem to be the ground of their own rights (rights to be unimpeded in performing their roles). Given this, we might wonder why we should call such cases 'rights' held by the parties in question at all, rather taking them to be undirected duties or, perhaps, to be rights held by the further group or individual that provides their ultimate justification. On the latter view, we would say that it is really *the people's* right that the prime minister not be impeded in declaring war; it is really something like *widespread economic actors'* right that the business manager's directive be acted upon; it is really *the patient's* right that the doctor be allowed to care for her, and so on.

---

[2] See also the discussion (at Section 7.6, penultimate paragraph, and Section 10.1, at note 11) of Raz's point about the wider benefits of my right to freedom of speech (1994, pp. 54–5).

[3] Readers might wonder whether the point developed in Section 8.3, at pp. 127–29, allows even the examples mentioned to qualify as 'for the right-holder's sake', but as explained at pp. 129–30, this is not the case. The good *to the prime minister* of the people's benefitting from her being unimpeded in declaring war—even just her intrinsic interest in her group's good—is no predominant justifier of our being duty-bound not to impede her. Only the good to the people is such a justifier.

Part III addresses this question: why call these 'rights', when they are held by a right-holder whose good does not justify them? Can we find reason for this use of the 'rights' concept—reason to refer as 'rights' to duties whose core ground is not the right-holder's good, reasons to set up the Addressive requirements that make the relevant duties directed? The answer is mixed, which is what we might expect given the messily broad range of instrumental reasons relevant to whether to create or sustain a legal or conventional duty's rights-type structure. But some notable points emerge. In Chapter 14, I focus on the important and universally held interest in fulfilling one's morally justified duties of office. This interest is served by others' duties that protect one's fulfilment of one's own morally justified duties of office. I argue that even though this interest can rarely play a predominant role[4] in justifying such protective duties, it plays enough of a role to make 'rights' language apt even though the rights in question do not exist for the right-holder's sake and hence must hold their rights status as a social creation. In the preceding chapters (Chapters 12–13), I focus specifically on property rights and here, I argue, our conclusions are especially mixed. Some property rights are natural or recognition-independent (Chapter 12), but many are not and insofar as their justification turns on how they serve the common or collective good *without* protecting the right-holder in perform-ing some duty of office, their status as rights should be questioned (Chapter 13).[5]

11.2 Why Property?

Property rights are, historically, among our canonical rights, and firmly at the heart of the history of rights theory.[6] But—with some notable exceptions[7]—they have not been central to philosophical discussion of modern human rights. There are two reasons why I focus on property. First, as mentioned at the end of the previous section, property rights do not specifically protect duties of office, and this makes them hard to conceive as justified fundamentally for the sake of parties beyond the right-holder. Compare again the prime minister's right to declare war or a business manager's right that her directives be followed—or a coach or train driver's right not to be distracted by over-chatty passengers, or a parking attendant's right to give someone a ticket. Each of these rights is normally *not* justifiable predominantly by

---

[4] By a 'predominant' role, I mean a STRONGEST or STRONG A role, in the language of Section 8.2.

[5] I could equally have focused on promissory and contractual rights, as distinct interesting cases in which the duties in question are not justifiable wholly or predominantly by what they do for the right-holder (even though I suspect that serving the right-holder is a condition on their bindingness (Raz 2012); but it is not what makes them morally binding; that is a matter of the promisor's and promisee's will independently of their good). Promissory duties, and their status as rights, are not natural in my technical sense, in that their existence and status depend on their being recognized as such, at least by promisor and promisee. But they do not depend, like legal rights, on wider social participation for their creation. I hope to return to these issues in future work (see also Section 8.3, p. 132.) For insightful extended discussion of the rights created by agreements, see Gilbert 2018.

[6] See their centrality in, e.g. the Franciscan poverty debates at the start of medieval rights discourse (Brett 1997; Tierney 1997; Garnsey 2007, ch. 4) and also in Hume's account of justice (1978 [1739–40], book III, pt. II), in Locke (1960 [1689]), Hegel (1991) [1821], Kant (1996 [1797]), and Fichte (2000) [1796–7]).

[7] Thomson 1990, Nickel 2000 and 2007, Ripstein 2009, Tomasi 2012.

how it serves the good of the right-holder (even though in most cases it will do this): neither their good as a specific embodied person, nor their generic good as a human being. One can plausibly say in each case that the right is justifiable by how it serves the right-holder's good *as a generic such-and-such* (elected national leader, business manager, coach or train driver, parking monitor); but we then have to explain that the reason to serve the right-holder's good *as a such-and-such* is because so doing serves others beyond the right-holder: the people, the business and its customers and wider economy, the coach and train passengers (and other drivers, in the coach case), the car park users. In our explanation, we cannot and should not 'stop' at the good of the right-holder in her role. Such rights thereby differ from those examined in Chapter 9: rights justifiable simply or predominantly in virtue of their relation to the right-holder's important human interests, or her good as a generic human, the importance of which needs no further explanation in terms of how serving it serves further goods.

But the role of 'owner' or 'holder of property rights' (which I shall take to be synonymous) is unlike the roles of prime minister, business manager, coach or train driver, or parking attendant because 'owner' carries with it no defining outward-serving duties. Instead, someone who owns something or has property rights over it can (within appropriate limits) permissibly use it to help others, themselves, or nobody. The idea of property rights therefore does not have naturally built into it the notion that such rights exist ultimately to serve others beyond the right-holder. Property rights do not wear on their face their grounding in the common good. In this way property rights are more like the human rights of Part II. And perhaps partly for this reason (and we will see further reasons in Chapter 12), it is contro-versial to regard property rights as rights that are justifiable primarily for the sake of the wider community rather than specifically for the right-holder's sake. In making this claim, at least regarding much modern property, I am contradicting Locke and Hegel, among others, and siding with Hume and Bentham.[8]

A second reason I focus on property is that it seems a particularly difficult right to justify. Many of the world's worst problems can be ascribed to poverty, and there is a sense in which property rights create poverty: were my and my neighbours' wealth at the disposal of those with very little, they would no longer be impoverished; abolish the trespassory duties protecting my house, car, and bank account, and some could be liberated, able to feed and educate themselves—and to protect themselves from exploitative violation of human rights not to be assaulted or abused—with the resources I and my neighbours currently use for luxuries.[9] Of course there is another plausible story in which property rights create wealth,[10] and certainly the mere abolition of my and my neighbour's property rights would not solve the world's problems but add to them. Abolition of *all* property rights would likely be signifi-cantly worse.

---

[8] Locke 1960 [1689], Hume 1978 [1739–40], Bentham 1987 [1789], Hegel 1991 [1821].

[9] See the figures on global wealth inequality in the UN's online materials on inequality and poverty.

[10] Compare the classical liberal arguments for private-property-defined free markets in Hayek 1960, Smith 1976 [1776], Hume 1978 [1739–40], and more recently in, e.g. de Soto 2000 or Cheneval 2019. Compare also Locke 1960 [1689], section 37, on the productiveness of acquisition.

Nonetheless, it is worth pausing on the way that specific property rights are an impediment to all except the owner. Others' rights not to be murdered or assaulted should not present themselves as impediments to a person: if they do appear in this way to someone, this is a sign that something is seriously morally awry with that person. Similarly, in a well-constituted, fair welfare state, the tax that must be paid as part of the social structure which ensures that inhabitants' human rights to education, to medical care, to political participation or to due process are fulfilled should again not present itself as an impediment to the person paying the tax.[11] If it does appear in this way to someone living in a fairly constituted state, this is again a sign of potentially serious moral error on the part of the duty-bearer. By contrast, it seems to me that even if they are fully morally justified, the property rights of others can often permissibly present themselves as a regrettable impediment to my plans. This is not to say that I can justifiably overlook them, but it is sometimes not morally reprehensible internally or among friends to bemoan how someone else's property limits one's options—especially the property of very wealthy people. And I think this is because– unlike in the human rights cases—what most property rights do for the owner (at least in the case of wealthy people (see Chapter 12)) is not what morally justifies them, and hence their impeding me is not, morally, their owner's own good impeding me. It is, rather, the chance playing out of interactions within a system that serves everyone which has resulted in my being impeded. This system can be justified yet I am allowed to bemoan its results because plans that would, were things otherwise, use what has turned out to be 'someone else's', are not in themselves morally suspect in the way that plans that would, if it were allowed, use others' bodies or their educational resources are.

11.3 Defining Property

A jurisprudential debate asks whether property rights are primarily rights of exclusion or of use, or whether there is no 'core' to property because it can be constituted by any bundle of rights in relation to a thing.[12] My view is that both exclusion and use must play a central role in an account of property, but rights of exclusion have some conceptual primacy.

I take a party's *rights of exclusion* over X to be constituted by the duties others owe to the party to refrain from using, handling or (in the case of land) crossing or occupying X. These are what we might call others' 'trespassory' duties, owed to the party in question, to keep off X. And I take a party's *rights of use* over X to be constituted by the party's Hohfeldian privileges, against all others, to use X, where this means the party's owing nobody duties not to use X. Rights of exclusion—

---

[11] Note that I do not say that the tax itself *funds* social provision. This is a common error, discussed in Section 11.4. Note also that I am here assuming a fair or just society which means—among other things—a society in which each person can readily afford to pay their tax burden. Tax is a justifiably bemoanable impediment in unjust societies, including (almost?) all societies through history.

[12] See the useful summary in Penner and Smith 2013; compare Munzer 1990, ch. 2; Penner 1997; Ripstein 2013. For a classic basis for the 'bundle' theory, see Honoré 1961; 'bundle' theorists like Munzer combine Honoré's analysis with Hohfeld 1964 (Munzer 1990, pp. 22–4).

trespassory duties—typically function to protect the party in exercising the privileges constitutive of her rights of use. Note that in many cases, the privileges constituting the right of use are legal but not moral, while the (exclusion-constituting) legal trespassory duties protecting these privileges are nonetheless morally justified. For example, I might owe my children a moral duty to turn my flowerbeds into a lawn on which they can practise football, and hence I might hold no *moral* privilege, against my children, to cultivate the flowers instead. Nonetheless my legal right of use of the garden will be rightly protected by others' duties to refrain from coming in and converting it into a football pitch: such trespassory duties are often morally justified even when they thereby protect me in committing a moral wrong.[13] (Of course, they would not require a neighbour to refrain from entering to prevent me *attacking* my children, or committing another serious moral wrong.)

This structure—trespassory duties owed to the owner that exclude others, protecting the owner's privileges of use—seems to be the conceptual core of property.[14] The point in parentheses at the end of the previous paragraph shows that neither the duties nor privileges in question need be 'absolute': I can own something even if many uses are legally as well as morally forbidden, and even if others are not excluded from stepping in to prevent such uses.[15] Furthermore, one can qualify as the owner of something without possessing straightforward rights of use or exclusion, if one is nonetheless suitably related to such rights, occupying a normative position suitably 'close' to them: e.g. as owner of an apartment that has been leased to someone else.[16] And of course further related rights—such as a (Hohfeldian) power to transfer exclusionary and use rights, and immunities protecting these rights—are often part of someone's ownership.[17]

Let us set aside complex possibilities involving neither straightforward exclusion nor use—cases like the lease just mentioned. Instead, let us isolate cases involving exclusion from cases involving use. I suggest that rights of exclusion without use rights would peripherally qualify as property. Suppose everyone owed a party a duty not to use some land, but that party was debarred from using it in any way. Some cases of ownership come close to this: suppose I own an artwork which is deemed a national treasure, in a jurisdiction in which this means that I have to display it in a public gallery and am banned from selling it. There is still a sense in which I own it, simply in virtue of my rights of exclusion—that is, in virtue of the fact that were others to steal or deface the artwork, I would be wronged. By contrast I suggest that

---

[13]   Compare Waldron 1993, ch. 3 on the right to do wrong.

[14]   Compare Snare 1972 for a non-Hohfeldian view in which use protected by exclusion is presented as the core of property (but which erroneously misses the Hohfeldian, directed character of trespassory duties); compare also Penner 1997, p. 152, for the centrality of exclusion.

[15]   Compare Plato on how one ought not return a borrowed weapon to a friend who has since gone out of their mind (Plato 1974 [*The Republic*], 331c).

[16]   See Honoré 1961 for the ideas of a right of 'reversion' and 'absence of term' as parts of 'full liberal ownership'. Even if we reject the 'bundle' view by giving the right of exclusion special status in relation to the concept of property (as I do in the main text), we should nonetheless see it as a family resemblance concept in which other rights cluster round this core—and enough of them can make a case of something like property, even without the core.

[17]   See Xu and Allain 2015, and (for focus that distinguishes rights to transfer and profit from rights of use), Christman 1994.

rights of use without the protection of rights of exclusion look less like property: suppose I held a privilege to use some land, but nobody owed me a duty to keep off the land in order to allow me to use it; this looks rather far from ownership for me.[18] These examples can be read in many ways, but I think they give some reason to conclude that the right of exclusion has a degree of conceptual primacy. On this view, the core of a party's owning X is when others' use of X qualifies as a violative trespass that wrongs the party in question. Without privileges to use X, the party's 'ownership' will be non-canonical, but the exclusion of others is core.[19]

Whether or not the details of this view are correct, the key point for my purposes is that trespassory duties constitutive of a right of exclusion—duties not to use X *owed to* X's owner—are central to ownership. This picture might seem inconsistent with the account of rights and directed duties developed in Chapter 4. For as Ripstein notes, 'it is trite law that you can commit a trespass even if you are in no position to know who the owner is. To take another's coat, innocently mistaking it for your own, you have a full defence to any criminal charge, but still commit a trespass against chattels.'[20] Chapter 4 says that for someone to owe someone else a duty not to take their coat, the duty-bearer must be under a formal requirement to conceive the coat's owner second-personally as a potential 'you'. And it might seem that this cannot be done without identifying the owner in the way Ripstein notes is unnecessary. But, as I noted in Section 4.6, I can conceive someone as 'you', and thereby in a sense identify them, without being able to point at them, identify them by description, or name them: I can simply think of them as 'you, whose coat I am not taking', just as one might coherently address in thought the owner of a meadow in which one is strolling ('you, the owner, ought to remove this dead tree') without knowing who that owner is.[21]

The question I address in the next chapters (12–13) is: when are property rights— which, we have seen, are centrally constituted by duties not to use or occupy things, whose violation counts as wronging the owner—morally justifiable, and why? Can such rights be grounded or justifiable primarily by what they do for the right-holder, and hence perhaps bear their rights status naturally? When must their status as rights be a social creation, and when can such creation be justified? Can we really justify thinking of them as rights—as constituted by trespassory duties *owed to* an owner?

11.4 Defining Money

Before I get to these questions, we should go over some rarely covered ground, which reveals the Hohfeldian power to be almost as central to modern property as the

---

[18] Compare Hohfeld's person who is told, with regard to a shrimp salad owned by others, 'eat the salad, if you can; you have our license to do so, but we don't agree not interfere with you' (1964, p. 41). This person's Hohfeldian privilege to use the salad, when unprotected by others' trespassory duties to exclude themselves, does not look much like property in the salad.

[19] In this discussion, I use 'right of use' rather differently to Ripstein 2013, who does not use Hohfeld's concepts, and seems mostly to construe 'use' narrowly as how the owner actually wants to use the item (see his dismissal of the 'Sartrean' view that failing to decide on a use is itself a use (p. 160) and his similar rejection of a broad interpretation of Katz's conception of use-qua-agenda-setting (p. 179)). I would endorse Ripstein's view that the right of use, as I have characterized it, is a formal one.

[20] Ripstein 2013, p. 159.   [21] See Chapter 4, note 38, and the opening of Section 4.6.

trespassory claim. It is central because it is constitutive of money. My arguments about the moral justification of property rights will apply as much to wealth in general—including the ownership of money, stocks and shares, options—as to land, chattels, or ideas. Money is clearly central to wealth in general, and the idea of a right of exclusion can be applied to money: if this £10 note is *mine*, then this means that, *ceteris paribus*, others will wrong me if they use it without my permission. But what exactly the money is (from which others are excluded) can seem metaphysically confusing, especially money in bank accounts.[22]

In my view, to have money is to have something whose essential character qua money is that it confers on its bearer a Hohfeldian power: a power to gain new rights including, among others, the power to make certain duties owed to one, such as trespassory duties constituting one's ownership of something and duties to provide services. To have £10 is to have the power to gain some among the vast range of claim-rights, power-rights, liberty-rights, and immunity-rights regarding goods and services that £10 can buy: to make that basket of food over there a basket regarding which others now owe me trespassory duties, or to make my hairdresser owe me a haircut, and so on. The Hohfeldian power which £10 confers on me is, for most of the rights over which it is a power, only conditional: it only creates new duties subject to the *consent* of the seller.[23]

Of course, to have property rights over any commodity whatsoever in a capitalist economy is to have a Hohfeldian power, as is any service one can offer for sale.[24] Rather than my £10, instead my chicken or my lectures could, with your consent, be exchanged for your basket of food or for your haircutting services. But unlike goods or services, money, I contend, *necessarily* confers a Hohfeldian power insofar as it is money.[25] If my chicken or my lectures do not simply lose market value but are made in principle unexchangeable, incapable of generating new rights over other things or services for me, then they do not stop being a chicken or a lecture, and my other rights over them would persist. They would simply lose their character as a saleable commodity or service, and the specific Hohfeldian power that involves. By contrast, if my £10 is made permanently in principle unexchangeable, losing its character as a Hohfeldian power (perhaps the bank note or coin is declared void, or all sellers and taxers decide not to accept pounds sterling in payment for anything, or my bank

---

[22] Note the small proportion of global money constituted by physical notes and coins. Note also that the legal relation between bank and depositor is not a fiduciary one; rather, the bank is a debtor which owes the depositor the money she has deposited: 'this trade of a banker is to receive money, and use it as if it were his own, he becoming debtor to the person who has lent or deposited with him the money to use as his own, and for which money he is accountable as a debtor', Foley v. Hill (1848) 9 E. R. 1002 (see http://www.uniset.ca/other/css/9ER1002.html).

[23] There could be economic systems and there might be some cases—e.g. the Scottish system of closed bids for house purchases—in which consent from the seller (either consent in general to sell, or to sell to this specific person) is not needed. One might wonder whether a *conditional* power really is a genuine power, but this is certainly possible in Hohfeldian terms: it is an ability, conditional on something, to alter certain duties, etc. Many Hohfeldian powers are conditional like this: e.g. the judge's power to sentence convicts is conditional on jurisdiction, on procedural requirements, etc.

[24] This is consistent with my earlier claim that the core of my property over X is others' duties to keep off X. Nonetheless, in *capitalism* the power to transfer these rights to others is central to property.

[25] In this respect it is similar to political power in a state governed by the rule of law.

account is declared no longer to be a bank account but simply a list of numbers unrelated to any duty on the bank's part to pay me or make payments for me), then my £10 is no longer money.

Further, it is I suggest *sufficient* for something to be money that it be a possessable thing (and not necessarily a *material* thing) that essentially confers on its possessor (a) a Hohfeldian power to create rights for the possessor over something over which someone else currently has rights (normally conditional on consent from that party) which is (b) internally rather than externally limited, on a numerical scale. By 'internal' limits I mean that the limit or extent of the disjunction of rights which my £10 constitutes a (conditional) power to create is not a limit or extent generated by some separate rule of the system, in the way that, say, the monarch's power to pardon convicts might be limited by a rule forbidding the issuing of pardons to pirates. It is instead akin to the way in which the monarch's power to pardon is limited to those people over whom she holds jurisdiction—so for example the British monarch could not pardon convicts convicted and imprisoned by Italy. Similarly, the Hohfeldian power conferred by my £10 cannot generate rights for me beyond those which I can get a seller to agree to give me for £10; the numerical value defines this limit.

This account of money might seem to overlook its role as an item of *exchange*.[26] Conditions (a) and (b) could be satisfied by ration tokens submitted to a shop which the unfortunate shop-keeper must then, after redeeming them to the agreed value, destroy. My sense is that bearers of such tokens would (unlike the shop-keeper) consider them money.[27] But if we think exchange is essential to money, then we should add a third clause: money held by party X is a possessable thing that essentially confers (a) a Hohfeldian power borne by X to create rights for X over that over which someone else Y currently has rights (normally conditional on consent from Y) which is (b) internally limited on a numerical scale, *and which (c) is in its exercise itself transferred to Y*.[28] Thus in buying Y's basket of food or haircutting service, my £10 augments Y's money stock—augments the numerical extent of Y's disjunctive Hohfeldian power of the type sketched.

Note that the 'itself' in clause (c) should be taken to refer to the possessable thing. When money's essential power (a) is exercised by X, the thing conferring this power is transferred to the party (Y) with whom it has been exchanged, who is thereby given (by the money) their own Hohfeldian power of types (a)–(c). Gifts transfer the thing that confers these powers without exercising them. Loans transfer it temporarily, and on conditions, etc.

My account makes it essential to money that it is a possessable medium of exchange, and my account might thereby seem akin to the common 'commodity' account of money. But unlike the standard commodity theorists, I do not maintain that money is a commodity just like any other.[29] When money takes physical form—

---

[26] And as a means for payment of tax, discussed in the text shortly.

[27] Compare Cohen 1995, pp. 57–9, on money as tickets to goods and services: money as freedoms.

[28] Note that without (b) and (c), there would be nothing to distinguish money on my account from other ceremonial items conferring Hohfeldian powers to make goods and services owed to the holder—such as legal powers of unlimited expropriation conferred by holding 'the king's crown', perhaps.

[29] For a sketch of this view, see e.g. Ingham 2004, ch. 1.

as notes or coin—the commodity account can seem attractive: my property rights over my pound notes entitle me stupidly to use them as kindling for my fire rather than to buy things. But the commodity account stumbles to explain the non-concrete money transferred electronically by banks.[30] Such transfers (as when one uses a debit card to make a payment) seem to involve transfer of a non-concrete 'thing' over which one holds rights even though the transferred 'thing' is not physical. Against this, one might say that what is transferred here is simply the right to be paid physical money by a bank: this right to be paid coins or notes to a certain value on demand is transferred from my bank to my shopkeeper's bank when I use my debit card to pay my shopkeeper.[31] But I think that conception of the purchase overstates the import-ance of coins and notes, at least in our everyday non-technical, non-legal thinking about money. We can imagine—and are sometimes rather close to realizing—a world in which there are no coins and notes. In what, then, do these non-material 'things' that are money consist? If one cannot access a cashpoint for physical money, then the only ways to use these things (i.e. the money amounts owed to one from one's bank account) is in exchange, gift, or loan. There seems to be no more to this non-physical 'thing' than its conferring the Hohfeldian powers defining these actions of exchange, gift, or loan—unlike more familiar commodities like coal, oil, or chickens. Further-more, construing money as a standard commodity makes mysterious the way that banks *augment* the money supply (i.e. create new money) simply through making loans or, in the case of central banks, through measures like 'quantitative easing'.[32] How can the supply of a commodity—even a non-concrete one—be generated simply through contract, agreement, accounting, and nothing more? My Hohfeldian account of money makes this easy to see: legal-conventional Hohfeldian powers can, as the positivists tell us, be created in a host of ways, just as any law or convention can be. Creating non-concrete objects that confer such powers is equally easy. Just as we can create new social roles or offices that confer new Hohfeldian powers on their holders (such as, say, a role of 'Health and Safety officer' with powers to cancel unsafe classes or exams), so we can create new non-concrete objects conferring new Hohfeldian powers on their holders.

My view that money is essentially something that confers a Hohfeldian power is in some respects more like the commodity theorist's standard rival: the view associated with 'Chartalists' and 'Modern Monetary Theory', the view that money consists in transferable debts or IOUs issued by the government.[33] To hold an IOU from someone is essentially to hold something that confers on the bearer a specific Hohfeldian power: the power to make the issuing party on demand duty-bound to deliver the service specified in the IOU, or to transfer to the holder rights of exclusion over the good specified. Douglas offers a nice outline of how such specific

---

[30] See again Ingham 2004.

[31] This would be supported by the legal conception of 'money in banks' as a debtor relationship, outlined in note 22 above.

[32] Ingham 2004, pp. 139–41; Werner 2014.

[33] For this contrast between commodity theorists and 'Chartalists', see Goodhart 1998; for the 'Char-talist' or IOU view, see especially Douglas 2016, pp. 76–9; see also Graeber 2011.

IOUs issued by particular people could, when transferable, become the kind of general Hohfeldian power that I have said money consists in:

Suppose you give me a fish and I issue you an IOU, promising to provide you with eggs upon request. If you don't want eggs, you can give the IOU to somebody else in exchange for what you desire. She might take the IOU even if she doesn't want eggs herself, since she knows she'll be able to swap it with somebody else who does want the eggs—with somebody else who knows the same thing she knows, and so on indefinitely. The IOU is, in this case, serving the function of a medium of exchange.[34]

Douglas adds that while personal IOUs of this type are unlikely to be trusted sufficiently to become a widespread medium of exchange, IOUs backed by the power of the state can perform this function. In particular, Douglas and related theorists claim that something that the state *guarantees to accept in payment of taxes*—a transferable IOU from the state whose content is a promise that this very IOU will be accepted in payment of taxes—can perform the requisite function:

If I seek to purchase something from you by using my IOU, it is your choice whether or not to take the deal; it will depend on how much you trust me [...] But if the government [through taxation] *imposes a debt burden upon you, which can only be settled with its own IOUs*, then you are pretty well guaranteed to accept its IOUs in payment. Thus the purchasing power of my IOUs is limited by my trustworthiness [...] while the value of the government's IOUs are limited only by its ability to impose a tax debt upon citizens by force.[35]

There are two major insights in this IOU theory. First, it highlights the important causal role of taxation in making something—pounds, dollars, or some other currency—widely accepted in exchange. Secondly, it facilitates a welcome reconceptualization of the relation between taxation and public spending. The reconceptualization in question is equally open to non-IOU theories, but the IOU theory is more likely to prompt it. The relevant reconceptualization observes that public spending need not be taken as funded by taxation, even in a state with a balanced budget. Instead, public spending can be equally appropriately conceived as funded by newly created money, with taxation's roles being simply (1) to control the overall money supply in order to limit the inflation that would otherwise ensue, and (2) to ensure that people want the money the state creates (because people will need it to pay taxes), and hence are willing to accept it in return for providing the services the state wants to fund.[36]

---

[34] Douglas 2016, p. 75.   [35] Ibid., pp. 81–2.

[36] Many think it obvious that taxation's role is to fund public spending. The IOU or 'Modern Monetary Theory' approach enticingly suggests that if, perhaps under the influence of a pervasive belief in the justness of current prices, economic actors could be relied upon to maintain the price level even while the state created significant amounts of new money to fund public services, then there would be no need for taxation, except at some minimal level in order to motivate people to accept the relevant currency. Note that much of what I have said works only for states in charge of their own currency, rather than those controlled by an external central bank like the European Central Bank or a Gold Standard. I also set aside complications about whether to conceive state creation of money as 'borrowing', and how this interacts with the issuing of government bonds. See Douglas 2016.

The IOU theory is especially likely to prompt this reconceptualization because its view of money—as state-issued IOUs that declare that they will be accepted in payment of taxes—entails it. For tax payments discharge the relevant IOUs, just as the IOU in Douglas's earlier example is discharged when someone finally presents it to him and insists on receiving the promised eggs. Once this has happened in this example, the IOU in question cannot then continue to be used as a means of exchange. New IOUs need to be issued for this purpose. The IOU theory of money implies the same about money when it is used for paying taxes: the IOU in which, so the theorists tell us, the money consists has now been discharged. So the money paid in taxes cannot be the same money—in the sense of the very same IOUs—used to fund public services.

As I noted before, one need not be an IOU theorist in order to reconceive taxation as not simply the very material of public spending in the way that my income is the very material of my private spending. And I cannot here assess the IOU view of money in detail, though it seems fairly plausible to me.[37] But I contend that even if it is true, it accounts only for the contingent form that modern money happens to take: we happen, via the social processes outlined by Douglas, to have endowed state IOUs with powers of the (a)–(c) type. But this is a contingent development. State-issued IOUs that promise to be received in tax payments *need not* be money: suppose these IOUs were not permissibly exchangeable, but had to be retained only by the party to whom the state issued them, for their own use in tax payment. More importantly, I think money could exist in a world without states or coercive tax extraction—for example, in an anarchistic world. So long as we manage to make some possessable 'object' (material or non-material) confer Hohfeldian power of type (a)–(c), it will be money. Its conferring such power is essential to its being money. While state-issued IOUs stamped on coins or notes, and owed to depositors by banks, might have gained this role in our world, I see no reason why, with appropriate social developments, alternative objects could not gain this role, independently of whether they are IOUs: objects including cowrie shells or bitcoins or electronic funds or other objects (material or non-material) that are independent of state IOUs. This is not to say that the nature of the particular possessable object conferring Hohfeldian powers which constitutes money makes no difference to money's place in the world. If there are resource limitations on the production of this object—as with gold rather than state IOUs—this will have profound implications for both commercial banks' creation of money by offering loans and central banks' 'printing' of money. But this is compatible with my claim that whether an object is money or not depends fundamentally on whether it is essentially an object of exchange, as encapsulated in Hohfeldian powers of type (a)–(c).

There is one condition to add to (a)–(c). The power in which money consists is conferred by a possessable and transferable object; hence it is not a power logically exerciseable only by a specific person. Rather, money is an object that can be

---

[37] If the IOU view is correct, then tax payments should, unlike other uses of money, be construed as not conferring the very same (a)–(c) powers on the state that they would confer when transferred to other bodies. For in relation to *the state*, money is, the IOU theorist tells us, like a (tax-paying) ration token, rather than a transferable means of exchange: it vanishes on receipt for tax payments.

detached from its owner and confers power of the (a)–(c) form on whoever has physical control of it—that is, of the coin or the money owed to depositors by banks. This makes it unlike, say, the judge's Hohfeldian power to sentence criminals. The latter power cannot be 'stolen' by someone who is not the judge. Even an impersonator who tricks a court into taking a convict away for the sentence she has chosen will not have genuinely exercised a Hohfeldian power. Instead, the purported 'sentencing' will be null and void, even if nobody grasps this. By contrast, someone can genuinely steal my money by taking my notes and coins, and they can fraudulently bring my bank to make payments I have not authorized. De facto control of money constitutes genuine possession of the relevant Hohfeldian powers—unlike in the judge case.

This fact brings in an important role for the right of exclusion which, I argued in Section 11.3, is central to property rights over ordinary chattels and land. Because money is detachable from its possessor (it is an object—coin, note, bitcoin, cowrie shell, state IOU—that essentially confers Hohfeldian power of types (a)–(c) on *whoever possesses it*), a party can hold rights of exclusion over it, constituted by others' trespassory duties, owed to the party, not to interfere with it. In this respect, it is like any other commodity. We can therefore ask, as with other property rights, whether the relevant exclusion-defining trespassory duties are justifiable predominantly by what they do for the money's owner, and hence whether these duties can qualify as naturally (recognition-independently) rather than constructedly owed to the owner—*justifying* a legal form that *reflects* rather than simply *constitutes* them.

Note that we can ask a similar question about the power itself, the Hohfeldian power defined by (a)–(c): is this power conferred on me by the £10 that I own justifiable predominantly on the basis of what the power does for me, or must any plausible justification for it refer centrally to what it does for others beyond me? Of course as a causal matter the power owes its existence to processes of social construction involving many people, such as the IOU circulation sketched by Douglas. But we might think we can still morally justify my possession of the power in question largely on the basis of what it does for me—for example, on the basis that my freedom requires it independently of whether this serves others. (We will see at the end of Section 12.3 that to regard a natural rather than a legal-conventional Hohfeldian power as grounded by its being good for its holder is to make the same category error I identified at the end of Section 7.4: that is, erroneously to infer that a right naturally exists from the fact that it would be good if it did. But we might still wonder whether an individual's freedom (or desert or some other good) can on its own, or in my STRONG B manner, justify our conferring on or creating for that individual some legal-conventional Hohfeldian power—including a power constitutive of money.)

I assess such arguments about property in general, including but not limited to money, in the next chapter. When are someone's ownership rights justifiable 'for the right-holder's sake'? In the first section of the next chapter (Section 12.1), I explain why it seems to me that they cannot always be so justifiable, even if (Sections 12.2–12.4) sometimes *some* property rights are, like our human rights, justifiable 'for the right-holder's sake'.

12

Modest Property Rights for the Right-Holder's Sake

12.1. Property Rights Not for the Right-Holder's Sake: The Property of Those with a Lot

This chapter explores arguments for and against the idea that some property rights are justifiable predominantly on the basis of the right-holder's own good, and hence (as Section 7.6 tells us) are constituted by duties naturally owed to the right-holder. I start, in the current section, by explaining why some of the property rights of those with much wealth cannot plausibly be grounded in this way. I realize that the ideas of 'a lot of' or 'much' wealth are vague. But here, I aim simply to show that *some* property rights cannot be justifiable for the right-holder's sake, and I understand 'the wealthy' in global terms which will include many readers of this book. Examples of the rights I have in mind include my ownership of the garden shed in which we store bicycles, or Bill Gates's ownership of $2 billion kept in one of his bank accounts.[1] Suppose that there is moral justification for respecting these legal property rights: that is, for people other than me to refrain from using the shed, and for people other than Gates to refrain from seizing control of his bank account. My contention is that *what such behaviour does for Gates and me* cannot be on its own sufficient to constitute a powerful case for people's being duty-bound so to behave. In a sense, such behaviour does *too much* for Gates and me for our good plausibly to be its ground.[2] We are already doing well enough that the extra interests, needs, or freedoms which such behaviour secures for us cannot plausibly function as the main ground for this behaviour.[3]

As it stands, the argument in the last sentence is flawed. The fact that one's life is going successfully even with a right violated does not entail that this right must be grounded primarily by what it does for others beyond the right-holder. One can have one's basic human rights violated—e.g. by being assaulted yet recovering, or by being denied political participation yet developing a flourishing career—but manage to live

---

[1] See Chapter 11, note 22 for the legal thesis that the money in Gates's account is not in the same way 'his'. I think that, except in moments of banking crisis, we tend to ignore this fact about money, and that this infuses our conceptual sense of what is 'ours'.

[2] This is not to overlook the important point, pressed by MacLeod (2015), that most property rights are held by groups or corporations, not individuals: families, businesses, churches.

[3] For an old argument to this effect, see Cruft 2006. I now think that argument fails because the non-interference/assistance distinction on which it trades cannot be made to do the work required.

a successful life.[4] (Note also that one can be very wealthy yet suffer human rights violations by, e.g. being denied political participation or education.) So we cannot infer from the fact that someone would be successful even without some of their wealth to the conclusion that the rights protecting this wealth cannot be grounded for the right-holder's sake.

But I nonetheless find it implausible that my property rights over my shed or Gates's over $2 billion could be justifiable primarily for my or Gates's sake. In both cases, there are powerful common good reasons (see Chapter 13) for other parties to respect the trespassory duties in question. But *do my own or Gates's own interests, needs, freedom, or 'good'* also on their own constitute powerful reasons for such 'non-trespassing' behaviour? Are the trespassory duties 'naturally' generated by our good? Might these duties legally operationalize or determine some such prior natural rights of ours? One might think that Gates's and my interests in autonomy, or in respect for what we have managed to gain through voluntary exchanges, or in getting what we deserve, or in respect for plans we have made, can constitute powerful reasons on their own for others to engage in the relevant non-trespassory behaviour. And in Sections 12.2–12.4, I find some merit in these arguments, and hence some reason to regard both certain specific property rights and some general rights to participate in property systems as justifiable for the right-holder's sake in a way that makes them natural or recognition-independent. But the reach of these arguments is limited. I do not believe they make my garden shed or Gates's $2 billion ours as a matter of natural right, nor even as a matter of legal right determining some natural right (even though perhaps my ownership of my shed *might* have been so justifiable if, say, it had been my life's work).[5]

To see why not, note that a party's good (e.g. her interests, needs, or freedoms), which is served by her property rights, can be served to a greater or lesser degree. We see a similar phenomenon with some 'standard' human rights: a right to higher education would do more to serve the interests which ground my right to a primary education; and perhaps a right not to be looked at or photographed without my consent would do more to serve some of the interests which ground my right not to be assaulted. These examples reveal that the relevant interest, need, or freedom of the individual can—as outlined in Chapter 8—on its own ground certain rights in a way that defeats almost all countervailing considerations (e.g. rights to a primary education or not to be assaulted), while *failing* to constitute such a strong case for further rights that would do more to serve it (e.g. rights to higher education or not to be looked at without consent). The same applies to levels of wealth. Even if my interest in owning the products of my labour on its own grounds certain property rights for me in a way that defeats almost all countervailing considerations (Section 12.3), it seems clear that this interest is *not* a powerful ground in favour of my property in my shed or Gates's in his $2 billion. The latter are like a right to higher education or a right not to be looked at: grounding such rights in what they do for the right-holder would take serving the relevant grounding interest to override a range of

---

[4] See my rejection of the 'guaranteeing' view of the relation between rights and their grounds, Section 7.3, p. 99. Compare Cruft 2015.

[5] See Sections 12.3–12.4 for more on the importance of personal connections and work.

countervailing considerations (notably, the costs the right imposes on everyone else as bearers of the relevant trespassory duties) which it should not always—or even just 'normally'—defeat. With the core of the interest secured (perhaps through *some* property rights, or a right to primary education or against assault), the case this interest can make for further rights augmenting extensive wealth for the right-holder is not on its own a powerful grounding case. To use the language of Section 8.2, the relevant interest cannot play a STRONGEST or STRONG A role in grounding the relevant duties.[6]

This argument is bolstered by a related thought about taxation. Part II can be seen as an extended argument for the claim that each state is duty-bound to set up and maintain a system upholding quite extensive human rights—to education, political participation, health care, due process, subsistence, free association, and much more. Such a system requires taxation that goes beyond that which a theorist merely willing to support police and courts to uphold property must countenance. (We might also agree with Waldron that each human has an important interest in being an owner—in owning some external material beyond their own bodies—and a system provisioning this will also require taxation.)[7] When such taxation is justified, the justifiably-taxable element in any legal holdings of wealth will constitute rights that are regularly extinguishable by the importance of something other than the right-holder's relevant good: the right-grounding needs, interests, or freedoms of others. It is implausible to regard rights that are so *regularly justifiably extinguishable for the sake of others* as grounded for the right-holder's sake. Such taxable property rights cannot be grounded by the right-holder's good in Section 8.2's STRONGEST sense, for rights grounded in this STRONGEST way obtain *whenever* the right-holder's relevant interest obtains, even if they are sometimes justifiably infringeable—and by contrast, taxable property rights vanish on taxation, rather than being justifiably infringed. Furthermore, taxable property rights cannot be grounded by the right-holder's good in Section 8.2's STRONG A or STRONG B senses, for if they were so grounded then their extinguishment by taxation would have to be an exceptional, non-'normal' occurrence. And taxation for the purposes outlined is instead surely regular and 'normal'.[8]

---

[6] One might retort that the relevant interest *does* play such a role in making the relevant duties *exist* (duties to supply higher education, or not to use my shed); it is just that such duties are often justifiably infringeable. But this strikes me as implausible: see the point about taxation immediately below. Thanks to Matthew Kramer for pressing this.

[7] Waldron 1988, ch. 9. See also this volume, Section 12.2. Note that the insight of 'Modern Monetary Theory' (Section 11.4) is that goods can be provisioned by the state without taxation being necessary except to control inflation and to maintain people's motivation to treat state IOUs as the medium of exchange. But this of course is not to say that taxation is unnecessary; it simply reconceives what might otherwise be considered redistribution. Despite the protestations of theorists like MacLeod, taxation either for the human rights listed or for Waldron's purposes does not threaten the values that ground private property (see MacLeod 2015, ch. 3, especially the strong claims at pp. 88–9).

[8] Note how the argument in the main text *allows property rights to plausibly be justifiable for the right-holder's sake in a* STRONG A *or* B *way if taxation is a rare or 'exceptional' circumstance*—as, maybe, libertarians (who would reserve taxation to support the court system only) might maintain. See also note 10 below for qualification of the idea of 'extinguishment'. Further, note that one alternative to the ideas in the main text would be to regard property rights over wealth that is regularly justifiably taxable as grounded for the wealth-holder's sake in Section 8.2's rare ACTUAL way. This view maintains that when the relevant wealth is *not* subject to taxation, other people's trespassory duties to exclude themselves from it are

The foregoing argument seems plausible to me in part because I simply do not find the owner's interests, needs, or freedoms served by her justifiably taxable wealth to be important enough on their own to generate or constitute reasons that qualify as duties in untaxed contexts. One response to the argument maintains that justified taxation does not extinguish but merely *justifiably infringes* the property rights of those who are taxed. If this were true, it would enable us to reconceive the property rights of those who are taxed as akin to, say, a human right to IVF treatment: a duty groundable predominantly (in my STRONG A sense) or even wholly (STRONGEST) on important interests of a given party, a duty that persists as a natural right of the party in question even when we cannot afford to fulfil it, but that in such a circumstance is regrettably unfulfillable.[9] But, as already suggested, this picture seems implausible as an account of taxation for the purposes sketched earlier. The 20 per cent of my income expropriated by the state in taxation does not in any sense persist as 'mine but regrettably infringed', nor trigger 'remainder' duties of apology from the state, say. This misconstrues the nature of taxation, and misconstrues the way the human rights for whose sake taxation is justified silence rather than simply outweigh the case against such taxation.[10]

A second response observes that taxation is often justifiable in part by what it does for the person taxed: by supporting public goods that could not be otherwise be provided, from which the taxed party will benefit, and by securing goods that the person would unwisely fail to choose to secure for themselves. If the interests, needs, or freedoms that would ground rights over property that would otherwise be taxed were regularly silenced *only* by other interests or goods *of the same right-holding person*, then the property rights in question could plausibly be conceived as justifiable for the right-holder's sake. For even though the grounds of such property rights would be regularly silenced, they would only be silenced by the right-holder's own good; they would always prevail against the good of *others*. But property rights over

---

groundable entirely by how they serve the wealth-holder; that is, the wealth-holder's good constitutes a fully sufficient case for generating such duties when they are not extinguished by taxation. It is just that this ground is regularly overridden or silenced—whenever taxation is justified. But this view strikes me as unlikely. It requires us to see the relevant wealth-holder's good (interest, need, freedom) in contexts without justified taxation as sufficient on its own to generate reasons which, because of their categorical, weighty, remainder-triggering, permissibly demandable character (see Section 7.2), are constitutive of trespassory *duties*. But it also requires us to see this duty-generative capacity of the wealth-holder's good as regularly silenced or overridden by the factors that justify taxation. If the wealth-holder's good is so regularly, 'normally' silenceable or overrideable, it seems unlikely that in contexts where it is *not* silenced or overridden it can succeed all on its own without the assistance of further positive grounds (e.g. based on the common good or others' interests in having a system of property) in generating the trespassory duties in question. Now I recognize that this argument is not unassailable: the ACTUAL reading of regularly-taxable property's ground remains open. I just regard it as unlikely.

[9] See Section 8.2 and, on the idea of a human right to IVF treatment, Tasioulas 2015 p. 62.

[10] Note that I am *not* here claiming that fulfilling human rights is the only reason for taxation. That is much too narrow a view. Note also that the view of taxation as a *justifiable infringement* of property rights rather than their *extinguishment* makes the same error as, e.g. Griffin's view of justified punitive imprisonment as a *justified infringement* rather than a *forfeiture* of the convict's rights (2008, pp. 65–6). Finally, note that perhaps total 'extinction' is the wrong way to conceive taxation's effect on taxed property, for while taxation triggers no 'remainder' duties, the taxing party nonetheless is under a demandable duty to explain and justify taxation to those who are taxed. Nonetheless, this is a much smaller 'remainder' than the 'justified infringement' view would warrant. See next footnote.

wealth that is justifiably subject to taxation are clearly not like this. Much of the relevant taxation would be justifiable, I contend, even if it was only for the sake of others beyond the person taxed. And even most of those cases that are plausibly construed as taxation for the sake of the taxed subject are best taken as cases in which the subject is taxed in order to serve the group of whom she is a part, and from which she benefits via the benefit to her group. Moreover the *individual subject's* interest in her group's good (as sketched in Section 8.3, pp. 127–29) would, I suggest, very rarely be sufficient on its own to justify the taxation in question. The good of the group taken in various ways collectively, and of all relevant individuals taken separately, are in my view the main grounds for taxation; the interests of the particular owner which are served by property subject to taxation cannot be regarded as regularly prevailing over such factors.

If these arguments are correct, then whatever level of wealth can regularly and frequently be justifiably taxed cannot be grounded primarily by what it does for the wealth-holder. These property rights must be justified in other ways, and hence they cannot be natural rights grounded by how they serve the right-holder, nor legal rights founded on and operationalizing such natural rights.[11] In Chapter 13, I will argue that they are legal-conventional rights justified by how they serve the common good—and I will suggest that throws some doubt on our conception of the relevant trespassory duties as *rights*. Beforehand, in Sections 12.2–12.4, I examine the limited place for some property rights that can, despite my argument above, be grounded for the right-holder's sake: property rights which, the argument tells us, we cannot see as regularly justifiably taxable.

12.2 Some (Non-Specific) Property Needed for Free Agency or Autonomy: Hegel

A position implicit in the last paragraph, one that seems attractive in light of the argument throughout Section 12.1, carves a distinction among property rights: *some*, namely the taxable, more extensive property rights of comparatively wealthy and 'middle income' people, are not groundable by what they do for the

---

[11] Antony Duff and David Owens have challenged my argument about taxation by observing that the permissibility of military conscription does not similarly throw doubt on the 'natural rights' or 'human rights' character of rights of free movement, control over one's body, etc. But I think there are relevant differences between the cases, differences that support my argument: (i) while taxation is not plausibly construable as a justified *infringement* of the property rights that are taxed, conscription *is* plausibly construable as a justified infringement of bodily control rights; (ii) while taxation largely extinguishes those property rights that are taxed, justified conscription is temporary, with the rights of bodily control restored at a later date; (iii) conscription—even non-military national service—is justifiable only on serious grounds such as to prevent war, while taxation is justifiable for more 'optional' or less important goods such as the provision of higher education or support for the arts (NB. This is not to deny the great importance of the latter goods.). These are perhaps differences of 'degree' rather than 'kind': taxation requires public justification to the taxed parties (see previous footnote), and perhaps milder forms of national service are justifiable for less-than-maximally-serious reasons, closer to those that can justify taxation. But even with the latter concessions, I believe the distinctions between taxation and conscription, as outlined above, support my claim that property rights subject to regular taxation are not plausibly justified for the right-holder's sake while bodily rights subject to conscription are.

right-holder, while *others* are. The latter—property groundable primarily for the given property-holder's sake—might include intellectual property (my rights over this text), property rights over particular goods with which one has a special relationship, perhaps by having infused one's labour in them (my rights over a sculpture I have made)[12] or through love or family association (my rights over the piano given to me by my grandfather), and perhaps property over goods essential for survival (my rights over the small amount of food in my cupboard). They might also include something like a right over whatever proportion of my overall property is necessary to meet further fundamental needs of mine. For those with little, the sum total of their property rights might not stretch beyond property in these categories. The trespassory duties constitutive of property in these categories will, if they really are groundable simply or predominantly on the basis of the owner's own good, naturally or recognition-independently constitute rights for the owner—while further property rights will not.

Several arguments might seem to support the idea that some property rights among those listed are groundable wholly or predominantly by how they serve the right-holder. One quick move frequently encountered claims that to use things requires that one own them, and of course each person has a fundamental interest in using things.[13] This argument's premise is false: one can use things without others holding trespassory duties excluding them from using the same things; instead, one might luckily hit on a use that others' use of the same thing would not impede, or one might decide on a joint use with others, or one might luckily hit on a thing that others do not try to use. Nonetheless, one can re-run the argument without reliance on the claim that our needs and interests in use *require* trespassory duties or property rights; the claim would rather be that the needs and interests of a given party make it *apt*, and thereby justified (along the lines sketched in Sections 7.2 and 7.6), for that party to hold property rights. Different versions of this argument can be found in Hegel and Locke. Locke's version would make property rights over certain *specific* items qualify as natural rights, groundable predominantly for the right-holder's own sake; I assess this in Section 12.3. Hegel's version would give a party a natural right to hold *some* property rather than none, without the argument favouring ownership of any specific item; I assess this in the current section.

In Brudner's Hegel, the person, in virtue of her 'inborn capacity for free choice', claims to be an unconditioned end, 'one that is neither relative to a subject (it is objective) nor valuable for the sake of some further end (it is final)'.[14] But because the person

depends for [her] identity on the world of contingent things, [a] disparity [...] opens between the person's subjective condition of end-status and the reality of [her] dependent existence. [...] This internal contradiction implies that the person *lacks* the world as that whose subordination to [her] ends validates the person's claim of final worth. Because [she] lacks the world, the person also desires it. This is [...] an intellectual desire of personality for validation as an end. To satisfy this desire, the person [...] must perform actions that put

---

[12] Compare Warnock's example of rights over a garden one has created (Warnock 2015, ch. 3), or Penner's example of a bird's right to its nest (Penner 2013, p. 266; see also Warnock 2015, p. 18).
[13] Locke 1960 [1689], section 26.   [14] Brudner 2013, p. 74.

objects into a relation of subservience to [her]. These actions will constitute a property because they will (partially or perfectly) *validate* a claim of end-status vis-à-vis a thing.[15]

Hegel himself writes:

The circumstance that I, as free will, am an object to myself in what I possess and only become an actual will by this means constitutes the genuine and rightful element in possession, the determination of *property*.[16]

These are difficult passages but I would suggest that they imply that for Hegel one's status as an unconditioned, self-choosing end makes one necessarily desire some kind of 'dominion' over or 'mastery' of things, where this involves not just chosen use of things, but exclusive use as a matter of right. No *particular* things are needed for this: just some of the unfree world of things must be within one's dominion.[17] Only such rights-protected use of some unfree stuff *validates* my end-status as a free will despite my dependence on such unfree things.

Hegel goes on:

My inner idea and will that something should be mine is not enough to constitute property, which is the existence of personality; on the contrary, this requires that I should take possession of it [and later sections show that *use* or *contractual exchange* work even better to constitute property as recognized personality]. The existence which my willing thereby attains includes its ability to be recognised by others.[18]

Brudner elaborates on this idea that validation of my end-status as a free will requires others to *recognize* my property as mine, and that this is most fully realized through my gaining property in a contractual exchange:

Because (assuming perfect information) all other persons have passed on the opportunity to acquire something offered for sale in a public market, indeed have registered the cost of their disappointment in the value I must relinquish to own it, recognition for holdings acquired through open exchange is omnilateral rather than bilateral.[19]

Brudner notes that this makes the realization of the person's end-status 'embedded in a common will wherein each recognizes and confirms the other as an owner'; yet 'the person who at this stage claims to be an absolute end also claims that [her] end-status is innate in [her] singular free will and so independent of any relation to another'.[20] This is inconsistent with the centrality of *omnilateral* recognition to the validation of the person's end status.[21] In overcoming this contradiction, property's recognition within a *rule of law*—necessitated if market recognition of ownership is to be recognized as normative by participants—involves recognizing each person not simply as free choosers but as *autonomous*, in the Kantian sense of being capable

---

[15] Ibid., p. 76; compare Waldron 1988, ch. 10 for a cognate interpretation of Hegel.

[16] Hegel 1991 [1821], section 45.

[17] Can the relevant need or desire be characterized without using the gendered and slavery-referencing notion of 'mastery', or the sovereignty-referencing notion of 'dominion'? I am unsure.

[18] Hegel 1991 [1821], section 51.   [19] Brudner 2013, p. 83.   [20] Ibid., p. 86.

[21] See ibid., p. 87.

of governing themselves *by law*.[22] When so conceived, people—it emerges—have a 'positive right to the conditions of autonomy [or self-determination]', in addition to their property rights.[23]

I have outlined this Hegelian argument sketchily and with quotations, and of course for any Hegel scholar there is much to fill in above. But my central concern is how the argument makes property an especially *core* human need. The argument maintains that persons as free beings necessarily desire something like subordinating control or dominion over at least some portion of the unfree world in the form of property rights; any particular portion will do, though a portion gained via a market is ideal because it involves omnilateral recognition of one's ownership. But the most important point is that lacking property leaves one unrecognizable as a free being. The twist at the end of Hegel's argument (the turn to the 'rule of law' to uphold omnilateral contracts) makes it necessary that everyone have 'the material and cultural preconditions of an autonomous life'.[24] Waldron interprets this as the contention that everyone should own property, and makes this itself a matter of right.[25] Brudner, by contrast, distinguishes social 'entitlements' to welfare from property rights, and takes the twist at the end to deliver only a universal entitlement to welfare rather than property. But we could take the argument's starting point (that free beings need at least some property) already to establish a Waldronian universal entitlement to own things. As noted in Section 12.1, if either a universal right to own some property or a universal right to welfare obtains, this will justify taxation extensive and regular enough that the taxable rights cannot be plausibly justifiable for the right-holder's own sake. More important for my purposes now, however, is the initial claim that there is a powerful case, grounded in the free agency or autonomy of the right-holder themselves, for the holding of *some* property by each of us.

I offer qualified resistance to Hegel's argument at its early stages.[26] First, a natural way to interpret Hegel sees him as making the same category error I ascribed to Scanlon, Kamm, Nagel, and Raz in Sections 7.4 and 7.7.[27] For Hegel on this reading, others excluding themselves from certain resources and thereby allowing me to use them is *not* what my interest in being validated as an unconditioned, free end asks for. Instead, that interest is specifically an interest in my *having rights*: in others excluding themselves from certain resources *as a matter of my right*. To my mind, this is what my *validation as an end* (to use Brudner's interpretation) would require. But I argued in Chapter 7 that the only thing which can place someone under a recognition-independent or natural duty to PHI is the good of PHI-ing (Section 7.2),

---

[22] '[T]he transition to a rule of law brings in its train a new conception of what is essential to agents and therefore a new conception of what is necessarily public: not only the agent's capacity for free choice but also [her] potential for self-determination [qua potential for self-government by law]' (ibid., p. 88).

[23] Ibid., p. 89.   [24] Ibid., p. 89.   [25] Waldron 1988, ch. 10.

[26] My opposition is not simply that control of external resources is not strictly necessary for free agency (the ability to converse or move might be enough). For the Hegelian could plausibly reply that control of external resources is so central to free agency that it makes duties protecting this control justified even though such control is not strictly *necessary*. See the second paragraph of the current section (12.2).

[27] For the ascription to Raz, see Section 7.7, note 50. The other authors are discussed more prominently in the cited sections.

and the only thing that can give someone a recognition-independent or natural right correlating with such a duty is PHI-ing's being good for that person (Section 7.6). The further good of *PHI-ing's being required by duty or right* is in the wrong category for grounding such a duty or right as a recognition-independent-matter: while PHI's value can place someone under a duty to PHI, the value of the existence of this duty cannot magically make that duty come into existence. Of course, I go on to affirm that the good of a right or duty's existence can give us reason to *create* (or, if it already exists, to *sustain*) such a right or duty as a legal or conventional matter. But we saw in Section 9.2 that only the good of *many* (or perhaps of the *generic* party) can normally give us reason to create or sustain a law or convention. So my own particular individual interest in others excluding themselves from certain resources *as a matter of my right* cannot primarily or on its own justify property rights over such resources for me either as recognition-independent natural rights, or as legal rights.[28]

Purged of the category error, Hegel's claim must be that others excluding themselves from certain resources[29] is, simply qua self-exclusion whether done as a matter of duty or not, an interest or need of my free agency in a way that makes the relevant others duty-bound, to me, to exclude themselves in the relevant ways. The relevant interest of mine is to be understood in terms of the validation of my end status as a free being.

I have doubts about these claims. I do not think they are false, but I question their centrality to human nature. It seems to me that my end status as a free being is most aptly validated by other free beings' engagement with me to work out how we will use the world together, rather than by all others excluding themselves from some material left as 'mine'.[30] Exclusion from some material which is thereby 'mine' seems not just unnecessary in order to meet my need to use material, but *inapt* as a response to this need in an ideal world; it divides me from other users in an unattractive way. An ideal world would involve others recognizing my end status, and my recognizing my own end status and others' such status, through communal agency in which others do not exclude themselves from any resources vis-à-vis me. This complaint can survive Macleod's insight that when assessing property, we should focus on property held by groups and communities.[31] 'Our' property will

---

[28] Against this concern, Hegelians might plausibly argue that the *value* of property rights to the owner is not what grounds them for Hegel, despite Brudner's claim that ownership fulfils a necessary *desire* (Brudner 2013, p. 76). Rather, their value-independent *importance* as generating an appropriate *status* for the owner grounds them. But I think this stance on close inspection collapses either into a version of the category error mentioned (something's *importance* can no more make it exist than its *value* can) or into an affirmation of the relevant rights as basic and ungrounded on anything other than themselves as our fundamental status (see my attribution of this view to Ripstein 2009, esp. pp. 34–5, and Zylberman 2016a in this volume, Section 7.3).

[29] For Hegel, these are resources I possess, use, or—best of all—gain through contract (Hegel 1991 [1821], sections 54–81), but I think the interesting claim for our purposes is simply that for each person, it is important that *some* resources are such that all others exclude themselves from them, leaving the person in question the only one permitted to use them without consent.

[30] In a sense, my claim here could be seen as the Fichtean one that *recognition by another free being through engagement and communication* is what realizes my end status as free, *not* recognition of my subordination of or dominion over what is unfree (Fichte 2000 [1796–7]).

[31] MacLeod 2015; see also Clarke 2015.

still involve exclusion of those who are not 'us'. An ideal world would involve *all* others recognizing my end status, and each of us recognizing each other's, through non-exclusionary fully joint use of resources.[32] There would be no need of exclusion of others from either 'my' or some restricted plural 'our' material in an ideal world. (Note that my claim is not that in an ideal world with *unlimited* resources, free use of resources would not require exclusion of others.[33] It is, rather, that even in an ideal world with *limited* resources, each individual's freedom would be most aptly served by an omnilateral communal decision on use of everything, a decision that was genuinely 'everyone's'.)

My references to an 'ideal' world in the foregoing paragraph signal my unwillingness to reject the Hegelian claim that others excluding themselves from resources vis-à-vis me is an important, right-grounding need *in the world as we know it, with people as we know them*. As things stand, people do not and will not agree on joint use of the entire world; private property seems here to stay in the short or medium term; fully joint agreement is not possible partly for psychological and institutional reasons about how people could come together to agree, but also for the epistemic reasons about how to comprehend the effects of multiple actions by many (for any joint action will comprise multiple individual actions) that Hayek highlights in his defence of the market.[34] It is worth noting that even omnilateral endorsement of the *market*, as supposed in Brudner's Hegel, is not forthcoming in the actual world: some try to evade the market (e.g. through theft or communist revolution), and many find themselves within it non-voluntarily. For these reasons, the individual's voluntary, communicative inclusion within a free and universal communal decision about how to use the entire world does not seem possible now, even though I think it would be the ideal way of meeting the individual's Hegelian need to be validated as a free chooser.

Instead, in the actual world, each individual's need for validation as free might indeed seem to require some resources from which others (perhaps *most* others but not one's immediate community or family) exclude themselves. Less Hegelian conceptions of freedom—focused not on the importance of validation through dominion over the unfree, but simply on the importance of having a sufficient degree of free or autonomous choice within one's life—generate a similar requirement. Others' duties to exclude themselves from some resources which I (or my group) can then use seem groundable in one of my STRONG ways by the importance of my (or my group's) freedom or autonomy. This sphere of protected resources constitutes a necessary buffer for the individual's or small group's freedom, a buffer against both the state and market forces.[35] Further, not just trespassory duties excluding others from goods but some Hohfeldian powers to make decisions about this property (the economic freedoms which capitalism secures) and enforcement of the relevant duties and powers again seem to be made apt, in the modern world, largely on the

---

[32] 'All' here means something like 'humanity' as sketched in Section 9.3.

[33] Compare Hume 1978 [1739–40], bk. III, pt. II, section II (esp. pp. 494–5) and Rawls 1971, pp. 126–7 on scarcity and the other 'circumstances of justice'.

[34] Hayek 1960, e.g. at pp. 27–35.   [35] Thanks to Sebastian Cruft for discussion.

basis of their role as protectors of the individual or group owner's freedom or autonomy[36]—though we will see at the end of Section 12.3 that the sense in which Hohfeldian powers of the requisite type are justifiable for the right-holder's sake is complex. Nonetheless in the modern world, the individual's autonomy arguably works on its own to ground at least some enforceable trespassory duties that serve the individual, largely independently of whether these duties and liberties serve others or the common good. I suggest that, in Section 8.2's terms, a person's free agency works in my STRONG A way by making others normally duty-bound to exclude themselves from some resources for the person. 'Normally' here means normal in the actual, non-ideal world even if an ideal world would involve humans omnilaterally controlling everything.

By maintaining that for each of us ownership of some resources—though not of anything in particular—is groundable for our own sake as an individual party, the previous paragraph makes such ownership recognition-independent or natural rights. This does not mean that it cannot be justifiably taxed or expropriated. But, given the relevant trespassory duties' STRONG A ground in the individual's good (qua free agent), taxation and other measures against the duties in question must be either rare (non-'normal') or must qualify as a justified infringement that leaves 'remainder' duties of apology or rectification. Section 12.1 showed that many property rights, especially of those who are comparatively wealthy, will not hold this special status as 'rights for the right-holder's sake'. But the discussion in the current section shows that some will: that each person's having *some or 'enough' property rather than none* is, in the modern world, justifiable for that person's sake, and hence bears the special status of human rights.[37]

12.3 Specific Property Earned through Labour: Locke

The Lockean argument that through labour-mixing one directly extends the natural recognition-independent rights one has over one's own body so that they encompass previously unowned external material has been ably criticised by Nozick, Simmons, Steiner, and Waldron.[38] In this section I focus on an alternative argument, much closer to Hegel's, which can be found in or developed from Locke. This argument maintains that the labourer, qua plan-maker or purposive agent (who might be an individual or a community) has an important interest, need, or freedom that favours others excluding themselves from *the specific objects* through which she carries out her plan or agency—an interest, need, or freedom which is important enough largely on its own to make others naturally duty-bound to exclude themselves, that

---

[36] For example, Nickel argues that property rights, including market powers to alienate property and negotiate for wages, plus further economic liberties to choose one's occupation and to profit from the products of one's labour, are justifiable primarily by how they serve the individual's autonomy (Nickel 2000). Compare also Tomasi 2012, pp. 76–81, on productive private property's vitally important role in enabling one to create one's own life. See this volume, Sections 12.3–12.4 for more on the status of economic liberties and powers.

[37] Of course I have not here discussed whether the right to some property as a freedom-protecting 'buffer' is a right that is 'everyone's business' in Chapter 10's sense—though I suspect it is.

[38] Nozick 1974, pp. 174–5; Waldron 1988, pp. 184–207; Simmons 1992, pp. 252–69; Steiner 1994, ch. 7.

is, duty-bound whether or not anyone has realized this, and hence which makes the relevant trespassory duties naturally owed to the labourer.[39] Unlike in Hegel's version, the agency interest in question is for Locke an interest in trespassory duties protecting *specific* objects: those bound up with the agent's specific plans. By contrast, for Hegelian arguments the relevant agency interest constitutes a non-specific case for *some* trespassory duties—the agent's benefitting from some such duties rather than none is what provides her with the necessary 'validation' or 'buffer'.[40]

The Lockean argument is standardly presented as justifying property rights in *what was previously unowned*. We are then to see modern holdings, if they are justified, as derived from long chains of voluntary transfers traceable to original acquisitions based on plan-incorporation.[41] The argument does not have to be taken in this way. One might see purposive, agential planning as a way of gaining property rights in what is currently the property of others if, say, those others do not themselves have plans for the relevant property nor need it for their survival or validation as a free agent.

One could pause at this point and focus critically on the claim that a party's purposive agency can function largely on its own to make others duty-bound to exclude themselves from its object.[42] But I propose a different critique: even if the Lockean approach can make some specific property rights over object O groundable for the right-holder's sake as 'natural' rights, *it cannot ensure that the same status attaches to rights over O after it has been voluntarily transferred.* Many of the rights in a property system allowing voluntary transfer will be unjustifiable on the basis simply of what they do for the right-holder—and hence they cannot be natural rights or forms of human right. Or so I will now argue.

My argument is a version of Nozick's famous 'Wilt Chamberlain argument'.[43] Suppose we start with some initial property rights over O, rights that are grounded, in Lockean fashion, simply by the importance of the right-holder's own interests or needs as a purposive incorporator of O into her plans. Such rights will exist for the right-holder's sake. Now suppose a *voluntary transfer* of O takes place, one that is legitimated by the consent of O's owner (the donor) and the recipient. The terms of

---

[39] For a strong version of this argument, see especially Simmons 1992, pp. 271–7; compare Penner 2013, pp. 265–67.

[40] An alternative reading of Locke takes him to argue that the labourer *deserves* others' self-exclusion from her product in a way that perhaps STRONG A grounds trespassory duties owed to the labourer (see Becker 1977). My own view is that this is a misreading of Locke, but one still might wonder why I do not pursue it for its independent attractions. I have two reasons. First, I am doubtful that desert is a morally fundamental principle. In particular, I am sceptical of the view that when we think of a duty as grounded by someone's deservingness, we are thereby ultimately grounding it on their own good. For I suspect that our reasons to respond to deservingness always turn on how principles of desert serve everyone including those beyond the particular deserving individual. Secondly, I suspect that even if desert arguments could show some property rights to be groundable for the right-holder's own sake, these would be weak arguments that were frequently overridden. For I share Stemplowska's sense that both needs and important freedoms outweigh desert-based claims, as do many other important goods (see Stemplowska 2015).

[41] Nozick 1974, pp. 150–3.

[42] Or, of course, one could pause on the importance that the historical-chain story gives to events in the distant past (Lyons 1981).

[43] Nozick 1974, pp. 160–4. See also Waldron 1988, pp. 259–62, for a similar question about whether Lockean labour-involvement could be preserved post-transfer.

voluntary transfer cannot guarantee that the recipient of O has incorporated O into her plans in a relevantly purposive way. More generally, a transfer simply by consent cannot guarantee that *the recipient* will have interests, needs, or freedoms (purposive-agency-related or otherwise) sufficient largely on their own to make it the case that others exclude themselves from the transferred item. One might think that the whole point of allowing free transfer is to enable transfers that need not meet this or any other condition beyond consent.[44] If this is correct, then *post-transfer* property rights will have to be grounded primarily on something other than the interests of the right-holder (such as the common good of having legal rights of transfer): they will not be 'rights for the rightholder's sake', and hence cannot exist recognition-independently as natural rights, even though the pre-transfer rights can.

A riposte to this observes that agreeing to receive O through voluntary transfer is itself a form of purposive activity. Why not take the recipient's interest in O *qua purposive agent who plans to receive O through voluntary transfer* to ground, in Lockean manner, natural rights over O for that recipient? One point to note, which does not impugn this riposte, is that the rights so generated cannot be recognition-independent, because transfer that is voluntary in the relevant way must involve recognition by the donor and the recipient that rights are being transferred. (If the donor gives O to the recipient without conceiving this—at least implicitly—to be a transfer of rights, the donor has not voluntarily agreed to the recipient now owning O; the donor might rather consider herself to have given the recipient use of what is still the donor's.) Despite the recognition-dependence of rights post-transfer, the riposte could still establish that such rights exist for their holder's sake, and are hence structurally morally continuous with the human rights of Part II.

The reason the riposte fails is that it is implausible to regard each and every recipient, following a voluntary transfer, to have interests, needs, or freedoms important enough on their own to constitute the primary ground for the post-transfer trespassory duties over the object transferred. For example, sometimes recipients will agree to a transfer absent-mindedly, with no plan for the object received. Furthermore, if the recipient's agency interests in the object really were as important as the riposte suggests, we should then wonder why *voluntary* transfer, involving permission of the donor as well as the recipient, was necessary. The necessity of the donor's permission perhaps suggests that the *joint* agency interests (or needs or freedoms) of donor-plus-recipient are together sufficient normally to ground the post-transfer trespassory duties. But if so, Section 7.6 tells us that those duties will be owed to donor and recipient together: on this view, when I voluntarily transfer O to you, the trespassory duties over O are naturally owed to both of us. This

---

[44] This is the thrust of Nozick's helpful characterization of post-transfer property distributions as 'unpatterned' (1974, pp. 155–64). Note that this point can also be used to reject both Raz's and Sreenivasan's accounts of the nature of rights. See this volume, Sections 2.2 and 3.4: neither approach allows that I could hold a property right (even a merely *legal* one) if the relevant trespassory duties (Raz) or my powers over them (Sreenivasan) were not grounded by my good: but surely voluntary transfer of property allows this: I can be a recipient of a voluntary transfer simply by agreeing to this, independently of whether it serves my good. Now we will see in Chapter 13 that calling property my 'right' when it is ungroundable for my sake might not be justifiable. But nonetheless it is surely conceptually permissible; Raz's and Sreenivasan's theories struggle to accommodate this.

would be an odd result, very odd indeed when we remember that most objects have gone through a long chain of voluntary transactions. This would make others' duties not to use the desk at which I am writing naturally owed jointly to me, to the Hume scholar A. E. Pitson (who gave it to me when I started at Stirling), to the shop from which Pitson bought it, and so on, covering all those with agency interests appropriately bound up at some point with the object. This is a *reductio ad absurdum*, suggesting we should abandon the idea that post-transfer property rights are groundable for the owner's sake.[45]

But a further move is available to the proponent of the riposte. This claims that the need for the donor's consent does not signal that *her (i.e. the donor's)* interests, needs, or freedoms play any positive role in favour of the post-transfer trespassory duties. Instead, the donor's consent merely lifts what would otherwise be an impediment to the post-transfer trespassory duties. On this view, the donor's consent shows that an impediment (namely, the donor's own agency interests in the object) has been 'removed', thereby allowing the recipient's agency interests (interests in the object to be transferred) to succeed as the positive case for trespassory duties that exclude all except the recipient from the object.[46] The trouble with this riposte is that voluntary consent does not have to line up with the good of either the donor or the recipient in this way. A donor can consent to a transfer in a legitimate, normatively effective way while having major ongoing plans for the transferred object which the transfer will thwart—perhaps the donor agrees on a whim, or out of weariness. And as noted earlier, the recipient can agree to a transfer without having any purposive involvement in the object's future. To repeat Nozick's message three paragraphs ago, the very point of a voluntary consent transfer system seems to be to allow ownership to be determined by bilateral agreements independently of any prior 'pattern', including the pattern of agency interests bound up with the object to be transferred.[47]

If this is correct, then even if some trespassory duties over specific objects are grounded in Lockean manner primarily by a party's agency interests, and hence qualify naturally as that party's property rights, an ownership system allowing

[45] Compare Waldron 1994, pp. 93–4.

[46] This could be taken as a version of the move made in Section 9.4 regarding the relative role of *the individual's good* vis-à-vis *principles beyond the individual's good* in grounding human rights to goods and services, and the similar move made in Section 10.3 regarding the relative role of *my friend's good* vis-à-vis *my own good* in grounding my duties to listen to my friend in need: in such cases, it looks as though within a grounding for the relevant duty's existence only the right-holder's good need function as *that which the duty-enjoined action serves*, and the duty therefore in a sense exists for the right-holder's sake even though the right-holder's good needs supplementation in order to ground the duty. But on inspection a similar claim fails in the case at hand: as noted in the main text above, there need be no sense in which *the owner's good* is served by others' non-trespass on her property, if she has gained it through voluntary transfer. For more discussion, including the sense in which the relevant non-trespass serves others as much as the owner herself, see Chapter 13.

[47] Nozick 1974, pp. 155–64; see also the classical liberal 'invisible hand' arguments for unpatterned free markets of Smith 1976 [1776] and Hayek 1960, explored in Chapter 13. My point in the main text marks a contrast between consent-based rights and duties, and those constituting personal relationships such as friendship. Once a friendship is established, a friend's consent to the non-performance of some duty of friendship need not always licence non-performance. The duty largely follows the interests, needs, or freedoms of the friend to whom it is owed, without always mapping onto the friend's consent, even though the fact of consent will always make a difference. See also Section 10.3, pp. 178–80.

voluntary transfers will be bound to result in many property rights that are not so groundable for the right-holder's sake—and hence that cannot naturally be rights but must bear their rights status as a matter of social creation.

A determined opponent—who still persists in wanting post-transfer property rights to be natural rights grounded for the right-holder's sake—might try a different strategy now, by focusing on the power to transfer. In the previous section, I highlighted the importance of the 'economic liberties' of modern capitalism, of which freedom of exchange is arguably the core.[48] This could have been taken simply as the claim that each individual's interests, needs or freedoms constitute powerful reasons (perhaps functioning in a STRONG B manner) to create *legal or institutional* Hohfeldian powers of free transfer. But my opponent might instead contend that some such powers are held naturally, independently of legal or institutional creation. And my opponent might argue that once natural property rights over O have been acquired in Lockean manner, transfers of O *effected by the natural transfer power* will surely preserve the natural status, as rights justifiable for the right-holder, of the post-transfer ownership of O.

Now I would endorse my opponent's claim that each of us hold some natural, uncreated Hohfeldian powers. We exercise these powers in creating institutions and laws. Without such powers, the possibility of duties so created would be mysterious.[49] We should note two points about these powers. First, even though they are natural in the sense of being uncreated, they include powers that are *recognition-dependent yet uncreated*: powers that themselves exist without anyone or any convention creating them for the power-holder, but that only succeed in creating new duties if they are taken by at least some (perhaps the exerciser and an uptaking promisee) to create such duties.[50] Secondly, Sections 7.4 and 7.7 tell us that such natural powers cannot exist simply because it would be good for the power-holder if they did. Their existence requires a different category of explanation, which I cannot offer here.

My opponent needs to claim that among our natural powers, we hold a power to transfer any property we own, or at least any natural property acquired in a Lockean manner. It is not clear to me that we hold this power naturally, that is, independently of wider social conventions constituting this power for us. We do indeed hold natural powers to issue promises, powers whose successful exercise requires (*ceteris paribus*)[51] only the consent or uptake of the promisee for them to succeed. But promising only creates a new duty *for the promisor*; this, I suggest, is one reason why, independently of wider conventions creating the power for us, we hold a power to promise conditional only on consent or uptake of the promisee. By contrast, transferring property involves changing everyone's duties, not just the duties of the transferor. For when I transfer O to a willing recipient, I place myself under new duties to exclude myself from O (so far, this is just like a promise), and I remove the recipient's pre-transfer duties to exclude themselves from O (and this looks just like natural consent, e.g. to someone's touching

---

[48] See Section 12.2, penultimate paragraph.

[49] One way to read Hart 1955 takes him to be arguing that such Hohfeldian power-rights are presupposed by the existence of other rights.

[50] They are thus not limited to powers of the type sketched at the opening of Section 7.7, p. 110.

[51] See Altham 1985 on wicked promises.

me), and I *also* 'redirect' everyone else's duties of self-exclusion from O so that they are, post-transfer, owed to the recipient rather than to me. The latter might look like a change that cannot be performed absent wider social creation of a power to perform it. I believe I might have *some* natural powers to place everyone under new duties, for example as exercised when I (for good enough reason) place myself in danger requiring others to rescue me.[52] But powers to create new duties simply via consent, independently of the good of the parties involved, and as an intentional, recognition-dependent creation of the duties in question, might seem unlikely as natural, uncreated powers.

But my opponent can respond that consent-dependent transfer of O does not really create any new duties for anyone other than the donor. The trespassory duties of others are *redirected*, owed post-transfer to the recipient rather than the donor, but what these others are duty-bound to do—namely, exclude themselves from O—remains the same pre- and post-transfer.[53] So perhaps this allows a power of voluntary transfer to bear the same 'natural', uncreated status as powers to promise—and indeed as powers to create further laws and institutions *ex nihilo* through joint action with others.

Personally, I am undecided about the issue above. I am inclined to think that the imbalances of (non-Hohfeldian) power that can be created for third parties through many innocent-seeming bilateral voluntary transfers of property make a natural power to transfer more problematic than a natural power to promise, even though I recognize that the latter can also create potential difficulties for third parties.[54] But for present purposes, I can afford to be concessive to my opponent. Let us suppose that there really is an uncreated, natural power to transfer property through the voluntary consent of donor and recipient. Such a power enables the transfer of property rights acquired as natural in a Lockean manner. But I contend that this does *not* confer natural rights status on post-transfer ownership. This is because any natural power to transfer, like the natural power to promise, is in a sense the power to do a little bit of two-person lawmaking: the power to create or alter duties in a way that is recognition-dependent, and that can involve *making* duties have a rights-type structure whether or not they serve the right-holder's interests. When I exercise this power by transferring O—which, let us suppose, I gained in Lockean manner by incorporating O into my projects, thereby making others naturally duty-bound to respect my good by excluding themselves from O—I with my recipient thereby *make it the case* that others' duties to exclude themselves from O are owed to the recipient

---

[52] Compare Waldron on the similarity between unilateral creation of property and the unilateral duty-creation involved in cry-for-help suicide attempts (Waldron 1988, p. 269; van der Vossen 2015 offers a defence of powers of unilateral appropriation). What Waldron does not notice is that just as *original* acquisition places everyone under new duties, there is a sense in which *transfer* does this too.

[53] Hohfeldian complications might require us to conceive this not as a redirection of duties, but as an extinguishment of duties-owed-to-donor to exclude oneself from O, accompanied at the same moment by a creation of duties-owed-to-recipient to exclude oneself from O. Despite Penner's arguments to the contrary (2013, pp. 246–248), I do not regard this Hohfeldian way of seeing the matter as problematic. The two positions look, rather, like a distinction without a difference—though I recognize that there is more to say to defend this.

[54] For this reason, one might be as sceptical of, say, a natural power that allows already-powerful families to ally themselves through marriage as one should be of a natural power of transfer.

rather than me, and I place myself under new duties to exclude myself. These changes are simply effected by the recipient's and my exercising our wills in the way that qualifies as our natural power of transfer. This means that the changes need not line up with either my or the recipient's good in any way—and hence the post-transfer duties need not be justifiable predominantly for the recipient's sake and cannot be natural but are rather created, in this case by the recipient and me.[55] Their status as owed to the recipient is a conventional creation of ours. So my argument succeeds: voluntary, consent-based transfer of Lockean natural property rights makes post-transfer rights lose their status as natural rights justifiable for the right-holder's sake.

12.4 Property as Protecting Other Human Rights: Nickel

Even if the Hegelian and Lockean arguments are correct, they do not get us far. At most, they establish that having some property rights rather than none is justifiable for the right-holder's sake (Hegel), and that some objects incorporated into our plans might be protected by property rights justifiable for the right-holder's sake (Locke). But I argued in Section 12.3 that post-transfer property will not inherit this status. And although I have not pressed this, the very bases of both Hegelian and Lockean arguments—the importance of free being's dominating or subordinating the unfree, and the importance of respect for unilaterally adopted plans—are not immediately intuitively attractive as grounds for duties. By contrast, Nickel argues for the import-ance of property as a means for protecting other human rights. This approach, I suggest, underpins the appeal of some of the examples with which I began Section 12.2, perhaps including property in the products of my artistic expression (as a means or determination of my human right to express myself (within appro-priate limits)), property over items with which I have some intimate relation (e.g. as bequeathed to me by a loved one—a determination of my human right to such intimate relations), and property over the items I need for survival.

Nickel makes much of the value—instrumental, determinative, constituting—to individuals' human rights, of *a system* of economic liberties borne by many.[56] But for such an approach to establish certain property rights as justifiable for the right-holder's sake, it must show the particular property rights in question to be of notable value to the specific owner's human rights. Showing a linkage between one person's property rights and *someone else's* human rights, or between human rights and a *multi-person system* of property rights, will fail to establish any given property rights as justifiable predominantly for the sake of the given right-holder—though such

---

[55] This is not to deny that our reason to respect post-transfer rights might be out of respect for the word (i.e. the power-exercising action) of the recipient and the donor. But similarly our reason to respect any morally justified legal rights is in part out of respect for the word or power-exercising action of those who sustain the laws. In neither case is the good of the right-holder (nor even *her word or will alone*) the predominant reason to respect the right. (Compare the discussion of promissory directedness in Section 8.3, p. 132.)

[56] Nickel 2000 and 2007, ch. 8.

linkages can justify property rights along the alternative lines explored in Chapter 13.[57] But to show property rights as natural, uncreated, and recognition-independent, we need to show that the property-holder's own good—in this argument, in terms of her own human rights—can constitute a predominate ground for the trespassory duties in question.

We might also, as Nickel does, highlight the way economic liberties including powers of transfer, powers to charge and keep profits from one's use of one's property, powers to borrow money, and many others are justifiable through their relation to the power-holder's other human rights. Now, towards the end of the last section (12.3) I pressed the point from Sections 7.4 and 7.7 that a Hohfeldian power's value to its holder (whether in terms of serving its holder's human rights or in other terms) cannot in itself make that power exist as a natural power. But we might rather take Nickel to be arguing for *legal* economic liberties as justifiable for the right-holder's sake. Chapter 9 showed that no single individual's interests, needs or freedoms are likely to be STRONG A or STRONGEST grounds for creating or maintaining a legal power.[58] But Nickel's point could be simply that legal-institutional economic liberties are justifiable as a determination or operationalization of a natural power constitutive of some of our natural human power-rights—or that human-rights-grounding interests, needs or freedoms are STRONG B instrumental grounds for legal creation and maintenance of the relevant economic liberties.

Nickel's approach arguably starts from a stronger premise—the importance of the individual's human rights—than either Hegel or Locke. And some conclusions are necessitated as tightly by this premise as Hegel's and Locke's are by theirs. For example, it seems to me that in the modern world others' self-exclusion from *some* property that I can use is an essential buffer justifiable by how it protects my ability to fulfil my own human rights.[59] Furthermore, if my human right to liberty includes natural Hohfeldian powers of transfer then legal economic liberties will be justifiable for my sake as founded on, reflecting, and operationalizing these natural powers.

Nonetheless, many of the conclusions that Nickel seeks to draw are less tightly necessitated by the owner's human rights. Two examples he offers are freedom of religion and freedom of movement:

Many activities protected by freedom of religion have important economic dimensions. Restricting economic activities in a wholesale way will accordingly restrict freedom of religion. Religious people frequently engage in activities such as (1) buying, renting, or constructing buildings for religious activities; (2) starting and running religious enterprises such as churches, schools, and publishing houses; (3) hiring employees to serve as religious leaders, editors, teachers, office workers, and janitors; (4) soliciting donations for religious causes; (5) saving, managing, and spending the funds coming from donations and the proceeds of religious enterprises; and (6) abandoning work or career to pursue religious study and callings. [...]

---

[57] If the linkages are sufficiently tight, they might also justify some property rights as human rights in Section 10.1's 'type (III)' sense.
[58] Again, compare Buchanan 2013, p. 62.
[59] See the final paragraphs of Section 12.2 for a sketch of this view.

There are also strong links to freedom of movement. Key parts of freedom of movement require economic activity. To illustrate this point we can use one particular important type of movement, namely internal or external migration to escape famine, severe poverty, or persecution. At the individual level success in such a migration requires quitting one's job (if any), converting any assets one has to money or things that can be carried or shipped, and buying supplies. If the process of travelling is extended, survival along the way will require finding places to sleep, eat and drink, and work or donations. Substantial restrictions on economic activities can impose restrictions on migration.[60]

Note that while Nickel's focus is specifically on the Hohfeldian *powers* constitutive of economic liberties, the same arguments also defend—as rights for the right-holder's sake—trespassory duties constitutive of property rights qua Hohfeldian *claims*: duties, for example, to exclude oneself from the money earned by the migrant in the example above (a duty owed to that migrant).

Compared to many of the human rights in Part II—rights to a PHI that is a direct object of interest, need, or important freedom for the human right-holder—the property rights and economic liberties in Nickel's examples are more loosely linked to the relevant important interests, needs, or freedoms. Migration is just one way to escape famine: other methods involve direct famine relief, democratic oversight of resource distribution, or welfare state benefits that enable purchase of expensive food.[61] The necessary links with religious freedom are perhaps harder to deny, but one might observe ascetic traditions in many religions that make control of external resources less than necessary. I do not intend here to revert to the thesis (discredited in Section 7.3) that respect for a right must either be *necessary* for or *guarantee* fulfilment of the interest, need, or freedom which grounds it.[62] But for an interest, need, or freedom to ground a duty in my STRONGEST or STRONG A sense, that interest, need, or freedom must always (STRONGEST) or 'normally' (STRONG A) make the duty *apt*, even in the face of powerful countervailing considerations or the absence of much further support. It is not clear that Nickel's cases fit the STRONGEST model. One might even wonder about the STRONG A model. Contextual factors—in particular, the existence of a free market system as opposed to, say, a planned economy, a medieval economy, or the kind of economy at work in a 'hunter-gatherer' society—whose status as 'normal' is unclear do necessary work *alongside* the relevant human-right-grounding interests, needs, or freedoms, in delivering Nickel's conclusions that property rights are made apt for the human-right-holder in the cases outlined.

This does not entail that the property rights in question are not justifiable for the right-holder's sake. For recall that there is a spectrum of degrees to which a right can be justified for its holder's sake.[63] The previous paragraph argues only that some of Nickel's examples of property rights appear justifiable *to some extent* for the right-holder's sake, but, at least, not to the STRONGEST extent possible. Their status as natural rights will be to that extent diminished.[64] In my view, this leaves Nickel's arguments with significant force: in the modern world, many property rights are

---

[60] Nickel 2007, pp. 129–31.   [61] Sen 1999, Reich 1964.   [62] Cruft 2015.
[63] See Section 8.2 and again in Section 9.4.   [64] Section 8.2.

justifiable to some extent for the right-holder's own sake, as apt means for protecting the right-holder's human rights—and are to that extent naturally their holders' rights.

This chapter has examined arguments for regarding property rights as 'rights for the right-holder's sake', and as thereby natural rights akin to our human rights. I have argued on Lockean- and Nickel-style grounds (Sections 12.3–12.4) that some property rights can be justified on this basis, as can a non-specific right to the ownership of some property rather than none (see Section 12.2's Hegelian argument).[65] But these conclusions do not undermine Section 12.1's argument that regularly justifiably taxable property cannot be grounded for the right-holder's sake. We are left carving a distinction among property: between property justifiable primarily for the right-holder's sake (and hence naturally its holder's right) and property whose justification depends in significant part on values beyond the right-holder's own good.[66] The next chapter considers the latter.

Before concluding, I venture a point that qualifies how we should think about those property rights that this chapter has shown to be justifiable for the right-holder's sake. Property's aptness for protecting the property-holder's human rights (Nickel), for meeting her autonomy needs (Hegel) or for respecting her projects (Locke) in the modern world seems *regrettable*, while the aptness of the objects of 'standard' human rights (e.g. to education, due process, non-assault) for meeting the right-holder's needs in the modern world is not regrettable. It is *not* that a better (though perhaps unattainable-with-people-as-we-know-them) world would have no need for education, due process or absence-of-assault; a world in which humans did not need these goods would not involve beings recognizable as human at all. Yet a human world without property, but in which the values (of freedom, autonomy, and recognition for labour, etc.) that property realizes for the property-holder in the modern world still obtain, seems in some sense possible. This is my complaint with Hegel and Locke: they make the good that property secures too fundamental to the modern owner's nature.[67] It is due to regrettable facts about modern human nature— facts that one might call 'contingencies' if one remembers that this does not mean they are easy or even possible to change, but simply that their changing would still leave humans recognizably as humans—that the individual needs some property.

A similar argument is sometimes made about due process: in an ideal world it would not be needed, because in an ideal world people would not commit the crimes for which systems of private or public law are needed. But it seems to me that this case is rather different from the property case. We do not have to believe in original sin in order to recognize with Pope that 'to err is human'. A world with no need for

---

[65] My view is that these arguments also ground many indigenous right claims, where natural property is held by a group: see Stilz 2017, pp. 4–5, 27, for a Nickel-style version of this argument, defending e.g. Native Americans' natural territorial rights (which she sees as property rights that fall short of Honoré 1961's 'full liberal ownership') against Columbus as a necessary instantiation of their human rights.

[66] Compare again Stilz's similar 'hybrid' view in her 2017. For differing forms of broadly similar bifurcations of property into two types, see e.g. Gould 1980 and Christman 1994.

[67] I would not make the same complaint about Nickel. He makes no claim that property rights or economic liberties are *fundamental* to any modern human, but only that they contingently serve important goods for the modern human. Tomasi 2012, however, does seem Hegelian in this regard.

due process rights would not involve beings recognizable as human. My claim, by contrast, is that a world without property, but with instead omnilateral shared communal decisions made about all external goods (as sketched in Section 12.2[68]) seems to me genuinely human, an ideal that is compatible with and would fully realize our humanity—even though it is unattainable. That is the sense in which property is regrettable. This does not impugn the arguments in the current chapter: that some property rights are, like human rights, justifiable for the right-holder's sake and hence natural rights. But it should dampen our applause for this conclusion.

[68] See four paragraphs from the end of that section.

13

Property Rights for the Common Good

13.1 Property as a System

Sections 12.2–12.4 suggested that *some* property rights might be groundable primarily by what they do for the individual (or group) right-holder, and hence qualify as natural rights for that party. Section 12.3 showed that post-market-transfer property rights cannot be grounded in this way (or at least their status as voluntarily transferred cannot supply such a grounding). This complements Section 12.1's claim that the property rights of those with extensive wealth—indeed any regularly justifiably taxable property—cannot be grounded by what they do for the right-holder. They must be grounded (if they are) in significant part by how they serve others beyond the right-holder. Such rights cannot be natural rights. Nor can they be social or legal determinations or operationalizations of prior natural rights on which they are founded.

Before explaining how some (legal or conventional rather than natural) property rights can be grounded in the common good, I introduce an orthogonal but related distinction. So far, I have focused on the distinction between rights justifiable primarily by what they do for the right-holder and rights justifiable primarily by what they do for others beyond the right-holder. The orthogonal distinction separates rights justifiable only systemically from those justifiable non-systemically: as I put it in earlier work, rights which are 'systemically justified [...] are justified by the value of the whole [...] system in which they are a part, rather than by their specific value independent of their role in the system as a whole'[1] Non-systemically justified rights can be justified independently of their role in any wider system.

The recognition-independent natural human rights of Part II appear non-systemically justified: my interest in not being tortured (or, perhaps, the generic human interest in not being tortured (see Chapter 9)) grounds your duty not to torture me independently of whether there exists any similar duty on you or others not to torture others, or any similar right not to be tortured borne by others. The importance of my political participation grounds duties on others to allow me to participate independently of whether there exist similar duties to allow others to

---

[1] Cruft 2010, p. 143. Compare Attas's related distinction between 'regime' and 'individual entitlement' approaches to property (Attas 2012)—though for Attas the latter must espouse Honoré's ideal of 'full liberal ownership', while the former need not; by contrast, my distinction between systemic and non-systemic justifications of property rights leaves open whether the rights to be justified are those of 'full liberal ownership'.

participate, or similar rights borne by others. I am not saying that the grounding for these human rights has *no implications* for whether others hold similar rights; we can infer that an interest which grounds a certain right for me will often ground a similar one for you (if you hold the same interest). But my point is that the relevant grounding interest, need, or freedom—whether taken as a specific or a generic human interest—will normally successfully ground (natural) rights for the bearer of the interest, need, or freedom *whether or not it successfully grounds rights for others*.

Some of the routes outlined in Chapter 12 to property rights for the right-holder's sake seem to be non-systemic. For example, if my plans for Greenacre justify your excluding yourself from Greenacre, or my other human rights (to political partici-pation, say) make such self-exclusion apt, or your self-exclusion makes Greenacre a useful 'buffer' for me against your and others' actions, then this would seem to work to ground my property rights in Greenacre independently of whether further acts of self-exclusion from further land or chattels were justified in relation to anyone else.[2]

As noted in Section 12.4, some of Nickel's arguments seem systemic: they turn crucially on the value, either to many human-rights-holders or to the generic human, of a *system* of property, rather than specifically on the value of her property holdings for the individual right-holder.[3] Similarly, my characterization of *legal rights in general* in Part II makes their justification systemic: we cannot ground a legal right for one person without thereby (and not through additional justificatory 'steps') grounding the same right for anyone who meets the relevant description.[4] In such cases involving large multi-person systems, Section 9.2 shows us that the good of an individual right-holder cannot plausibly ground—nor even play a major role in grounding—the system as a whole, and the relevant duties therefore cannot consti-tute duties owed naturally to the relevant right-holder as her natural rights. Before assessing systemic arguments for property in Section 13.2, we might therefore conclude that systemic justifications are possible *only* for legal or conventional systems of rights and not natural rights.

Yet while this is correct, we should note that there is still logical space for systemic justifications for large, multi-person systems of natural *duties*, natural duties that—because their systemic justification means a particular party's good cannot work largely on its own to ground them—cannot take the form of natural rights.[5] Someone who wanted most property to have a 'natural' status might try to regard the property that cannot fit Chapter 12's natural rights model like this: as a large system of *natural* trespassory duties grounded on the common good (in ways to be outlined in

---

[2] Similarly, Owens forthcoming sketches a defence of some property rights as justifiable simply by how the specific rights for the individual serve that individual's interests in controlling the items protected by the rights. Such interests are served by the individual's property rights independently of whether anyone else holds property rights.

[3] For example, see the centrality—to Nickel's defence of economic liberties as necessary for free movement—of others holding property with which I can make exchanges (Nickel 2007, p. 131).

[4] See Section 9.2.

[5] Such systems of duties could perhaps take the form of natural rights borne by a group: the group whose good grounds the system.

Section 13.2), which we have decided, through legal-conventional creation, to regard as directed duties—i.e. a system of common-good-grounded natural duties falling on X not to trespass on O, on Y not to trespass on P, and so on, but natural duties whose *direction* as correlating with *rights* for the parties allowed to use O and P is a legal-conventional creation. Now in my view, such an approach to property is incorrect. When it comes to property, both the rights *and the trespassory duties with which they correlate* should be regarded as legal-conventional creations—except in the case of those property rights that fit Chapter 12's natural rights models.

I use the remainder of the current section to explain this. First, note that we can make sense of the idea that the potential value of a behavioural system involving interlocking coordinated action by several parties could make the relevant parties naturally duty-bound to perform the relevant valuable coordinated behaviour. For example, I argued at the start of Section 7.7 that two people might jointly hold a duty to coordinate their behaviour to lift a log off someone's leg, a natural joint duty entailing individual natural duties requiring highly specific individual actions from each: this could be seen as a small (two-person) natural system of duties (and in this case it can plausibly be regarded as grounded in a STRONG way by the injured party's good).

But the likelihood of successful grounding for natural, recognition-independent interlocking duties falling on many, which essentially require each party to perform specific parts within a large overall pattern of coordinated behavior, seems low. This is partly because when my duty depends on you playing your part, the duty vanishes if you will not play your part. For example, if you cannot be persuaded to do your bit to lift the tree off Joe's leg, I have no duty to try pointlessly to do what would (if you were doing yours too) be 'my' bit. (Instead, presumably I have a different duty to do something else.) It seems very unlikely that absent a conventional-legal normative system, others could be relied on to play their parts in an interlocking complex behavioural system in a way that would make any person naturally duty-bound to play theirs.

Furthermore in many cases of coordinated behaviour—especially a property system—it is not at all clear what the coordinated behaviour would be without a socially recognized normative system to create it. The recognized conventional or legal system enables the coordinated behaviour to emerge through people's choices. Without the system recognized, there is no answer (beyond that already given by the human rights of Pt II) to the question what specific set of coordinated behaviours for many people in relation to the use of resources would be relevantly valuable and hence required by duties.[6] Instead, the value lies in the existence of a recognized conventional-legal normative system. And it would be a category error (as outlined in Sections 7.4 and 7.7) if the value of such a system was taken to make it exist. Instead, it gives us reason to create, sustain and respect it. We should therefore conclude that systemic justifications for large multi-person systems work best for legal-conventional systems of rights and duties. Justifications of *property* as a

---

[6] Hayek 1960; see also Buchanan 1988, pp. 15–18. Compare the absurdity of saying that the precise coordinated set of behaviour generated by a town's parking system was pre-institutionally required before the system had been created.

wide-ranging social system can, I think, only be justifications of legal-conventional rather than natural property. (Note that this is not to dismiss *non-systemic* justifications for some (limited) natural property rights, as in the strategies outlined in Chapter 12.)

13.2 Property's Systemic Justification as a Common Good Justification

So: what (if anything) justifies those property rights that cannot be justified for the right-holder's own sake? The property rights in question include holdings justifiable solely as the result of market transfers (Section 12.3) and those property rights at the outer edges of wealthy people's wealth, including all regularly justifiably taxable property (Section 12.1). If they cannot be justified for the right-holder's own sake, then Part II told us that they cannot be human rights, nor naturally or recognition-independently qualify as rights; rather, their status as *rights* must be a socially created, legal, or conventional matter. Section 13.1 adds that their justification must be systemic, and that given their large multi-person systemic grounding, the trespassory duties with which they correlate must also be legal-conventional creations. Do we have good reason to create such a system of duties—i.e. a property system that goes beyond the limited property rights groundable as natural rights in Chapter 12's manner? I answer this question affirmatively in the current section, before going on in Section 13.3 to ask whether we should regard these legal-conventional trespassory duties as constituting *rights*, even though—unlike natural rights—they are not grounded by the right-holder's own good.

My view is that we have common good reasons to create and sustain the systems of trespassory duties and economic liberties broadly constitutive of modern free markets: systems that give individual people and corporate entities property over much more than those few property rights (and few economic liberties) that can be grounded for the right-holder's own sake along the lines explored in Chapter 12. The notion of 'common good' in play here will be examined in a moment, but my broad claim is the classical liberal one, articulated by David Hume, Adam Smith, and Friedrich von Hayek, and developed in the fundamental theorems of welfare economics, that all or most people benefit from property systems enabling free market transfers. The benefits come from how market interactions harness our limited altruism, limited knowledge, and limited resources to deliver an efficient, productivity-generating allocation of resources.[7] I have sympathy with this orthodox story, which I will call 'the classical liberal case for property':[8] the argument that relatively free markets (constituted by relatively unlimited economic liberties

---

[7] See Hume 1978 [1739–40], bk III, pt. II, section II; Smith 1976 [1776]; Hayek 1960; see perhaps especially the 'invisible hand' argument encapsulated in Smith's much-quoted claim about how free market exchanges harness human selfishness to each party's benefit: 'It is not from the benevolence of the butcher, the brewer, or the baker, that we expect our dinner, but from their regard to their own interest. We address ourselves [in market exchange], not to their humanity but to their self-love' (Smith 1976 [1776], bk. I, ch. II, p. 18). See also Buchanan 1988, ch. 2 and de Soto 2000.

[8] Note that on this account neither Locke nor Nozick are classical liberals; rather, in my usage the classical liberals are Hume, Smith, and Hayek: those who focus on the efficiency and stability delivered by market exchanges starting from an initial property distribution. Compare Tomasi's 2012 use of the phrase.

enabling relatively unrestricted ownership of resources) are a way of ensuring the creation of enough social wealth both to secure many people with significant well-being, and to allow satisfaction of everyone's human rights (as sketched in Part II).[9]

But I think there is a real risk of unquestioningly rationalizing the actual here. Is my acceptance of the orthodox classical liberal story, my willingness to see broadly free market property systems as in some sense serving the common good, simply a product of my immersion in post-Cold War ideology? A product of my lack of imagination when it comes to alternative possibilities such as communism or anarchism?[10] A product, even, of my over-generalizing from the (limited) success of Chapter 12's arguments that there are *some* natural property rights and natural Hohfeldian powers to exchange those rights? Answering these questions requires more wisdom than I can offer. Instead, I will take the classical liberal case for broadly free market systems of property as given, and I aim in the remainder of the current section (13.2) to clarify the sense in which this case justifies property systems as serving the *common good rather than the individual right-holder*—before going on in Section 13.3 to show the surprisingly radical doubt that a proper appreciation of the classical liberal case should throw on non-natural property's status as a *right*.

A brief note before examining the common good argument in detail: taking the classical liberal case for broadly free market property systems as given is not to dismiss the powerful limitations of the market proposed, for example, by Anderson or Reiff.[11] Nor is it to rule out the kind of market socialism defended by Miller, in which 'the market mechanism is retained as a means of providing most goods and services, while the ownership of capital is socialised'.[12] I focus on the classical liberal common good case for having *some property system involving broadly free markets*; this might include systems in which all businesses are worker-owned.

We can distinguish several senses of 'common good'. One is the distinctive good of a particular group or 'commons', independently of how this relates to the good of its members. While I think that some 'common goods' in this sense might be morally important, I do not think the efficiency, productivity, or peace that the classical liberals tell us are secured by property systems are sufficient, when construed simply as *goods of a group conceived independently of their good to its members*, to justify the creation and maintenance of the relevant property systems.[13]

A second conception of the 'common good' takes it as a good common to all members of the group. Thus on this conception, the efficiency, productivity, or peace

---

[9] Compare the argument in Cheneval (2019), that capitalist liberties are justifiable as necessary means to ensure societies have enough wealth to fulfil everyone's welfare rights. Section 11.4 showed us that this should not be conceived as an argument in favour of creating the wealth necessary for tax payments to fund welfare rights; for strictly speaking tax payments do not fund government spending. Nonetheless, I noted that taxation is normally a necessary concomitant to wide government spending: necessary for macroeconomic stability.

[10] It seems very likely that many of us will over-generalize from the failure of Soviet regimes, and the horrors documented in, e.g. Alexievich 2016. (The sense in which China's economy is a free market one, and the extent to which its success depends on this, should of course affect our assessment of the classical liberal argument.)

[11] See Anderson 1993, Reiff 2013.   [12] Miller 1989, p. 10.

[13] Compare Murphy 2005, p. 154, for a similar claim against the moral importance of the common good when conceived as a good distinct from the good of its members.

secured by property systems justifies their creation and maintenance because efficiency, productivity, and peace are good for each and every member of the relevant group. If it works, this is a very powerful justification for property systems. It does not say that one individual's good on its own is sufficient to justify the creation or maintenance of a property system. But it says that the fact that a property system is good for each and every person falling under it justifies our creation and maintenance of it. In Section 8.2's sense, this approach makes each person's good play a STRONG B role in justifying the creation and maintenance of the conventional-legal property system. Even though we have seen in Chapter 12 that there will rarely be natural property rights underlying the relevant conventional-legal property rights, nonetheless if conventional-legal property rights are justified in this STRONG B way, this explains some of the appeal in seeing them as akin to human rights: my good (alongside everyone else's) plays a central role in justifying the creation and maintenance of the system. This second conception of the common good is broadly akin to Murphy's or Finnis's—the difference being that the approach to property under consideration takes it as a human creation rather than natural law. The similarity is that for Murphy and Finnis, a law is grounded in the common good when it serves each and every person within its scope.[14]

A third conception of the common good takes it as the aggregated good of all people within the relevant scope. As is well known, such a utilitarian approach allows trade-offs when an institution or course of action could be adopted even though it would harm or sacrifice some, if in so doing it would secure the greatest aggregated sum of good.[15]

It is not always clear whether a defender of a property system on common good grounds means the 'common good' in my second or my third sense (use of the first sense is rare). The aspects of Nickel's linkage and autonomy-based arguments that focus on how a property system as a whole serves the common good (as opposed to those aspects which defend property rights as natural rights for the right-holder's sake) can plausibly be read in my second sense, as showing the system to serve *each and every member's* autonomy and other human rights. Tomasi's, de Soto's and MacLeod's various claims about the importance of property can be given a similar reading: on this reading, they claim that each and every person's practical reason (MacLeod), self-construction (Tomasi), or interests which ground other human rights (Nickel, de Soto) are well served by a system of free market property rights.[16] Similarly, Hume and Smith sometimes seem to defend property systems as in each and every individual's interests.[17]

---

[14] See Murphy 2005 and Finnis 1980, ch. VI. See also Murphy's arguments for what he calls an 'aggregative' rather than Finnis-style 'instrumental' conception of the common good (Murphy 2005, pp. 139–48).

[15] I take 'aggregated' here to mean summed in a way that allows tradeoffs, unlike Murphy's distinctive tradeoff-resistant use of 'aggregative' in his 2005; compare Rawls's famous concerns about utilitarianism (1971, p. 27).

[16] Nickel 2000 and 2007, ch. 8; de Soto 2000; Tomasi 2012; MacLeod 2015.

[17] E.g. Hume 1978 [1739–40] writes: 'Every member of society is sensible of this interest [served by a property system]' (p. 498); compare Waldron 1994, reading Hume as taking a property system to benefit each and every participant. Insofar as Hayek is Paretian, the same can be said for him.

Yet at times authors in this tradition seem to opt for the third, aggregative interpretation instead.[18] This aggregative approach might seem both necessary and problematic for those who defend systems of property rights on common good grounds. It seems problematic because a property system grounded by how it serves the aggregate even at the expense of minorities should command significantly less respect—both in terms of the efforts we should put into respecting it, and in terms of its priority in conflicts with other considerations[19]—than a property system grounded by how it serves *every* person within its scope (unless that scope is itself unjustifiably limited, as e.g. in societies that legalize slavery). But the aggregative approach might seem necessary because it is implausible that any property system serves each and every person falling under it, including for example people with no property whatsoever beyond that required as a natural right in Chapter 12's sense. Imagine some family whose human rights (in the Part II sense) and natural property rights (in Chapter 12's sense) are fulfilled, but who have nothing more than that, and who live alongside people who have become significantly wealthier than them as a result of the (welfare-state-limited) free market.[20] Can we really confidently say that the impediments (both direct and, through relative market power, indirect) that others' wealth presents to the family in question are the result of essential parts (e.g. free bilateral transfer) of a system that serves *their own interest or need* by securing peace, efficiency, and productivity? Is peace, efficiency, and productivity worth these impediments, to the family who faces them? Only the aggregative version of the common good approach, which allows us to see these people's suffering as *outweighed* by the benefits the property system delivers for *others*, seems likely to be able to justify the system.

This concern is tempered by the fact that a property system can serve the common good in my second sense without serving *on balance* each and every member living within it. It is arguably sufficient, for the system to be justified by how it serves the common good in my second sense, that some important good for each is secured by the system, even if for some individuals—such as the members of the family in the previous paragraph—that property-secured good (e.g. peace, efficiency, productivity) is outweighed by the costs the system imposes on her.[21] If the important good secured by the property system is good enough, perhaps—so the response goes— the second-type common good justification of the system goes through even though some are damaged on balance by it.

I am unsure how persuasive the last point is: do you better address my concern that others' property impedes me severely by telling me that I myself nonetheless have an (outweighed pro tanto) interest in the property system, or by telling me, along utilitarian-aggregative lines, that others will benefit from the system that leaves me suffering? Further, one might anyway worry—along the lines sketched in

---

[18] This is evident in the pre-Paretian, proto-utilitarian conceptions of the common good to be found, sometimes, in Hume and Smith, and the subsequent welfare economics tradition.

[19] See Kamm 1996, p. 321, for cases where these dimensions diverge.

[20] The living arrangements in contemporary urban UK are a near example. Except that not all human rights are fulfilled there.

[21] Compare this volume, Section 2.2 and Raz 1986, p. 180.

Section 9.1's Varied Specific view—about individuals who are in *no way* served by, say, peace or efficiency, not even merely pro tanto. But I will not pursue further the fault line between my second and third forms of common good justification. I will assume that one or other of these often succeeds in justifying a system of property rights that goes beyond the natural property defended in Chapter 12—even if the third approach offers a comparatively weak justification.

Instead, I want to remind the reader again that on either common good approach, the good (to each or to the aggregate) of *the overall property system* is what justifies it, not simply the good of *a single given person's right*. Each right within the system— whether borne by me, you, or someone else—is justified by what it does either for each and every one of us humans within the system, or for our interests aggregated. This, I think, is entailed by what MacLeod and Tomasi say about the human values served by property: free exchange, along with other ways of negotiating *others'* property, are essential to the exercise of practical reason and the self-creation that these authors highlight as the values served by a property system.[22] Similarly, the classical liberal defence of property (Hume, Smith, Hayek) highlights not just the value of one's own property to oneself, but the value of the system as a whole to oneself as a means of efficiently serving one's wants while similarly serving others. Consider, for example, Hayek's insight that it is not just my rights, but others' rights and my capacity to exchange things in order to make them mine, which serve my human interest in getting what I want. For Hayek, this market mechanism serves these wants more efficiently than would direct rights to whatever I want: 'The benefits I derive from freedom are [...] largely the result of the uses of freedom by others.'[23] This marks a key distinction between systemically justified property rights—in which the system as a whole serves the common good—and the human rights of Part II and natural property of Chapter 12, where each person's right is justified by how it serves the interests of that person.[24] It means that the benefits any one person's property brings to people beyond that person (benefits through its role as part of an efficient system, for example) are essential and central to the justifiability of that person's property.

Someone who wanted to challenge this, and who wanted more natural property rights than those allowed by Chapter 12, might try to argue that even if the system as a whole is justified by how it serves the common good, this still allows each particular right within the system to be justified *in an intrasystemic sense* by how it serves the individual right-holder.[25] This idea might seem akin to the argument I used in Section 9.4 about natural socio-economic rights: I said that because only a particular party's good need play the role, in the grounding of a given duty to ensure someone has subsistence supplies (say), of 'good to be served by the dutiful action', then even if

[22] Tomasi 2012, MacLeod 2015.   [23] Hayek 1960, p. 29.

[24] Compare Finnis 2011, p. 5, for the claim that some goods are 'good for me and anyone like me'. In my view, *human rights* are justified by how they are good for the person in the right-holder position; while most *property rights* (setting aside those in Chapter 12) are justified by how they are good for anyone in any position, not just right-holder position.

[25] Thanks to Matthew Kramer for pressing this concern—inspired in part by e.g. Hart's attempt to distinguish the justifying aim of a system of punishment from the grounds for individual punitive acts within the justified system (Hart 1968).

the duty's grounding required other principles or values beyond that party's good, it could still be taken as naturally owed to the party in question.[26] Similarly, one might argue that if the property system allocates Greenacre to me, then only my good need play the role of 'good to be served' by your keeping off Greenacre. Even if the good of others is part of the justification of the system, your duty to keep off seems, in an intrasystemic sense, to be based primarily on my good: why not see the relevant duty as naturally owed to me?

There are several reasons why this response fails. One is that, as argued in Chapter 12 and Section 13.1, the relevant trespassory duty—to keep off Greenacre— is unlikely to be a *natural duty* (even before we consider its status as a right). Another more interesting reason is that even if respect for my interest (as owner of Greencare within the system) might be psychologically-causally sufficient to keep you off Green- acre, the classical liberal case for property tells us that the moral justification for this trespassory duty of yours, and the moral justification for your fulfilling it, is not simply to serve my interest: it is central to this justification that the duty, and respect for it, positively serves other interests too—including the interests of others who might want to buy Greenacre from me, or who might want to buy Greenacre from them, or who benefit in more general ways from the efficiency and peace of the system, including from others doing what they want with Greenacre. In the common good classical liberal case for property, all these interests figure as 'to be served' in justifying your being duty-bound to keep off Greenacre, and if you are fully virtuous you should take your self-exclusion from Greenacre as an action serving these many common good interests. The grounding of the relevant duty is therefore sharply distinct from that of the human rights of Part II, including those discussed in Section 9.4: rights that it is possible to ground morally largely (or even wholly) by what they do for the right-holder's good, or at least that can be grounded by justifications in which the right-holder's good is the sole good positively 'to be served' by respect for the right. Unless it is one of the cases considered in Chapter 12, your duty to keep off Greenacre cannot be grounded like this. Rather, in this duty's justification the good of others alongside the right-holder must be part of what is to be positively served by your keeping off Greenacre; that is what the classical liberal common good justification tells us.[27]

---

[26] See Section 9.4, pp. 158–60.

[27] A proponent of the version of the Generic Human view of the grounds of human rights developed in Chapter 9 might object that a whole system of property is justifiable primarily by what it does for the right- holder's own interest as a generic human, *just like the legal human rights of Part II* (see Section 9.2 for the argument that the Generic Human view allows systems of legal human rights to be justified by the very same *generic human goods* that justify natural human rights). The claim would be that the individual human's *generic human interest* (in, say, autonomy (Nickel), practical reason (MacLeod), self-construction (Tomasi)) is sufficient on its own normally (in my STRONG A sense) to justify the creation and maintenance of a free market system of property. This looks like a 'rights-for-the-right-holder's-own- sake' justification of a full legal system of property. Any person living within the legal system could then see their own *interest/need as a generic human* as the primary ground for the system, and hence as the ground for their legal rights within that system—even those of extremely wealthy people, or those gained through bilateral transfers made for reasons independent of the recipient's own good. We could respond effectively to this objection by noting the many problems of the Generic Human view (see especially Sections 9.1, 9.2 and 9.6), or by denying that all really do, *qua generic human*, hold an interest in the existence of a system of

13.3 Do We Need Property *Rights* for the Common Good?

There can seem an odd sort of doublethink in conceiving property rights as grounded for the common good. It requires the owner to think both that she is the right-holder, the person who will be legally and morally wronged[28] if others fail to exclude themselves from Greenacre, and at the same time that her own good (interests, needs, freedom) plays no special role in making this the case but rather the property rights she holds are justified because they serve the common good (construed in one or other of Section 13.2's second or third ways). We have seen back in Chapter 2 that Raz's theory of rights makes this impossible: for Raz, to hold a right one's own interests have to be the ground of the relevant duty.[29] But my conception of rights as Addressive duties, as developed in Part I, allows that people can hold rights even if their own interests, needs, freedom, or good are not the ground of these rights. Nonetheless, we have also seen in Chapter 7 that recognition-independent, natural rights have to fit Raz's model. This leaves conceptual space for the classical liberal position sketched in Section 13.2, which maintains that most property rights are non-natural legal rights grounded for the common good. But even though there is conceptual space for this position, the doublethink involved should give us pause. In particular, are the common good grounds for property systems genuinely grounds for taking trespassory duties to be owed to specific owners in the manner we (who live in free market property societies) currently assume?

The common good position I associated with Murphy and Finnis makes each person's legal property rights grounded on their good for everyone, through their role in a system that is good for everyone. On this basis, might our legal property system

property. But even if we set these responses aside, we can also note that if it works, the Generic Human view maintains that the generic human interest in not being tortured justifies a system of legal rights not to be tortured whose purpose is to serve each human's generic interest *as a potential object of torture*; similarly, the generic human interest in free speech justifies a system of legal rights to speak freely whose purpose is to serve each human's generic interest *as a potential speaker or communicator*. By contrast, the generic human interest in the existence of a legal system of free market property rights is not fundamentally a generic interest *against theft or other incursions on the property of the owner*. It is, rather, a generic interest in the system as a whole, not just in the legal rights the individual will hold under the system. The relevant generic human interests do not pick out the role of *owner independently of the existence of other owners* as the important locus of human interest or need, in the way that *potential victim of torture* or *potential speaker/ communicator* is an important locus of human interest or need in a way that does not depend on the existence of other potential victims or speakers. Thus even the Generic Human approach to property is a common good justification—even if it grounds property systems on a single generic human interest. On this view what my rights over Greenacre do on their own for me as a generic human is not sufficient to ground such legal rights; it is what my rights over Greenacre as part of a property system do for the shared generic human interest of each and every member of the system which grounds them. Systemic justifications, even based on a single generic human interest, do not justify rights 'for the right-holder's sake'.

[28] See Section 5.3 for defence of the idea that any morally justified duty owed to me—including legally and conventionally created duties—is such that its violation wrongs me morally.

[29] Raz 1986, p. 166. See this volume, Section 2.2 for discussion. We also saw (in Section 3.4) that Sreenivasan's hybrid theory cannot accommodate property rights involving control powers justified for the common good. See Chapter 12, note 44 above. Kramer's and Wenar's versions of the Interest Theory, and all versions of the Will Theory, can accommodate this but suffer other problems (see this volume, Chapters 2–3).

more honestly reflect its underlying grounds if we took all trespassory duties (or at least those for which right-holder-based justifications of the types examined in Sections 12.2–12.4 cannot be found) to be owed to each and every person, rather than just to the person currently conceived as the owner? This would be an extremely radical change, entailing, for example, that others' duties to exclude themselves from 'my' shed were actually owed to everyone, and not just me—so someone who trespassed on my shed would wrong everyone, with me bearing no special status as especially wronged. Similarly, this radical change would entail that others' duties to exclude themselves from Bill Gates's bank account were not specially owed to Gates but to everyone, with all of us wronged by a theft from his account and no special wrong accruing to Gates alone. Even if hints of this way of thinking can be found in, for example, communist conceptions of ownership as fundamentally collective and aristocratic conceptions of ownership as stewardship, it would be an extremely radical change.[30]

Equally radical change would follow if we tried to make legal property systems reflect the underlying grounds that utilitarian aggregative rather than common good justifications offer. This would suggest making trespassory duties over my shed or Gates's money owed to the aggregated collective, rather than Gates and me.

To justify eschewing these radical changes, we need to look closely at how important or valuable it is for the duties constitutive of a legal property system to be *Addressive* duties correlating with *rights* borne by the person (or group) non-excluded from the relevant item ('item' here being land, chattels, money, ideas, etc.). In doing this, we cannot look simply to the good of the relevant PHI (in this case, people excluding themselves from an item) as the source of the directedness of duties to PHI: PHI's goodness only makes duties-to-PHI owed to some person or group if that person or group's good is what makes others duty-bound to PHI,[31] and we have ruled out that possibility by establishing that most property rights are not grounded primarily by what they do for the right-holder in particular (but rather by what they do for the common good of which the right-holder is just one part). Instead, we should look at the value of people's *thinking and acting* on the basis that trespassory duties are owed to owners as right-holders. (Note that this is not vulnerable to the category error mentioned earlier[32] because the value of people's so thinking and acting would here be our reason to *create and sustain a system of legal property rights*, rather than being something that would magically makes recognition-independent natural rights exist *ex nihilo* because it would be good if they did.)

So: do the common good benefits which a legal property system brings depend on its involving trespassory duties that are *owed to right-holders*? It is not clear that they do. Let us imagine in more detail the 'radical change' sketched a few paragraphs back. Imagine a property system almost identical to our own, but in which all trespassory

---

[30] Compare Ihara's view that Confucian philosophy would conceive most duties as undirected, uncorrelating with rights, and that the idea of a right 'should not be promoted if moral systems that do not involve the notion of individual rights can serve as well or better' (Ihara 2004, p. 28). Ihara does not consider *property*, and my argument in the current section can be seen as sketching what Ihara might take to be a Confucian view of the classical liberal case for property.

[31] See Section 7.6.   [32] In Sections 7.4 and 7.7.

duties are taken to be owed not to particular right-holders but to the common good (perhaps with 'the community' or 'everyone' as right-holder). Such a system, let us suppose, would involve the same trespassory duties that exist in the actual world, but these duties would be owed to the community; it would also involve the same particular people holding the same Hohfeldian powers over trespassory duties which they hold in the actual world; it is just that these trespassory duties would be owed to the community. For example, in this imagined scenario everyone except me would, as in the real world, hold legal duties to exclude themselves from the shed in my garden, and I would, as in the real world, hold powers to adjust these duties for example by 'giving' the shed to you so that now you need not exclude yourself but the rest of the world including me is now duty-bound to do so. The only difference with the real world in this case would be that the trespassory duties in question would, both pre- and post-transfer, be owed to the community rather than, as in the real world, to first me and then you.

Note that 'the community' in the sketch above need not signify a close-knit group or a group with a sense of its own identity: it refers simply to whatever collective constitutes the domain whose members' good—either taken together individually or aggregated with trade-offs[33]—is what justifies, in our common good terms, the property rights in question.

Now the sketch above shows that we can make sense of the existence of powers of transfer held by individual people or small groups, regarding specific delimited items, without having to see the power-holders as those who hold rights correlative to the trespassory duties excluding others from the relevant items. And we can also see the power-holders as holding Hohfeldian privileges to use the relevant items from which others must exclude themselves. This structure can obtain even without the relevant trespassory duties being owed to the holder of the powers and privileges in question.

Furthermore, the holders of the relevant transfer powers and exclusive use privileges (concerning my shed or Greenacre, say) can be endowed with further powers to *demand fulfilment* of the trespassory duties protecting the relevant item, again without us having to see these trespassory duties as owed to the power holder. Such demanding could not be performed by the power holder on her own behalf as the person to whom the trespassory duties are owed, but it could be performed on behalf of the community, or the demand could simply be issued by the power holder without it being on behalf of anyone.[34]

Furthermore again, the holders of all the aforementioned powers and privileges regarding Greenacre could also hold powers to bring in force (e.g. the police) in order to uphold the trespassory duties protecting Greenacre. Or the state could hold this power. Either way, compensatory, rectificatory, and apologetic duties could be triggered by violation of the relevant trespassory duties, and these compensatory, rectificatory, and apologetic duties could involve actions done for the benefit of or towards the person holding the powers and privileges regarding Greenacre—all of this is possible without the relevant trespassory duties, or the relevant compensatory, rectificatory, and apologetic duties, being *owed to* that person and correlating with a

---

[33] See Section 13.2.   [34] Compare Section 3.3.

right held by that person. For example, in this imagined scenario your duty to pay £100 to me in compensation for stealing the roofing felt from the shed in my garden will be a compensatory duty that *benefits* me but is *owed to* (and correlates with a *right* held by) the community or everyone. Although the money is to be paid to me and hence in one sense is 'owed to' me, the duty to make this payment will be addressed to or owed to the community, in the sense that the community is the subject who will be wronged if payment is not made.[35]

Let us call the person (or group) who is not subject to trespassory duties to exclude herself from a given item while all others are, and who bears powers to control and make demands in relation to others' trespassory duties to keep off this item, but who does not hold rights correlating with these trespassory duties because the duties are not owed to her, a 'controller' of the item.[36] Do the common good grounds for a legal property system favour a system like our own, involving individually held ownership rights correlating with trespassory duties, a system in which trespass wrongs the individual privileged to use and control the item in question? Or would these common good grounds be equally well served by a legal 'controllership' system in which a trespass on any given item wronged the community rather than wronging the item's 'controller'?

In my view, most of the strongest common good grounds for a property system are served equally well by a 'controllership' system as by one like our own involving individually held *rights* of ownership. For example, the benefits of a property system highlighted by the classical liberals—the way in which a property system enables a multiplicity of diverse people's desires to be fulfilled despite our limited altruism[37] and our limited capacities to know how to satisfy multiple varying desires[38]—would seem to be delivered by any system that gives individuals transferable protected exclusive privileges to use specific items. This is what is necessary for a free market in which bilateral exchanges would (ignoring informational deficiencies and third party effects) deliver Pareto gains.[39] And the 'controllership' system can do this just as well as our current ownership system. 'Controllers' have the Hohfeldian powers to exchange in order to ensure that the post-exchange items they 'control' satisfy their desires better than before the exchange. It looks, therefore, as though the benefits of a free market system can be delivered by free market controllership as much as free market ownership.

Another closely related[40] and frequently cited common good benefit of property systems is the way they deal with the 'tragedy of the commons': the security that property rights provide to individual owners can make cultivation or development of items worthwhile for the owner in a way that they would not be if the item was not privately owned.[41] But again a 'controllership' system would seem able to deliver the

---

[35] Compare Section 3.5.   [36] See Cruft 2013, pp. 219–22, for an initial sketch of this notion.

[37] See again the famous quotation from Smith 1976 [1767] at note 7 above.

[38] Hayek 1960, ch. 2; Buchanan 1988, pp. 16–17.

[39] See the fundamental theorems of welfare economics.

[40] Some might see this as just another version of the point about the market's efficient handling of limited altruism noted above.

[41] Hardin 1968. Note that this seems highly context-dependent. See the emerging work on the tragedy of the anticommons.

same benefits. The system ensures that the 'controller' has secure use of the item she 'controls' unless she chooses to transfer the relevant trespassory duties. And as noted above, rectificatory and compensatory duties can be set up in such a way that the 'controller' can be confident that efforts she puts into developing the relevant item will reap benefits usable by her the 'controller', even if the trespassory duties are violated—for rectificatory and compensatory duties can be set up to ensure the 'controller' is not at a loss as a result of violation. All of this is compatible with both the trespassory and the rectificatory/compensatory duties being owed, qua duties, to the community, even though they function to the benefit of the 'controller'.

Furthermore, the benefits of free market property systems that MacLeod and Tomasi cite again seem to be provided by the 'controllership' system: Macleod highlights the way that property systems enable and foster the exercise of practical reasonableness, and Tomasi highlights the way that property systems enable one to see oneself as a primary cause and creator of one's own place in society.[42] A 'controllership' system could deliver both these benefits. Both the 'controller' of an item and others contemplating using it or bargaining for it through exchange have to negotiate the system in the same way that they would if they lived in a 'normal' property system. The forms of practical reasonableness involved will be almost identical, the only difference being that controllers will not conceive trespassory duties regarding the items which they can use and control as owed to them.

Tomasi's benefit might seem harder to replicate under 'controllership'. How can I consider myself the author of the life I have ended up with if the items I have come to control, as a result of my free market activities, are not ultimately 'mine' because violation of the trespassory duties protecting them wrongs the community rather than just me?

In response, we should note first that what I come to 'control' on the basis of my extended free market activities within a 'controllership' system will be the very same result of my decisions and efforts as the result that I would have reached within a free market private property system while making the same decisions and efforts.[43] My eventual holdings as a 'controller' can be seen as my own creation in the same way that my holdings as an 'owner' could.

Secondly, we should note that even within the 'controllership' system the privileges of use and powers of transfer regarding items I 'control' are genuinely *my* privileges and powers. They are not privileges or powers held by the community: it is not that the community can enter or sell Greenacre if I merely 'control' it; only I can do this. The classical liberal and other common good cases for private property insist on this by highlighting the problems associated with communal use and control.[44] Further-more, under the 'controllership' system it is not even the case that I have to exercise my use privileges and transfer powers regarding Greenacre in a way that I think will, or that actually will, serve the community or the common good. Again, the classical

[42] Tomasi 2012, MacLeod 2015.

[43] The only possible difference would be psychological effects—on exchange and on the eventual result—of everyone's conceiving the relevant trespassory duties as correlating with 'rights' held individually by the relevant 'owners'. I discuss this possibility shortly below.

[44] See Hayek 1944.

liberal and other common good cases for private property highlight the benefits of each owner being able to use their property for whatever end they please: their own, someone else's, or for no particular end. 'Controllership' replicates this too by allowing me to use my use privileges and transfer powers over Greenacre entirely at my discretion (within the familiar limits). There is therefore a real sense in which the items I end up 'controlling' are *mine*, even within the 'controllership' system in which others' trespassory duties not to use them are owed to the community rather than me.

A final point in favour of my claim that a 'controllership' system could deliver the same benefits—in terms of enabling people to consider themselves the authors of their own lives—that Tomasi claims for private property systems is that the privilege of use that goes with controlling an item enables the controller (and, if she wants, *only* the controller) to be the consumer of that item. We should take consumption here in a very broad sense that might include gaining knowledge from a book, as well as more familiar forms of consumption involving, say, gains in nutrition or pleasure. In consuming an item, a controller gains something that is undeniably 'hers' from what she 'controls', and the extent and nature of her consumption will be determined by what she has been able to come to 'control'. All of this is still compatible with the relevant trespassory duties over what she 'controls' being owed to the community, not to her.

There might seem to be one benefit of private property systems that a parallel free market 'controllership' system could not deliver. This is the benefit of people truthfully thinking of themselves as the specific right-holders who are wronged when trespassory duties protecting a given item are violated. This entails further that the sphere of disrespect for the individual right-holder is constituted in part by the relevant trespassory duties.[45] The 'controllership' system disallows me from thinking this about 'my' shed, and disallows Gates from thinking this about 'his' money: trespass on these items wrongs the community and thereby shows disrespect to them but not specifically to me as someone with a special status beyond my membership of the community.

It is not clear that there is any value or importance *as such* in people conceiving themselves as right-holders (and hence as potentially wronged and disrespected) in cases beyond the human rights sketched in Part II (and perhaps also in the case of those property rights that are grounded as rights for the right-holder's own sake (see Sections 12.2–12.4)). But it might turn out that there are important further instrumental or derivative benefits of people thinking of themselves as right-holders—and others thinking of them in this way—with regard to any specific items gained within what would otherwise be a 'controllership' system. For example, as a psychological matter people might be more willing to police and uphold trespassory duties which they consider *owed to them*, correlating with *their rights*, constituting *respect for them*, than to police and uphold trespassory duties over items for which they were the

---

[45] See Section 5.3.

mere 'controller'. Or they might gain greater psychological consumption benefits from goods they consider theirs as a matter of ownership rather than 'control'.[46]

I am unconvinced by the claims in the previous paragraph. Further, even if there were such benefits they would have to be weighed against the cost constituted by the fact that a legal private property system with trespassory duties owed to owners fails, as it were, to wear its grounding moral purpose on its face.[47] There are many other conventional and legal rights grounded by how they serve parties or values beyond the right-holder: I have already mentioned the prime minister's right to declare war, or a teacher's right to timely submission of work from their pupils, or a business manager's rights (within limits) to allocate tasks and recruit new people (and to be unimpeded in doing so). But each of these rights, unlike property rights, is by its very nature clearly aimed at enabling the right-holder to perform duties of office or duties that go with her role, duties that are themselves clearly grounded in values other than simply the right-holder's own good. So even though a business manager or a teacher might sometimes wrongly or absurdly fixate on the rights given to her by her role, and thereby fail to remember the grounding of her role in values other than her own good, the nature of the rights and the role involved makes it readily possible to see that this is an error. The prime minister's rights wear their ground in the nation's good on their face, as do the teacher's rights in the good of education. The business manager's rights similarly wear their ground in the good of the business on their face—though here matters are closer to the private property case, because the good of the business is not ultimately the ground for the relevant rights, but rather common goods like efficiency and personal self-creation ground the whole system of businesses. Still, because a business is obviously a human conventional creation that could be configured in many ways and whose 'good' is obviously of at most only instrumental importance, I think the link from a business manager's rights to the good of the business to the common good is not too difficult to see. The manager's right does not seem likely to tempt us to regard it as grounded ultimately by the good of the business, because it is not tempting to see a business's good as of ultimate right-grounding importance.

This is a major contrast with private property rights. The common good case for legal private property systems requires property rights that do *not* protect some other-directed duty of office: it is not that being an 'owner' (or indeed a 'controller') is defined by duties of world stewardship or concern for others, say. The common good case for private property systems is specifically opposed to this and allows owners to use their property entirely at their discretion (within the familiar limits). Of course,

---

[46] Compare the similar discussion, not focused solely on *property*, in Section 5.1. It would be interesting to explore how far the positive psychological aspects of ownership highlighted in Rose 2013 accrue to one's being *owed* trespassory duties, and how far they could equally accrue to being 'controller' in my technical sense. Note that one further purported cost of regarding property as 'controllership' might be thought to be that it belies the directedness inherent in promissory relationships of gift or contract (see Section 8.3, p. 132). But I can promise to give you what I currently 'control', and my duty to deliver be therefore owed to you, even while the trespassory duties constitutive of this 'control' that I transfer are owed neither to me (pre-transfer) nor you (post-transfer), but are rather owed to the community throughout.

[47] Again, with the exception of those property rights grounded in the manner outlined in Sections 12.2–12.4.

one might try to argue that a better property system would confer duties of office on owners—perhaps duties of stewardship or concern or, to take Katz's suggestion, duties to decide 'what constitutes a worthwhile use of a thing'.[48] But I am convinced by the classical liberal case that the important common goods of efficiency, peace, and stability are best secured by generally allowing owners to use their property as they wish (within obvious limits) rather than placing them under a duty to serve particular ends with their property.[49] If this is correct, then the common good case makes private property rights importantly distinct from the rights of the previous paragraph—the prime minister's or business manager's. Both the latter and property are justified by how they serve goods beyond the right-holder but unlike the prime minister's rights or the manager's rights, ownership rights do not function to protect the kind of other-directed duty of office that would make obvious that rights of ownership are there to serve others beyond the owner.

Within a system of private property rights, then, it is very easy to slip erroneously into thinking that the individual owner's good is the ground for her property rights. This slip is made even harder to avoid by the fact that—as outlined in Sections 12.2–12.4—*some* property rights really are so grounded. But making this error will lead one to misclassify property rights by lumping them *all* into the same category as the human rights of Part II, resulting in a misconception of both their moral importance (an importance which should depend on their common good role rather than primarily their good to the individual right-holder) and their metaphysics (as rights which, due to their unjustifiability simply or primarily by their good to the right-holder, cannot be natural and recognition-independent).

I think we therefore have quite powerful reason to favour a radical shift in our conception of free markets: reason to see free markets as involving 'controllership', with trespassory duties owed to the community rather than to particular individual or group owners.[50] The trespassory duties within such a system wear on their face their ground in the common good. As sketched, such a controllership system will still be recognizably a free market with the same bilateral transaction structures and private use privileges that we know. But it will avoid some of the misconceptions we see at present: misconceptions that I would diagnose in common divisive proto-libertarian phrases such as 'taxpayer's money'—a phrase whose overtones suggest that taxation requires a justification of the type needed to justify infringing the human rights of Part II. I would even diagnose such overtones in the recently popular phrase, 'giving back to the community': I recognize this is a controversial interpretation but it seems to me often to be used to justify charitable giving by someone who

[48] Katz 2013, p. 1483. Thanks to Mark Reiff for pressing me with his view that a stewardship duty would be appropriate for owners.

[49] Note that the same common good case would ground just the same latitude for anyone who held *controllership* powers that did not qualify as ownership: powers to use the items they control as they see fit. I endorse this position: recall that 'controllership' does not mean stewardship; it means all the same powers and duties as accrue to an 'owner', the only difference being that the relevant trespassory duties are not owed to the controller.

[50] A very interesting question which I cannot go into here is what the limits of the relevant community are; this correlates with the individuation of property systems. These issues and related questions about inter- rather than intrasystemic trade are questions I cannot address here.

erroneously conceives her rights over her own wealth as akin to her other human rights. Both phrases, I suggest, implicitly assume that all property rights are grounded ultimately by how they serve the property holder.[51]

However, the powerful case for reconceiving free markets as 'controllership' is tempered by the fact that any property rights justified by the common good will be part of a legal system that is continuous with those specific, limited property rights which can be grounded—as in Sections 12.2–12.4—primarily in what they do for the individual right-holder. A 'controllership' system would risk misclassifying the latter, or else complicatedly distinguishing the two types of property where, as we saw in Chapter 12, this distinction is a vague matter (when exactly has something been incorporated into a person's plans in a way that merits respect? When exactly does someone own enough to validate their freedom status?).

Furthermore, it might seem hard to stabilize the concept of 'controllership' so that people genuinely conceive the relevant trespassory duties as owed to the community rather than the 'controller'.[52] Because of the classical liberal's case to allow any given controller to do what she wants (within limits) with her item rather than using it specifically for the community, 'controllership' will typically benefit the 'controller'. Duties whose fulfilment is necessarily a result that is typically of benefit to some person are normally rights for that person—even though (contra Kramer) this is not entailed by such benefits.[53] This might seem to make it likely that there will be a natural slide from 'controllership' back to 'ownership'. On the other hand, one might take heart from, for example, Ihara's claim that Confucian systems of duties— including duties whose fulfilment benefits particular people—can survive without a place for the concept of rights. If this is humanly sustainable, then so might be a reconception of property as 'controllership' rather than rights-based ownership.[54]

Whether or not a move to 'controllership' is possible, I hope to have established in Chapters 12–13 that even if some property rights are natural, recognition-independent rights grounded primarily for the right-holder's own sake, many are justifiable (if at all) only as legal or social creations: systems for the common good, construed either as a shared or an aggregated good.

In addition, the point raised at the end of Section 12.4 bears repeating in this context. Like Chapter 12's arguments, the common good arguments examined in Chapter 13 depend partly on features of humans that seem regrettable and inessential to the valuable characteristics that make humans human. In particular, limits on our altruism and also on our communicative capacities (i.e. our inability to have an all-involving conversation in deciding what to do) are limits necessary to the classical liberal case for private property, but limits that in an ideal-utopian but still in some

---

[51] I will not give references for these generic phrases; I advise readers to look in contemporary British news media.

[52] See Cruft 2013, pp. 220–1.

[53] See Section 5.4: most morally justified duties that are owed to someone necessarily place that party in a position that would typically be beneficial, but there are exception cases like my odd military officer's right to be saluted in the heat of battle.

[54] Ihara 2004.

sense recognizably human world we would largely overcome.[55] By contrast, our need for education, for political participation and for the other goods secured by the human rights of Part II are not regrettable aspects of our humanity; or insofar as they are regrettable (as in the needs generating rights to due process), they are nonetheless unavoidable aspects of our humanity. The needs, interests, or freedoms generating both natural rights and common good cases for property seem, instead, regrettable and not absolutely unavoidable aspects of our human lives. This feature of the cases for property—whether construed as a right or as controllership—need not affect the moral importance or metaphysical status of the trespassory duties and economic liberties justified by these cases. But it should affect our thinking about the possibilities, and should warn us to avoid assuming in all contexts that something like property (as a common-good-grounded system or as an individualistically grounded natural right) is what humans need.[56]

---

[55] The epistemic limitations Hayek highlights (those overcome by a price system) look different to me: less regrettable and more essential to the very nature of humanity.

[56] A large omission in the foregoing is the relation between the natural rights and common good cases for property, and modern environmental problems. Part of the issue concerns the relation between other human rights which environmental problems threaten—human rights to life, health, security—and property rights. But there might also be distinct environmental values that can conflict with property rights. I set this aside for future work. (See e.g. Warnock 2015.)

14

Rights Protecting Performance of Duties

14.1 Do We Need *Rights* Protecting Other-Directed Duties of Office?

Where Chapter 12 defended the possibility of *some* (limited) natural property rights, Chapter 13 argued that *most* trespassory duties are justified by their place within a legal or institutional free market system that serves the common good. And Section 13.3 cast doubt on the claim that this common good justification supports making the relevant trespassory duties correlate with individually held *rights*. Instead, a rival 'controllership' system would more honestly wear its common good grounding on its face. As outlined in Section 13.3, such a 'controllership' system would involve a distribution of Hohfeldian powers and privileges identical to that of the free market system in which we live at the moment (and hence the 'controllership' system would deliver the benefits of the free market highlighted by classical liberals); the only difference would be that trespassory duties would be owed not to the party with the privileges to use the object they protect, and the powers to transfer them, but would instead be owed either to nobody or to the common whose good justifies the system. I doubted whether any instrumental benefits of people's thinking of what they control as protected by *their individual rights*, rather than by *trespassory duties owed to the common*, could justify favouring a system of individual property *rights* instead of 'controllership'.[1]

A central component of my case for 'controllership' is that conceiving common-good-justified property as a *right* is especially likely to be misleading because ownership is not a role defined by duties to use one's property in specific ways. Many other rights justifiable only by how they serve people or values beyond the right-holder protect that right-holder in performing duties of office, duties justified by how they serve others. For example, I mentioned politicians' rights protecting their exercise of duties owed to the people, and doctors' rights protecting their exercise of duties owed to patients. Because the trespassory duties constitutive of ownership protect no such other-directed duty of office, I believe we are especially likely to misconceive property rights as akin to the human rights of Part II: that is, to misconceive them as justified primarily by what they do for the right-holder, as rights justified for the right-holder's sake and hence potentially as natural rights.

---

[1] See Section 13.3.

To avoid this misconception, I believe that common-good-justified property should be reconceived as 'controllership'. I am doubtful that use of the rights concept is fully defensible in conceiving trespassory duties grounded by the common good.

In the current chapter, I ask whether these doubts should also apply to further rights justified by the common good, even those that protect other-directed duties of office. The grounding of these sorts of rights in values and interests beyond the right-holder's good—politicians' rights, doctors' rights, parents' rights, bus drivers' rights, business managers' rights, etc.—should be evident to participants in the system: it is clear that these rights' aim is to protect the right-holder in performing duties whose purpose is to serve others. This is an important point of contrast with common-good-grounded property rights, which do not protect any duty of office for owners. But we might still wonder why the duties in question—duties to allow politicians, doctors, bus drivers, and managers to perform their roles—should be taken as *owed to* the relevant individual parties, rather than as owed to the common good or other further interests or values (health, efficiency) that justify these duties by justifying our creating and sustaining the roles.

This question presses when we note the relationship between being owed a duty (or holding a right) and being respected. When I hold a right or am owed a duty, violation of the duty wrongs me, and Sections 2.4 and 5.3 showed that when the right or duty in question is morally justified, such wronging is *moral* wronging that shows me moral disrespect; and the fact that I would be wronged generates in me a status-based interest in the relevant duties' fulfilment. This is as true of rights or directed duties morally justified by how they serve people or values beyond the right-holder, as it is of those morally grounded for the right-holder's sake. But *why* does impeding the prime minister's declaration of war, or failing to honour a doctor's recommended treatment of someone, or failing to do what one's manager reasonably demands, qualify as disrespect to and wronging of the people who are prime minister, doctor and manager? This seems puzzling when we remember that these people's own good is not what grounds the directed duties in question.[2] Should we rather see the wrongs here as 'really' wrongs to 'the people' (in the PM case), 'the patient' (in the doctor case), or wrongs against the business or against efficiency (the manager case)—and *not* wrongs to the right-holders in question? The case for 'controllership' involved making this move in relation to property rights. Why not make it in all the other cases too?

---

[2] For an initial statement of this puzzle, see Cruft 2013. Someone committed to Owens's Humean conception of resentment mentioned in Chapter 3, note 18, could try to explain this phenomenon by accepting that the duties in question are not *owed to* the relevant parties (prime minister, doctor, manager, etc.) as their rights, but maintaining nonetheless that such parties' resentment at the relevant duties' violation is possible because these are justified duties whose violation harms the parties in question. In effect, this would be to pursue a 'controllership'-type approach to all apparent 'rights' that are justifiable only by factors beyond good to the right-holder—while at the same time carving out a place for resentment of such duties' violation by those who are harmed by the violation. My sense is that this move would be quite radical: it involves denying that the prime minister, the doctor, and so on really have rights here, and thereby involves making their resentment akin to the resentment of Kramer's local shopkeepers when his employer fails to pay his salary (see p. 18). In Section 14.2, I defend a place for genuinely directed duties correlating with rights for the prime minister, the doctor, and so on.

It seems to me unproblematic to regard the parties which the relevant role aims to serve (e.g. people, patient) as owed the duties in question; but why also see the role-bearers (politician, doctor) as right-holders? Of course, cases like the prime minister or the doctor and so on, unlike the property case, do not involve the same risk that we will come to see the rights in question as grounded, like fundamental human rights, primarily by what they do for the right-holder. Nonetheless, we might still ask why we see the relevant duties as owed to (and correlating with rights held by) the office-holders at all, with the attendant implications for wronging, disrespect, and status interests and desires. Are there instrumental or other benefits of seeing the relevant role-protecting duties as correlating with rights for the role-bearer, benefits absent in the property/'controllership' case?

14.2 The Right-Grounding Importance of One's Morally Justified Duties

One distinctive feature of the rights highlighted in the previous section emerges when we notice that all humans have a powerful interest in performing their morally justified duties.[3] The rights highlighted serve this interest: they allow politicians, doctors, parents, managers, etc. to do their morally justified jobs.[4]

We can distinguish unspecific from specific versions of this interest. The unspecific version is the general interest in performing whatever morally justified duties one happens to bear. The specific version is, for example, the prime minister's particular interest in declaring war now, because war is morally required and she has a duty to declare it.

The general, unspecific interest in performing whatever one's morally justified duties require of one is, I venture, a universal human interest: a form or variant of our broad interest in responding to moral reasons (of which morally justified duties are one type—see Section 7.2). Even proponents of the Varied Specific view of the human good sketched in Section 9.1—say, those who deny that all humans share a basic need for political participation or education—must accept that all humans have an interest

---

[3] As before (see Section 8.1), this could be restated in terms of a need or an important freedom.

[4] Wenar's theory of the nature of rights makes role-based interests central (2013). For discussion, see this volume, Sections 2.3–2.5. Wenar claims that 'the historical unity of rights [...] is that rights enabled role-bearers to do their jobs. Divide any office into, first, the duties of that office and, second, the normative features of the office that enable the office-holder to do those duties. Historically, rights formed that second category' (Wenar 2013, p. 206). The striking plausibility of this historical claim should press us to explain these 'enabling' rights, which is my aim in the current chapter: can we justify seeing them as rights, correlating with duties owed to the office-holder? Of course, as Wenar acknowledges, nowadays enabling rights are no longer the core of the rights concept. I am unsure about the historical claim, even though it seems appealing—perhaps it depends partly on the conceptions of property at work in the Franciscan debates on which I am no expert (did early conceptions take property to enable owners to do god's will, unlike in the Hume–Smith–Hayek classical liberal conception?); see also, e.g. Siedentop's claim that Tertullian's translators find 'one of the earliest assertions of a basic right' in the second or early third century as a right to be 'free to worship according to [one's] own convictions' (Siedentop 2014, p. 78, citing Wiles and Santer 1975, p. 227); compare also the apocryphal text, Ecclesiasticus 3:2, referring, according to its translators, to the (enabling?) 'rights of a mother over her son' (thanks to Matthew Kramer for the example). See also Brett 1997 and Tierney 1997.

in acting in the ways required of them by morally justified duty. Of course, not everyone accepts this.[5] But to me it seems undeniable. Someone who claims that the success of her life is entirely independent of whether she fulfils the morally justified duties that bear on her must misunderstand morality, success, or both.

This general, unspecific interest in doing one's duty is not only universal, but also of right-grounding importance in its own right. That is, I suggest the general interest in fulfilling one's morally justified duties is sufficiently important to ground—in Section 8.2's STRONGEST or STRONG A senses—certain uncreated, recognition-independent duties on others to enable or allow one to fulfil one's duties. Section 7.6 tells us that these latter duties, because they are grounded primarily in one's own good, naturally take the form of rights for one. They might include one's natural rights to education and freedom: rights that enable one to be the sort of person who could fulfil whatever morally justified duties (and other moral reasons) happen to bear on one.[6]

Now, one might try to develop these thoughts into an argument that the interest in doing one's duty grounds all the purportedly problematic rights of the previous section (14.1): politicians', doctors', parents', managers' rights to be unimpeded, protected, or assisted in fulfilling their duties. One such line of argument—which I will label (A)—would maintain that the rather specific duties that protect or enable people to fulfil their roles (e.g. our duties not to impede the prime minister's declaration of war, a doctor's assistant's duty to help with a diagnosis, an employee's duties to implement her manager's directives) are institutional or legal determin-ations or operationalizations of a very general rights-correlative duty to help people perform their morally justified duties (whatever they happen to be), or at least to refrain from impeding them, a duty grounded by the *unspecific* interest in doing whatever will turn out to be one's duty—rather as legal human rights determine or operationalize more general natural human rights grounded on important interests, as outlined in Sections 9.3–9.5. This argument might be bolstered by the related claim—here labelled (B)—that *specific* interests in doing one's particular morally justified duties naturally justify (in one of my STRONG senses) specific duties on others to protect or enable one to do one's particular duties, which again institutions or law determine or operationalize. If this paragraph's lines of argument succeed, they would require a significant change in how I have presented politicians' rights, doctors' rights, parents' rights, and bus drivers' rights. These would turn out, despite my earlier claims, to be justifiable for the right-holder's sake; hence their vindication

---

[5] See e.g. Nietzsche 2011 [1895], pt 11.

[6] This is not to deny either that other interests, needs or freedoms also work in a STRONGEST or STRONG A way to ground rights to education and freedom, nor is it to deny that duties to educate and allow people freedom can be justified on powerful common good grounds and related grounds other than the right-holder's good (see penultimate paragraph of Section 8.2). Some might also worry that allowing my interest in doing my duty to ground further duties for others generates a regress: for these further duties will be duties that the relevant others have the same interest in performing, thereby generating further duties to allow others to perform these duties. I see no harm in this regress.

as rights would be akin to the vindication I offered for applying the rights concept to human rights—indeed they might seem to be forms of human right.[7]

In what follows, I reject (B) but give a limited endorsement to (A). Either approach might seem prey to the problems I identified for Raz's attempt to argue that, e.g. parents' interests justify duties because serving parents' interests serves children.[8] But the approaches under consideration do *not* say that a given interest justifies a duty (and hence qualifies the interest-bearer as a right-holder correlative to that duty) simply if it is served by that duty—that would multiply rights absurdly in the manner outlined in Section 2.2. Nor do they say that being served *necessarily* by a duty must make the duty owed to one.[9] Instead, the approaches under consideration maintain that an interest in doing one's duty (either (A) unspecific or (B) specific) genuinely *grounds or justifies* further duties—e.g. to assistance as a doctor—rather than simply being served by them. This claim can seem rather plausible, thereby delivering the conclusion that, say, the doctor's right to assistance is justified for the doctor's own sake (as well as for the patient's sake).

But I think on close inspection that the (B) approach is mistaken and the (A) approach is important but limited in its implications. In the current paragraph and the following two I look at approach (B), before returning to (A). We can begin to see what is wrong with approach (B) by noting that anyone who focuses on *the doctor's* specific interest in doing her duty by diagnosing the patient in front of her seems to be focused on the wrong person: surely someone who wants to understand why the assistant should help the doctor needs to focus on *the patient's* interests, rather than the doctor's. Furthermore, the doctor's specific interest in doing her duty in this context should in a sense be no more than an interest in whatever interests or goods ground the duty in question—which in this case will be the patient's interests, plus perhaps wider health values. A focus on her own role as a duty-bearer would be an aberrant self-focus on the part of the doctor.[10]

As offered, these remarks do not explain what is wrong with regarding the doctor's rights to assistance in performance of her duties of office as rights grounded for her sake on her specific interest in doing the particular duty she faces in context. But they hint at the following explanation. For a doctor's interest in fulfilling her duty to diagnose a particular patient to take the contextually specific form it actually takes, a complete moral justification of that specific duty has to be in place. To avoid circularity, this justification must be based on goods or interests *other than* the doctor's own specific interest in fulfilling the duty in question: typically the

---

[7] See Chapters 9–10; perhaps the rights in question would not be 'everyone's business'. I would also have to retract Section 2.5's claim that whether, say, legal rights to child benefit payments are borne by parents or only by children is a matter lawmakers can simply decide as they wish.

[8] See discussion in Section 2.2.   [9] See Kramer's theory, as discussed in Section 2.3.

[10] In the particular circumstances, the doctor might turn out to have additional interests at stake in doing her duty: she might stand to earn a lot from the diagnosis, or she might care especially for this patient compared to others; we should set aside these additional contingent interests as irrelevant to the question of whether, in general across the board, we can justify regarding duties that allow or help a doctor to do her duty as *owed to* that doctor. For we cannot be confident that these additional contingent interests will accompany every specific duty determined by the doctor's role; by contrast a specific moral interest in performing her specific particular duty accompanies every one of her morally justified duties: this, I have said, is a moral interest in the further interests and values that justify her particular justified duty.

justification might be determined by how the relevant diagnostic behaviour by the doctor will in this context serve both the patient's interests and the interests of the wider public in permissible ways of delivering health (perhaps conjoined with the fact that the doctor was not forced into her profession). These factors work together morally to justify the doctor's specific duty to diagnose the patient in front of her. Now, importantly, they might *also* work together as a full moral justification for the further enabling or assisting duties borne by the doctor's assistant, duties to assist the doctor in performing the diagnosis. In particular, *if* the doctor's specific or particular interest in doing her duty in this context justifies such enabling-assisting duties borne by her assistant, then the factors justifying the original duty (the doctor's duty to diagnose) must *already* have justified the relevant enabling-assisting duties. This is because a specific interest in performing a specific duty is 'transparent': it amounts to no more than an interest in the factors that justify the duty: in the case of the doctor's interest in diagnosing the patient, it amounts to an interest in the patient's interests and perhaps also in the wider public's interests. For this interest of the doctor's to justify the assistant's enabling-assisting duties, these assistant's duties have to have already been justified by the interests (of patient and public) that justify the doctor's initial specific duty.

To put this in general terms, I claim that whatever factors make it the case that someone has a specific, particular moral interest in fulfilling one of their specific morally justified duties (i.e. whatever factors ground the specific duty for that person) must, if that specific interest justifies further assistive duties borne by others, at the same time already justify these further assistive duties. To deny this, and hence to allow that the specific, particular interest in doing one's specific duty could play an independent role in justifying others' duties to assist one in performing one's own duty, would belie the interest's specific, particularized character as simply a moral interest in whatever moral factors ground one's own duty in the context. It would be to give this interest separate moral weight of its own.[11] But a doctor's specific interest in doing her duty by the patient in front of her cannot have a life of its own like this.[12] Instead it must be 'transparent', comprising no more than the interests and values that justify the original duty itself; it follows that for it to ground assistive duties to help the doctor the relevant interests and values must already succeed in justifying such assistive duties. We should conclude that even if assistive duties to aid the doctor in performing her role (or similar assistive duties aiding others in doing their

---

[11] At worst, giving this interest-in-doing-one's-duty-in-this-particular-context separate moral weight might involve in principle allowing that the interest could weigh against the interests grounding the initial duty. This would be absurd. It would be like allowing the possibility that the doctor's interest in 'doing her duty by the patient' could justify an invasive diagnostic procedure that would damage the patient (and perhaps also damage wider health values). I recognize that the idea of giving the relevant interest 'separate moral weight of its own' need not be taken in this most absurd way; but my view is that *any* approach which offers some reasonable account of giving the relevant interest 'moral weight of its own' will fail, because the interest should be 'transparent' in the manner outlined in the main text.

[12] By contrast, I suggest that it is not absurd, as Section 8.3 suggests at pp. 127–29, to allow that some individual's interest in their group's self-determination could have weight independent of the weight of the group's interest in self-determination. An individual's interest in her group's success need not, in my sense, be 'transparent' relative to the group's interest, in the way that one's specific interest in doing one's duty is 'transparent' relative to the goods which morally justify the duty.

duty) can be justified by the doctor's (or other role-bearer's) specific, particular interests in fulfilling the morally justified duties she bears in context, such assistive duties are not therefore justified for the doctor's (or other role-bearer's) sake. For their grounding by the role-bearer's *specific interest in fulfilling her original duty* presupposes their grounding on other grounds—namely, by those goods or values (of patient, people, common good) that justify the original duty. The role-bearer's own specific interest in fulfilling the original duty can play no independent role in grounding the assistive duties.

So much for approach (B). But what about approach (A), based on the unspecific interest in fulfilling whatever duties one happens to bear? I allowed at the start of this section that that can have a distinct weight of its own, justifying some duties that plausibly constitute the agent's human rights to education and minimal freedom: preconditions for pursuing any morally justified duty that might bear on one. Should we see the doctor's assistant's duty, or the people's duty not to impede their politicians, and so on, as conventional determinations of a general right justified 'for the right-holder's sake' on this general unspecific interest? I think we can indeed see the unspecific interest as playing a role in justifying a general, unspecific natural right (to respect for and assistance in carrying out one's role as a moral agent) that the relevant precise rights determine. The fact that these precise rights are also justifiable on other grounds (such as on grounds of the patient's interests and wider health values, in the example introduced earlier) does not exclude a justification in which the unspecific interest plays a role. (Compare my claim, in Section 8.2, that human rights to free speech can be justified on the basis of the right-holder's interests in speaking even though alternative common good justifications for the same rights—in which the right-holder's interests need play no part—also succeed.) The key point is that the unspecific interest in fulfilling one's morally justified duties whatever they are is, unlike its specific siblings, not wholly 'transparent' relative to the interests and values that ground those duties. It is an interest in being able to play one's part whatever that part might be, an interest in one's own moral agency, in a sense an interest in being a full active member of society. It can thereby play a relevantly independent duty-grounding part, and it can play this part recognition-independently.

Nonetheless many of the particular determinations of the general natural right to respect and assistance for one's moral agency considered in this section—such as the doctor's particular right to her assistant's aid, or the teacher's right to timely submission of work—are *not required* if the general right in question is to be fulfilled. In this respect, the relation between the relevant determinations and the general right might seem like that between particular institutional welfare rights and the natural human right to welfare, as outlined in Sections 9.3–9.5. But I think the relation between the determining rights and the general one is weaker in most of the cases under consideration in the current section. Some among a range of possible institutional or social determinations—say, an institutional right to unemployment payments, or to state-supplied paid employment, or to a healthy private employment market providing many opportunities, or to alternative non-employment ways of contributing to our social good that will provide one with a livelihood—need to be adopted if our human welfare rights are to be fulfilled. Abolishing one such way of delivering the natural welfare right without replacing it with another will leave the relevant welfare right violated. By contrast, it is not clear that a doctor's natural right to respect and assistance with her moral agency requires a right that her assistant aid her diagnosis *or any similar duty at all that would assist her specifically in performing her duties to her patient.* A system without such assistive duties might be bad for patients and wider health values, but the harm and difficulty it would present to doctors would not constitute a violation of the natural right generated by the doctor's unspecific interest in fulfilling her moral duties.

The argument of the previous paragraph depends on the claim that the relevant assistive duties are not sufficiently tightly necessitated by the party's unspecific interest in doing her duty to be grounded or justified predominantly by this interest. Now in Section 7.3 (p. 99), I argued that a party's interest can naturally ground a duty to perform some action PHI even if PHI is not strictly *necessary* to the serving or securing of that interest. Nonetheless, PHI has to be in some sense made naturally apt by the interest: as respecting, instantiating or serving it (among other options). My claim in the previous paragraph is that the doctor's unspecific interest in doing her duty does not naturally make her assistant's action apt in such an unavoidably duty-generating way. Nor does it make such action part of a disjunction that is naturally required.

This is an important point of contrast with the legal human rights of Chapters 9–10, but it is a non-sharp contrast of degree. As noted in Section 10.1, some legal human rights might be our local optional way of adding further determinate protection to some natural human right that could as readily be secured without any such protection.[13] In most of the cases at hand in the current chapter—the doctor's right to her assistant's work, the tutor's right to timely submission of work, the business manager's right to issue specific directives—the relation between the specific determinate right and the unspecific natural right to do one's duty is loose and optional. A morally justified system could but need not adopt some such assistive or similar rights. Of course a lot turns on the precise cases: secretly replacing the doctor's medicine with arsenic would be a direct attack on her general interest in doing her duty, and this grounds a duty not to do this which is naturally, non-optionally owed to the doctor (as well, obviously, as to the patient). Similarly, some might think that preventing the prime minister from declaring war when her power to do so is a morally justified power and she has a duty to do so does impede her general interest in doing her duty in a way that violates her general, unspecific right—but this is complicated by many issues including epistemic concerns about whether war is ever justifiable. Nonetheless, the assistant's duty to help the doctor, or the student's duty to submit work to the tutor on time, are in my view clearly not so tightly required by the doctor's or tutor's unspecific interest in doing their duty or right to be able to do their duty, and hence they are duties whose direction (as owed to the doctor or tutor) is an optional matter: we can choose to make them owed to the doctor and tutor as their rights, but we need not.

---

[13] See the cases discussed at pp. 170–71.

In the latter cases, then, this might seem to leave us with Section 14.1's question unanswered: why should we regard the relevant assistive duties—of the doctor's assistant to help with the diagnosis, or of the tutor or the business manager—as *rights borne by the relevant role-occupier*? Perhaps the arsenic case can be explained as the doctor's right because of its tight relation to her unspecific natural right to do her duty.[14] But why not instead regard the duties to assist the doctor in her diagnosis or to submit work to the tutor on time as owed to the patient or the student and not the doctor and tutor? Similarly, why not regard duties to do as the business manager specifies as owed to the wider economy whose good plays the major role in justifying the duties in question—and *not* to the manager? These duties are not necessitated tightly enough by the relevant parties' general unspecific interest in doing their duties for us to be conceptually compelled to regard them as their rights.

Here we might look for instrumental benefits in doctors, tutors, etc. conceiving as 'their rights' the duties others bear to assist or enable them to pursue their roles. Perhaps this makes them better at pursuing their roles.[15] But we can also find non-instrumental reasons to favour the use of the rights concept here. When we create or sustain a role defined by a duty (such as the roles of doctor, politician, or bus driver), this has a major effect on the moral agency of those who come to occupy the role: the role-defining duty becomes one of the role-occupier's main morally justified purposes. We have seen that her important human interest in doing her morally justified duty is shaped or concretized by this role. Now, if optional, non-necessary assistive duties supporting the performance of the relevant role-defined duty are *rights* for the role-occupier, Chapter 4 shows us that this means that we who bear the assistive duties are required to conceive the role-occupier second-personally as a 'you' who our protective-enabling action affects, and the role-bearer is required to conceive herself first-personally as so affected by us. Even if the parties whose good justifies the role (e.g. patients, students) are also right-holders (thereby reflecting their good's role-justifying status), by making the duty-bearing role-occupier a right-holder we fittingly mark the distinctive, major moral importance of her moral agency—that is, the moral importance of her interest in doing her moral duty, an interest given shape by the relevant role. Even though—as argued in the current section—this interest in doing her duty will in many cases not play a large grounding part in justifying the assistive duties in question, it is such an important and distinctive interest, and one that is shaped so decisively by the duties in question, that we do well to reflect this fact by characterizing these duties as the role-bearer's rights.[16]

---

[14] Thanks to Antony Duff for pressing me on this case.

[15] Compare the similar possibility that conceiving items of property as protected by 'my rights' has instrumental benefits—see Section 13.3, pp. 245–46.

[16] Note that Wenar's theory of the nature of rights accommodates rights to perform role-based duties especially well, for any role-based duty confers on the role-bearer a role-based desire to perform it; hence any duty to enable or refrain from impeding such performance will be owed to the role-bearer, on Wenar's theory (2013). Earlier, I argue that Wenar's theory wrongly ascribes rights even when a possessor of a role-based want is not a party owed the duty in question—as in the case of a duty-to-salute-military-officers owed solely to the monarch and not officers, or a duty-to-make-child-benefit-payments owed solely to children and not parents (see Section 2.5). But the strong appeal of and insight in Wenar's theory, I suggest, lies in the appeal of regarding duties which assist a role-bearer in performing her duty of office as owed to

This is not to revert to the general position, rejected in Chapter 2, that any duty whose fulfilment serves someone's important interests must be *owed to* that party as her right. Rather, it reflects the very special importance of the universal interest in doing one's morally justified duty, and the distinctive relationship between this interest and the legal or institutional roles which give it a particular shape for a particular moral agent. It is not conceptually compulsory to regard the relevant assistive duties as the role-bearer's rights, as it would be if they were fully groundable for the role-bearer's sake.[17] If this were conceptually compulsory, then we would always have to conceive useful duties to salute military officers as owed to such officers, and duties to make child benefit payments as owed to parents—as denied in Section 2.5. Instead, making such duties *rights* for the relevant role-bearer is a good idea, but not required: it fittingly reflects their relation to the role-bearer's interest in doing her duty. We should *choose* to make such duties rights, even though this is not conceptually required, because the role-bearer's interests are not what justify the duties in question.

14.3 Property as an Outlier

If the argument of the preceding section is correct, then property rights on the classical liberal conception—unlike, say, property protecting the owner's fulfilment of her duties of stewardship or of Lockean divine commands to use resources and not waste them—are a real outlier. Other than the cases discussed in Chapter 12 (which, we should remember, might well be quite common), they are not justified for the owner's own sake like the human rights of Part II, but nor are they justified specifically to protect the owner in performing some further morally justified duty, such as the duties of office of Sections 14.1–14.2. It is doubtful to me that their status as individual legal-institutional 'rights' can therefore be fully justified (except perhaps occasionally on contingent, instrumental grounds) even if a conceptual switch to controllership would be difficult to effect.

Now, it might seem that we could run the same argument defending common-good-grounded property as a right that we ran in Section 14.2 defending duties to assist the doctor as her right. For don't trespassory duties protecting objects one can use help one pursue and fulfil one's own morally justified duties?[18] But if they do this, they do so contingently. As noted in Sections 13.3 and 14.1, ownership on the classical liberal conception carries no defining other-directed duty of office that the owner must fulfil, as the roles of doctor or politician do, for example. The classical liberal case for property claims that the most efficient and productive results are obtained when owners are free to do what they wish (within familiar limits) with their property. For trespassory duties defended on this basis, there is no *necessary*

---

that role-bearer. We can often choose whether to make them so owed, and frequently we would be justified in so choosing.

[17] See my defence, in Section 7.6, of the thesis that duties justified for some individual's (or specific group's) sake must be that person's rights. This is the idea that Raz's account of rights in general succeeds as a sufficient but not a necessary condition on a duty's being someone's right.

[18] For arguments broadly along these lines, see MacLeod 2015 and Schaab 2017.

relation between the trespassory duties protecting objects one can use and one's pursuit of one's own morally justified duties. Any such relation depends on contingencies and is thus much less solid a ground for taking trespassory duties as their beneficiary's rights. The case for regarding common-good-grounded trespassory duties as 'controllership' rather than as the individual beneficiary's rights remains strong, I think.

In defence of this pro-'controllership' conclusion, consider the modern political cliché which decries 'rights without responsibilities'.[19] Of course this can mean many things, but it is often used to attack the idea that one could justify a right for a particular party without also justifying duties borne by that party. In response to this, Part II can be read as a defence of the idea that sometimes the good of an individual can indeed on its own be sufficient to make others duty-bound to that individual, independently of whether the individual themselves bears any duties. But Section 14.2 might make us wonder whether the politicians' criticism has more force against rights that do not fit Part II's model: rights that are not justifiable for the right-holder's own sake, but that also—as 'rights without responsibilities'—do not protect the right-holder in pursuing her own further morally justified duties, such as duties of office. I would suggest that the property rights of the classical liberals are problematic 'rights without responsibilities' *par excellence*: rights that are not justified by their importance to the right-holder but rather by their importance to the common good, but that do not protect any morally justified ownership-defining duty to serve the common good. We would better register such rights' grounds, and their relation to the right-holder, if we conceived them along the controllership lines of Section 13.3, rather than making them individually borne rights.

A 'controllership' system that would more honestly reflect property's common good grounding could take trespassory duties to be undirected, or to be owed to the community of which the 'controller' is a part. Either way, violation of these duties would not wrong or show disrespect to the 'controller' beyond the disrespect shown to the community within which the controller lives. It is worth noting that this position can still make some moral sense of the psychological feeling of violation people report on being burgled or having their pockets picked. For the property rights in these cases—at least if they do not involve some lavish palace but rather a modest home—can plausibly be accommodated as 'rights for the right-holder's sake' along the lines of Sections 12.2–12.4. Furthermore, it is also worth noting that even within the 'controllership' system, the trespassory duties over which I am a 'controller' will implicate my interests, for the common good is essentially comprised by my interests—alongside everyone else's (see Section 13.2).[20]

Note that the previous section (14.2) established that we need not make this move for many other rights grounded by how they serve the common good, or other values beyond the right-holder's good. For most of these further rights are not 'rights without responsibilities', but rather rights protecting role-defined duties, where both the duties and their protective rights are justified by the same common good

---

[19] As with Chapter 13, note 51 above, a glance at the British media should supply examples. For a precursor, see perhaps Bradley 1962 [1876].

[20] See Owens's Humean conception of resentment at note 2 above.

or further value beyond the right-holder's good. Perhaps there are some cases to put alongside property: I wonder about rights that accrue to a monarch who, in a modern constitutional setup, no longer holds any duties of office. But with the exception of property, I think such outliers are rare, at least among rights held by individual humans. Most rights held by individuals—or at least most Hohfeldian claim-rights held by individuals—justifiable primarily by how they serve values beyond good to the right-holder are legal or institutional rights protecting role- or office-based duties, in which the relevant role or office gives shape to the right-holder's important interest in fulfilling her moral duties. As such, the 'rights' concept is apt for characterizing the rights in question.

We should end by asking what this implies about the rights of groups and of artificial entities, such as business corporations. My argument, I suggest, favours regarding businesses, like individuals, as 'controllers' rather than right-holders *in relation to all the trespassory duties over which free market capitalism gives them control*. Because any given business's interest or 'good' lacks moral importance in itself, businesses cannot hold natural property rights of the kind defended in Sections 12.2–12.4—though by contrast some natural groupings including families and nations perhaps can. Yet for the latter groups, as for individual humans, property that cannot be grounded as a natural right will be best conceived as 'controllership'. What about further duties that serve such groups, duties not groundable in the group's own good and that are different from the trespassory duties constitutive of controllership? Examples include duties of political obligation to the state, and employees' duties to do as asked by a business that employs them. Where such obedient or assistive actions help the group or corporate entity in question to fulfil their own morally justified duties, we can then run Section 14.2's argument in favour of regarding the relevant duties of obedience or assistance as owed to the entities in question (state, business) as their 'rights', even though their interests do not ground the relevant duties to obey or assist. I think this approach can vindicate our use of the rights concept in relation to the rights of states and businesses.

But it is worth noting that the business case is particularly debatable. This is partly because it is unclear what the morally justified duties specific to businesses qua businesses are: are legal or conventional duties requiring maximization of shareholder value, or production of profit, morally justified? Does the classical liberal argument that we get best results if we take individual owners to be allowed to do what they want with their property (within familiar limits) apply as readily to businesses' actions? If so, we might begin to doubt whether businesses themselves (as opposed to their members) bear the kind of morally justified duties of office needed to underpin an argument like that in Section 14.2.[21] And even if the latter worry can be addressed, we might also ask whether the moral agency of businesses deserves the respect that individuals' interests in fulfilling their moral duties clearly do.

---

[21] This, of course, is not to reject the idea of businesses possessing the same duties as others to respect human rights, plus further duties of corporate social responsibility. I simply question whether businesses bear distinctive morally justified duties qua businesses, as doctors do qua doctors or politicians do in their role, etc.

The latter points tell against conceiving our duties in relation to businesses as owed to them as their 'rights'. I do not see the points as decisive, but this clearly requires more discussion, including consideration of reasons beyond those considered in the current chapter for the use of the 'rights' concept in relation to duties ungroundable by the right-holder's interests. Nonetheless for present purposes we can already draw the conclusion that in many cases we can justifiably use the concept of 'rights' even when the duties in question are not groundable by what they do for the right-holder. This will include rights borne by individuals, groups and corporate entities like states—and, more arguably, businesses—which protect the right-holder in performing their own morally justified duties.[22]

---

[22] I would add that we can also use it to refer to the rights of humanity, in Section 9.3's sense: rights to the 'assistance' of its members through actions that will help humanity fulfil its duties.

15

Conclusion
A Partial Vindication of Rights

So: how defensible is our use of the concept of a right? In Part I, I developed a new Addressive first-/second-personal analysis of this concept, and explained that, so analysed, legal-conventional rights can exist wherever we choose to create and sustain them, while natural rights—that is, duties whose status as someone's right is recognition-independent—exist for a party whenever that party's good grounds the relevant duties. In Part II, I defended our use of this rights concept to refer to human rights, conceived both as natural rights that owe their existence to the right-holder's good, and as legal-conventional rights that are founded on and determine or operationalize these natural rights. And I added that distinctively *human* rights are plausibly conceived as 'everyone's business' in Chapter 10's various senses. Further, my defence of human rights encompasses socio-economic rights to goods and services as readily as civil and political rights, and, in Section 9.4, I stressed the importance of the state's role as duty-bearer. Now, in Part III, I have argued that while the rights concept is appropriate when applied both to assistive duties that serve the right-holder's interest in doing her duty, and to a small but notable class of natural property rights, it is harder to defend its use to refer to trespassory duties justified along classical liberal lines by how they serve the common good. The latter property 'rights' are, I argue, better conceived as 'controllership': as trespassory duties that are justifiably personally controlled by someone in a role akin to that of 'owner', but whose violation would wrong the community at large rather than the specific 'controller'.

The result is a partial vindication of the rights concept: it is appropriate in human rights contexts but not in referring to some cases of property. Nonetheless, on the latter point about property it is worth recalling my claim, in Sections 5.1 and 7.7, that we can justifiably create duties as rights whenever so doing would be useful for any plausible instrumental reasons, and there might be as yet unexplored instrumental cases for the psychological usefulness of thinking of property as 'mine by right'.[1] I would, however, register my concern about the likelihood of any assessor's (including my own) potential willingness to rationalize the status quo.

There are two important qualifications to add to Part II's claim that we are justified in using the rights concept to refer to human rights. One is that this is not a defence of the ideological misuses to which the concept is often put: for example, misuses as a

---

[1] See Section 13.3; compare also the discussion of businesses' rights at the end of Section 14.3.

pretext for war, or misuses which overlook a particular agent's lack of standing to use the concept (e.g. suppose a state criticizes others for human rights violations but is itself a violator), or misuses which embody morally pernicious conceptions of the relationships between relevant parties.[2] Related cases are uses of the human rights concept which overlook some agent's or group's justifiable framing of the issues in non-rights terms. I have argued that in cases where a party's good naturally grounds duties borne by others—and in cases in which legal duties are founded on such natural duties—use of the rights concept is illuminating as a way of drawing attention to the moral structure in question, in particular, to the Addressive relationship between the party and duty-bearers that this moral structure entails. Use of the rights concept in such cases deepens our understanding and is to that extent justifiable. But it does not follow that alternative conceptual schemes will not illuminate other features that rights language obscures.

A second qualification involves recalling Section 8.3's point that theorists who question the very idea that we can—at least on some formal level—distinguish an individual's good from wider values and goods will be unpersuadable by my defence of the rights concept. I have assumed that we can make sense of the individual–group distinction underpinning my defence. But it is important to remember this limitation.

Suppose my conclusions are correct. What does this imply for our behaviour? Interestingly, my defence of the rights concept works primarily in terms of its contribution to our understanding rather than to our behaviour. As noted at the outset, whether trespassory duties or duties to allow someone to speak freely (to take two examples) are rights or not need make no difference to our overt behaviour, but only to how we should *think* about the parties involved. We might disappointedly conclude that there is no direct practical payoff. That would not mean no payoff whatsoever, though. Recognizing that rights are constituted by the requirements of Addressive first- and second-personal apprehension outlined in Chapter 4 involves recognizing that the practical normative realm is not perfected simply by people's doing their duty, nor even simply by—as Hills would have it[3]—people's acting on their duties while understanding these duties as theirs. If rights are constituted by formal requirements of Addressive first- and second-personal conception, then the practical normative realm formally requires capable parties who are owed duties first-personally to recognize their 'acted on' position in relation to these duties, and it formally requires the relevant duty-bearers to conceive those they act on second-personally as addressees, as potential 'yous' with their own first-personality. Vindicating a place for rights in our world therefore involves vindicating a place for a formally connected, non-alienated conception of normativity: a distinctive form of normativity that speaks to the agent in her guise as 'acting-on-others-conceived-second-personally'.[4] This is not a purely esoteric, intellectual payoff: getting our thinking right about our relationships to each other is enormously important. And

---

[2] One instance would be the 'savages–victims–saints' construction which Mutua plausibly finds in many uses of the idea of human rights: a construction in which violators are taken as 'savages', right-holders as 'victims' and enforcers or upholders of the rights as 'saints' (Mutua 2002, ch. 1).

[3] Hills 2015.   [4] See Section 7.4, p. 102.

of course getting our thinking right has knock-on effects for our actions. I outline some of these effects through Parts II and III—by highlighting the importance of recognizing that natural human rights are groundable relatively independently of goods beyond the right-holder's,[5] and by highlighting the dangers of mistakenly taking all property rights to be akin to such human rights.[6]

But we might still wonder: what can we conclude, from my argument in partial vindication of the rights concept, about the relative importance of different rights or of rights vis-à-vis undirected duties and undemandable reasons? We should not conclude that natural rights grounded for the right-holder's sake must necessarily take priority over created conventional rights, nor indeed over undirected natural duties, if they conflict. What my argument tells us, instead, is where to look when wondering about the relative importance of a right. Rights' importance depends on the goods or values they serve, the goods or values that justify our respect for them and (in the case of legal-conventional rights) our creating and sustaining them. My argument tells us that to examine these values, we should look at the right-holder's own good, if the right is a human right of the type discussed in Part II, or at wider values if it is one of the common-good-grounded property rights (better construed as 'controllership') considered in Chapter 13, or one of the role-supporting rights considered in Chapter 14. We should thus avoid fixating on the right-holder's own good when judging the relative importance of property rights or the rights protecting duties of office; but such a focus of attention is *not* out of place—despite conservatives' protestations to the contrary—when judging the importance of our basic human rights.

---

[5] See Section 10.6.
[6] See the discussion of proto-libertarian misconceptions at the end of Section 13.3.

Bibliography

Ajei, Martin Odei. 2015. 'Human Rights in a Moderate Communitarian Political Framework', *South African Journal of Philosophy* 34, 491–503.

Alexievich, Svetlana. 2016. *Second-Hand Time*, trans. B. Shayevich (London: Fitzcarraldo).

Altham, J. E. J. 1985. 'Wicked Promises', in I. Hacking, ed., *Exercises in Analysis: Essays by Students of Casimir Lewy* (Cambridge: Cambridge University Press), 1–22.

American Anthropological Association. 1947. 'Statement on Human Rights', *American Anthropologist* 49, 539–43.

Anderson, Elizabeth. 1993. *Value in Ethics and Economics* (Cambridge, MA: Harvard University Press).

Anscombe, G. E. M. 1981a. 'Rules, Rights and Promises', in her *Ethics, Religion, and Politics: Collected Philosophical Papers, Vol. III* (Oxford: Blackwell), 97–103.

Anscombe, G. E. M. 1981b. 'The First Person', in her *Metaphysics and Philosophy of Mind: Collected Philosophical Papers, Vol. II* (Minneapolis: University of Minnesota Press), 21–36.

Applbaum, Arthur Isak. 1999. *Ethics for Adversaries: The Morality of Roles in Public and Professional Life* (Princeton, NJ: Princeton University Press).

Aristotle. 2002. *Nicomachean Ethics*, trans. Christopher Rowe, intr. and commentary Sarah Broadie (Oxford: Oxford University Press).

Arpaly, Nomy. 2003. *Unprincipled Virtue: An Inquiry into Moral Agency* (Oxford: Oxford University Press).

Ashford, Elizabeth. 2015. 'A Moral Inconsistency Argument for a Basic Human Right to Subsistence', in R. Cruft, S. M. Liao, and M. Renzo, eds, *Philosophical Foundations of Human Rights* (Oxford: Oxford University Press), 515–34.

Attas, Daniel. 2012. 'Private Property', in A. Marmor, ed., *The Routledge Companion to Philosophy of Law* (London: Routledge), 277–90.

Babb, Matthew. 2016. 'The Essential Indexicality of Intentional Action', *The Philosophical Quarterly* 66, 439–57.

Baldwin, James. 1979. 'On Language, Race and the Black Writer', *The Los Angeles Times* 29 April, available at http://marktwainstudies.com/wp-content/uploads/2017/02/Baldwin-1979-.pdf.

Barry, Christian, 2005. 'Applying the Contribution Principle', *Metaphilosophy* 36, 210–27.

Becker, Lawrence C. 1977. *Property Rights: Philosophic Foundations* (London: Routledge & Kegan Paul).

Beitz, Charles. 2009. *The Idea of Human Rights* (Oxford: Oxford University Press).

Benhabib, Seyla. 1992. 'The Generalized and the Concrete Other', in her *Situating the Self: Gender, Community and Postmodernism in Contemporary Ethics* (Cambridge: Polity), 148–77.

Bennett, Jonathan. 1974. 'The Conscience of Huckleberry Finn', *Philosophy* 49, 123–34.

Bentham, Jeremy. 1987 [1789]. 'Anarchical Fallacies', in J. Waldron, ed., *'Nonsense Upon Stilts': Bentham, Burke, and Marx on the Rights of Man* (London: Methuen), 29–76.

Benvenisti, Eyal and Alon Harel. Forthcoming. 'Embracing the Tension between National and International Human Rights Law: The Case for Discordant Parity', *International Journal of Constitutional Law*.

Besson, Samantha. 2015. 'Human Rights and Constitutional Law: Patterns of Mutual Validation and Legitimation', in R. Cruft, S. M. Liao, and M. Renzo, eds, *Philosophical Foundations of Human Rights* (Oxford: Oxford University Press), 279–299.

Bowen, Joseph. 2020. 'Beyond Normative Control: Against the Will Theory of Rights', *Canadian Journal of Philosophy* 50: 427–43.

Bowen, Joseph. ms. 'Why More Than What Happens Matters: Robust Rights and Harmless Wronging'.

Bradley, F. H. 1962 [1876]. 'My Station and Its Duties', in his *Ethical Studies* (Oxford: Clarendon).

Brett, Annabel. 1997. *Liberty, Rights and Nature: Individual Rights in Later Scholastic Thought* (Cambridge: Cambridge University Press).

Broome, John. 2013. *Rationality through Reasoning* (Oxford: Blackwell).

Brownlee, Kimberley. 2016. 'The Lonely Heart Breaks: On the Right to be a Social Contributor', *Aristotelian Society Supplementary Volume* 90, 27–48.

Brudner, Alan. 2013. 'Private Property and Public Welfare', in J. E. Penner and H. E. Smith, eds, *Philosophical Foundations of Property Law* (Oxford: Oxford University Press), 68–98.

Buchanan, Allen. 1988. *Ethics, Efficiency, and the Market* (Totowa, NJ: Rowman and Littlefield).

Buchanan, Allen. 2013. *The Heart of Human Rights* (Oxford: Oxford University Press).

Buss, Sarah. 2012. 'The Value of Humanity', *Journal of Philosophy* 59, 1–39.

Bykvist, Krister. 2009. 'No Good Fit: Why the Fitting Attitude Analysis of Value Fails', *Mind* 118, 1–30.

Carter, Ian. 2011. 'Respect and the Basis of Equality', *Ethics* 121: 679–710.

Chambers, Clare. 2013. 'The Marriage-Free State', *Proceedings of the Aristotelian Society* 113, 123–43.

Chan, Joseph. 1999. 'A Confucian Perspective on Human Rights for Contemporary China', in J. R. Bauer and D. A. Bell, eds, *The East Asian Challenge for Human Rights* (Cambridge: Cambridge University Press), 212–37.

Cheneval, Francis. 2019. 'Entrepreneurial Rights as Human Rights', in J. Queralt and B. van der Vossen, eds, *Economic Liberties and Human Rights* (London: Routledge), 114–132.

Christman, John. 1994. *The Myth of Property: Toward an Egalitarian Theory of Ownership* (Oxford: Oxford University Press).

Clarke, Alison. 2015. 'Property, Human Rights and Communities', in T. Xu and J. Allain, eds, *Property and Human Rights in a Global Context* (Oxford: Hart), 19–40.

Cohen, G. A. 1995. *Self-Ownership, Freedom, and Equality* (Cambridge: Cambridge University Press).

Collins, Stephanie. 2013. 'Collectives' Duties and Collectivization Duties', *Australasian Journal of Philosophy* 91: 231–48.

Cornell, Nicolas. 2015. 'Wrongs, Rights, and Third Parties', *Philosophy and Public Affairs* 43, 109–43.

Cranston, Maurice. 1973. *What Are Human Rights?* (London: Bodley Head).

Cruft, Rowan. 2004. 'Rights: Beyond Interest Theory and Will Theory?', *Law and Philosophy* 23, 347–97.

Cruft, Rowan. 2006. 'Against Individualistic Justifications of Property Rights', *Utilitas* 18, 154–72.

Cruft, Rowan. 2010. 'On the Non-instrumental Value of Basic Rights', *Journal of Moral Philosophy* 7, 441–61.

Cruft, Rowan. 2012. 'Human Rights as Rights', in G. Ernst and J.-C. Heilinger, eds, *The Philosophy of Human Rights* (Berlin: de Gruyter), 129–57.

Cruft, Rowan. 2013. 'Why is it Disrespectful to Violate Rights?', *Proceedings of the Aristotelian Society* 103, 201–24.

Cruft, Rowan. 2015. 'From a Good Life to Human Rights: Some Complications', in R. Cruft, S. M. Liao, and M. Renzo, eds, *Philosophical Foundations of Human Rights* (Oxford: Oxford University Press), 101–16.

Cruft, Rowan. 2017. 'The Circularity of the Interest and Will Theories of Rights', in M. McBride, ed., *New Essays on the Nature of Rights* (Oxford: Hart), chapter 8.

Cruft, Rowan, S. Matthew Liao, and Massimo Renzo. 2015. 'The Philosophical Foundations of Human Rights: An Overview', in R. Cruft, S. M. Liao, and M. Renzo, eds, *Philosophical Foundations of Human Rights* (Oxford: Oxford University Press), 1–42.

Darby, Derrick. 2004. 'Rights Externalism', *Philosophy and Phenomenological Research* 68, 620–34.

Darwall, Stephen. 1977. 'Two Kinds of Respect', *Ethics* 88, 36–49.

Darwall, Stephen. 2006. *The Second-Person Standpoint: Morality, Respect, and Accountability* (Cambridge, MA: Harvard University Press).

Darwall, Stephen. 2012. 'Bipolar Obligation', in R. Shafer-Landau, *Oxford Studies in Metaethics, Vol. 7* (Oxford: Oxford University Press), 333–58.

Davidson, Donald. 1984. 'On the Very Idea of a Conceptual Scheme', in his *Inquiries into Truth and Interpretation* (Oxford: Clarendon), 183–98.

Dempsey, Michelle Madden. 2011. 'Public Wrongs and the "Criminal Law's Business": When Victims Won't Share', in R. Cruft, M. H. Kramer, and M. R. Reiff, eds, *Crime, Punishment, and Responsibility: The Jurisprudence of Antony Duff* (Oxford: Oxford University Press), 254–72.

Dietz, Alexander. 2016. 'What We Together Ought to Do', *Ethics* 126, 955–82.

Donahue, Charles Jr. 2010. '*Ius* in Roman Law', in J. Witte, Jr. and F. Alexander, eds, *Christianity and Human Rights* (Cambridge: Cambridge University Press), 64–80.

Donnelly, Jack. 2003. *Universal Human Rights in Theory and Practice*, 2nd edn. (Ithaca, NY: Cornell University Press).

Douglas, Alexander X. 2016. *The Philosophy of Debt* (London: Routledge).

Duff, R. A. 2001. *Punishment, Communication, and Community* (Oxford: Oxford University Press).

Duff, R. A. 2010. 'Towards a Theory of Criminal Law?', *Aristotelian Society Supplementary Volume* 84, 1–28.

Duff, R. A. 2011a. 'Responsibility, Citizenship, and Criminal Law', in R. A. Duff and S. Green, eds, *Philosophical Foundations of Criminal Law* (Oxford: Oxford University Press), 125–48.

Duff, R. A. 2011b. 'In Response', in R. Cruft, M. H. Kramer, and M. R. Reiff, eds, *Crime, Punishment, and Responsibility: The Jurisprudence of Antony Duff* (Oxford: Oxford University Press), 351–80.

Duff, R. A. 2014. 'Aut Dedere Aut Judicare', Minnesota Legal Studies Research Paper No. 14–04. Available at https://papers.ssrn.com/sol3/papers.cfm?abstract_id=2387719.

Duff, R. A. and Sandra E. Marshall. 2010. 'Public and Private Wrongs', in J. Chalmers, F. Leverick, and L. Farmer, eds, *Essays in Criminal Law in Honour of Sir Gerald Gordon* (Edinburgh: Edinburgh University Press), 70–85.

Dworkin, Ronald. 1977. *Taking Rights Seriously* (London: Duckworth).

Dworkin, Ronald. 1986. *Law's Empire* (London: Fontana).

Dworkin, Ronald. 2011. *Justice for Hedgehogs* (Cambridge, MA: Harvard University Press).

Eide, Asbjørn. 1987. *Report on the Right to Adequate Food as a Human Right*, UN Doc E/CN.4/Sub.2/1987/23.

Engstrom, Stephen. 2009. *The Form of Practical Knowledge: A Study of the Categorical Imperative* (Cambridge, MA: Harvard University Press).

Etinson, Adam (ed.). 2018. *Human Rights: Moral or Political?* (Oxford: Oxford University Press).

Fabre, Cécile. 2000. *Social Rights Under the Constitution* (Oxford: Oxford University Press).

Fabre, Cécile. 2006. *Whose Body is it Anyway?* (Oxford: Oxford University Press).

Feinberg, Joel. 1970. 'The Nature and Value of Rights', *The Journal of Value Inquiry* 4, 243–57.

Fellmeth, Aaron Xavier. 2016. *Paradigms of International Human Rights Law* (Oxford: Oxford University Press).

Fichte, J. G. 2000 [1796–7]. *Foundations of Natural Right*, ed. Frederick Neuhouser, trans. Michael Baur (Cambridge: Cambridge University Press).

Finnis, John. 1980. *Natural Law and Natural Rights* (Oxford: Clarendon Press).

Finnis, John. 2011. *Human Rights and Common Good: Collected Essays, Vol. III* (Oxford: Oxford University Press).

Fiss, Owen. 2011. *The Dictates of Justice: Essays on Law and Human Rights* (Dordrecht: Republic of Letters).

Flikschuh, Katrin. 2015. 'Human Rights in Kantian Mode: A Sketch', in R. Cruft, S. M. Liao, and M. Renzo, eds, *Philosophical Foundations of Human Rights* (Oxford: Oxford University Press), 653–70.

Flikschuh, Katrin. 2017. *What is Orientation in Global Thinking? A Kantian Inquiry* (Cambridge: Cambridge University Press).

Forst, Rainer. 2012. *The Right to Justification*, trans. J. Flynn (New York: Columbia University Press).

Frydrych, David. 2017. 'Kramer's Delimiting Test for Legal Rights', *American Journal of Jurisprudence* 62, 197–207.

Gardner, John. 2002. 'Reasons for Teamwork', *Legal Theory* 8, 495–509.

Gardner, John. 2008. 'Simply in Virtue of Being Human: The Whos and Whys of Human Rights', *Journal of Ethics and Social Philosophy* 2, 1–23.

Gardner, John. 2011. 'Relations of Responsibility', in R. Cruft, M. H. Kramer, and M. R. Reiff, eds, *Crime, Punishment, and Responsibility: The Jurisprudence of Antony Duff* (Oxford: Oxford University Press), 87–102.

Garnsey, Peter. 2007. *Thinking about Property: From Antiquity to the Age of Revolution* (Cambridge: Cambridge University Press).

Gearty, Conor. 2016. *On Fantasy Island: Britain, Europe, and Human Rights* (Oxford: Oxford University Press).

Geuss, Raymond. 2001. *History and Illusion in Politics* (Cambridge: Cambridge University Press).

Gewirth, Alan. 1978. *Reason and Morality* (Chicago, IL: University of Chicago Press).

Gewirth, Alan. 1982. *Human Rights: Essays on Justifications and Applications* (Chicago, IL: University of Chicago Press).

Gilbert, Margaret. 2018. *Rights and Demands* (Oxford: Oxford University Press).

Goldberg, John C. P. and Benjamin C. Zipursky. 2010. 'Torts as Wrongs', *Texas Law Review* 88, 1–71.

Goodhart, Charles A. E. 1998. 'The Two Concepts of Money: Indications for the Analysis of Optimal Currency Areas', *European Journal of Political Economy* 14: 407–32.

Gostin, Lawrence. 2014. *Global Health Law* (Cambridge, MA: Harvard University Press).

Gould, Carol C. 1980. 'Contemporary Legal Conceptions of Property and Their Implications for Democracy', *Journal of Philosophy* 77, 716–29.

Gould, Carol C. 1988. *Rethinking Democracy: Freedom and Social Cooperation in Politics, Economy, and Society* (Cambridge: Cambridge University Press).

Gould, Carol C. 2004. *Globalising Democracy and Human Rights* (Cambridge: Cambridge University Press).

Gould, Carol C. 2014. *Interactive Democracy: The Social Roots of Global Justice* (Cambridge: Cambridge University Press).

Gould, Carol C. 2015. 'A Social Ontology of Human Rights', in R. Cruft, S. M. Liao, and M. Renzo, eds, *Philosophical Foundations of Human Rights* (Oxford: Oxford University Press), 177–95.

Graeber, David. 2011. *Debt: The First 5,000 Years* (Brooklyn, NY: Melville House).

Green, Mitchell. 2015. 'Speech Acts', *The Stanford Encyclopedia of Philosophy* (Summer 2015 Edition), ed. Edward N. Zalta. https://plato.stanford.edu/archives/sum2015/entries/speech-acts/.

Grice, H. P. 1957. 'Meaning', *The Philosophical Review*, 66: 377–88.

Griffin, James. 1986. *Well-Being: Its Meaning, Measurement and Moral Importance* (Oxford: Clarendon).

Griffin, James. 2008. *On Human Rights* (Oxford: Oxford University Press).

Griffin, James. 2010. 'Human Rights: Questions of Aim and Approach', *Ethics* 120, 741–60.

Griswold, Charles. 2007. *Forgiveness: A Philosophical Exploration* (Cambridge: Cambridge University Press).

Gyeke, Kwame. 1997. *Tradition and Modernity: Philosophical Reflections on the African Experience* (Oxford: Oxford University Press).

Gyeke, Kwame. 1998. 'Person and Community in African Thought', in P. H. Coetzee and A. P. J. Roux, eds, *The African Philosophy Reader* (London: Routledge), 317–36.

Haase, Matthias. 2012. 'Three Forms of the First Person Plural', in G. Abel and J. Conant, eds, *Rethinking Epistemology, Vol. 2* (Berlin: de Gruyter), 229–56.

Halpin, Andrew. 1997. *Rights and Law: Analysis and Theory* (Oxford: Hart).

Hardin, Garrett. 1968. 'The Tragedy of the Commons', *Science* 162, 1243–8.

Harel, Alon. 2011. 'The Triadic Relational Structure of Responsibility: A Defence', in R. Cruft, M. H. Kramer, and M. R. Reiff, eds, *Crime, Punishment, and Responsibility: The Jurisprudence of Antony Duff* (Oxford: Oxford University Press), 103–21.

Harel, Alon. 2014. *Why Law Matters* (Oxford: Oxford University Press).

Hart, H. L. A. 1955. 'Are There Any Natural Rights?', *Philosophical Review* 64, 175–91.

Hart, H. L. A. 1968. *Punishment and Responsibility* (Oxford: Oxford University Press).

Hayek, F. A. 1944. *The Road to Serfdom* (London: Routledge).

Hayek, F. A. 1960. *The Constitution of Liberty* (London: Routledge).

Hayward, Tim. 2013. 'On Prepositional Duties', *Ethics* 123, 264–91.

Hegel, G. W. F. 1991 [1821]. *Elements of the Philosophy of Right*, trans. H. B. Nisbet, ed. Allen W. Wood (Cambridge: Cambridge University Press).

Hills, Alison. 2015. 'The Intellectuals and the Virtues', *Ethics* 126, 7–36.

Hobbes, Thomas. 1968 [1651]. *Leviathan* (London: Penguin).

Hohfeld, Wesley N. 1964. *Fundamental Legal Conceptions*, ed. W. W. Cook (New Haven, CT: Yale University Press) [reprinted from *Yale Law Journal* 1913 and 1917].

Holmes, Stephen and Cass R. Sunstein. 1999. *The Cost of Rights: Why Liberty Depends on Taxes* (New York: Norton).

Honoré, A. M. 1961. 'Ownership', in A. G. Guest, ed., *Oxford Essays in Jurisprudence* (Oxford: Clarendon), 107–47.

Hope, Simon. 2013. 'Subsistence Needs, Human Rights, and Imperfect Duties', *Journal of Applied Philosophy* 30, 88–100.

Hume, David. 1975 [1777]. *Enquiries Concerning Human Understanding and Concerning the Principles of Morals*, ed. L. A. Selby-Bigge, 3rd edn. P. H. Nidditch (Oxford: Clarendon).

Hume, David. 1978 [1739–40]. *A Treatise of Human Nature*, ed. L. A. Selby-Bigge, 2nd edn. P. H. Nidditch (Oxford: Clarendon).

Ihara, Craig K. 2004. 'Are Individual Rights Necessary? A Confucian Perspective', in K.L. Shun and D. B. Wong, eds, *Confucian Ethics: A Comparative Study of Self, Autonomy, and Community* (Cambridge: Cambridge University Press), 11–30.

Ingham, Geoffrey. 2004. *The Nature of Money* (Cambridge: Polity).

James, Susan. 2003. 'Rights as Enforceable Claims', *Proceedings of the Aristotelian Society* 103, 133–47.

Jones, Charles. 2013. 'The Human Right to Subsistence', *Journal of Applied Philosophy* 30, 57–72.

Jones, Peter. 1994. *Rights* (Basingstoke: Palgrave).

Jones, Peter. 1999. 'Group Rights and Group Oppression', *Journal of Political Philosophy* 7, 353–77.

Julius, A. J. 2016. 'Mutual Recognition', *Jurisprudence* 7: 193–209.

Kagan, Shelly. 1991. 'Replies to My Critics', *Philosophy and Phenomenological Research* 51, 919–28.

Kagan, Shelly. 1998. *Normative Ethics* (Boulder, CO: Westview).

Kahn, Elizabeth. 2018. 'A Structural Approach to the Human Right to Just and Favourable Working Conditions', *Critical Review of International Social and Political Philosophy*. https://doi.org/10.1080/13698230.2018.1448152.

Kamm, Frances M. 1996. *Morality, Mortality. Vol. 2: Rights, Duties, and Status* (Oxford: Oxford University Press).

Kamm, Frances M. 2007. *Intricate Ethics* (Oxford: Oxford University Press).

Kant, Immanuel. 1996 [1797]. *The Metaphysics of Morals*, ed. and trans. Mary Gregor (Cambridge: Cambridge University Press).

Kant, Immanuel. 1997 [1785]. *Groundwork of the Metaphysics of Morals*, ed. and trans. Mary Gregor (Cambridge: Cambridge University Press).

Katz, Larissa. 2013. 'Spite and Extortion: A Jurisdictional Principle of Abuse of Property Right', *Yale Law Journal* 122, 1444–83.

Kramer, Matthew H. 1998. 'Rights without Trimmings', in M. H. Kramer, N. E. Simmonds, and H. Steiner, *A Debate Over Rights: Philosophical Enquiries* (Oxford: Oxford University Press), 7–112.

Kramer, Matthew H. 2001. 'Getting Rights Right', in M. H. Kramer, ed., *Rights, Wrongs and Responsibilities* (Basingstoke: Palgrave), 28–95.

Kramer, Matthew H. 2009. *Moral Realism as a Moral Doctrine* (Oxford: Blackwell).

Kramer, Matthew H. 2010. 'Refining the Interest Theory of Rights', *American Journal of Jurisprudence* 55, 31–9.

Kramer, Matthew H. 2017. 'In Defence of the Interest Theory of Right-Holding: Rejoinders to Leif Wenar', in M. McBride, ed., *New Essays on the Nature of Rights* (Oxford: Hart), chapter 3.

Kramer, Matthew H. and Hillel Steiner. 2007. 'Theories of Rights: Is there a Third Way?', *Oxford Journal of Legal Studies* 27, 281–320.

Kramer, Matthew H., N. E. Simmonds, and H. Steiner. 1998. *A Debate Over Rights: Philosophical Enquiries* (Oxford: Oxford University Press).

Kurki, Visa. 2018. 'Rights, Harming, and Wronging: A Restatement of the Interest Theory', *Oxford Journal of Legal Studies* 38, 430–50.

Lafont, Cristina. 2012. *Global Governance and Human Rights* (Amsterdam: Van Gorcum).

Lawford-Smith, Holly. 2015. 'What "We"?' *Journal of Social Ontology* 1, 225–50.

Leonard, James S., Thomas A. Tenney, and Thadious M. Davis (eds). 1991. *Satire or Evasion? Black Perspectives on Huckleberry Finn* (Durham, NC: Duke University Press).

Liao, S. Matthew. 2010. 'The Basis of Human Moral Status', *Journal of Moral Philosophy* 7, 159–79.

Liao, S. Matthew. 2015. 'Human Rights as Fundamental Conditions for a Good Life', in R. Cruft, S. M. Liao, and M. Renzo, eds, *Philosophical Foundations of Human Rights* (Oxford: Oxford University Press), 79–100.

Lippert-Rasmussen, Kasper. 1996. 'Moral Status and the Impermissibility of Minimizing Violations', *Philosophy and Public Affairs* 25, 333–51.

List, Christian and Philip Pettit. 2011. *Group Agency: Possibility, Design, and Status of Corporate Agents* (Oxford: Oxford University Press).

Locke, John. 1960 [1689]. *Second Treatise of Government*, ed. P. Laslett (Cambridge: Cambridge University Press).

Luban, David. 2015. 'Human Rights Pragmatism and Human Dignity', in R. Cruft, S. M. Liao, and M. Renzo, eds, *Philosophical Foundations of Human Rights* (Oxford: Oxford University Press), 263–78.

Lyons, David. 1981. 'The New Indian Claims and Original Rights to Land', in J. Paul, ed., *Reading Nozick: Essays on Anarchy, State and Utopia* (Totowa, NJ: Rowman and Littlefield).

McBride, Mark. 2017. 'The Tracking Theory of Rights', in M. McBride, ed., *New Essays on the Nature of Rights* (Oxford: Hart), chapter 7.

MacCormick, Neil. 1977. 'Rights in Legislation', in P. M. S. Hacker and J. Raz, eds, *Law, Morality, and Society* (Oxford: Clarendon), 189–209.

MacCormick, Neil. 1982. *Legal Right and Social Democracy: Essays in Legal and Political Philosophy* (Oxford: Clarendon).

McDowell, John. 1998. *Mind, Value, and Reality* (Cambridge, MA: Harvard University Press).

MacLeod, Adam J. 2015. *Property and Practical Reason* (Cambridge: Cambridge University Press).

McMahan, Jeff. 2016. 'On "Modal Personism"', *Journal of Applied Philosophy* 33, 26–30.

Marshall, Sandra E. 2014. '"It Isn't Just about You": Victims of Crime, their Associated Duties, and Public Wrongs', in R. A. Duff, Lindsay Farmer, S. E. Marshall, Massimo Renzo, and Victor Tadros, eds, *Criminalization* (Oxford: Oxford University Press), 291–306.

Marx, Karl. 2000. 'On the Jewish Question', repr. in D. McLellan, ed., *Karl Marx: Selected Writings*, 2nd edn (Oxford: Oxford University Press), 46–70.

May, Simon Căbulea. 2012. 'Moral Status and the Direction of Duties', *Ethics* 123, 113–28.

May, Simon Căbulea. 2015. 'Directed Duties', *Philosophy Compass* 10, 523–32.

May, Simon Căbulea. 2017. 'Desires, Interests and Claim-Rights', in M. McBride, ed., *New Essays on the Nature of Rights* (Oxford: Hart), chapter 4.

May, Simon Căbulea. ms. 'Rights, Wrongs, and Demands'.

Mbiti, John S. 1970. *African Religions and Philosophy* (New York: Doubleday).

Menkiti, Ifeanyi A. 1984. 'Person and Community in African Traditional Thought', in R. Wright, ed., *African Philosophy: An Introduction* (Lanham, MD: University Press of America), 171–82.

Mensh, Elaine and Harry Mensh. 2000. *Black, White & Huckleberry Finn: Re-Imagining the American Dream* (Tuscaloosa: University of Alabama Press).

Mill, John Stuart. 1987 [1863]. 'Utilitarianism', in J. S. Mill and J. Bentham, ed. A. Ryan, *Utilitarianism and Other Essays* (Harmondsworth: Penguin), 272–338.

Mill, John Stuart. 1991 [1859]. 'On Liberty', in J. S. Mill, ed. J. Gray, *On Liberty and Other Essays* (Oxford: Oxford University Press), 5–130.

Miller, David. 1989. *Market, State, and Community: Theoretical Foundations of Market Socialism* (Oxford: Clarendon).

Miller, David. 2007. *National Responsibility and Global Justice* (Oxford: Oxford University Press).

Miller, Fred D. Jr. 1995. *Nature, Justice, and Rights in Aristotle's Politics* (Oxford: Oxford University Press).

Moyn, Samuel. 2012. *The Last Utopia: Human Rights in History* (Cambridge, MA: Harvard University Press).

Munzer, Stephen R. 1990. *A Theory of Property* (Cambridge: Cambridge University Press).

Murphy, Mark C. 2005. 'The Common Good', *The Review of Metaphysics* 59, 133–64.

Mutua, Makau. 2002. *Human Rights: A Political and Cultural Critique* (Philadelphia: University of Pennsylvania Press).

Nagel, Thomas. 1979. 'What is it Like to be a Bat?', in his *Mortal Questions* (Cambridge: Cambridge University Press), 165–80.

Nagel, Thomas. 1986. *The View from Nowhere* (Oxford: Oxford University Press).

Nagel, Thomas. 2002. *Concealment and Exposure & Other Essays* (Oxford: Oxford University Press).

Nagel, Thomas. 2005. 'The Problem of Global Justice', *Philosophy and Public Affairs* 33, 113–47.

Narveson, Jan. 1988. *The Libertarian Idea* (Philadelphia, PA: Temple University Press).

Neuman, Gerald. 2003. 'Human Rights and Constitutional Rights: Harmony and Dissonance', *Stanford Law Review* 55: 1863–900.

Nickel, James W. 2000. 'Economic Liberties', in V. Davion and C. Wolf, eds, *The Idea of a Political Liberalism* (Lanham, MD: Rowman & Littlefield), 155–75.

Nickel, James W. 2007. *Making Sense of Human Rights*, 2nd edn (Oxford: Blackwell).

Nickel, James W. 2008. 'Rethinking Indivisibility: Towards a Theory of Supporting Relations between Human Rights', *Human Rights Quarterly* 30, 984–1001.

Nicol, Danny. 2011. 'Business Rights as Human Rights' in T. Campbell, K. D. Ewing, and A. Tomkins, eds, *The Legal Protection of Human Rights: Sceptical Essays* (Oxford: Oxford University Press), 229–43.

Nietzsche, Friedrich. 2011 [1895]. 'The Anti-Christ', in *The Anti-Christ, Ecce Homo, Twilight of the Idols and Other Writings*, ed. A Ridley (Cambridge: Cambridge University Press), 1–68.

Nozick, Robert. 1974. *Anarchy, State, and Utopia* (Oxford: Blackwell).

Nussbaum, Martha. 2000. *Women and Human Development: The Capabilities Approach* (Cambridge: Cambridge University Press).

Nussbaum, Martha. 2002. 'Capabilities and Human Rights', in P. De Greiff and C. Cronin, eds, *Global Justice and Transnational Politics* (Cambridge, MA: MIT Press), 117–49.

Nussbaum, Martha. 2006. *Frontiers of Justice* (Cambridge, MA: Harvard University Press).

Nussbaum, Martha. 2011. *Creating Capabilities: The Human Development Approach* (Cambridge, MA: Harvard University Press).

Oberdiek, John. 2004. 'Lost in Moral Space: On the Infringing/Violating Distinction and its Place in the Theory of Rights', *Law and Philosophy* 23.

Oberdiek, John. 2008. 'Specifying Rights Out of Necessity', *Oxford Journal of Legal Studies* 28, 127–46.

O'Neill, Onora. 1996. *Towards Justice and Virtue: A Constructive Account of Practical Reasoning* (Cambridge: Cambridge University Press).

O'Neill, Onora. 2000. *Bounds of Justice* (Cambridge: Cambridge University Press).

O'Neill, Onora. 2015. 'Response to John Tasioulas', in R. Cruft, S. M. Liao, and M. Renzo, eds, *Philosophical Foundations of Human Rights* (Oxford: Oxford University Press), 71–8.

Owens, David. 2012. *Shaping the Normative Landscape* (Oxford: Oxford University Press).

Owens, David. 2017. 'Wrong by Convention', *Ethics* 127, 553–75.

Owens, David. Forthcoming. 'Property and Authority', *Journal of Political Philosophy*.

Parekh, Bhikhu. 2004. *Rethinking Multiculturalism: Cultural Diversity and Political Theory* (Basingstoke: Palgrave).

Peach, Lucinda Joy. 2005. 'Feminist Reflections on "Women's Rights as Human Rights"', in David A. Reidy and Mortimer N. S. Sellers, eds, *Universal Human Rights: Moral Order in a Divided World* (Lanham, MD: Rowman and Littlefield), 81–108.

Penner, James E. 1997. *The Idea of Property in Law* (Oxford: Oxford University Press).

Penner, James E. 2013. 'On the Very Idea of Transmissible Rights', in J. E. Penner and H. E. Smith, eds, *Philosophical Foundations of Property Law* (Oxford: Oxford University Press), 244–71.

Penner, James and Henry E. Smith 2013. 'Introduction', in J. E. Penner and H. E. Smith, eds., *Philosophical Foundations of Property Law* (Oxford: Oxford University Press), xv–xxvii.

Perry, John. 1979. 'The Problem of the Essential Indexical', *Noûs* 13, 3–21.

Plato. 1969. *The Last Days of Socrates (Euthyphro, The Apology, Crito)*, trans. H. Tredennick (Harmondsworth: Penguin).

Plato. 1974. *The Republic*, trans. D. Lee, 2nd edn (Harmondsworth: Penguin).

Quinn, Warren. 1993. *Morality and Action* (Cambridge: Cambridge University Press).

Rachels, James. 1979. 'Killing and Starving to Death', *Philosophy* 54, 159–71.

Railton, Peter. 1984. 'Alienation, Consequentialism, and the Demands of Morality', *Philosophy and Public Affairs* 13, 134–71.

Rainbolt, George. 2006. *The Concept of Rights* (Dordrecht: Springer).

Rawls, John. 1971. *A Theory of Justice* (Oxford: Blackwell).

Rawls, John. 1999. *The Law of Peoples with 'The Idea of Public Reason Revisited'* (Cambridge, MA: Harvard University Press).

Raz, Joseph. 1975. *Practical Reason and Norms* (London: Hutchinson).

Raz, Joseph. 1984. 'Legal Rights', *Oxford Journal of Legal Studies* 4, 1–21.

Raz, Joseph. 1986. *The Morality of Freedom* (Oxford: Clarendon).

Raz, Joseph. 1994. 'Rights and Individual Well-Being', in his *Ethics in the Public Domain* (Oxford: Oxford University Press), 44–59.

Raz, Joseph. 2010. 'Human Rights without Foundations', in S. Besson and J. Tasioulas, eds, *The Philosophy of International Law* (Oxford: Oxford University Press), 321–38.

Raz, Joseph. 2012. 'Is there a Reason to Keep Promises?', Columbia Public Law Research Paper 12–320. https://papers.ssrn.com/sol3/papers.cfm?abstract_id=2162656.

Raz, Joseph. 2015. 'Human Rights in the Emerging World Order', in R. Cruft, S. M. Liao, and M. Renzo, eds, *Philosophical Foundations of Human Rights* (Oxford: Oxford University Press), 217–31.

Raz, Joseph and Avishai Margalit. 1994. 'National Self-Determination', in J. Raz, *Ethics in the Public Domain* (Oxford: Clarendon), 125–45.

Reich, Charles. 1964. 'The New Property', *Yale Law Journal* 73, 733–87.

Reiff, Mark R. 2013. *Exploitation and Economic Justice in the Liberal Capitalist State* (Oxford: Oxford University Press).

Reilly, Niamh. 2009. *Women's Human Rights* (Cambridge: Polity).

Reinecke, Juliane and Shaz Ansari. 2016. 'Taming Wicked Problems: The Role of Framing in the Construction of Corporate Social Responsibility', *Journal of Management Studies* 53: 299–329.

Renzo, Massimo. 2015. 'Human Needs, Human Rights', in R. Cruft, S. M. Liao, and M. Renzo, eds, *Philosophical Foundations of Human Rights* (Oxford: Oxford University Press), 570–87.

Rippe, Klaus Peter. 1998. 'Diminishing Solidarity', *Ethical Theory and Moral Practice* 1, 355–73.

Ripstein, Arthur. 2009. *Force and Freedom: Kant's Legal and Political Philosophy* (Cambridge, MA: Harvard University Press).

Ripstein, Arthur. 2013. 'Possession and Use', in J. Penner and H. Smith, eds, *Philosophical Foundations of Property Law* (Oxford; Oxford University Press), 156–81.

Rödl, Sebastian. 2014. 'Intentional Transaction', *Philosophical Explorations* 17, 304–16.

Rose, Carol M. 2013. 'Psychologies of Property (and Why Property is not a Hawk/Dove Game)', in J. Penner and H. Smith, eds, *Philosophical Foundations of Property Law* (Oxford; Oxford University Press), 272–88.

Ruggie, John Gerard. 2013. *Just Business: Multinational Corporations and Human Rights* (New York: Norton).

Sandel, Michael. 1982. *Liberalism and the Limits of Justice* (Cambridge: Cambridge University Press).

Sangiovanni, Andrea. 2016. 'Are Moral Rights Necessary for the Justification of International Legal Human Rights?', *Ethics and International Affairs* 30, 471–81.

Sangiovanni, Andrea. 2017. *Humanity without Dignity: Moral Equality, Respect, and Human Rights* (Cambridge, MA: Harvard University Press).

Sartre, Jean-Paul. 1948. *Existentialism and Humanism*, trans. P. Mairet (London: Methuen).

Sartre, Jean-Paul. 1958 [1943]. *Being and Nothingness*, trans. H. E. Barnes (London: Methuen).

Scanlon, T. M. 1984. 'Rights, Goals, and Fairness', in J. Waldron, ed., *Theories of Rights* (Oxford: Oxford University Press), 137–52.

Schaab, Janis. 2017. 'Why it is Disrespectful to Violate Rights: Contractualism and the Kind-Desire Theory', *Philosophical Studies* 175, 97–116.

Schwenkenbecher, Anne. 2013. 'Joint Duties and Global Moral Obligations', *Ratio* 26, 310–28.

Sen, Amartya. 1999. *Development as Freedom* (Oxford: Oxford University Press).

Sen, Amartya. 2004. 'Elements of a Theory of Human Rights', *Philosophy and Public Affairs* 32, 315–56.

Shue, Henry. 1980. *Basic Rights: Subsistence, Affluence, and US Foreign Policy* (Princeton, NJ: Princeton University Press).

Siedentop, Larry. 2014. *Inventing the Individual: The Origins of Western Liberalism* (London: Allen Lane).

Singer, Peter. 1972. 'Famine, Affluence, and Morality', *Philosophy and Public Affairs* 1, 229–43.

Simmons, A. John. 1992. *The Lockean Theory of Rights* (Princeton, NJ: Princeton University Press).

Simmons, A. John. 2015. 'Human Rights, Natural Rights, and Human Dignity', in R. Cruft, S. M. Liao, and M. Renzo, eds, *Philosophical Foundations of Human Rights* (Oxford: Oxford University Press), 138–52.

Skorupski, John. 2010. *The Domain of Reasons* (Oxford: Oxford University Press).

Smith, Adam. 1976 [1776]. *An Inquiry into the Nature and Causes of the Wealth of Nations*, ed. E. Cannan (Chicago, IL: University of Chicago Press).

Snare, Frank. 1972. 'The Concept of Property', *American Philosophical Quarterly* 9, 200–6.

de Soto, Hernando. 2000. *The Mystery of Capital* (London: Random House).

Sreenivasan, Gopal. 2005. 'A Hybrid Theory of Claim-Rights', *Oxford Journal of Legal Studies* 25, 257–74.

Sreenivasan, Gopal. 2010. 'Duties and their Direction', *Ethics* 120, 465–94.

Sreenivasan, Gopal. 2012. 'A Human Right to Health: Some Inconclusive Scepticism', *Aristotelian Society Supplementary Volume*, 86, 239–65.

Sreenivasan, Gopal. 2017. 'Public Goods, Individual Rights, and Third Party Benefits', in M. McBride, ed., *New Essays on the Nature of Rights* (Oxford: Hart), 127–48.

Steiner, Hillel. 1994. *An Essay on Rights* (Oxford: Blackwell).

Steiner, Hillel. 1998. 'Working Rights', in M. H. Kramer, N. E. Simmonds, and H. Steiner, *A Debate Over Rights: Philosophical Enquiries* (Oxford: Oxford University Press), 233–302.

Stemplowska, Zofia. 2009. 'On the Real World Duties Imposed on Us by Human Rights', *Journal of Social Philosophy* 40, 466–87.

Stemplowska, Zofia. 2015. 'Can Moral Desert Qualify or Justify Human Rights?', in R. Cruft, S. M. Liao, and M. Renzo, eds, *Philosophical Foundations of Human Rights* (Oxford: Oxford University Press), 166–75.

Stilz, Anna. 2017. 'Property Rights: Natural, Conventional, or Hybrid?', in J. Brennan, B. van der Vossen, and D. Schmidtz, eds, *The Routledge Handbook of Libertarianism* (London: Routledge), 244–58.

Stilz, Anna. Forthcoming. *Territorial Sovereignty: A Philosophical Exploration* (Oxford: Oxford University Press).

Strawson, P. F. 1962. 'Freedom and Resentment', *Proceedings of the British Academy* 48, 1–25.

Supiot, Alain. 2007. *Homo Juridicus: On the Anthropological Function of the Law*, trans. S. Brown (London: Verso).

Tasioulas, John. 2007. 'The Moral Reality of Human Rights', in T. Pogge, ed., *Freedom from Poverty as a Human Right: Who Owes What to the Very Poor?* (Oxford: Oxford University Press/UNESCO), 75–102.

Tasioulas, John. 2012. 'On the Nature of Human Rights', in G. Ernst and J.-C. Heilinger, eds, *The Philosophy of Human Rights* (Berlin: de Gruyter), 17–59.

Tasioulas, John. 2015. 'On the Foundations of Human Rights', in R. Cruft, S. M. Liao, and M. Renzo, eds, *Philosophical Foundations of Human Rights* (Oxford: Oxford University Press), 47–70.

Tasioulas, John. 2017. 'Exiting the Hall of Mirrors: Morality and Law in Human Rights', King's College London Dickson Poon School of Law Legal Studies Research Paper Series, Paper No. 2017-19. https://papers.ssrn.com/sol3/papers.cfm?abstract_id=2915307.

Tasioulas, John and Effy Vayena. 2016. 'The Place of Human Rights and the Common Good in Global Health Policy', *Theoretical Medicine and Bioethics* 37, 365–82.

Taylor, Charles. 1985. 'Atomism', in his *Philosophy and the Human Sciences: Philosophical Papers, Vol. II* (Cambridge: Cambridge University Press), 187–210.

Teitel, Ruti G. 2011. *Humanity's Law* (Oxford: Oxford University Press).

Thompson, Michael. 2004. 'What is it to Wrong Someone? A Puzzle about Justice', in R. J. Wallace, P. Pettit, S. Scheffler, and M. Smith, eds, *Reason and Value: Themes from the Moral Philosophy of Joseph Raz* (Oxford: Oxford University Press), 333–84.

Thompson, Michael. 2012. 'Propositional Attitudes and Propositional Nexuses: A Hieroglyphical Elucidation', in S. Rödl and H. Tegtmeyer, eds, *Sinnkritisches Philosophieren* (Berlin: de Gruyter), 231–48.

Thomson, Judith Jarvis. 1990. *The Realm of Rights* (Cambridge, MA: Harvard University Press).

Tierney, Brian. 1997. *The Idea of Natural Rights* (Grand Rapids, MI: Emory University Press).

Tomalty, Jesse. 2014. 'The Force of the Claimability Objection to the Human Right to Subsistence', *Canadian Journal of Philosophy*, 44: 1–17.

Tomasi, John. 2012. *Free Market Fairness* (Princeton, NJ: Princeton University Press).

Vasek, Karel. 1977. 'A 30-Year Struggle: The Sustained Efforts to Give Force of Law to the Universal Declaration of Human Rights', *Unesco Courier* 30, 28–9, 32.

van der Vossen, Bas. 2015. 'Imposing Duties and Original Appropriation', *The Journal of Political Philosophy* 23, 64–85.

Van Duffel, Siegfried. 2012. 'The Nature of Rights Debate Rests on a Mistake', *Pacific Philosophical Quarterly* 93, 104–123.

Waldron, Jeremy. 1984. 'Introduction', in J. Waldron, ed., *Theories of Rights* (Oxford: Oxford University Press), 1–20.

Waldron, Jeremy. 1988. *The Right to Private Property* (Oxford: Clarendon).

Waldron, Jeremy. 1993. *Liberal Rights* (Cambridge: Cambridge University Press).

Waldron, Jeremy. 1994. 'The Advantages and Difficulties of the Humean Theory of Property', in E. F. Paul, F. D. Miller Jr., and J. Paul, eds, *Property Rights* (Cambridge: Cambridge University Press), 85–123.

Waldron, Jeremy. 2010. 'Two Concepts of Self-Determination', in S. Besson and J. Tasioulas, eds, *The Philosophy of International Law* (Oxford: Oxford University Press), 397–414.

Waldron, Jeremy. 2018. 'Human Rights: A Critique of the Raz/Rawls Approach', in A. Etinson, ed., *Human Rights: Moral or Political?* (Oxford: Oxford University Press), 117–44.

Warnock, Mary. 2015. *Critical Reflections on Ownership* (Cheltenham: Edward Elgar).

Weinrib, Ernest J. 1995. *The Idea of Private Law* (Cambridge, MA: Harvard University Press).

Wellman, Carl. 1995. *Real Rights* (Oxford: Oxford University Press).

Wellman, Carl. 2011. *The Moral Dimensions of Human Rights* (Oxford: Oxford University Press).

Wenar, Leif. 2005a. 'The Value of Rights', in M. O'Rourke, ed., *Law and Social Justice* (Cambridge, MA: MIT Press), 179–209.

Wenar, Leif. 2005b. 'The Nature of Rights', *Philosophy and Public Affairs* 33, 223–52.

Wenar, Leif. 2007. 'Responsibility and Severe Poverty', in T. Pogge, ed., *Freedom from Poverty as a Human Right* (Oxford: Oxford University Press/UNESCO), 255–74.

Wenar, Leif. 2013. 'The Nature of Claim-Rights', *Ethics* 123, 202–29.

Wenar, Leif. 2015. 'Rights', *The Stanford Encyclopedia of Philosophy* (Fall 2015 Edition), ed. Edward N. Zalta. https://plato.stanford.edu/archives/fall2015/entries/rights/.

Werner, Richard A. 2014. 'Can Banks Individually Create Money Out of Nothing? The Theories and the Empirical Evidence', *International Review of Financial Analysis* 36, 1–19.

Wiles, Maurice and Mark Santer (eds). 1975. *Documents in Early Christian Thought* (Cambridge: Cambridge University Press).

Wong, David B. 2004. 'Rights and Community in Confucianism', in K.-L. Shun and D. B. Wong, eds, *Confucian Ethics: A Comparative Study of Self, Autonomy, and Community* (Cambridge: Cambridge University Press), 31–48.

Wringe, Bill. 2005. 'Needs, Rights, and Collective Obligations', *Royal Institute of Philosophy Supplement* 57, 187–208.

Wringe, Bill. 2010. 'Global Obligations and the Agency Objection', *Ratio*, 23, 217–31.

Xu, Ting and Jean Allain. 2015. 'Introduction: Property and Human Rights in a Global Context', in T. Xu and J. Allain, *Property and Human Rights in a Global Context* (Oxford: Hart), 1–16.

Young, Iris Marion. 2011. *Responsibility for Justice* (Oxford: Oxford University Press).

Zylberman, Ariel. 2016a. 'Why Human Rights? Because of You', *Journal of Political Philosophy* 24, 321–43.

Zylberman, Ariel. 2016b. 'Human Rights, Categorical Duties: A Dilemma for Instrumentalism', *Utilitas* 28, 368–95.

Index